Deciphering the Global

Deciphering the Global

Its Scales, Spaces and Subjects

Edited by Saskia Sassen

Routledge
Taylor & Francis Group
New York London

Routledge
Taylor & Francis Group
270 Madison Avenue
New York, NY 10016

Routledge
Taylor & Francis Group
2 Park Square
Milton Park, Abingdon
Oxon OX14 4RN

Routledge is an imprint of Taylor & Francis Group, an Informa business

Printed in the United States of America on acid-free paper
10 9 8 7 6 5 4 3 2 1

International Standard Book Number-10: 0-415-95733-8 (Softcover) 0-415-95732-X (Hardcover)
International Standard Book Number-13: 978-0-415-95733-5 (Softcover) 978-0-415-95732-8 (Hardcover)

Library of Congress Cataloging-in-Publication Data

Deciphering the global : its scales, spaces and subjects / edited by Saskia Sassen.
p. cm.
Includes bibliographical references and index.
ISBN-13: 978-0-415-95732-8 (hb)
ISBN-13: 978-0-415-95733-5 (pb)
1. Globalization--Social aspects. 2. Culture and globalization. 3. Acculturation. 4. Transnationalism. 5. Cosmopolitanism. I. Sassen, Saskia.

HM841.D43 2007
306.01--dc22 2006033652

Visit the Taylor & Francis Web site at
http://www.taylorandfrancis.com

and the Routledge Web site at
http://www.routledge.com

Contents

Preface

Deciphering the Global: Its Spaces, Scalings and Subjects is a project developed through the doctoral work of students. Today is a time of growing interest in the research and ideas of the younger generations, partly because the significant dislocations we are living through signal the need for new concepts and framings. Since I arrived at the University of Chicago in fall 1998, I have had a chance to work with a variety of doctoral students interested in one or another version of globalization or transnationalism. Eventually it became clear to me that a pattern in these dissertations makes for a rather original approach to the subject of broadly understood globalization. It is a pattern that breaks with the typical approach in the literature, which has been to start with the self-evident scale of the global — global markets, the International Monetary Fund (IMF), the World Trade Organization (WTO), not to mention the ubiquitous McDonald's and Nike. That approach has made important contributions, but it is ultimately a partial view of the larger transformation.

In sharp contrast to the prevailing scholarship, the starting point in each of these chapters is a thick, complex, messy environment where the global needs to be detected, decoded, discovered, and then constructed as an object of study. This type of approach asks what it is we are trying to name with the term *globalization*. Each of these chapters recognizes we are living through a transformation that, though partial, is epochal. But each chapter also assumes that we might not have fully understood its characteristics and its locations. All chapters are based on original dissertation research; they capture only some of what the dissertations address. They include diverse types of research and theorization. Together these chapters show that confining the characteristics and locations of that epochal transformation to the self-evident scale of the global and to self-evident supranational institutions is profoundly inadequate.

The analytics in each chapter contribute to raise the level of complexity and ambiguity in the study of globalization. This is in good measure a function of the way the object of study is constructed. Each chapter focuses on a type of issue rarely seen in the prevailing literature on globalization. This in turn demands distinct methodological and interpretive instruments. The outcome is an expansion of the analytic terrain and interpretive tools for studying the global.

What brought us all together over the years was one of those old University of Chicago institutions: the workshop. This is a labor of love. It works. Workshops are meant to be multidisciplinary. Indeed, the authors in this volume come from anthropology, sociology, political science, history of culture, and political economy. With Arjun Appadurai and Neil Brenner, both then at Chicago, we began to organize this workshop as soon as I had decided to come to Chicago. We have been meeting regularly since fall 1998. We have heard each other's papers over and over again as the research progressed over the years. The authors in this volume are among the first cohort of the workshop. Three of them were workshop coordinators, each for a full academic year: Heather Hindman, Anne Bartlett, and Rachel Harvey. There is a second workshop cohort at various stages of their research: Danny Armanino, Eric Boria, Jennifer Buntin, Chi-chen Chiang, Kathleen Fernicola, Zack Kertcher, Greg Liegel, David Lubin, Sheldon Lyke, Daniel Menchik, Yuki Ooi, Michal Pagis, Nilesh Patel, Lorraine Mora, Xuefei Ren, Rachel Rinaldo, Liza Weinstein, Robert Wyrod, Alvaro Santana and Satomi Yamamoto. I look forward to their contributions for a second collection. Several in this second cohort have been workshop coordinators: Kathleen Fernicola, Jennifer Buntin, Michal Pagis, Liza Weinstein, and Chi-chen Chiang and Greg Liegel, who co-coordinated. They are all to be thanked for making this collective project possible. We greatly appreciate the ongoing support of the University of Chicago and several of its programs.

Critical help came from the two or three scholars we invited to each of our annual globalization conferences over the last eight years: John Agnew, Arjun Appadurai, Swapna Banerjee-Guha, Seyla Benhabib, Judit Bodnar, Linda Bosniak, Neil Brenner, Michael Burawoy, Craig Calhoun, Karin Knorr Cetina, Terry Nichols Clark, Jean Comaroff, Michaeline A. Crichlow, Michael Dawson, Michael Goldman, David Harvey, Patricia Fernandez-Kelly, Uma Kothari, Scott Lash, James H. Mittelman, Aihwa Ong, Bryan R. Roberts, Warren Sack, Leslie Sklair, Maria Sergeevna Tysiachniouk, and John Urry. They were invited to deliver a public talk and then, the next day, in a seminar setting, to discuss a chapter from the particular doctoral students in the workshop chosen to present their work on a given year. We owe great thanks to the generosity, depth, and precision of the comments our distinguished discussants gave to these students.

We want to thank David McBride, now at Oxford University Press, for believing that a volume of student work could succeed and helping launch this project when he was still at Routledge. Angela Chnapko took over and worked scheduling miracles, fully supported by the project editor Jennifer Genetti. Danny Armanino, from the University of Chicago, helped with research, the bibliography, editing, proof-reading , and generally managed the whole process. We all owe him a huge thank you.

The authors in this volume and the cohort that follows it are part of a new generation of young researchers keen on confronting today's world through new types of analytics. The starting points are complex and somewhat hermetic settings, rather than the more common self-evident global institutions. There are growing numbers of scholars working on globalization from the perspective developed in this volume, but as of now they often lack the clear reference points present in the scholarship about self-evident global institutions. Much of this research is now often homeless, given the prevailing emphases in the literature and the dominant conceptual understanding of the character of the global. This volume offers a framing and an intellectual "home" for a broad range of substantive projects across several disciplines. The authors in this volume have left their elders behind. They have new ideas and new discoveries. It is precisely this condition that contributes to the value of the volume.

Saskia Sassen

University of Chicago

Introduction: Deciphering the Global

SASKIA SASSEN

Transnational processes such as economic, political, and cultural globalization confront the social sciences with a series of theoretical and methodological challenges. Such challenges arise out of the fact that the global — whether an institution, a process, a discursive practice, or an imaginary — simultaneously transcends the exclusive framing of national states, yet partly inhabits, and gets constituted inside, the national. Seen this way, globalization is more than the formation of global institutions and growing interdependence of what can remain fairly unchanged nation-states. As developed in this book, globalization signals a possibly deeper unsettlement.

If the global partly inhabits and arises out of the national, it becomes evident that globalization in its many different forms directly engages two key assumptions in the social sciences. The first is the proposition about the nation-state as the container of social process, with the implied correspondence of national territory with the national; that is, if a process or condition is located in a national institution or in national territory, it must be national. The second, also implied by the first, is that the national and the global are two mutually exclusive entities. Both propositions describe conditions that have held, albeit never fully, throughout much of the history of the modern state, especially since World War I, and to some extent continue to do so. What is different today is that these conditions are partly but actively being unbundled. Different also is the scope of this unbundling.

Conceiving of globalization as partly inhabiting and even getting constituted inside the national opens up a vast research agenda that remains largely unaddressed. The assumptions about the nation-state as container of social process remain useful for much of what is studied in the social sciences and have, indeed, allowed social scientists to develop powerful methods of analysis and the requisite data sets. But these assumptions are not helpful in elucidating a growing number of questions about globalization and transnational processes coming onto the research and theorization agenda of the social sciences. Nor are those assumptions helpful for developing the requisite analytics.

Conceptual frameworks that rest on the assumption that the nation-state contains society and that it is mutually exclusive with the global cannot fully accommodate the critical proposition organizing this book. This proposition might be formulated as follows: The fact that a process or entity is located within the territory of a sovereign state does not necessarily mean it is a national process or entity; it might be a localization of the global or a denationalized instance of the national. Though most such entities and processes are likely to be national, there is a growing need for empirical research to establish the range of instances which are not, from materialities to imaginaries. Much of what we continue to code as national today may well be precisely such a localization or denationalized instance. Developing the theoretical and empirical specifications that allow us to accommodate such conditions is a difficult and collective effort.

This book seeks to contribute to that collective effort by mapping an analytic terrain for the study of globalization predicated on such a more complex understanding. It includes, but also moves beyond, understandings of globalization that focus on growing interdependence and self-evident global institutions. Thus, part of the research work entails detecting the presence of such globalizing and denationalizing dynamics in thick social environments which mix national and non-national elements. Such a framing of the global allows us to use many of the existing research techniques and data sets in the social sciences developed with national and subnational settings in mind. But we would still have to elaborate new conceptual frameworks for interpreting findings — frameworks that do not assume the national is a closed system, mutually exclusive with the global, even when subject to growing interdependence. Surveys of factories in global commodity chains, in-depth interviews that decipher individual imaginaries about globality, and ethnographies of national financial centers all expand the analytic terrain for understanding global processes. Expanding that analytic terrain opens up the research agenda for the social sciences in general and, perhaps especially, for more sociological and anthropological types of questions.[1]

What Are We Trying to Name?

What is it, then, we are trying to name with the term globalization? In my reading it involves two distinct sets of dynamics. One of these involves the formation of explicitly global institutions and processes, such as the World Trade Organization, global financial markets, the new cosmopolitanism, and war crimes tribunals. The practices and organizational forms through which these dynamics operate constitute what is typically thought of as global. Although they are partly enacted at the national scale, they are to a very large extent novel and self-evident global formations.

But we are beginning to understand that there are processes that do not necessarily scale at the global level as such, yet are part of globalization. These processes can take place deep inside territories and institutional domains historically constructed as national in much, though by no means all, of the world. Localized in national and subnational settings, these processes are part of globalization in that they insert localities in global production, organizational, cultural, social or political processes; or involve transboundary networks and entities connecting multiple local or "national" processes and actors; or involve the recurrence of particular issues and dynamics in a growing number of countries or localities, with subjective recognition of this recurrence. Among these we can include, for instance, cross-border networks of activists engaged in specific localized struggles with an explicit or implicit global agenda, as is the case with many human rights and environmental organizations; localities with significant concentrations of globally oriented operations, such as export-processing zones and financial centers, both of which articulate global processes with national economies; particular aspects of the work of states (e.g., monetary and fiscal policies critical for the operation of global financial markets that a growing number of states are implementing, often under pressure from the IMF and the United States); and the use by national courts of international legal instruments, whether human rights, international environmental standards, or WTO regulations, to address issues once exclusively handled through national instruments. These types of conditions and processes partly denationalize the national, even when it all continues to be coded as national.

When the social sciences focus on globalization it is typically not on such national and subnational processes and entities but rather on the self-evidently global scale.[2] The social sciences have made important contributions to the study of this self-evident global scale by establishing the fact of multiple globalizations and by making it increasingly clear that the dominant form of globalization — the global corporate economy — is but one of several. Political science, specifically international relations, has a strong canonical framing of the international, with the national state as a key actor. The strength of this canon poses difficulties when it comes to opening up to the possibility of global formations and their multiscalar character. The same can be said for sociology. The strength of its research methods and data sets has rested to a very large extent on the type of closure represented by the nation-state. This holds particularly for the more quantitative types of sociology, which have been able to develop increasingly sophisticated methods predicated on the possibility of closed date sets. Though it uses very different methods and hypotheses, applied economics is similarly conditioned on data sets that presume closure in the underlying reality. Measuring interdependence from such a perspective tends to be a function of transactions among unitary nation-states. This concept of interdependence captures processes that may have existed for centuries and hence are not particularly useful to specify what is distinctive about the current epoch. On the other hand, although still maintaining similar assumptions about the nation-state, more historically inflected forms of sociology and political science have made significant contributions to the study of international systems; notable here is the work on world-systems and on cross-border migrations.

Two disciplines more than any others have contributed significantly to the study of the global as it gets constituted subnationally. They are geography and anthropology, specifically, particular branches of each. Economic and political geography have done so especially through a critical development of scale and scaling. This work recognizes the historicity of scales and thus resists the reification and naturalization of the national scale so present in most of social science. Anthropologists have contributed studies of the thick and particularistic forces that are also part of these dynamics, thereby indirectly alerting us to the risks of exclusively scalar analytics that disregard the complexity of environments. Without wanting to generalize, it seems to me that the analytic and interpretive tools of these two disciplines have been at an advantage compared to sociology, political science, and economics when it comes to studying the global through the more expanded approach developed in this book.

From Older Scalar Hierarchies to Novel Scalings, Topologies, and Assemblages

Global and subnational processes and formations can, and are, destabilizing scalar hierarchies centered in the nation-state. Historically, the formation of European nation-states in turn destabilized the scalar hierarchies of the preceding period — typically constituted through the practices and power projects of past eras, such as the colonial empires of the sixteenth and subsequent centuries, or the medieval towns that dominated long-distance trading in certain parts of Europe. Most notable today is what is often seen as a return to older imperial spatialities for the economic operations of the most powerful actors: the formation of a global market for capital, a global trade regime, and the internationalization of manufacturing production. It is, of course, not simply a return to older forms.

It is crucial to recognize the specificity of today's practices and of contemporary capabilities enabling these practices. This specificity partly consists of the fact that current cross-border spaces have to be produced in a context where most territory is encased in a thick and highly formalized national framework marked by the exclusive authority of the national state. The fact of the preeminence of the national scale and of the exclusive authority of the state over its territory is, in my reading, one of the key contexts within which the current phase of globalization takes off. And it is a key feature distinguishing the current phase from earlier global eras which lacked such nation-states. This angle on the global question allows us to recognize a foundational tension easily overlooked in globalization studies centered on interdependence of what might be basically unchanged nation-states. Thus, insofar as the global gets partly constituted inside the national, the institutional preeminence of the national brings with it a necessary participation of national states in the formation of global systems

Notwithstanding different origins and starting times across the world, the history of the modern state can be read as the work of rendering national just about all crucial features of society: authority, identity, territory, security, law, and economic accumulation. Periods preceding those of the ascendance of the national state saw rather different types of scalings, with territories typically subject to multiple systems of rule rather than the exclusive authority of the state. Global firms, global markets, global subjectivities, human rights, and other kindred figurations entail the denationalizing of at least some components of the national. Thus, even entities structured inside thick or highly formalized national settings can undergo foundational transformations. What we easily refer to as global and see as outside the national can actually arise out of the national. This type of focus allows us to capture the enormous variability across countries regarding the incorporation of, or resistance to, globalization. These processes are partly shaped by the specifics of each country, whether formal and *de jure* or informal and *de facto*. At the same time, this type of approach avoids the trap of comparative studies — which puts countries on parallel tracks and tends to compare what can be standardized — because it starts from the insight that the conditionalities of a global system are multisited and hence need to be partly met through the specific structuration in each country (see Sassen 2006, chap. 1).

Today's global and denationalizing dynamics cut across institutional hierarchies and across the institutional encasements of territory historically produced by the formation of national states. This does not mean that the old hierarchies disappear but rather that novel scalings emerge alongside the old ones and that the former can often trump the latter. Older hierarchies of scale constituted as part of the development of the nation-state continue to operate, but they do so in a far less exclusive field than they did in the recent past. This holds even when factoring in the hegemonic power of a few states, which meant and continues to mean that most national states were in practice not fully sovereign.

Existing theory is not enough to map today's multiplication of practices and actors contributing to these rescalings. Included are a variety of nonstate actors and forms of cross-border cooperation and conflict, such as global business networks, the new cosmopolitanism, nongovernmental organizations (NGOs), diasporic networks, and spaces such as global cities and transboundary public spheres. International relations (IR) theory is the field that, to date, has had the most to say about cross-border relations. But current developments associated with various mixes of globalization and the new information and communications technologies point to the limits of IR theory and data. Several critical scholarships have examined how its models and theories remain focused on the logic of relations between states and the scale of the state at a time when we see a proliferation of nonstate actors, cross-border processes, and associated changes in the scope, exclusivity, and competence of state authority over its territory.

A second feature is the multiscalar character of various globalization processes. A financial center in a global city is a local entity that is also part of a globally scaled electronic market. We might think of this as an instance where the local is multiscalar, not simply part of a nested scalar hierarchy. Similarly, the WTO is a global entity, but it becomes active once it gets inserted into national economies and polities and can thus also be conceived of as multiscalar. These instances cannot easily be accommodated into older nested hierarchies of scale, which position everything that is supranational above the state in the scalar hierarchy and what is subnational beneath the state. In such hierarchies, the subnational needs to run through the national state if it is to function globally.

A more complex multiscalar configuration can be seen in the operational space of multinational firms: It includes as key components both far-flung networks of affiliates and concentrations of strategic functions in a single or a few locations. Perhaps most familiar here is, again, the bundle of conditions and dynamics that marks the model of the global city. In its most abstract formulation this is captured in one of the key organizing hypotheses of the global city model, to wit, that the more globalized and digitized the operations of firms and markets become, the more their central management and specialized servicing functions — and the requisite infrastructures and buildings — become strategic and complex, thereby benefiting from agglomeration economies. To variable extents these agglomeration economies are still delivered through territorial concentrations of multiple resources; that is to say, they are delivered through cities. That variety of multiscalar dynamics points to conditions that cannot be organized as a hierarchy, let alone a nested hierarchy. This is a multiscalar system, operating across scales and not, as is so often said, merely scaling upward because of new communication capabilities.

Alternative approaches that go beyond older scalar hierarchies, micro/macro analyses, and container categories such as nation–states are gaining traction. Here I would like to single out analyses that emphasize topological patterns rather than nested scalar hierarchies, actor networks rather than actors per se, and the disassembling of familiar, often naturalized national arrangements and their reassembling into novel global and denationalized formations. The chapters in this book contribute to these alternative approaches.

The Subnational: A Site for the Global and the Translocal

Studying the global, then, entails not only a focus on what is explicitly global in scale. It also calls for a focus on locally scaled practices and conditions articulated with global dynamics; perhaps the most developed scholarships with this type of focus are those on global cities and commodity chains. And it calls for a focus on the multiplication of cross-border connections among subnational localities where certain conditions recur, such as the conditions for capital accumulation required by today's economy, the conditions for expatriate enclaves, human rights abuses, environmental damage, and community mobilizing around certain struggles. Finally, it entails recognizing that many of the globally scaled dynamics actually are partly embedded in subnational sites and move across these differently scaled practices and organizational forms.

The chapters in this book variously illustrate some of the conceptual, methodological, and empirical issues in this type of study.

The first part, "Scalings: Global Microspaces" contains chapters on a neighborhood, a public space, a landmarked historic district, an evangelical community, and a favela. What they share is that the locality is not simply a microcosm of some larger macroscale or an entity subsumed in scalar hierarchies. These localities are productive in that they make possible processes and conditions that situate them in often complex scalar interactions and translocal networks. They are not simply sites for the extraction of value by national and global actors —as might have been a mine or a plantation in a colonial empire or in today's neocolonialisms. Even when they have suffered severely, as in the favelas of São Paulo studied by Simone Buechler, they are also the sites for making conditions for survival and politics. Richard Lloyd and Matthew Hill show how localities can develop the conditions that allow them to draw the global economy into some of their concrete and specific processes: the creative economy in Lloyd's study of Wicker Park in Chicago and global tourism in landmarked Old Havana in Cuba. Marina Peterson shows how public concert programming in downtown Los Angeles intersects with defining features of globalization concerning the economy, politics and state scaling, and media. Sarah Busse Spencer shows how missionaries and NGOs bring the global in bits and pieces into the living rooms and lives of locals in Novosibirsk, Russia.

The second part, "Translocal Circuits and Their Mobilities," also plays on places but as components of translocal circuits and multiple mobilities. A focus on places here allows us to detect the diverse circuits constitutive of economic, political, cultural, social, and subjective globalization. Rachel Harvey shows us how a global financial market is constituted both through global electronic networks and through local cultures. But also the Techno and New Age neo-nomads examined by Anthony D'Andrea navigate both globe-spanning circuits and very specific places: Goa, Ibiza, and kindred sites. Heather Hindman's mid-level expatriate communities in Nepal are by definition geographically mobile, but they are so through movement among a series of fixed places with an infrastructure that creates continuity. No matter how transnational their struggles, Evalyn Tennant's activist networks pivot on face-to-face interactions. Gracia Farrer's Chinese immigrants in Japan find their specific advantage in the frontier of a fast growing transnational economy between the two countries.

The third part of this book, "The Political: Shifting Spaces and Subjects," examines the rearticulation of the political focusing specifically on novel types of spaces, scalings, and actors. Together these chapters underline the particular diversity of the political today. Anne Bartlett shows how the struggle in Darfur extends into London as the city becomes part of the political field within which the conflict gets enacted. Rami Nashashibi examines the intersection of Islam with a Chicago street gang and hiphop in the contemporary American ghetto as a site for a novel type of cosmopolitanism. Jennifer Johnson studies the emergence of extralegal community policing in Mexico's coffee-growing highlands arising out of farmers' struggles for economic survival and the options for exiting state-sanctioned choices that are introduced in their lives by human rights NGOs. Moving into the state, Josh Kaplan investigates whether human rights struggles can succeed under conditions of a permanent state of emergency in Israel. Kamal Sadiq shows how in a developing country such as Malaysia, the question of who is a citizen and who is an immigrant does not follow the prevailing theories on the matter. Finally, going against the common notion of states dominated by global actors, Giselle Datz demonstrates how heavily indebted national states keep securing financing from their global creditors in spite of recurrent defaults.

Behind these empirical cases, each based on original research in the field and in archives, lies an engagement with conceptual and methodological questions. The next section revisits each of these chapters in more detail, focusing on this engagement.

Elements for Mapping a Field of Inquiry

Studying global processes and conditions that get constituted subnationally has some advantages over studies of self-evident global entities, but it also poses specific challenges. It makes possible the use of long-standing research techniques, from quantitative to qualitative, in the study of globalization. It also provides a bridge for using the wealth of national and subnational data sets as well as specialized scholarships such as area studies. However, as indicated earlier, both types of studies need to be situated in novel conceptual architectures; the researchers who generated these research techniques and data sets pursued questions that mostly had little to do with globalization.

As already indicated, the first part brings together studies where the key conceptual, methodological, and empirical effort is to detect how localities or local conditions are productive in the shaping of an articulation with global dynamics rather than merely victimized by the global. Neither this articulation nor the productivity of the local is self-evident. Seeing them entails constructing conceptual architectures that allow a researcher using ethnographies, surveys, or archival research to detect them. Not only the object of study but also the distinct scholarships each author engages varies across chapters.

Lloyd contests the common notions that globalization homogenizes place and that it subsumes the local in hierarchies of extraction. He counterposes the notion of local space as productive. He posits the possibility that local space in a global city can, under specific conditions, incorporate a mode of spatial practice that materializes at the intersection of global economic forces and postindustrial urban restructuring. To capture this possibility Lloyd chooses to focus on a specific cultural-economic formation, one he calls *neo-bohemia*. He conceptualizes neo-bohemia as a mode of spatial practice increasingly central to current strategies of capital accumulation in particular types of urban neighborhoods in global cities. The cities that have such bohemian enclaves have changed sharply over the last few decades. A central thesis in Lloyd's work is that the interaction between this neo-bohemia and the new urban economy cannot be read through the premises of older bohemia's cultural autonomy and economic marginality. In revealing the economic centrality of neo-bohemia, Lloyd's study contributes to the economics of bohemian space. This is a subject long neglected in the literature; its recent recovery has mostly been through the more limited concept of artists and bohemia adding value to real estate. Lloyd expands the analytic terrain within which to study these trends by noting the economic value of artists' work itself to the corporate economy. He uses ethnography, but his aim is to construct an analytics. The potential of this study is further strengthened by the fact that it is an ethnography of a neighborhood in Chicago, the emblematic national and industrial city. Beyond this historical fact, today's new scholarship about the spaces of global urbanism represents Chicago's urban form as obsolete and juxtaposes it to the decentered sprawl of Los Angeles, the new postmodern urban form.

Peterson's research examines the vast multiscalar and largely invisible social, political, and financial infrastructure set in motion through what on the surface appears to be a rather simple series of public performances. Her research shows how a modest urban intervention in a city with large numbers of immigrants draws global dimensions into the concentrated and confined site of a public concert. The public performance is the beginning of a thread that moves through multiple domains and ultimately scales globally because of the type of city in which it originates. The city is Los Angeles, with its many connections to places and peoples around the world. The locality — downtown Los Angeles — in part produces these global articulations through the work of developing a public performances project. In this process the global is drawn into that local environment. Much making takes place. The focus is on the making of public space and the making of new kinds of civic subjects. Peterson notes that "these are civic subjects simultaneously marked as minority, part of a multicultural civic body, and transnational." The mix of themes she brings to bear on her examination have mostly been the objects of "separate literatures in the analysis of globalization and the global city." Insufficient attention has gone to their intersection and to how they contribute to constitute the global city — alongside the more familiar actors such as the new transnational professional class and global firms. Even less attention has gone to the ways in which public concerts emerge as translocal civic spaces through their articulation with global processes and the figuring of local multiculturalism as international. Thereby, the global is brought to the city, and the city is made global.

Hill examines yet another mechanism launched by localities to become articulated with global projects. The mechanism is heritage preservation, and the global project is tourism. The fact that Hill focuses on heritage in socialist Cuba adds a third critical actor in the larger process: the national state. This mix of conditions remains understudied. It becomes a lens through which to analyze the structural and contingent forms of scale-making in the late socialist global periphery. Hill identifies three scale-making projects that partly constitute and make visible a reshaping of the experience of place in late socialist Cuba: the cosmopolitan project of the United Nations Educational, Scientific, and Cultural Organization (UNESCO) to unite the entire world through the creation of a global heritage network; the efforts of urban conservationists to transform Old Havana into a distinctive place through the restoration of the colonial city center; and the socialist state project of maintaining hegemony through its allocative power. Using ethnography, interviews, and archival research, Hill examines the multiple tensions that emerge out of the intersection of these three projects.

Spencer examines the process of becoming global in a place where the outside world is still remote and the state prefers it that way. The place is Novosibirsk, and the state is Russia. She identifies two distinct components in this process: (1) the interaction with the global other; and (2) the adoption of foreign behaviors and attitudes through face-to-face contact with outsiders. She posits that the first involves the globalization of a person's social networks, whereas the second involves, to some extent, the adoption of a global habitus. Newly globalizing settings make legible the effect of globalizing agents on the process of becoming global. In Russia, long closed to the outside world, individuals in local settings can be seen to choose whether to become global, and how extensively so, as they are confronted with global influences and presences. Using ethnography, Spencer examines a U.S.-based missionary Christian church and an NGO support center founded and funded by U.S. and British sources.

Buechler addresses the fact that individuals, households, and neighborhood communities remain insufficiently studied as part of major global processes that have often devastating socioeconomic effects. When the globalization literature focuses on the local it has tended to focus on how local actors enter the global arena, most notably through NGOs. In contrast, Buechler focuses on local actors working at the local level to address global conditions that affect their local conditions, particularly the level and quality of employment. To that end, she deconstructs the local scale into three organizational levels: the individual low-income worker, community associations, and municipal governments. One question here is whether the devolution of power from the national state to municipalities has made a difference in the ability of individual workers and community associations to confront the degradation of their livelihoods by aligning themselves with their municipal government. Buechler posits that if municipal governments are made up of similar elites as those of national governments, it cannot be assumed that they will have an exclusively local agenda. They may or may not respond to the new global political and ideological pressures with distinctively local interests in mind; they might also support the global neoliberal agenda of the national state for their own self-interest. The fact that they are local elites does not necessarily mean that they know the needs of their constituents or, even if they do, that they will act in the latter's interest. Understanding the conditions for local empowerment requires disaggregating the local in terms of the different social classes and interests that comprise it.

Part Two begins with the chapter by Tennant. She contests what is today the prevalent analytic distinction in the study of social movements and activism: national versus transnational movements. She posits that whether national or transnational, it is analytically more productive to distinguish social movements in terms of face-to-face versus translocal mediated forms of interaction. Further, insofar as the interactions within a social movement can produce multiple scalings, one critical question becomes whether such a movement functions through nested scalings or cuts across the traditional hierarchies centered in national states. Understanding today's social movements through this more complex analytic grid entails contesting three common assumptions about space, scale, and organization. One assumption conflates the local and the national: local collective actors and movement dynamics are seen as mere micro-instantiations of the national. The second assumption, which partly contradicts the first, represents people as embedded within local territorial contexts; access to the national or global is mediated through nested scalar hierarchies running through national states. The third assumption, though closely related to the second, concerns social networks and has different implications. People are presented not only as embedded in particular, located social contexts but also as stuck there — immobilized. In her research Tennant finds that many recent and contemporary movements are organized across, rather than within, these nested scalar hierarchies centered on national states. Her thesis is that these movements can thus be more productively understood as the translocal collection of distributed forms of locally organized collective action.

D'Andrea examines cultural globalization as a domain where new forms of subjectivity and identity are being developed in complex interactions with familiar major global processes. He sees in this focus one way of redressing the often residual character given to the cultural in globalization research, with culture reduced to reactive identities and ideologies, instruments for adapting to major global figurations. Building on what he sees as the relations of affinity between globalization and countercultures, he focuses on mobile expatriates involved in a cosmopolitan culture of expressive individualism. The empirical cases he uses for this examination are Techno and New Age transnational countercultures. He conceptualizes these particular countercultures as expressing and amplifying global processes but in a contestatory mode. Thus, while they produce sociocultural patterns marked by fluidity, changeability, and reflexivity, they do so as a global counterculture, a type of negative diaspora that rejects their homelands. The research project is a multisited ethnography of these countercultures as produced within specific worlds of artists, therapists, bohemians, and expatriates; these typically inhabit peripheral zones of global cities and global tourist regions. Given their marginal and hypermobile character, D'Andrea develops the thesis that these countercultures are one empirical instance of a form of *global neonomadism*. Understanding how these global neonomads interact with local economies and moral orders is a lens into the cultural logics constituting globalization.

Hindman examines the growing world of globalization's middlemen to understand how questions of culture are and are not accommodated by global processes of specialized outsourcing. To do this she uses the case of expatriate training and compensation systems and illustrates how the creation of a generic process limits the space allowed for difference. More so than other professionals, expatriates are expected to have a significant engagement with the culture of the countries where they are posted. The mission of the expatriate worker is to be loyal to a home nation and a home company and to act as the embodiment of a presumed organic connection of nation, state, culture, and identity. The value of the expatriate employee is precisely their ability to act as translators of difference, without "going native." Hindman questions the value of "culture general" approaches to training and raises the hypothesis that valuing the culture of the place where the expatriate is posted is a façade for a process of creating an acultural space for business, be it a government's or multinational firm's agenda. The empirical focus is on the institutions that frame the expatriate's experience and that bring consistency across the many different locations of expatriate life. Hindman examines the agents and instruments, amounting to a whole new industry of specialized services that forms expatriates through testing, calculations of hardship, and an emerging discourse on both expatriate failure and the possibility of creating an unmoored, international employee. This shaping of the expatriate becomes a lens through which

Hindman explores how culture is codified within what is represented as a seemingly cosmopolitan and multicultural population.

Farrer engages the proposition that immigrants' transnational entrepreneurship is a form of adaptation, the prevailing explanation in the literature. She posits that though born out of immigrant-specific conditions, this entrepreneurship cannot be simply treated as yet another mode of adaptation. Adaptation does not sufficiently capture the scope, content, and significance of immigrant entrepreneurship. Farrer counters the prevalent explanation with the thesis that besides striving to survive and adapt, transnational immigrant entrepreneurs are also active facilitators of transnational economies with the potential to change and develop the global economy. The concepts of scale and network help explain the ways immigrants manage not only to participate in global processes but also to contribute to these through their grassroots efforts and often haphazard enterprising. The task for Farrer is to find out how they enter the process of transnational capitalism. The most common understanding is that immigrants do so through their demand for goods and services from their home countries; this becomes a driving force for some industries to expand their production and markets globally. This view presents immigrants' effect on transnational corporations and the global economy mainly as a function of their consumption capacity. She sets out to establish how immigrants become active participants in the producing of globalization. She uses interviews and a survey of Chinese immigrants in Tokyo who have become transnational entrepreneurs between the two countries.

Harvey contests the notion that global financial markets exist outside the institutional matrices and sociocultural milieus of the national, in a sort of "grand victory of time over space." She posits that national and subnational processes are necessary for constituting and running global financial markets. The empirical case she uses to explore this thesis is the London Gold Fix, which emerged as a global market between 1950 and the mid-1990s. That this particular market should have become global is particularly intriguing given its character. It was neither an electronic market nor a continuous pricing mechanism, unlike the ideal typical global financial market of much of the globalization literature. The Gold Fix set the price of gold twice a day from the offices of one of the market makers in London's financial district, in a slow-motion overlap of local, national, and global scalings. Through archival research and interviews with key actors in today's Gold Fix, Harvey seeks to establish the specific role of national and subnational processes in the making and running of this global market.

The third part begins with the chapter by Bartlett. She posits that the city is a vital space for the emergence of new political practices and subjects at a time when national political conflicts can enter translocal circuits. The lens Bartlett uses to get at this possibility is how the politics of global south countries are "brought to life on the streets of Western cities" and how immigrant groups in these cities become political. As these cities receive large numbers of foreign nationals and can accommodate multiple forms of political action, the possible roles of cities in producing the conditions for political action expand to include a growing array of transnational struggles. Given the variable outcomes of these struggles — from emancipatory and inclusive to reactionary and exclusive — Bartlett sets out to understand what drives these diverse possibilities. These political practices and subjects are not necessarily transparent. She proposes to research "microclimates of politics" within the larger political grid of a complex city. This brings to the fore questions of boundaries and of the existence of informal politics that are not necessarily aligned with the politics of the host city and country, or with the formal political system of the home country. Bartlett posits that this possibility makes cities productive politically, as in the making of new political practices and subjects. Her empirical focus is on the Darfur crisis and Darfurian immigrants in London who are politically engaged by the crisis back home. In this research she uses participant observation and ethnography to analyze the processes through which some of these Darfurian immigrants become new types of political subjects in London and how the city becomes a specific type of political field for that far-away crisis.

Nashashibi takes on a space and subject that have so far been rarely linked to the global: the ghetto and the gang. His thesis is that the presence of Islam in a black U.S. ghetto and the globalizing trends of hip-hop unsettle the common view of the ghetto as a hyperisolated and parochial space. Nashashibi wants to go beyond the growing consensus among urban social scientists that a new set of dynamics marks the modern ghetto — captured in concepts such as the *third ghetto*, the *postindustrial ghetto*, the *excluded ghetto*, and the *hyperghetto*. As much as they advance our understanding of the particular kind of space that is the modern ghetto, these concepts do not extensively theorize the presence of the global through these changes. Nashashibi advances the notion of *ghetto cosmopolitanism* to capture a multilayered space anchored within the periphery of today's global city. In considering aspects of contemporary ghetto space the most unlikely source for alternative notions of cosmopolitanism, Nashashibi expands on work that deciphers the global within local and seemingly very provincial spaces. He uses archival and ethnographic research to understand this evolution of a legendary Chicago black street gang and within the world of hip-hop.

Johnson explores what happens to institutions and practices foundational to liberal democracy when the market becomes the preferred mechanism for addressing social issues. The particular institutional domain through which she studies the larger question is that of the legitimacy of state control through policing. Johnson contests particular aspects of the scholarship that sees economic globalization as deeply implicated in the development of a new penal state. Rising rates of incarceration, the expansion of prison facilities and personnel, increasingly punitive sentencing laws, and more intrusive correctional practices have contributed to the notion of the penal state. This process is marked by a simultaneous retreat of the state from economic regulation and its reentrenchment in the sphere of crime control and punishment. Johnson engages this scholarship by positing that concurrent to the overarching expansion of state regulatory power in the penal realm, the global ascendancy of the market paradigm has set in motion countervailing forces that also erode the national state's monopoly on the legitimate means of coercion. Her empirical research focuses on new subnational forms of political community that effectively claim the right to make and enforce penal law over and against opposition from recognized state institutions. Insofar as these subnational entities displace the national state as the fulcrum for claims making, we can posit that state transformation is occurring. But it is happening in a radically different way than the penal state literature suggests. She examines this possibility through an ethnography of an extralegal community policing movement in Mexico.

Kaplan examines the limits of state power in emergencies, that is to say, when the state's very existence is threatened and, hence, exceptional measures can be invoked legally. His window into this question is the existence of transnational regimes and international norms that can, in principle, legitimately contest state abuse of its power. The empirical case he uses is the human rights regime in the state of Israel in the current period. Few states under the rule of law have gathered as much power as Israel with its permanent state of emergency already in place before its founding in 1948. But Israel also has standing as a state under the rule of law. These two conditions set up a strong tension between state rights and human rights that can illuminate the possible existence of limits to such state power. States of exception in response to threats to the existence of a state justify by law government actions that would otherwise be considered unacceptable and morally reprehensible, illegal, and contrary to human rights. Further, the human rights regime is commonly recognized to be a weak regime. It has weak enforcement options, depending as it does on enforcement by the state, and also provides for exceptions to its implementation in the face of existential threat. This means that any indication of its capacity to contest or contain state power can be seen as an indicator of limits to that power. Kaplan uses research on the jurisprudence of Israel's High Court, one that has at least at times successfully challenged various decisions and practices of the executive branch and has ruled in favor of Palestinians. And he uses ethnographic research and interviews to study a transnational human rights movement in Israel.

Sadiq engages the question of citizenship through the lens of immigration. He contests the proposition that citizenship is a privilege the state bestows on people within its borders. This proposition is foundational to much of the scholarship on citizenship and immigration. Traditional understandings of citizenship continue to assume that only legal immigrants — not illegal immigrants — are eligible for naturalization and thereafter various privileges, notably voting. Sadiq's central concern is to detect the possible limits of citizenship as traditionally understood. He uses the case of developing countries under the rule of law to examine whether it is indeed the case that democratic states protect the privilege of national and state-level voting for their citizens. His empirical research on the intersection of citizenship and immigration in Malaysia contrasts with the usual focus on highly developed countries in the scholarship on citizenship and immigration. Sadiq uses archival research about granting citizenship documents to residents in a particular region of Malaysia, as well as ethnographic research and interviews with political officials, residents, and immigrants in that same region. This research illuminates the possibility that citizenship ceases to be a clear-cut, well-defined category at a time when globalization is redefining various features of the nation-state. His central claim about the increasing dependence on paperwork to identify individuals results in what Sadiq conceives of as the *documentary citizenship* of illegal immigrants. He expects documentary citizenship will increase in developing countries as more states rely on paperwork to identify their members.

Datz contests the prevailing notion in the scholarship that under the current neoliberal regime developing country states confront overwhelming constraints in their policy options. She uses as her empirical case states facing demands from their global creditors that they restructure their debts subject to IMF conditions. Datz hypothesizes that the view of overwhelming constraints on these states' policy options does not align well with the extensive evidence of successful debt restructurings by developing countries that have defaulted more than once. Few instances diverge as sharply from the preferences of financial markets and the supranational financial system as the suspension of payments on debt owed to private creditors who purchase government bonds both domestically and internationally. Datz sets out to understand what these cases of successful debt restructuring in the face of recurrent defaults tell us about state autonomy in today's world, where global institutions have the power and authority to impose often extreme conditions on states, particularly developing country states. Her empirical cases are sovereign default and debt restructurings of Ecuador, Russia, and Argentina. She posits that we need far more refined conceptualizations of scalar interactions producing opportunities and constraints for both state and nonstate actors, domestically and globally. To that end she advances an approach for analyzing the outcome of debt restructuring processes that combines a macrolevel understanding of lending cycles with the microeconomic sociology of financial markets.

The chapters in this book show us the breadth of the research and theorization agenda on globalization and denationalization. They make legible features not usually addressed in the pertinent scholarships.

Notes

1. The scholarship alluded to in this brief introduction is vast. It seems best to direct the interested reader to the bibliographic materials in each chapter of this volume, as well as to Sassen (2006), which contains detailed discussions of the key points raised here and extensive citations to further literature.
2. For an elaboration of how the social sciences, especially sociology, could develop their existing empirical and interpretive tools to address the question of the global see Sassen (2007).

Works Cited

Sassen, Saskia. 2006. *Territory, authority, rights: From medieval to global assemblages.* Princeton, NJ: Princeton University Press.

——— 2007. *A Sociology of Globalization.* New York: Norton.

PART 1
Scalings: Global Microspaces

CHAPTER 1

Postindustrial Bohemia

Culture, Neighborhood, and the Global Economy

RICHARD LLOYD

If it is the case, as Walter Benjamin claimed, that "every epoch...dreams the one to follow," (1999, p. 13) then perhaps we need to think of that space of the urban avant-garde called bohemia not as a thing erased by globalization — with its presumed leveling and homogenizing tendencies — but rather as a mode of spatial practices whose true importance is only fully realized in the intersections of global economic forces and postindustrial urban restructuring. For Benjamin, the nineteenth-century Parisian arcades were dreamworlds anticipating the onset of the mass spectacles of consumer capitalism (Benjamin 1999). Also in the nineteenth century, the throng of underemployed artists and intellectuals colonizing the garrets, cabarets, and cafés of the French capital hatched a durable dream of the artist in the city, with all the romanticized lifestyle connotations attached to this position: heroic self-sacrifice, rejection of bourgeois morality, art for art's sake. This dream remains alive, only now contributing to the production of a symbolic economy that commands ever greater attention in the contemporary metropolis.

Indeed, though the cultural legacy of bohemia has long been considered to be disproportionate to its size and frequency, until recent decades its economic impact has been little treated. After all, the field of cultural production, and especially the position staked out by the avant-garde, operates according to principles that seem to reverse ordinary economic logic (Bourdieu 1992). But macrostructural transformation at the *fin-de-millenaire* confounds this popular judgment. Elements of the modernist bohemia persist; as Brooks (2001, p. 67) points out, "The French intellectuals designed ways of living that are by now familiar to us all," and in fact, bohemia and its familiar lifestyle affectations are only more frequent in the present period. But the cities that host these enclaves have changed dramatically, and the interaction between bohemia and the new urban economy requires that old premises of bohemia's cultural autonomy and economic marginality be retired.

To capture the intersection of cultural continuity and structural change, I advance the concept of neo-bohemia, identifying a mode of spatial practices increasingly central to strategies of capital accumulation in select urban neighborhoods. Neo-bohemia signals both continuity and change. There is sufficient resonance between the ideologies and practices of contemporary urban artists and those of previous generations to render them legibly bohemian. Still, the new bohemia also contributes to novel outcomes under the conditions of structural transformation associated with economic globalization. These conditions are (1) new geographies of industrial production, transforming the economic base underlying neighborhood formation in older cities; (2) a changing urban occupational structure favoring educated and adaptable workers and demanding greater flexibility at all levels of the occupational hierarchy; (3) increased polarization, as the older blue-collar middle class is squeezed and as the city becomes hardened into stark contrasts of privilege and devastation; and (4) increased emphasis on the immaterial attributes of the commodity form, that is on symbolic value generated via aesthetic differentiation.

Among urban scholars, the most noted element of the new bohemia has been the correspondence between the agglomeration of artists and alternative subcultures in a district and the subsequent local improvements in amenities and class of residents known as gentrification. But if this is the most obvious contribution made by the artist in the city to capital valorization, it is nonetheless typically not well understood in terms of its broader spatial and historical context. Analysis of artist-led gentrification suffers from an overemphasis on spectacle and a tendency to treat residents strictly as consumers, failing to grasp that they are simultaneously workers in a reconstituted urban occupational structure.

The problem is not that urban scholars have failed to notice the proliferation of new bohemias but rather that they are too often blinded to the real importance of these spaces. Scholarly judgment is impaired by nostalgic commitment to the modernist bohemia that leads contemporary heirs to be quickly dismissed as shallow and inauthentic, by the conviction that the logic of gentrification is already known and is apparently unchanging, and, finally, by a notion of what constitutes *production* that is still locked in industrial-era modes of categorization and analysis. All of this amounts to a missed opportunity, for the new bohemia is a particularly sharp lens onto the dynamic interplay between the forces of economic globalization and the existing forms of both built environment and cultural styling within the city.

Neo-bohemia signals a mode of spatial practices central to new strategies of capital accumulation, confounding notions of bohemia's social alterity and economic marginality. Shifting relations of production in the global city entail a new workforce, amenable to post-Fordist contingency and competent to the requirements of an increasingly aesthetic economy. As in the modernist bohemia, creative individuals derive benefits from urban association. Global shifts in capitalism elevate the importance of these practices to the reconfiguration of the neighborhood as a site of accumulation. The concept of bohemia retains utility, but its contribution to the contemporary production of neighborhood space must be reexamined in geohistorical context.

This proposition finds support in the most unlikely of case studies for a volume that purports to navigate the labyrinth of scales and spaces through which the global economy is actively produced. In addition to rebooting a concept — bohemia — typically taken as a quintessential artifact of modernism, this chapter, though primarily analytic rather than descriptive, derives from ethnographic work, a method usually considered by its very nature to be local and ahistorical (Burawoy 2000). Moreover, this ethnographic work is undertaken at the neighborhood level in the city of Chicago, the prototype of a metropolis forged by the dynamics of the national, mass-production society. In fact, leading attempts to capture the signature spaces of global urbanism insist — explicitly or implicitly — on Chicago's morphological obsolescence, focusing instead on Manhattan's hypervalorized financial district (Sassen 2001) or on the decentered sprawl of Los Angeles — almost metaphorically mirroring the dispersals of global capital (Dear 2002; Soja 1996) — or more recently on the proliferating slums of the developing world (Davis 2006). But as we see in Chicago — or in Brooklyn or a range of other anachronistic places — former industrial neighborhoods, once strongholds of white ethnics, political machines, and organized labor, are now playing a new role in the global economy, ironically drawing on the legacy of the old bohemian dream.

From Sweatshop to Distraction Factory

A relatively nondescript brick building in Chicago's Wicker Park district, once a white ethnic enclave and site of light industry nestled along the

El line on the near northwest side of downtown, tells a surprisingly rich tale of social transformation. Erected in the early twentieth century, this building housed a dressmaker's sweatshop where young immigrants, most likely Polish women living in walking distance toiled (Coorens 2003). It captures the character of place and period. Chicago, the shock city of the frontier, was a national center of industry whose explosive growth was fueled largely by European immigration. The sweatshop, with its cramped work conditions, piece-rate compensation, and intimate scale, is a signature space of early twentieth-century laissez-faire capitalism.

By midcentury, the building and its surrounding district were already growing increasingly anachronistic. The hyperexploitative labor relations were undermined by government regulation, labor union power, and the end of the stream of new European immigrants whose daughters might be slotted into the line. Chicago's identity as an industrial titan now rested on the hulking steel mills of the South Shore, not the West Side's comparatively puny industry. Of course, the economic hegemony of even these large-scale enterprises would prove stunningly fragile, as would the institutional arrangements at both the municipal and national scales that characterized mature Fordism. The 1970s were a period of extreme crisis, in Chicago as elsewhere, that we now understand as the birth pangs of the reregulations associated with globalization and an increasingly neoliberal mode of governance.

Mirroring the malaise of the industrial order, the building had fallen into disrepair, languishing underused as a storage facility, while the neighborhood around it was steadily losing population. By the 1980s, it housed a "shooting gallery," where heroin and other narcotics were sold and ingested. Outside, street prostitution thrived. This seedy commerce might be read as the consequence of an economic shift that could only leave this building a relic, a sign of the progressive displacement of industry that robbed the neighborhood of a more legitimate economic base.

But in 1989, the old brick building became home to a new occupant, the Urbus Orbis Café, which catered to and helped to make visible the growing number of young people, many with artistic aspirations, who were moving into the neighborhood. The opening of Urbus Orbis marked a new turn in the neighborhood's identity, and in its modest lifetime the café was hailed as a premier site in the constitution of Chicago's new bohemia. Wicker Park had languished in obscurity throughout the 1980s, its mostly Latino population struggling to make a community within an increasingly derelict urban landscape, but by the middle of the next decade it was a widely recognized site of cultural innovation and a generator of urban cool in which artists, musicians, and young professionals sipped coffee and admired the locally produced artwork decorating Urbus Orbis's exposed brick walls.

Despite its popularity, in 1998 Urbus Orbis succumbed to the many perils that beset small businesses, including in this case the gentrification of the neighborhood, which made operation increasingly expensive. An antique store followed with an even shorter tenancy in the same space. In 2001 a tenant with considerably deeper pockets rehabbed the building into an odd combination of television studio and residential space. It became home for an installment of MTV's popular program *The Real World*, a pioneer of the reality television wave. *The Real World* sets up an eclectic cast of young people in a domicile of putative urban cool and turns cameras on their presumably unscripted experience for the vicarious entertainment of a global audience.

If the hip was once constituted in connection with outlaws and alienation, it is now an urban amenity, exportable through the circuits of the global commodity chain. MTV's selection of the loft to stage its exercise in cinema semi-verite ratifies the ongoing status of the neighborhood as hipster ground zero in Chicago, a designation Urbus Orbis once helped facilitate. Meanwhile, local artists and hip kids have been markedly ambivalent toward MTV's cooptation of a neighborhood aesthetic over which they feel proprietary (Kleine 2001). This is characteristic of new accumulation strategies, with bohemian activity in the city translated into a means to profit for other interests, even against the ideological opposition of those who make the scene.

The strange odyssey of this squat brick structure from light industry to residential media object is as good a place as any to begin examining the new role of old neighborhoods and cultural tropes in the shifting geography of capitalist accumulation. Whereas the story in Chicago was once steel and stockyards, now it is culture and technology. Inherited structures of the industrial past are marked by the new spatial practices characterizing this shift. The building has gone from sweatshop to postmodern distraction factory, where everyday life, leisure, and image production merge. Trendy nightclubs, artists' lofts, and the offices of multimedia design firms currently occupy similar structures around the neighborhood. Local residences that once housed a blue-collar labor force now accommodate artists, students, and educated young professionals thriving on the local ambiance of urban cool.

These transformations are fully decipherable only by taking account of forces that are global in scope. Against traditions of neighborhood study in Chicago that tended to treat local communities as "mosaic little worlds" (Hannerz 1980, p. 19-58), making sense of the emergent culture of Wicker Park requires a multiscalar and historically sensitive conceptual frame.

Industry displacement and the decline of blue-collar community is one obvious outcome of macrostructural transformation. So is the breakdown of the institutions of the urban industrial order, replacing welfare state liberalism with a more entrepreneurial, or neoliberal, mode of local governance. New modes of interurban competition now revolve around the signature enterprises of the global city — corporate administration, but even more the production of innovations in a range of producer services and creative industries (Florida 2002; Sassen 2001). In this environment, new strategies of good government promote privatization and the production of lifestyle amenities geared to the specific tastes of a new class of knowledge workers, whose interests soundly trump those of working class or minority coalitions (Clark et al. 2002; Sites 2003).

As Sassen (2001) documents, a chief characteristic of the global city is the elevation and overvalorization of finance and other high-end producer services; indeed, these sectors provide a better measure of the coordination of global economic activity from big city perches than does the standard indicator of corporate headquarters (Sassen 2001). These highly specialized and innovative sectors are particularly reliant on the advantages of dense urban agglomeration and are therefore resistant to the dispersal seemingly enabled by telematics and digital communication. To these exemplars of postindustrial production must be added the production of culture — a sector of increasing import to first-world economic fortunes and one equally bound to urban locales, by both long tradition and immediate requirements. The hypermobility of capital — increasing the complexity of financial instruments and transactions and requiring a host of specialized services — has also been accompanied by the heightened aestheticization of the economy. As Jameson (1991, p. 4) notes, "What has happened is that aesthetic production today has become integrated into commodity production generally: the frantic economic urgency of producing fresh waves of ever more novel-seeming goods…at ever greater rates of turnover, now assigns an increasingly essential structural function and position to aesthetic innovation and experimentation." Rather than being merely anachronistic, neighborhoods like Wicker Park, once predicated on the spatial practices of blue-collar manufacturing, are reconfigured as strategic sites in the novel economy of the aesthetic.

Spatial Practices

Henri Lefebvre's (1974) concept of spatial practices highlights the active and dialectical nature of this socially produced space. A neighborhood like Wicker Park is not an empty container in which social processes unfold. Elements of the neighborhood's cumulative character, including its old brick buildings, are a source of opportunity and constraint that actively structure a trajectory of activities across time, even as such activities transform the neighborhood. Moreover, just as the concept of spatial practice avoids discounting the contributions of space to process, it also resists the ecological fallacies associated with many past conceptions of neighborhood, privileging space over time. The ecological properties of the Wicker Park neighborhood are not sufficient to compel the outcomes I document. Neo-bohemia is produced in the dialectical interplay between the structuring influences of local exigencies and the needs of particular global forces for hitting the ground in specific types of thick environments. Thus, social theory cannot confine observation only to the neighborhood space but must continuously take into account the structuring forces of history and the wider social field.

The richness of the unadorned brick building on North Avenue is found in its continual reinscription by the social dynamics in which it is embedded, the active social reproduction of the building and the neighborhood by shifting social practices. Social space is inscribed by history and remains a dynamic and dialectical work in progress. Just as the exemplary building in discussion here is not reduced to relic, neither is the neighborhood. To understand the new relevance of Wicker Park to the contemporary mode of accumulation, we must consider the spatial practices that produce it, practices rooted in long-standing advantages of the urban form not only for durable manufacturing but also for aesthetic innovation. Cities, after all, have been sites not only for the production of steel and automobiles but also of the blues and abstract expressionism. In an aestheticized economy, this element of urban life grows more essential as a structuring principle, one that helps us to grasp postindustrial modes of production and the corresponding organization of labor power.

These practices are directly linked to the contemporary moment of capitalism; they express a relationship between a mode of accumulation that is global in scope and spatial outcomes at the local level. This does not mean that Wicker Park directly expresses the global economy; "the macro-micro link refers not to such an expressive totality, but to a structured one in which the part is shaped by its relation to the whole" (Burawoy 2000, p. 27). This is not to be confused with models that posit the subsumption of the *space of place* by the *space of flows* (Castells 1989). Instead, the place idiosyncrasy of Wicker Park, generated by local history and long-standing tropes of the urban cultural milieu, and the deracinated economy of global commodity exchange operate in a kind of tandem. Wicker Park is not merely strip mined by global capital; its neo-bohemian economy is simultaneously local and global in its costs and its rewards. In the neighborhood, familiar elements of the modernist bohemia acquire new meanings in relation to the structuring forces of the social field, with the global dispersal of production and the heightened aestheticization of the economy creating the context for former Chicago sweatshops being turned into coffee shops, television studios, or the loft offices of Internet design firms. To examine neo-bohemia as an instantiation of spatial practice is to foreground its relationship to a mode of accumulation rooted in aesthetic production, in which the immaterial attributes of the commodity form — the symbolic expressive content — become foregrounded in the chain of value added.

The factory, as the spatially grounded, materialized form of the mode of production, recedes in explanatory power for spatial production in the postindustrial West. However, the economy of informational flows and of signs circulating in space still involves material space — locations — of symbolic production, a point lost in much contemporary analysis. In neighborhoods like Wicker Park, the built environment of a past epoch may be reimagined in the service of new productive processes. Spatial practice "embraces production and reproduction, and the particular locations and spatial sets characteristic of each social formation" (Lefebvre 1974, p. 33). The relationship to space is active and dialectical; practice is conditioned by spatial configurations, and space is produced through practice. As we trace the history of Wicker Park, we see disjuncture and reconfiguration of spatial practice linked to global shifts in the social formation.

Rethinking Neighborhood

The discontinuities of sociospatial restructuring associated with globalization, neoliberalism, and post-Fordism pose a challenge to contemporary urban theorists, who struggle to separate neighborhood analysis from the industrialized mode of production that motivated Chicago's massive growth and initial morphology. As the social formation changes, so do relevant spatial practices. The cumulative character of the neighborhood endures,[1] and at the same time it interacts with the dynamics of a restructured social field. Industrial capitalism was the organizing principle behind Chicago's explosive growth, and the implicit background to the neighborhood morphology developed by the ethnographers working out of the University of Chicago in the first half of the century. Their diligent ethnography provides an irreplaceable record of that stage of urban development. However, their ecological functionalism lacks an account of contradiction and has proven poorly suited to account for the cluster of crises that beset the industrial city in the postindustrial period.

The crisis of the mass-production economy had significant impact on urban fortunes in the United States. The spatial practices appropriate to industrial production — the specific organizations of space and everyday life — came into conflict with new imperatives of the accumulation process. The flight of industry from the urban cores of cities like Chicago represents what Harvey (1982) refers to as a *spatial fix,* in which capital strives to circumvent the burdens of the outmoded production strategies and the relatively empowered labor that characterized Fordism. This disjuncture creates severe structural mismatch, marginalizing large portions of the urban landscape and population.

Old manufacturing cities like Chicago or Detroit were especially damaged in the wake of this capital flight, a far more damaging development for the core city than the white flight that accompanied industrial disinvestment. The burdens of urban decay are largely shouldered by African Americans in cities like Chicago and by newer immigrant groups, including the Puerto Ricans and Mexicans whose population quickly achieved majority status in many neighborhoods on Chicago's West Side after 1970. Wilson (1987, 1996) has extensively documented the economic devastation on Chicago's segregated South Side, with the loss of the manufacturing base contributing to unprecedented concentration of poverty and social isolation.

Similar effects are evident on the West Side, with the losses mostly in light industry rather than the monolithic steel mills. Indeed, Wicker Park lost manufacturing jobs at a rate in excess of the city as a whole: In the six-year period from 1977 and 1983 alone, 12,543 such jobs disappeared from the area. By 1990, the West Town poverty rate stood at 32 percent (Lester 2000). This was not as severe as some South Side neighborhoods, where the poverty rate climbed over 50 percent, but it was still substantially higher than the 21.6 percent rate for the city as a whole. Although in 1990 there were already signs of the incipient neo-bohemia in the neighborhood, few would have anticipated that Wicker Park would shortly be anointed "cutting edge's new capital" by *Billboard Magazine* (Boehlert 1993, p. 1) or that in 2001 the technology-sector magazine *Industry Standard* would hail it as "the best new place for media companies" (Jaffe 2001, p. 1).

During the 1990s, Wicker Park was effectively reinvented as a site of aesthetic innovation, incubating the work of artists and musicians and also attracting participants in design intensive economic activities, including an increasing presence in "media driven Internet companies" (Jaffe 2001, p. 1) These enterprises in graphic design and Internet content provision also use the spaces of production from an earlier era, while organizing a much different kind of labor force. The labor relations of late capitalism are characterized by the pressures of flexible accumulation, replacing the standardization of employment with more contingent and precarious arrangements (Beck 2000). This destabilizing of work is evident in both the degraded service sector to which the structurally disadvantaged turn after the flight of industry and in more elite sectors of the economy. Neo-bohemia comprises an intermediate space between deprivations of the service proletariat and the privileges of the professional class, displaying high levels of creativity and flexibility, and trading both compensation and security for rewards of status and lifestyle. The traditions of bohemia thus abet the flexible post-Fordist economy, facilitating aesthetic competencies and undergirding an ideology amenable to contingency and self-sacrifice.

The association of Wicker Park's gritty spaces with creative energy has helped initiate a new identity and concomitant development, which frequently does not benefit the populations who endured the hardships of post-Fordist restructuring. Yet the advantages the neighborhood space provides for new accumulation strategies are necessarily precarious even for the new worker populations. The reorganization of the neighborhood in the context of aesthetic production creates new conflicts and contradictions — and therefore ongoing dynamism. Neighborhood spatial practices organized around cultural production, entertainment, and technology may attract participants in part with the allure of glamour and riches, but as a practical matter contingency and instability characterize these strategies. Multiple interests intersect within the neighborhood — interests that are often incompatible. Neo-bohemia is a kind of spatial fix, creating new opportunities for capital accumulation. But, consistent with Harvey's argument (1982), such a magical solution to the problems of capital can never be completely successful: Neo-bohemia entails fresh contradictions played out in dynamic neighborhood space.

A number of scholars have identified the usefulness of artists to property speculators, for example on Manhattan's Lower East Side (Deutsche and Ryan 1984; Mele 2000; Smith 1996). However, their emphasis on land-based entrepreneurs does not address the extent to which the practices of neo-bohemia contribute to other strategies of capital valorization in the postindustrial city. Spatial practices linking the constitution of everyday life to labor relations and productive processes are subordinated in gentrification theories to the abstract space produced by relations of exchange. In effect, the artists are treated as placeholders — unwitting shock troops of gentrification paving the way for nebulously defined yuppies to follow on their heels. This mode of analysis does not adequately address changes in the urban occupational structure and the often contradictory processes of the aesthetic economy. Instead, gentrification is reified as a natural process, much like the Chicago School's old invasion succession model, only now in reverse. As in Wilson's underclass arguments (1987; 1996), the temporal dimensions of gentrification disappear along with attention to the structuring influences of external forces, leaving an apparently homogenized and self-reproducing space ultimately devoid of contradiction.

Shifts in the occupational structure of the city are discounted in these models, and competing interests of local residents are either ignored or rendered grossly simplistic. The pitiless yuppies who replace indigenous residents are analyzed essentially as consumers rather than as participants in the shifting urban occupational structure, one characterized by structurally inscribed precariousness and its own forms of exploitation. These theories reduce capital interests to a single voice. However, analysis of neo-bohemia shows that such a reduction is not appropriate. The production of space is not only a matter of narrow property speculation; space is also essential to the organization and deployment of labor power and productive processes. This point seems easy to grasp when we look at the organization of the blue-collar neighborhood during Fordism, but it remains salient in the context of global restructuring, where labor relations are complicated in new ways.

Neo-Bohemia

Though cities throughout history have played a role as incubators of cultural innovation, in the nineteenth century new ideas about the nature of artists and their relation to the city began to be elaborated. This was particularly true in Paris — for Benjamin (1999, p. 3-13) "the capital of the 19th century" — the platform for many of the cultural innovations that would constitute European modernism. Drawing on the freshly minted example of the Romantic poets, artists began to be thought of not as skilled craftsmen, integrated into the social system, but as exalted and often tortured geniuses, liable to be alienated from a society unable to grasp the contents of their sensitive souls. What Parisians such as poet Charles Baudelaire and painter Edouard Manet added to the Romantic paradigm was a distinctively urban vision, both in terms of the works of art they produced and the lifestyles they adopted.

By the mid-nineteenth century, Paris was flooded with adherents to this design for urban living. This overabundance of intellectual and creative fervor in Paris can be attributed to the general tumult of the period: the spatial revolution spurring the spectacular growth of the great city and the political and economic upheavals transforming the nature of social-class relations (Seigel 1986). Bohemians blurred the boundaries in an emergent society, evincing the commitment to cultural distinction of the fading aristocracy, the individualism of the ascendant bourgeoisie, and the hedonism and licentiousness of the urban demimonde. Perhaps because so many were frustrated applicants to the professions, overeducated and undernourished within the new urban economy, bohemians became known for their fierce antipathy toward the bourgeoisie — which in this case refers to both the entrepreneurial and professional classes in Paris — and the ethics of instrumental labor (Grana 1964).

But aesthetics, not politics, is the calling card of bohemia. Seigel (1986, p. 4) notes of the Parisian bohemians, "Ambitious, dedicated, but without means and unrecognized, they turned life itself into a work of art." This propensity persists, as new generations of spectacular urban subcultures lay claim to their own spaces of performance. Moreover, though successive bohemian movements continue to buttress their distinction via repudiation of the mainstream, the middle class, the yuppie, or whatever, these efforts at boundary maintenance need not signal economic marginality for bohemian signs and spaces, especially as the symbolic economy of cities grows in practical importance (Zukin 1995).

The past practices of artists in the city contribute to the foundations of ongoing cultural innovations that feed into the global economy, with contemporary urban spaces serving as critical sites for the manufacture of cultural desire. Media outlets like MTV broadcast this urban aesthetic to a much wider audience than ever before. This media diffusion of the bohemian aesthetic becomes a crucial component in the global culture, the corporate dissemination of the hip. The cumulative traditions of the modernist bohemia thereby play a new role in global capitalism. Bohemian spaces have impacted cultural production and have created a durable mythology of artistic practice in the urban context, a mythology that informs the strategies of contemporary social actors participating in an aestheticized urban economy.

In this sense it no longer seems wise to speak of bohemia as marginal to the wider capitalist economy. As the urban field changes in response to the global reconfiguration of capitalism, so does the meaning of bohemia. Contemporary capitalism is predicated on the "rapid flow of signs and images which saturate the fabric of everyday life" (Featherstone 1991, p. 67), extending the aestheticization of everyday life beyond the realm of urban artists, even as they continue to take a lead role in the constitution of these signs and images.

In the postindustrial economy, culture cannot be dismissed as reflective superstructure but rather is a crucial dimension in dynamics of capital valorization. As Anderson (1998, p. 55) puts it, "Culture has necessarily expanded to the point of where it has become virtually coextensive with the economy itself, not merely as the symptomatic basis of some of the largest industries in the world — tourism now exceeding all other branches of global employment — but much more deeply, as every material object and immaterial service becomes inseparably tractable sign and vendible commodity."

The congregation of artists in a neighborhood like Wicker Park abets new accumulation dynamics in an economy predicated on mechanisms that extract value added from aesthetic dimensions at multiple scales, local and global. Lifestyle scenes produced by urban subcultures are reconstituted as local consumption amenities, and they explode local boundaries through the circuits of fashion and media. An explosion of cultural commodities has occurred in the past half-century, in fashion, film, advertising, and countless new media, as well as at the local level where entertainment and tourism become central features of urban economies. The culture industries identified by Horkheimer and Adorno (1994) have grown both more powerful and at the same time more nimble, disseminating a remarkable diversity of products and modes of mass cultural practices of identification.

The cultural production done in locales like Wicker Park helps create conditions of possibility for this diversity. Rather than cultivating talent in house, the music industry can access a neighborhood like Wicker Park that condenses aspirants who bear their own start-up costs. From the countless bands that thundered nightly in local venues, music labels in the 1990s were able to glean a handful that would go on to wider success. The congregation of artists also nurtures creative talent that may be portable, a kind of urban finishing school for cultural producers. This development of new products and talent is accomplished at little or no cost to the corporate interests that may benefit, as artists willingly bear the costs, in keeping with the bohemian ethic of contingency and self-sacrifice, with dim prospects of fame, wealth, and beautiful lovers as added incentive.

Cultural production in the traditional sense is only one way neo-bohemia now interacts with the city's economy. Artists evince high rates of education and wide-ranging aesthetic competence. These traits are useful for labor in enterprises that are gaining ascendancy in the postindustrial city. The Chicago Artists Survey of 2000 indicated that 87 percent of respondents had at least a college degree, an impressive amount of formal education. At the same time, incomes are low; more than half reported annual household incomes under US$40,000. Only a minority makes a substantial portion of their living from practicing their craft, and most subsidize arts incomes with other jobs. Thus, the growing artistic population is available as flexible labor for a variety of postindustrial enterprises. The expanding demand for inserting design features and cultural tropes in a wide array of settings, goods, and displays further swells this labor market. They may work in temporary positions for white-collar enterprises or as subcontracted labor in graphic-design or media-content provision. As the new economy proliferates opportunities to find work that valorizes aesthetic competence, many artists sell out by taking jobs in advertising or information technology, often justifying this move by averring that they are only doing so to support their real work, for which market demand is minimal.

Frequently, young artists find employment in an aestheticized service sector, where their bohemian self-work, transforming life into a work of art, becomes a source of added value for enterprises like bars, boutiques, and nightclubs producing a marketable ambiance of urban cool. The overall ethos produced in neo-bohemia is demonstrably attractive to professionals in the growth industries of the global economy, individuals also evincing substantial education and cultural capital. As Mele (2000) showed in his study of Manhattan's East Village, the veneer of hipness is a resource in new strategies to sell urban space to residential consumers, leading to substantial new development in formerly decaying neighborhoods and corresponding increases in ground rents.

Many local artists in neighborhoods take an ahistorical stance toward this development, assuming it to be simply natural and inevitable that the urban middle class will take their consumption and residential cues from starving artists. This is not the case. Postindustrial restructuring, with the rising import of educated professionals and the declining number, income, and status of blue-collar workers, is essential to understanding both contemporary gentrification and new trends in amenity provision. Florida (2002) has been at the popular forefront in identifying the consumption habits of contemporary professionals, whom he refers to as the *creative class*. These include the quirky diversions of the bohemian neighborhood, and in fact Florida demonstrates correspondence between the density of artists, writers, and performers in a region with that of professionals in area like high technology. In a move that would have been unimaginable to his father, Chicago's current mayor Richard Daley has made amenity provision for yuppies a central plank of his governance strategy, and the Chicago Department of Cultural Affairs strives to nurture the city's bohemian distinction.

This bohemian ethos as an urban amenity is constructed through the practical activities of artists and other young people committed to an aestheticized urban experience, now differentiated from a parodic image of suburban Babbitry. In this fashion, creative efforts become valorized indirectly, with little benefit enjoyed by the artists. Indeed, such processes often produce outcomes that confound the artists' ideological dispositions, such as the displacement of non-white, working-class neighbors by rising rents. Now, as MTV — a division of the global media conglomerate Viacom — intervenes to broadcast Wicker Park's hip urban scene beyond neighborhood boundaries, the young artists and hipsters stand as the essential but essentially uncompensated local color.

Insofar as they contribute to the neighborhood ambiance of creative energy, even types of creative production expressly antagonistic to the capitalist order can be viewed as resources for neighborhood enterprises with clear aesthetic dimensions, including the design community. The concentration of various forms of cultural production, ranging from pop efforts to more esoteric or folk offerings, are inscribed on the habitus of local participants, whose own creative efforts are inflected by the diversity of the field. As Molotch (1996, p. 225) describes, "Local art is a factor of production…Every designer's hand…draws from the surrounding currents of popular and esoteric arts and modes of expression — verbal, literate, and plastic — that makes up everyday life. These interpenetrations of daily rounds and high culture, ways of life and circulating beliefs, are raw materials of what can come from place."

The local creative and lifestyle subcultures are raw materials of what can come from place that underlie Wicker Park's strategic advantage as a site for new enterprises, supporting the image production that feeds what Frank (1997) refers to as *hip consumerism.* Capitalist enterprises exploit consumer desire generated from the accentuation of trivial differences in the commodity marketplace; capital, for all its homogenizing tendencies, finds useful the imagery of diversity and nonconformity generated from the representational spaces of neo-bohemia.

Despite the fact that the majority of Americans now live and work in what Gottdeiner (1985, p. 3) describes as "deconcentrated urban realms," cultural production still privileges the old center city as a generative milieu and site of fantasy brokering consumer desire, particularly for consumers in the coveted youth demographic extending to age thirty-five. In the 1990s, major trends of youth fashion — including grunge, hip-hop, and heroin chic — were clearly sold as emerging organically from street culture, and each came with its own musical soundtracks and celebrity icons. The suburbs, with their strip malls and "virgin sidewalks" (Duany, Plater-Zyberk, and Speck 2000, p. 14) generate no such alluring associations. A neighborhood like Wicker Park, put on the cultural map in the 1990s by rock-and-roll culture and its associated street aesthetic, can be a real-world model for constructing the image of a hip downtown scene that becomes pseudo-universalized as it enters the global swirl of commodified signifiers.

Transitional neighborhoods — where old brick warehouses, once the wreckage of industrial disinvestment, are converted into trendy nightclubs or high-tech design offices — motivate aesthetic associations of the derelict with the mysterious and the desirable. Wicker Park, like the East Village in New York, features both bag ladies and fashion models, and both are components of the neighborhood's neo-bohemian aesthetic.

Though Chicago persists as among the most segregated metropolitan areas in the United States, Wicker Park accommodates a reasonable amount of social diversity. The neighborhood continues to feature a significant population of working-class Latinos who share the sidewalks with artists and young professionals. Young artists, likely to be socially liberal, find this aspect of neighborhood life attractive, and the diversity is part of the daily street vista that inflects aesthetic dispositions. However, liberal ideology translates into interaction only in a limited fashion. As a practical matter interactions between the Latino population and mostly white local artists or young professionals are cursory and superficial. Much as Sennett (1994, p. 357) writes of Greenwich Village, "Difference and indifference co-exist…the sheer fact of diversity does not prompt people to interact." Like Sennett's Greenwich Village, Wicker Park's street scene is "a visual agora" (idid., p. 357), belying Jacobs's (1961) more utopian interpretation of difference fusing into community on tightly-packed city streets. The diverse pedestrian life is crucial to the construction of the representational space of neo-bohemia, but everyday diversity is appropriated by participants as lived aesthetic rather than a social principle.

These multicultural elements of the neighborhood scene are also sources of strategic advantage for the design enterprises that cluster there. Younger generations in the United States, particularly the huge marketing demographic — which is what a generation practically amounts to in late capitalism — born between 1977 and 1997 and variously known as Millenials, Generation Y, or the Echo Boom (Howe and Strauss 2000), are becoming far more racially diverse. "Well aware that this racially mixed group of Gen Y'ers is fast becoming one of the nation's largest consumer blocks, marketers are now grappling with the multi-billion dollar challenge of wooing and defining them" (Takahashi 2001, p. 1) Thus local cultural amenities can abet new strategies of youth-oriented marketing, contributing the hybrid culture Def Jam Records founder Russell Simmons recently referred to as the "best brand-building culture in America today" (ibid., p. 1). Corporate interests are embracing a particular image of diversity as part of mass-marketing strategies, that is, diversity as an aesthetic rather than a political principle. Writes Klein (1999, p. 115), "The $200 billion culture industry — now America's biggest export — needs an ever changing, uninterrupted supply of street styles, edgy music videos and rainbows of color." These do not emerge from thin air, and so the emergence of multicultural marketing creates distinct demands for image production. The proliferation of multicultural images depicts multiple races, ethnicities, and cultural styles, often juxtaposed in striking ways. To revisit Sennett's (1994) term, it is a visual agora, but the aesthetic cosmopolitanism of brand culture neither requires civic community nor challenges the prevailing global relations of power.

Workers in arts occupations are a growing population in cities throughout the United States even in older industrial cities not commonly linked with bohemian traditions (Markusen 2004). Even where their products are only locally consumed, artistic efforts contribute to the constitution of cosmopolitan city space, responding to the needs of highly educated workers in the global city. Moreover, new economy enterprises in media and information technology increase not only the products but also the occupations that have a significant aesthetic dimension. In the milieus of neo-bohemia, we can identify the cross-fertilization of traditional arts activities with growth sectors in the urban economy. Like manufacturing, this aesthetic production requires workers, and insofar as this production feeds capitalist accumulation it entails the extraction of surplus value with differential effects across the still visible, and somewhat fetishized, class structure. Neo-bohemia cannot be analyzed only in terms of consumption; it also organizes the reproduction and deployment of flexible labor for the realization of profit.

Conclusion

Deciphering the global — the challenge posed by this volume — requires multipronged research strategies. The study of globalization is not the same as the study of the capitalist world system, done primarily through historical comparative method, in which nation-states remain essential units of analysis. The spaces of globalization, and the circuitry connecting them, can operate both above and below the scale of nation. Moreover, early propositions in the globalization debate, such as Castells's (1989) famous assertion that the *space of flows* now overwhelms the *space of places* — that is, the space of embedded identity and lived experience — cannot withstand careful scrutiny. Constructing a conceptual template that understands a locality like Wicker Park and similar districts as both structured by and structuring of global processes allows us to deploy ethnographic observation in a manner both historically sensitive and cognizant of the multiscalar nature of globalization in which place continues to play a vital role.

Wicker Park is in these ways an exemplary space in which to explore the intersection of the arts and new categories of capital accumulation, recovering the neighborhood as a site for study of the operations of a post-Fordist, global economy. This art/design/entertainment matrix is an emergent spatial theme in a variety of cities around the United States, and similar trends can be demonstrated in Williamsburg of New York, the Mission District of San Francisco, Deep Ellum in Dallas, and East Nashville and other city locales. Because of Chicago's status as a long-standing laboratory for urban studies and an exemplar of industrial organization, the neighborhood allows for rich comparisons between industrial and postindustrial spatial practices. Wicker Park has emerged from the wreckage of postindustrial restructuring, with the aesthetic demands of global capitalism creating the context for new spatial practices and new strategies of capital accumulation, without obviating, but rather outsourcing, many of the old. Ironically, former sweatshops are now being put to use in the manufacture of images for an economy of aesthetics.

Notes

1. Such cumulative character combines the elements that Lefebvre (1974) identifies as representations of space, with reference to spatial design and the built environment, and representational spaces, with regard to the everyday sentiments that permeate a social environment over time.

Works Cited

Anderson, Perry. 1998. *The origins of postmodernity*. London: Verso.

Beck, Ulrich. 2000. *Brave new world of work*. Cambridge, UK: Polity Press.

Benjamin, Walter. 1999. Paris, capital of the nineteenth century. In *The arcades project*, 3–26. Cambridge: Harvard University Press.

Boehlert, Eric. 1993. Chicago: Cutting edge's new capital, *Billboard Magazine*, August, 1, 6–7.

Bourdieu, Pierre. 1992. *The field of cultural production*. New York: Columbia University Press.

Brooks, David. 2001. *BoBos in paradise*. New York: Simon and Schuster.

Burawoy, Michael. 2000. *Global ethnography*. Berkeley: University of California Press.

Castells, Manuel. 1989. *The informational city*. Oxford: Blackwell.

Clark, Terry Nichols, Richard Lloyd, Kenneth Wong, and Pushpam Jain. 2002. Amenities drive urban growth. *Journal of Urban Affairs* 5:517–22.

Coorens, Elaine. 2003. *Wicker Park from 1673–1929*. Chicago: Old Wicker Park Committee.

Davis, Mike. 2006. *Planet of slums*. New York: Verso.

Dear, Michael. 2002. *From Chicago to LA: Making sense of urban theory*. Thousand Oaks, CA: Sage.

Deutsche, Rosalyn and C.G. Ryan. 1984. The fine art of gentrification. *October* 31:91–111.

Duany, Andres, Elizabeth Plater-Zyberk, and Jeff Speck. 2000. *Suburban nation: The rise of sprawl and the decline of the American dream*. New York: North Point Press.

Featherstone, Mike. 1991. *Consumer culture and postmodernism*. London: Sage.

Florida, Richard. 2002. *The rise of the creative class*. New York: Basic Books.

Frank, Thomas. 1997. *The conquest of cool*. Chicago: University of Chicago Press.

Grana, Cesar. 1964. *Bohemia versus bourgeois*. New York: Basic Books.

Gottdiener, Mark. 1985. *The social production of urban space*. Austin: University of Texas Press.

Hannerz, Ulf. 1980. *Exploring the city*. New York: Columbia University Press.

Harvey, David. 1982. *Limits to capital*. Chicago: University of Chicago Press.

Horkheimer, Max, and T.W. Adorno. 1994. *The dialectic of enlightenment*. New York: Continuum.

Howe, Neil, and William Strauss. 2000. *Millenials rising: The next great generation*. New York: Vintage.

Jacobs, Jane. 1961. *The death and life of great American cities*. New York: Basic.

Jaffe, Matthew. 2001. Best new place for media companies. *Industry Standard: Intelligence for the Internet Economy*, February 12: 1–4.

Jameson, Fredric. 1991. *Postmodernism: Or, the cultural logic of late capitalism*. Durham, NC: Duke University Press.

Klein, Naomi. 1999. *No logo: Money, marketing, and the growing anti-corporate movement*. New York: Picador.

Kleine, Ted. 2001. Reality bites: The battle for Wicker Park. *Chicago Reader*, August 31, 6–10.

Lash, Scott, and John Urry. 1994. *Economies of signs and space*. Thousand Oaks, CA: Sage.

Lefebvre, Henri. 1974. *The production of space*. Cambridge UK: Blackwell.

Lester, Thomas W. 2000. Old economy or new economy? Economic and social change in Chicago's West Town community area. Master of urban planning and policy, University of Illinois–Chicago.

Markusen, Ann. 2004. Targeting occupations in regional and community economic development. *Journal of the American Planning Association* 70(3): 253–268

Mele, Christopher. 2000. *Selling the Lower East Side*. Minneapolis: University of Minnesota Press.

Molotch, Harvey. 1996. L.A. as design product: How art works in a regional economy. In Allen J. Scott and Edward W. Soja, eds., *The city: Los Angeles and urban theory at the end of the twentieth century*, 225–277. Berkeley: University of California Press.

Sassen, Saskia. 2001. *The global city: New York, London, Tokyo*. Princeton, NJ: Princeton University Press.

Seigel, Jerrold. 1986. *Bohemian Paris*. Baltimore: Johns Hopkins University Press.

Sennett, Richard. 1994. *Flesh and stone: The body and the city in western civilization*. New York: Norton.

Sites, William. 2003. *Remaking New York: Primitive globalization and the politics of urban community*. Minneapolis: University of Minnesota Press.

Smith, Neil. 1996. *The new urban frontier*. New York: Routledge.

Soja, Edward. 1996. *Thirdspace: Journeys to Los Angeles and other real imagined places*. Cambridge, MA: Blackwell.

Takahashi, Corey. 2001. Selling to Gen Y a far cry from Betty Crocker. *New York Times*, April 8, p. C1.

Wilson, William Julius. 1987. *The truly disadvantaged*. Chicago: University of Chicago Press.

———. 1996. *When work disappears*. New York: Vintage.

Zukin, Sharon. 1995. *The cultures of cities*. London: Blackwell.

CHAPTER 2

Translocal Civilities

Chinese Modern Dance at Downtown Los Angeles Public Concerts

MARINA PETERSON

As the sun set behind the skyscrapers, the director of Grand Performances presented the Beijing Modern Dance Company: "Please help me welcome 'Beijing shi-en di hu tuan.'" The audience members' faces were obscured by darkness, but their applause on hearing the company introduced in Mandarin sonically marked the event as a space of translocal civilities. The evening was part of Grand Performances' free summer concert series in downtown Los Angeles. As civic events, public concerts are sites of both city and civic subject making.[1] The concept of translocal civilities captures the ways public concerts emerge as sites of global city and translocal civic subject making. Intended to help create a multicultural audience that reflected the diversity of the city, the Beijing Modern Dance Company's performances internationalized that audience, constituting new kinds of civic subjects that were simultaneously marked as minority in the United States, part of a multicultural civic body, and transnational.[2] Global cities are key locales for citizenship that is organized around informal practices and forms of belonging (Sassen 2003, p. 5). Public concerts, the result of complex multiscalar planning processes, are shaped by and contribute to the formation of globalized subjects, cities, and spaces.

After roughly three decades of globalization in fact and theory, it is possible to recognize the global both empirically and theoretically. Certain processes are now by definition global, whereas others become global as they take on the scalar character or ideological foundations of globalization. China and Los Angeles are heightened locales in the current formation of globalization.[3] Free trade, the production of consumer goods and media, increasing inequalities in wealth, and the privatization of public services are only some of the markers of globalization of which China and Los Angeles are at the forefront. These serve as the framework through which the public concert-planning practices became global. At the same time, though those defining features of globalization are largely established and recognizable, they neither exhaust the global nor account for the range of practices that are part of globalization.

Multiscalar-*scapes* (Appadurai 1996) provide an analytic tool for assessing how a particular case relates to a range of processes that are both congruent with and in excess of defining paradigms and features of globalization.[4] The multiscalar nature of scapes suggests how the global is produced in places (Sassen 2001) at the same time as it is inherently uneven (Appadurai 1996). Thus scapes allow for an examination of how local practices might be part of globalization in multiple and as of yet unknown ways. Scapes are differently global in relation to scale, place, and medium, suggesting the presence and production of different globalizations and of differently global places. Difference, therefore, is not only something that resides in the domain of the local as a means of altering the global but is also in and of the global. The ability to decipher globalization*s* has the potential to bring new insight into the nature and content of the global, allowing for the development of an ongoing understanding of globalization as it unfolds.

The ways in which multiscalar practices articulate with and help shape scapes indicates how particular cases become translocal in relation to specific, discrete, yet intersecting global processes. The Beijing Modern Dance Company's weekend performances marked the culmination of more than a year of planning that entailed programming decisions, political negotiations, fund-raising, and marketing. The articulation of these practices with a complex web of global flows or scapes that included artscapes, politicoscapes, financescapes, and mediascapes (Appadurai 1996) helped figure the public concert as a translocal civic space. Thus, California Plaza — already an icon of neoliberal capital (Davis 1992; Loukaitou-Sideris and Banerjee 1998; Soja 1996) — became constitutive of the global city anew as the site for the intersection of divergent artistic, political, economic, and social global and globalizing processes.[5]

Modernism's Global Stage

Grand Performances' decision to program the Beijing Modern Dance Company was made after the presenters traveled to China the previous year. They visited Hong Kong, mainland cities of Beijing, Shanghai, and Zhengzhou, and the Hunan province where, as guests of members of the Chinese Friendship Association, they were treated to performances of local dance and theatrical groups. The trip and the subsequent performances were part of a three-year project funded by the James Irvine Foundation to present performing artists from "so-called developing countries that have had major immigration to Southern California in the last twenty-five years" (Grand Performances, Irvine Foundation grant application, internal document, 2001).[6] The goals of this project focused on the impact the performances would have in Los Angeles and included the promotion of "better understanding between communities," civic engagement by recent immigrants, and an awareness of a wider variety of art forms than those presented as stereotypical of a country (Grand Performances, Irvine Foundation grant application, internal document, 2001). Moreover, the artists presented should "use a contemporary genre to address their societies' current issues and/or tell their 'stories'" and "be considered among the best in their countries for artistic merit and excellence" (Grand Performances, Irvine Foundation grant application, internal document, 2001). Presenting the Beijing Modern Dance Company was construed as a perfect means by which Grand Performances could fulfill the artistic and social aims of the project: a contemporary art form with traditional content that would represent Angeleno Chinese Americans, newly including them in the civic body and helping others obtain increased cultural understanding.[7] For its American premiere, the company performed a program that featured an original work set to Igor Stravinsky's *Rite of Spring*. As modern dancers performing a standard of the repertoire, they fused their Chinese roots with a "sophisticated" European art form, defying stereotypes that Chinese artistic performance is only Peking opera or martial arts.

Modern dance was most appropriate for achieving these goals because, as the director of Grand Performances stated, modern dance is a "distinctly contemporary art form that can be influenced by the culture of the country" (Michael Alexander, personal communication, August 24, 2003). For Grand Performances, the influence of the country of origin of the dancers is apparent when a company presents dances that incorporate a narrative about events or issues from their country or choreograph pieces to music from that country. Evoking a definitively modernist paradigm, the presenters argued that modern dance is the most universal performing art form because it does not depend on a specific language to convey a message. Unlike music, they said, which might depend on audiences having more specialized knowledge of the form to understand an extramusical message in it, or theater, which depends on knowledge of the language spoken, modern dance can convey a story or other kind of message to a general audience.

The programming decisions of Grand Performances intersected with an artscape of actual and potential circulation of forms and ideologies. The relation between artistic modernism and international relations is most often periodized in terms of either colonialism or Cold War politics, the former linked especially to early twentieth-century primitivism and the latter to universalist notions of modernist form. Modernism, in these cases, is framed as a Euro-American project that, as primitivism, draws on the rest of the world to appropriate content (Flam and Deutch 2003; Torgovnick 1990) or, as cultural imperialism, sends out cultural products in a spirit of progress and universalism (Thompson 2002; Von Eschen 2004). Though it has been argued that globalization, or late capital, corresponds to an aesthetics of postmodernism (Harvey 1990), the case of Grand Performances presenting the Beijing Modern Dance Company suggests that even in the context of globalization, modernism is very much still alive. The modernist paradigms driving the programming choices of Grand Performances are implicated in distinctly contemporary flows of economics and politics and are central to the refiguring of a local multiculturalism — a hallmark of the postmodern city — as global. Rather than creating Los Angeles as a global city through cultural exports like Hollywood and American popular music (Scott 2000), these public concert-planning practices reach out and capture global culture in their web of associated ideologies.[8]

The universal aspect of the modern form provided a framework of quality and judgment within which the chosen art form should fit, while at the same time the art would have content reflecting an authentic Chineseness as determined by the presenters. Specific aesthetic choices were made in programming modern dance from China to support the general aims of Grand Performances to present a contemporary art form with traditional content. Much of what the presenters were shown did not meet their criteria for style or quality. In China, the director of Grand Performances and the director of programming were mainly taken to tourist-oriented performances of Peking opera and acrobats, which because of their stereotypical nature did not fit the needs of the Irvine project. The director of programming was shown "a kind of constructed village, almost a Disneyfication of the arts, but nowhere near that in terms of production values;" appalled by the "commodification of the traditional work" and distressed at "Broadwayed" versions of "traditional work" she searched, nearly in vain, for the traditional art in what she considered its pure form (Leigh Ann Hahn, personal communication, January 6, 2003). Finally, at a reconstructed Tujen village she saw a trio of old men. "One played a gong and vocalized, the other played a drum and vocalized, and the third juggled knives. Not like any kind of slick, well, it was just a folk kind of thing" (Leigh Ann Hahn, personal communication, January 6, 2003). It had been difficult to convince her hosts she was actually interested in performers like these old men. The difference in aesthetic judgment between the director of programming and her Chinese hosts reflected an imbalance of power due to the role of Grand Performances as gatekeeper, in which programming staff's judgment and evaluation of artwork defined the parameters of taste from the position of aesthetic norms and values that were projected as universal rather than relative.

Programming the Beijing Modern Dance Company reflects a Euro-American art field of evaluatory frameworks (Bourdieu 1993) gone global within an ideological framework of universal difference. Describing modern dance from non-U.S. or European countries as using a contemporary form with traditional elements draws on the binaries of the high modernist paradigm: modern versus traditional, present versus past, and the West versus the rest. Authenticity is found in raw sounding folk music but is lost in a performance that appears commodified because of its similarity to Disney or Broadway. Yet in the articulation of an artscape organized around modernist forms and ideologies the particularity of these evaluations are glossed as universal. A norm from one context became globalized when a judgment of quality as an arbiter of international art forms was not considered to be relative. The Irvine grant promoted this universalizing logic in form and content. The grant was not specifically intended for programming Chinese performing artists but came to fit a Chinese case.

China as nation imbued the performance and its people with culture, allowing the Beijing Modern Dance Company to represent Southern California Chinese Americans by extension. Intended to reflect and produce a multicultural city whose members, attending the performances, would become more tolerant and understanding of each other, performers throughout the season marked a serial multiculturalism by which this process could occur group by group. In this case, Chinese Americans were intended to feel included in the civic body by seeing artists from their home country on a downtown stage.[9] For others, the recognition of the representation of Chinese Americans by the dancers was to be achieved in part through an acknowledgment of the value of an art form. In other words, it was hoped that non-Chinese Americans would gain respect for Chinese Americans by discovering that Chinese art is sophisticated. Thus, though the multicultural project of Grand Performances was framed around the participation and recognition of Chinese Americans, the process of representation shifted the focus to China. Following Ong (1999, p. 111), "an essentializing notion of Chineseness continues to dog the scholarship because the Chinese past, nation, singular history, or some 'cultural core' is taken to be the main and unchanging determinant of Chinese identity." Even as the value came from the attachment of a universalized arbiter of modernism to culture, it was this unchanging cultural core of Chinese identity that enabled modern dancers from Beijing to represent Angeleno Chinese Americans. Through this process of representation, Chinese Americans became translocalized and multicultural Los Angeles was made global.

International Politics of Presenting

The Beijing Modern Dance Company's performances became a space for making international politics at the local level with valences evocative of contemporary U.S.–China relations. The politics of presenting reflected strategic choices that smoothed economic, artistic, and social relations. Such choices included not only which art to present but also where the performers should come from. The Beijing Modern Dance Company was chosen over a Hong Kong group because, with Beijing the political capital of China, it was considered best able to represent the Chinese nation-state. That these processes would take place in the space of the city by specifically urban actors is congruent with trends of neoliberalism and globalization. According to Brenner (2004), one aspect of late twentieth-century rescaling of state power is the uneven territorialization of capital, which provides the conditions of possibility for the emergence of global cities that can bypass the nation politically and economically. As Sassen (n.d.) elucidates, globalization has entailed a rescaling of state space in which cities "exit hierarchies historically centered in the nation-state" and urban regions become "key…sites for a rescaling of national state power" (see also Sassen 2000, 2001, 2003). At the same time, cities are productive of new kinds of global spaces that are at times congruent with national spaces and at times are divergent.

Following the logic of global trade, for international performing arts presenters all countries are not equal. The uneven ability of artists to move around the world reflects a politics of art that is intertwined with the ways processes of economic globalization affect international migration (Sassen 1998). In the United States, the Department of Homeland Security screens artist visas, determining whether or not a person can enter the country. The evaluations are based on a set of criteria about the cultural uniqueness of the art as well as the person's likelihood of leaving the country at the end of the tour (see Peterson 2003 for a lengthier discussion of this evaluation process). Money helps speed movement, and expedition fees — lower for China than other countries — facilitate visa approval.[10] At the same time, movement is conducive to trade relations insofar as it reflects a semblance of social freedom that both justifies and provides evidence of the purported ideological effects of free trade. Freedom of movement was important for the dance company as a means of validation in an international art world. Earlier instances of defection by dancers touring abroad were frowned on by the company director. Aspiring for international recognition as a Chinese modern dance company, the dancers now abide by the prerogative of the Chinese government in order to secure freedom of movement.

In the translocal space of the public concert a range of global politics is expressed, reflecting the smoothing of foreign relations as well as contestations over governmental policies that may not be possible within particular national spaces. Precautions taken by Grand Performances not to offend the Chinese government meant there was a risk that others would be offended. Kaplan (1992) describes how Chinese politics, in particular the tension between Taiwan and mainland China, are played out in Chinese diasporic communities around the world in immediate and intense forms that include both newspaper articles and murders. This dynamic was enacted when a Taiwanese cultural center in Chinatown in Los Angeles would not accept the programs for the group from Beijing; explicitly because of the season-long relationship with the Chinese Embassy resulting largely from this performance, at a later concert that season of Chinese, Japanese, Korean, and Tibetan artists, language in the printed program about the oppression of Tibetans by the Chinese government was toned down. Reminiscent of protestations that China should not be granted most-favored-nation status because of its human rights abuses, after this performance an audience member complained saying that presenting the Chinese artists after the Tibetan singer reflected a hierarchizing of the two countries, with China privileged over Tibet. Expressing her position in a larger politicoscape of Anglo-American activists represented by the slogan "Free Tibet," she asserted that given the treatment of Tibetans by the Chinese government this hierarchization was inappropriate. Yet, just as with U.S.–China relations in which human rights abuses and government repression are overlooked to maintain and foster neoliberal free trade relations, these politics were glossed by the presenters to maintain smooth diplomatic and economic relations between Grand Performances and China.

A Creative Economy

The choice by Grand Performances to present Chinese artists, and the Beijing Modern Dance Company in particular, was imbued with dynamics guiding late twentieth-century U.S.–China relations. Economic concerns motivated much of Grand Performances' planning and provided a justification for presenting Chinese artists that was supplemental to the aim of reflecting the diversity of the city. Late capital and its scaling as the global economy in many ways defines and drives neoliberal globalization, as evidenced in part by the United States granting most-favored-nation status to China.[11] Arguments in favor of granting China most-favored-nation status suggest economics directly influence the social, as discussion of the cost of imports and exports shift seamlessly to assertions that free trade promotes peace and democracy (Larson 1997). However, though economics provided a foundation for Grand Performances' programming decisions, capital did not necessarily drive its artistic and social concerns. Rather, following the logic of -scapes, financescapes — materialized through actual and desired funding from sources with differing motivations and demands — intersected with artscapes, politicoscapes, and mediascapes in multiple and uneven ways.

A report on state arts agencies argues that "international exchanges mean the opening up of whole new markets for artists and arts organizations" (Warshawski n.d., p. 4).[12] The money coming into Los Angeles from China, especially through trade, was a significant part of the decision to present Chinese performing artists. Following the capitalist logic of cultural policy, which posits economic justifications for the arts and positions the arts within larger capitalist projects, Grand Performances drew on trade figures[13] as part of its efforts to obtain more support for the Beijing Modern Dance Company's performance, arguing that the arts are an important aspect of international trade. Ultimately, though this tactic might have contributed to local political support, it did not yield direct financial results. The staff of Grand Performances also hoped the Beijing Modern Dance Company's performance would provide access to new funding for the organization from sources in China, the city of Los Angeles, the Port of Los Angeles, wealthy Chinese Americans in Los Angeles, and individuals at concerts.

The social and artistic demands of philanthropy suggest how financescapes — as articulated by nonprofit fund-raising — can be imbued with other ideals, in this case a rhetoric of equality and cross-cultural understanding that is neither identical to nor necessarily directly compatible with the logic of capital even as it is implicated in global economic processes. The Irvine Foundation, as the major funder of the three-year project of which this performance was part, defined many of the parameters of the Beijing Modern Dance Company's performances. Concerned with California as a whole, the Irvine Foundation's mission emphasizes improving the social and economic well-being and civic participation of a state marked by diversity and inequality (James Irvine Foundation 1997, inside cover), positing a dystopic multiculturalism that has the potential of becoming utopic through the foundation's interventions. Grand Performances supports the Irvine Foundation's goals of providing "equal opportunity" by presenting free concerts and encourages "communication, understanding, and cooperation among diverse cultural, ethnic and socio-economic groups" (James Irvine Foundation 1997, inside cover) through programming and postperformance discussions. Performances such as those of the Beijing Modern Dance Company "involve young people…, promote cross-cultural understanding, and…nurture tolerance and mutual respect," thereby connecting people "through cultural participation" at the same time as they showcase artistic creativity (James Irvine Foundation 2001, p. 26). The fact that the work of international relations was done by private actors — a philanthropy and a nonprofit organization — is consistent with the shifting of state functions to nongovernmental organizations. Moreover, funding from the California philanthropy exemplified a multiscalar federalism in which institutions at the state and city level were the primary negotiators with the Chinese nation-state. Reflecting the scaling of state power that is considered a key element of economic and political globalization, funding by the Irvine Foundation helped constitute Grand Performances' concerts as translocal (Brenner 2004).

A media sponsorship by KSCI, a Los Angeles-area pan-Asian television station, marked the intersection of financescapes and mediascapes, as Asian American television viewers were available as capitalist consumers and public concert audience members. KSCI's donation to Grand Performances was in the form of advertising. A promotional commercial about Grand Performances that highlighted the Beijing Modern Dance Company was intended to help attract Chinese Americans to the free concerts in California Plaza. In exchange for the media sponsorship valued at $39,000, KSCI's logo was included in the season collateral of Grand Performances and the station was thanked during the director's preperformance announcements. KSCI attracts viewers from this kind of advertising, banking on the consumer power of southern Californian Asian Americans to attract their own advertisers, which as major multinational corporations are actors with amassed capital in the global economy. KSCI's material explains that the Asian market is "a young, rapidly growing and affluent consumer market. Delivering a marketing message through Asian-language media connects a company to the hearts of Asian-American consumers. In an age where…new market growth is key, Asian consumers are a critical group that has the elements to increase a company's profits" (KSCI-TV 2002b, p. M13). As its advertisement in *Advertisement Age* asserts, KSCI offers "your direct connection to Asian American consumers" (KSCI-TV 2002b, p. M13), a consumer segment on the rise. Through KSCI's media sponsorship of Grand Performances, ethnicized television viewers as capitalist consumers and public concert audience members were exchanged through advertising. A charitable contribution by KSCI, itself a form of civic involvement, was intended to draw Asian American television viewers to the Beijing Modern Dance Company's performances, turning television viewers into public concert audience members and, by extension, civic participants. This exchange hinged on ethnically marked Asian American television viewers as alternately previously excluded from Los Angeles civic life and as already existing market consumers. Through this exchange, the multicultural aspirations of a free concert presenter intersected with financescapes and mediascapes, scaled to a regional audience whose members were connected to international flows of economics and media.

Marking the localization of financescapes, the performances of the Beijing Modern Dance Company were also an opportunity for Grand Performances to make connections with important Chinese in Los Angeles. Ong (1996, p. 737) describes how ethnicity and class intersect in the ranking of immigrant populations, providing uneven access to "key institutions in state and civil society." The special access at Grand Performances' concerts was provided in the form of reserved seating for audience members with capital. Class, along with other forms of capital, became a means of organizing a stratified audience — as opposed to the ideal of a unified general public — in relation to the economic interests of the concert organization. Financescapes were concretized in the audience, as actual or potential donors, and those with access to other sources of funds were rewarded for that fact. At the Beijing Modern Dance Company's performances seats were reserved first for donors. The rewarding of audience members with capital then extended from economic capital to political and social capital (Bourdieu 1984). Reserved seats were provided for local and international political figures, creating a translocal political space through the presence of a Chinese American staff member from the mayor's office, the Chinese consul general, and Chinese consulate staff members. As a means of giving special status to the Chinese Consulate, controlling the interpretation of the event, and maintaining the political relationships of the company, the staff person in charge of the reserved seating area was directed to seat the Beijing Modern Dance Company's public relations person — who traveled with the company and wrote program notes and press releases in conjunction with local consulate officials — next to a Chinese Consulate staff member. The privileged position of the company's public relations person indicated how financescapes elided into a melding of politicoscapes and mediascapes. As economic capital shifted to social and political capital in the space of reserved seating, seating arrangements tangibly supported and reinforced the mutually constitutive relationship between political representation, capital, and publicity at stake in these performances of Chinese modern dancers in downtown Los Angeles.

Translocalizing Multiculturalism

To achieve the aims of Grand Performances of reflecting the diversity of Los Angeles at its concerts and to fulfill the terms of the Irvine Foundation grant of including previously excluded immigrant populations in the civic body, the Beijing Modern Dance Company's performances needed to attract a significant amount of Chinese American audience members. Marketing, which entailed hooking into multiscalar mediascapes through the use of ethnic media, was essential for making this underserved audience aware of the performance. Ethnic media, which helps channel marketing to groups bounded by nationality and ethnicity, was key for the production of a translocal multiculturalism. KSCI's media sponsorship was a central component of this process. KSCI, like transnational television more generally, "is fed primarily by products imported from the homeland.... These programs locate their homeland outside the United States" (Naficy 1993, p. 62). Thus, through KSCI's broadcast area, Asia becomes located in Los Angeles, in turn producing Los Angeles as a translocal media space through the localization of global mediascapes. Beyond KSCI's donated advertisements, mediascapes were accessed through multiscalar marketing techniques that included distributing flyers around Chinatown, creating links from Chinese cultural center Web sites, advertising in Chinese newspapers, and airing ads in Mandarin on the radio.

Language is central to producing the audience of the media source, helping turn an ethnoscape, a nationality, and translocal civic subjects into an identity group, whose members consume products, media, and concerts marked as exclusive to them. A market survey conducted by KSCI found that "only 13% of Chinese and Korean respondents said that their household speak either all English or predominantly English, and 10% of Vietnamese said the same. Therefore, not surprisingly," the research report concludes, "in-language media from TV, newspapers, radio to internet play a major role in their life," moreover, "a dominant majority of them consume in-language media everyday" (KSCI-TV 2002a, p. 2). In Los Angeles, ethnic media outlets target different segments of the Chinese

American and Asian population, helping construct the Chinese American population along linguistic divisions that reflect Chinese politics and U.S. immigration patterns.

Southern California Chinese-language radio stations in particular are marked by linguistic divisions that reproduce Chinese politics and social dynamics in the United States. KAZN AM1300 was originally K-Asian, which programmed in "Korean, Cantonese, Japanese, Mandarin, Polynesian, Tagalog (Filipino), Thai and Vietnamese" (KAZN AM1300). Reflecting Chinese national language policies, in 1993 it shifted to all Chinese programming in Mandarin, the dominant language of China. Gladney (1991, p. 307) writes, "The development of the 'common language'...based on Beijing Mandarin was indispensable to the development of China as a unified nation. The denial of differences among the Chinese languages was thought to be critical to the legitimation and modernization of the nation." In extending this practice to Los Angeles, a Chinese nation-state-making project is replicated in the United States, subsuming differences between Chinese Americans by hierarchizing through language. As KAZN's Web site explains, "One must realize and understand that even though many of these listeners may not speak Mandarin as their primary household language, Mandarin is considered to be the 'universal' dialect or language among all Chinese, so, Radio Chinese attracts a broad spectrum of the Chinese demographics" (KAZN AM1300). KMRB AM1430 (2003), on the other hand, broadcasts in Cantonese and Mandarin; its assertion that the station is filling an "ever-expanding...Cantonese market" marks a recognition and production of a minority Chinese population in the Los Angeles area, thereby emphasizing a pattern that is local to Los Angeles.

Ethnic media sources, by providing the forum for advertising the Beijing Modern Dance Company's performances to Los Angeles-area Chinese Americans, were key to making the public concert a translocal space through language (King and Wood 2001). After radio announcements on Chinese AM radio stations in Mandarin were aired, many Mandarin-only speaking people called the office of Grand Performances to inquire about the performance. With the help of a native speaker, a transliterated cheat sheet was made for staff members answering the phone to be able to say that the performance of the Beijing Modern Dance Company (*Beijing xian de wu*) was at 8 p.m. (*bath di em*), parking was $8 (*pa chuh bath quai*), and no tickets were needed (*bu yau peyau*) because it was free (*sui beyan lai*). We (I was volunteering) practiced saying the words with the correct intonations, but only the staff member with knowledge of Cantonese was able to remember how to pronounce the Anglified text. Those who called Grand Performances speaking Mandarin extended their membership as ethnic media consumer to public concert audience member.

The inclusion of Mandarin-speaking and -reading Chinese Americans continued at the performances. A bilingual program with Mandarin and English text was intended to integrate audiences and to make Mandarin readers feel included. Signs for the restrooms were printed in Mandarin and English. At each of the three evening performances, the director of Grand Performances ended his announcements by saying *Beijing Modern Dance Company* in Mandarin. On the third night, he started his announcements by saying *Ni hao!* To which the audience responded *Ni hao!*. The director's gesture was an acknowledgment of the Chinese speakers in the audience at the same time as it marked Angeleno diversity as international. The audience applause at his statements registered a civic inclusion based on translocal identities.

The presence of Chinese Americans in the audience at the Beijing Modern Dance Company's performances marked the success of Grand Performances' project of reflecting the diversity of the city in downtown Los Angeles. The specific links between media and ethnic or national groups helps draw local ethnic groups to performances by artists from their native countries, creating a multicultural audience that connects the city to another country and hence the world — bypassing the national space of the United States — through the national and ethnic backgrounds of its residents. Articulating with global mediascapes through ethnic media unlinks the Chinese nation from the state, as nation becomes identity for those in diaspora and the city of Los Angeles becomes a site for the production of an American multiculturalism now understood as transnational. That Chinese Americans were attracted to the performance of a Chinese modern dance company indicates how these civic subjects are members of an urban multicultural community and of international diasporas, constituting the multicultural and the global city.

Conclusion

The convergence of multiscalar processes at the Beijing Modern Dance Company's performances in downtown Los Angeles helped shape public concerts as translocal civic spaces, sites for the emergence of translocal civilities. Through a complex scaling process, public concert planning intersected with defining parameters of globalization such as free trade, denationalization and regionalization, city-to-city networks that bypass the nation-state, immigration, and transnational media. Yet, as the case of Los Angeles public concert planning suggests, the global is constituted through a range of practices that both articulate with and exceed the economic, political, and technological. The diversity of the global can be captured by the rubric of multiscalar scapes, which, operating with different social and ideological logics, intersect in and through specific geographies, practices, institutions, processes, and underlying ideologies. In planning the performances of the Beijing Modern Dance Company, multiscalar -scapes were accessed and created in the Port of Los Angeles, the homes or cars of all those listening to Chinese-language AM radio in Los Angeles, the traveling itineraries of the staff of Grand Performances and the mayor of Los Angeles, California Plaza, Chinatown, the cities of Los Angeles and Beijing, and the nation-states of the United States and China. The public concert, though existing only as the moment and place of the performance, contained practices that originated across an ocean — spoken Mandarin — and were produced through historical processes, such as the history of European modern dance in China. The multiscalar nature of these practices suggests how the global comes into being in spaces of translocal civilities such as these public concerts.

Cities have become sites for the enactment of global processes and the emergence of new forms of citizenship. These domains imbue each other, such that the global is a space in which new kinds of subjects are shaped at the same time as citizenship is increasingly bound to the global. As the site for the negotiation of these processes, the global city is a translocal locality, produced through and productive of local subjects who are both local and nonlocal — who are of Los Angeles and of some other country. These civic subjects are performed through participation and recognition, creating and reflecting spaces and forms of belonging that, though located in the city, span scales from the body to the global. As multiscalar spaces for civic belonging are formed, the inhabitants of those spaces and the cities in which they are located become part of emergent translocal civilities.

Notes

1. Grand Performances' concerts are a civic proxy. Continuing the form of free concerts sponsored by municipal governments in American cities and towns for centuries, these particular concerts are one example of the privatization of public services that is a feature of neoliberal globalization. The term *civic subjects* describes these city residents who are included in the civic body through events like public concerts that are not spaces of legal or formal citizenship but work alongside such spaces.
2. Multiculturalism and immigration are usually discussed separately as markers of globalization and the global city (see, respectively, Castles and Miller 2003; Isin 2000; Sassen 2000, 2001). Their intersection, and accompanying rhetorical strategies of city making and marketing as means of constituting a global city, has been addressed less often (Lowe 1996).

3. The fact that China is a country and Los Angeles a city reflects different aspects of the dynamics of globalization, with a national economy now at the center of global manufacturing chains and the consumer economy at stake for the former and global city formation around cultural export of concern for the latter. Juxtaposed, they mark two aspects of the debate over the extent to which globalization has resulted in denationalization (Ferguson and Jones 2002).
4. It is common to define globalization as a shift in the nature of the capitalist economy facilitated by technology and national policies (Castells 1996; Harvey 1990). Culture, the arts, and social movements are taken as effects of this shift. Though the question of what drives globalization can be addressed empirically, the concept of scapes enables the preliminary disarticulation of global flows in order to begin such a historical and philosophical investigation. While capital may ultimately be instrumental to transformations of other global processes, the force of these flows and the relationships between them might change in different times and spaces, with arts or social networks or ideologies of a cultural bent becoming predominant in certain instances.
5. Characteristics of the global city that are reflected in Grand Performances' programming of the Beijing Modern Dance Company include the tendency for the city to bypass the nation politically and economically (Brenner 2004; Sassen 2000, 2001); a large number of international residents who are part of diasporic networks, especially ones located in part in the Third World (Castles and Miller 2003; Hannerz 2006; Isin 2000); neoliberal trends of the rise of public–private partnerships (Brenner and Theodore 2002; Harvey 2001, p. 352; Whitt 1987, pp. 21, 29); and an emphasis on cities as sites for the consumption of cultural events (Harvey 2001; Whitt 1987). Though other work on Los Angeles as a global city emphasizes the city as a site for the export of global cultural forms (Scott 2000), the case examined here reflects a bringing of the global to the space of the city, producing a global city — and globalization — through localized practices (Flusty 2004).
6. Though the staff of Grand Performances never provided evidence of immigration patterns to support their choice of country, census data show that after 1980 Chinese immigration to Los Angeles surged and that between 1980 and 1990, 150,512 Chinese migrated to Los Angeles County, more than any other Asian nationality (Ong and Azores 1994, p. 104). The previous year a Mexican modern dance company performed as part of the Irvine project.
7. Elsewhere I discuss how the performance was interpreted as representing Angeleno Chinese Americans (Peterson 2005, chap. 4).
8. The case also suggests the possibility for the presence of multiple modernisms, as the use of modernist forms by Chinese dancers has the potential to reconfigure the wider ideological framework insofar as they bring a history that alternately shares features of and diverges from defining aspects of modernism (Peterson 2005, chap. 4).
9. Throughout a season, Grand Performances presents artists that are intended to represent a selection of Los Angeles' demographic groups, ranging from jazz to mariachi to European classical music.

10. Expedition fees make visa applications move through the U.S. Department of Homeland Security more quickly. The Grand Performances' director was informed that visa approval fees for Chinese were lower than for other countries because China charged the United States less.
11. Most-favored-nation status, otherwise known as normal trade relations, regulates and equalizes tariffs on imports and is granted by the United States to most countries in the world.
12. Current cultural policy is largely concerned with economic justifications for the arts, whether around urban development or increased government arts funding (Bradford, Gary, and Wallach 2000). Critiques, though rare, interrogate the capitalist logic of the field (Evans 2001).
13. According to the Los Angeles County Economic Development Corporation (2003), in 2002 China was the number one trading partner in two-way trade with Los Angeles. Much of this trade comes through the Port of Los Angeles, "ranked third in the world on the basis of containers handled in 2002" behind only Hong Kong and Singapore (Los Angeles County Economic Development Corporation 2003).

Works Cited

Appadurai, Arjun. 1996. *Modernity at large: Cultural dimension of globalization.* Minneapolis: University of Minnesota Press.

Bourdieu, Pierre. 1984. *Distinction: A social critique of the judgment of taste.* Trans. Richard Nice. Cambridge, MA: Harvard University Press.

———. 1993. *The field of cultural production: Essays on art and literature.* New York: Columbia University Press.

Bradford, Gigi, Michael Gary, and Glenn Wallach, eds. 2000. *The politics of culture: Policy perspectives for individuals, institutions, and communities.* New York: New Press.

Brenner, Neil. 2004. *New state spaces: Urban governance and the rescaling of statehood.* Oxford: Oxford University Press.

Brenner, Neil, and Nik Theodore, eds. 2002. *Spaces of neoliberalism: Urban restructuring in North America and Western Europe.* Oxford: Blackwell.

Castells, Manuel. 1996. *The rise of network society.* Oxford: Blackwell.

Castles, Stephen, and Mark J. Miller. 2003. *The age of migration: International population movements in the modern world.* New York: Guilford Press.

Davis, Mike. 1992. *City of quartz: Excavating the future in Los Angeles.* New York: Vintage Books.

Evans, Graeme. 2001. *Cultural planning: International perspectives.* London: Routledge.

Ferguson, Yale H., and R.J. Barry Jones. 2002. *Political space: Frontiers of change and governance in a globalizing world.* Albany, NY: State University of New York Press.

Flam, Jack with Miriam Deutch. 2003. *Primitivism and twentieth-century art: A documentary history.* Berkeley: University of California Press.

Flusty, Steven. 2004. *De-coca-colonization: Making the globe from the inside out.* New York: Routledge.

Gladney, Dru C. 1991. *Muslim Chinese: Ethnic nationalism in the People's Republic.* Cambridge, MA: Harvard University Press.

Hannerz, Ulf. 2006. The cultural role of world cities. In Neil Brenner and Roger Keil, eds., *The global cities reader,* 313–18. New York: Routledge.

Harvey, David. 1990. *The condition of postmodernity: An enquiry into the origins of cultural change.* Cambridge, MA: Blackwell.

———. 2001. From managerialism to entrepreneurialism. In *Spaces of Capital: Towards a Critical Geography,* 345–68. New York: Routledge.

Isin, Engin F., ed. 2000. *Democracy, citizenship and the global city.* London: Routledge.

James Irvine Foundation. 1997. *Sixty years: For the people of California, annual report.* San Francisco: James Irvine Foundation.

———. 2001. *Celebrating California, annual report.* San Francisco: James Irvine Foundation.

Kaplan, David E. 1992. *Fires of the dragon: Politics, murder, and the Kuomintang.* New York: Atheneum.

KAZN AM1300. About KAZN AM1300. http://www.mrbi.net/Share/am1300.com/aboutus/1300-eng.htm.

King, Russell, and Nancy Wood, eds. 2001. *Media and migration: Constructions of mobility and difference.* New York: Routledge.

KMRB AM1430. 2003. Background of KMRB AM1430. http://www.am1430.net/about/about.htm.

KSCI-TV. 2002a. *KSCI Research Brief, 2d quarter.* KSCI-TV: Los Angeles.

———. 2002b. KSCI-TV reaches millions of Asian-Americans. *Advertising Age's Multicultural Guide, Special Advertising Section,* November 4:M13

Larson, Allen P. 1997. Remarks before the U.S.–China business council, Washington, DC, June 5, http://www.state.gov/www/regions/eap/970605_larson_china.html.

Los Angeles County Economic Development Corporation. 2003. 2003 international trade trends and impacts report says "made in china" is the new #1 trading partner, news release, http://www.laedc.org/data/press/PR74.html.

Loukaitou-Sideris, Anastasia, and Tridib Banerjee. 1998. *Urban design downtown: Poetics and politics of form.* Berkeley: University of California Press.

Lowe, Lisa. 1996. Imagining Los Angeles in the production of multiculturalism. In Avery Gordon and Christopher Newfield, eds., *Mapping multiculturalism,* 413–23. Minneapolis: University of Minnesota Press.

Naficy, Hamid. 1993. *The making of exile cultures: Iranian television in Los Angeles.* Minneapolis: University of Minnesota Press.

Ong, Aihwa. 1996. Cultural citizenship as subject-making: Immigrants negotiate racial and cultural boundaries in the United States. *Current Anthropology* 37(5):737–62.

———. 1999. *Flexible citizenship: The cultural logics of transnationality.* Durham, NC: Duke University Press.

Ong, Paul, and Tania Azores. 1994. Asian immigrants in Los Angeles: Diversity and divisions. In Paul Ong, Edna Bonacich, and Lucie Cheng, eds., *The new Asian immigration in Los Angeles and global restructuring,* 100–29. Philadelphia: Temple University Press.

Peterson, Marina. 2003. "World in a weekend": Public concerts and the emergence of a transnational urban space. *Journal of Popular Music Studies* 15(2):121–39.
———. 2005. *Sounding the city: Public concerts and civic belonging in Los Angeles.* Ph.D. dissertation, Department of Anthropology, University of Chicago.
Sassen, Saskia. n.d. Scaling State City. PowerPoint presentation.
———. 1998. *Globalization and its discontents: Essays on the new mobility of people and money.* New York: Free Press.
———. 2000. *Cities in a world economy,* 2d ed. Thousand Oaks, CA: Pine Forge Press.
———. 2001. *The global city: New York, London, Tokyo,* 2d ed. Princeton, NJ: Princeton University Press.
———. 2003. The repositioning of citizenship: Emergent subjects and spaces for politics. *New Centennial Review* 3(2):41–66.
Scott, Allen J. 2000. *The cultural economy of cities.* London: Sage.
Soja, Edward W. 1996. *Thirdspace: Journeys to Los Angeles and other real and imagined places.* Oxford: Blackwell.
Thompson, Emily. 2002. Wiring the world: Acoustical engineers and the empire of sound in the motion picture industry, 1927–1930. In Veit Erlman, ed., *Hearing cultures: Essays on sound, listening and modernity,* 191–210. Oxford: Berg.
Torgovnick, Marianna. 1990. *Gone primitive: Savage intellects, modern lives.* Chicago: University of Chicago Press.
Von Eschen, Penny M. 2004. *Satchmo blows up the world: Jazz ambassadors play the Cold War.* Cambridge, MA: Harvard University Press.
Warshawski, Morrie. n.d. *Going international: Case statement.* Washington, DC: National Assembly of State Arts Agencies.
Whitt, J. Allen. 1987. Mozart in the metropolis: The arts coalition and the urban growth machine. *Urban Affairs Quarterly* 23(1):15–36.

CHAPTER 3

Reimagining Old Havana

World Heritage and the Production of Scale in Late Socialist Cuba

MATTHEW J. HILL

> *If ... urban entrepreneurialism ... is embedded in a framework of zero-sum inter-urban competition for resources, jobs, and capital, then even the most resolute and avant-garde municipal socialists will find themselves, in the end, playing the capitalist game and performing as agents for the very processes that they are trying to resist (Harvey 1989a).*

In October 1993 the Colegio Santo Angel, an eighteenth-century merchant's house recognized by the World Heritage Committee of the United Nations Educational, Scientific, and Cultural Organization (UNESCO), collapsed in a pile of dust while awaiting restoration. The implosion nearly killed a British journalist as well as a leading Cuban conservationist who was extemporizing at that moment on the past glories of the 'Colonial Williamsburg-style structure (see Glancey 1993, p. 22; Scarpaci 2000, p. 727). Fortunately, no one died in the incident, as the building had been previously declared uninhabitable and evacuated. The collapse of the Colegio and of a second building that fell victim to torrential rains later that evening were not unusual occurrences in Old Havana. Official documents suggest that two such cave-ins take place every three days due to age, heavy rains, and a lack of adequate maintenance (Rodríguez Alomá and Alina Ochoa Alomá 1997, p. 86). But the loss of a building with a top-level protection category located in an internationally recognized plaza made its demise noteworthy. The fate of the Colegio was a direct result of another collapse — the dissolution of the Soviet Union, which in turn dried up state funding for restoration work in the Old City. Restoration work that had begun in 1989 was halted in 1991 due to a lack of financing and the prioritizing of other projects in the Old City. In the intervening two-year period, the Colegio was cannibalized by vandals in search of scarce building materials. Theft combined with a partially exposed roof and heavy rains contributed to its ultimate demise (see Sansen 2000, pt. 2, p. 66).

The collapse of the Colegio reverberated to the highest levels of government. Over the preceding fifteen years, the Cuban state had dedicated considerable technical, legislative, and financial resources to the restoration of the Plaza Vieja. Moreover, it had invested substantial political capital, including a promise to UNESCO's director general that the "Cuban people would work tirelessly to rescue and revalorize the Plaza Vieja" as part of Cuban National and World Patrimony (UNESCO 1983, p. 6). As images of the collapsed structure spread across European newswires, the state was placed in a difficult position. Since state parties to the World Heritage Convention are legally required to protect designated properties in their territory, the collapse potentially threatened Old Havana's World Heritage status.

Faced with this impasse, it is rumored that President Fidel Castro summoned the historian of the city, Eusebio Leal, to his office for a meeting, asking what could be done to hasten the restoration work in the Old City. Leal purportedly suggested that if the state would allow him to operate the state-owned restaurants and hotels in Old Havana, he would use the money to fix up the Old City. In the aftermath of this conversation, it is said that Cuba's highest government echelon passed a decree (Decree Law 143) transforming the Office of the Historian of the City of Havana (OHCH) from a provincial-level cultural institution into a decentralized state agency subordinated directly to the Cuban Council of State. The OHCH was also granted the legal power to commercially redevelop state properties in the historic center and to tax state companies operating in the zone. This legal measure was to enable the OHCH to act as its own investor, thereby allowing it to self-finance the rehabilitation of the historic center. This was the first time that a quasi-independent government agency was granted such absolute control over a tract of urban territory. The scope of its authority encompassed not only the public administration and financial management of the district, but decisions about zoning, land use, housing, and practically every public investment.

The collapse of the Colegio is significant because it prompted the reorganization of a series of social relationships and thus, intersecting geographical scales, that led to the globalization of Old Havana. By globalization I refer to processes of capitalist expansion, the flows of international capital, tourists, commodities, and information technology that more readily situate Old Havana in relation to these forms of circulation rather than to the context of the Cuban nation-state. I argue that these flows are not the evolutionary byproduct of transformations in the nature of markets and capital taking place on a planetary scale, but the contingent outcome of a dialectical process that operates at multiple levels simultaneously. Moreover, I suggest that heritage is one means of producing new articulations between disparate spatial scales that ultimately constitute a global project.

It is within the context of this global project that the significance of the Colegio can be read at each of these interlocking spatial scales. At the local level, its facades form part of a cultural frame that structure the way in which residents and visitors experience and understand the plaza (and Old Havana) as a place. At the national level, the Colegio is one of a series of protected properties that taken together constitute the identity of the nation by defining its national culture or patrimony. In the wake of the Colegio's collapse, and the state's unbundling of Old Havana, it also comes to comprise part of a series of internationalized zones that are officially known as "zones of high significance for tourism" and unofficially as "islands of capitalism." By promoting commercial activity within these zones, the state seeks to accumulate the hard currency needed to maintain its allocative power, and to further the socialist project in a post-socialist world.[1] Finally, at the global level, the Colegio is a concrete instance of the assemblage of heritage objects through which UNESCO's global geography of World Heritage cities and sites is comprised. Through the particular experience of the Colegio and its immediate environment, the Plaza Vieja, the cosmopolitan observer can experience and know the "universal history of humankind," and through it, the "common humanity" that comprises the world as a community. Through the intersection of these scales (local, national, global) a new dynamic of capital investment is created.

Heritage Preservation as Scale-Making

In the Cuban context, where the revolution interrupted the speculative processes of modernization and urban renewal that remade other Latin American cities in the 1960s and 1970s, colonial architecture emerged as a global economic resource in the late socialist period. It included "built forms," comprising both "building types" such as houses, temples, and meeting places created to enclose human activity and defined but "open spaces" such as plazas, streets, or markets (Low 1990, p. 454). At the same time, these colonial forms could be remolded to create a landscape or set of symbols whose circulation is mediated by a range of institutionally located heritage actors (e.g., architects, developers, urban planners, nongovernmental organizations) (Schein 1997, p. 660; Zukin 1995, p. 265). Looking at globalization as situated in this way prevents treating it as a universal process that remakes place in a uniform manner regardless of historical context and geographic location. Rather, it turns attention to specific locational strategies, institutional linkages, and place-making projects that are realized in particular times and places with the symbolic resources of the built urban form (Tsing 2000).

I see these linkages being constructed through scale-making practices that create articulations between different communities or groups of cultural producers like urban conservationists, government bureaucrats, and global heritage actors. By *scale making,* I refer to the ways these groups seek to imagine or represent space in ways that advance their particular interests and turn these representations into a dominant mode of seeing or knowing the world. Moreover, through this renegotiation, territories get reinserted into new networks which shift the coordination and control of those territories (Dicken, Kelly, Olds, Yeung 2001, p. 97) This process of representing space is a highly charged process in which the producers and readers of space construct and negotiate conflicting representations. Finally, the power and coherence of a particular vision or representation of space can be strengthened by linking it up to the visions set forth by other scale-making projects, whether global or local (Jones 1998; cf. Cox 1998). The constructed nature of scale does not mean then that scales are purely representational. It is in the embeddedness of these representations in material social relations, which are set in flux by globalization, that scales become meaningful (Kelly 1999, p. 381).

Rebuilding the Colegio, Conjuring Scale

Three years after the Colegio's collapse, the piles of rubble, rebar, and cement block had been cleared, and plans were initiated to construct a replica of the original merchant's house from the ground up. At the same time, the protection category of the original structure had been downgraded, allowing for several commercial modifications: the construction of an additional floor, the use of contemporary materials such as modern bathroom fixtures, and the introduction of a restaurant, outdoor café, and gift shop. The colonial-era house — used in the republican period as a school for orphans and during the revolution as public housing — was now restored with hard currency for service as a luxury apartment hotel. Where thirty-six families, many of them rural migrants, once lived in crowded flats as *usufructuarios gratuitos* (rent-free leaseholders), eleven European nationals, including a tourism agent and director of an art school, now resided in large, air-conditioned rental apartments. Meanwhile, the building's former rural residents were relocated to shelters (*albergues*), temporary dwellings, or replacement housing in East Havana.[2]

The urban conservationists who ultimately rebuilt a replica of the original Colegio Santo Angel conjured up an image of a colonial building situated in the midst of an eighteenth-century plaza — in lieu of a run-down block of tenement houses surrounding a modern underground parking structure. The power of this representation was strengthened by linking it to UNESCO's vision of a world of global heritage objects of outstanding universal significance, preserved in the name of the world community. Other representations of space that were excluded in the process were those of plaza residents, who lost access to the plaza as a public space and, in some instances, to their homes, which were expropriated for use as tourist hotels, restaurants, and shops. Scale making then is also the conflicted process in which competing groups present alternative ways of knowing or apprehending space and attempt to normalize these ways of knowing through institutional practices such as urban conservation. As in the case of the Plaza Vieja, the power of scale-making projects can be enhanced by linking them up with other, more extensive scale-making projects. In fact, the most powerful scale-making projects are those that create productive linkages, no matter how tentative, with other scale-making projects, such as the linkage between World Heritage and the local conservation movement in Old Havana.

UNESCO and the Global Heritage Grid

> It is true that, in many countries, remarkable efforts have already been made to protect those monuments which are endangered; and there is no nation today which is not proud of its artistic heritage and conscious of the importance of that heritage in its cultural life. But UNESCO, which … is called upon to ensure the conservation and protection of the world's heritage of works of art and monuments, had a duty to take its own steps to bring these national efforts into a world-wide scheme, and to show the key role that may be played in the cultural formation of contemporary man [sic] by communion with the works produced, through the centuries, in the various centers of civilization which cover the surface of the globe like so many volcanos of history. — UNESCO General Director René Maheu[3]

Having defined globalization in terms of the articulations between various scale-making projects, I turn to the role of UNESCO and its global project to incorporate the cultural and natural heritage sites of the world into a kind of global imaginary that binds places of outstanding universal significance into a geographic space or circuit that I name the *global heritage grid*. In the case of Old Havana, this global project articulates with the aims of the Cuban socialist state that, in the late socialist context, seeks to use tourism as a means of generating hard currency. Finally, the dreams of UNESCO and the socialist state articulate with those of urban conservationists whose primary concern is to salvage historically significant buildings and architectural styles considered to be important markers of national identity. In the course of over three decades, the interests of these different groups converged in Old Havana, transforming the state from a primary financier of urban conservation to a beneficiary of that process and urban conservationists from a class of political outsiders to a managerial class. This section explores the way UNESCO's World Heritage Convention and its global vision of uniting the planet through a shared cultural heritage linked up with this more local-level process.

UNESCO's vision of World Heritage is set forth in a variety of contexts, including the World Heritage Convention, the operational guidelines for the implementation of the convention, and the public pronouncements of UNESCO's director general and the World Heritage Committee.[4] Taken together, these international legal texts and public statements comprise the discourse of World Heritage. The network of cultural and natural heritage sites that are subsequently conjured into existence through this discourse become the symbolic glue through which the idea of humankind's belonging to a cosmopolitan community is cemented (Turtinen 2000). This discourse consists of a set of norms and categories that define what counts as global heritage, the procedures and practices for protecting that heritage, and the system of governance for monitoring, assessing, and propagating information about that heritage.

A key concept is UNESCO's notion of *outstanding universal value*. Outstanding universal value is a fuzzy construct based on an eclectic assortment of values including masterpieces of human genius, important interchanges of human values, unique testimonies to cultural tradition, outstanding examples of buildings and landscapes, and, tautologically, even ideas "that possess outstanding universal value (UNESCO 2005:19). What is significant in this assemblage of criteria is their "high cultural orientation," that is, the "school mediated, academy supervised idiom" (Gellner 1983, p. 55) of letters, fine art, and material culture that is evident in UNESCO's emphasis on masterpieces, monumental arts, civilizations, and artistic works of outstanding universal significance. [5] In particular, the notion of outstanding universal value is dependent on an enlightenment notion of universal history, with its teleological assumptions about human reason, progress, and perfectibility. This idea of a single global viewpoint through which all human history can be understood is in keeping with UNESCO's mission of creating solidarity by promoting an awareness of the unity of humankind. Yet it is also constitutive of a master narrative in which heritage properties are situated within an evolutionary framework in which human history can be considered to unfold in stages. World Heritage exists then within a geography of imagination that seeks to disembed heritage sites "from former times and spaces in nations" and to reembed them in a global framework that ties them to an "evolutionary history of humankind" (Turtinen 2000, p. 19). In the post-colonial context of the Americas, this evolutionary history is actually the history of European economic expansion and conquest, a history that has been written by Europe, and later "by those who have adopted Europe's history as their own" (Asad 1987, p. 604).

Seeing Old Havana as a part of UNESCO's global heritage grid requires an act of conjuring spatial scale. If we think of scale as a "spatial dimensionality necessary for a particular type of view" (Tsing 2000, p. 120), we can easily see how scale is brought into being through the discourse of World Heritage. This is clearly evident in a 1983 speech delivered by UNESCO's director general in the context of UNESCO's international campaign to save the Plaza Vieja (Rigol and González 1983). In the context of that speech, the director general looked beyond the weeds, crumbling tenements, collapsed buildings, and modern parking structure that rose out of the center of the plaza to see a space that was "one of the most representative architectural works" to emerge from the encounter of many cultures — Spanish, African, and indigenous — in the crucible of the Antilles (ibid.: p. 7). The plaza he envisioned was an idealized nineteenth-century square, when the plaza "remained the center of the city" and a "new type of spot in the Americas" — a spot set aside for social life — and a product of "the first attempt at urban planning in this part of the world" (ibid.). It is this idealized plaza that, together with Old Havana, for him represented a "mosaic" of all the Spanish Colonial cities that served as "milestones in the saga of the Americas" and part of a "single history": that of humanity (ibid., p. 8). Through his speech, the director general then lifted an aging plaza, which had gone through a continuous process of transformation over four centuries, out of its contemporary surroundings. In so doing, he fixed the identity of the plaza in terms of a nineteenth-century square that fit into a universal narrative about a particular moment of world history making: the Spanish conquest. Subsequent transformations that failed to fit with this idealized image were either dismissed as inauthentic accretions, or read out of the field of vision altogether.

Contrary to popular belief, UNESCO provides little in the way of financial resources to support urban conservation in places such as Old Havana — a costly process with a price tag that could easily run into the billions of dollars. In the Cuban case, this financial support amounted to a million-dollar loan to create a laboratory and training facility for technical specialists, scholarships to study restoration abroad, and technical assessors to evaluate the restoration process. Far more importantly, what UNESCO provides are the norms and categories through which the built environment is reimagined as belonging to the global heritage grid and the technical training and expertise necessary for nationals to realize these categorizations in local settings. The fact that World Heritage, on the surface of things, is a highly depoliticized discourse about civilizations that have disappeared enabled UNESCO to make these categorizations in Cuba, where outside political intervention is strictly controlled. The colonial past was also ultimately perceived as a safer past than its republican counterpart, a period associated with political corruption, economic underdevelopment, and foreign domination at the hands of an imperial power, the United States (cf. Pérez 1986). As the following section attempts to show, the Cuban state used these UNESCO categorizations in different ways in response to the contingencies of particular historical moments. In the 1970s and 1980s, when the state was more concerned with consolidating the identity of the revolution, urban patrimony together with museums served an important pedagogical function. In the 1990s, when the state's concern shifted to the attraction of hard-currency resources required to sustain a socialist project, World Heritage provided the brand that helped in the marketing of Old Havana as a global tourist destination.

Late Socialism and Shifting Scale of Governance

To provide an example of this shift in official attitudes about conservation, consider the words of a prominent Cuban conservationist whom I interviewed in the late 1990s:

> In the 1960s, when someone spoke of saving Old Havana it seemed crazy (*parecía una locura*); Old Havana was so old, it was necessary to think in terms of the future. What were we going to save? What kind of thing was it? It was the house where a colonizer, a slave trader, an exploiter once lived. On the contrary, we had to create a new house where there were no slaves; that is, in terms of the political discourse [of the period]. I remember at the University [of Havana] there were professors who said that the *Capitolio* had to be demolished, because this architecture possessed no value...[M]any of the professors of

> architecture in the seventies, who were formed in the fifties and saw eclecticism as an evil, also saw colonial architecture as an evil. In due time, these [attitudes] coincided with the new political attitude (*el nuevo concepto político*), which viewed the architecture of all these periods as bad architecture since they coincided with bad [historical] periods.[6]

In other words, the Cuban revolution was fashioned in terms not of saving the past but of a radical break with the past, which was associated with a panoply of social injustices, including colonialism, slavery, and exploitation. By contrast, the future was seen as an arena of possibility, one in which "scientifically designed schemes for production and social life" would replace received tradition (Scott 1998, p. 94). This took the territorial form of massive industrial, transportation, and housing projects aimed at urbanizing the countryside while relocating the disenfranchised in Havana and Santiago de Cuba — squatters, slum dwellers, and shanty-town residents — to newly constructed socialist housing blocs on the urban fringe (cf. Butterworth 1976; Eckstein 1981, 1994; Hardoy and Acosta 1973). The futurist ideology of the revolutionary reformers is illustrated in this passage by the radical call, on the part of a number of prominent revolutionary architects, for the destruction of an Old Havana landmark, the *Capitolio* — the former state capital completed under the republican reign of dictator Gerardo Machado (1924–1933).[7]

The shift from a futurist to a past orientation was generated in part through the efforts of an iconoclastic group of urban conservationists who participated in international conferences on historic cities in the former Soviet bloc and the European meetings of international heritage organizations like UNESCO and the International Council on Monuments and Sites (ICOMOS). Originally, they consisted of a small group of architects and historians who worked together on the National Monuments Commission (1963–1976) with little budget or recognition. They spent a majority of their time identifying, cataloging, and studying historic buildings and preventing them from being demolished by local governing bodies known as *Juntas de Coordinación, Ejecución e Inspección* (Soviets for Coordination, Inspection and Execution or JUCEI). According to an architect who served on the commission, these early restoration efforts were isolated affairs that focused on colonial buildings that were the oldest and most affected by the passage of time—military fortresses, government palaces, and palatial mansions, structures that were considered important because they were tied to an important figure or architectural style in Cuban history. As a result of these efforts, this architect noted, "The work of restoration began to gain ground. There was a growing awareness on the part of the authorities and the population that didn't exist in the beginning...that there were values that had to be preserved, ... places that were very valuable that we had to conserve, protect, and restore."[8]

This growing recognition on the part of government leaders led to the passage of the first two heritage laws enacted by the Cuban National Assembly: the National Cultural Heritage Law and the National Monument Law (1977). These laws established a registry of historic landmarks together with extensive guidelines for their protection and safeguarding. A year later, the National Monuments Commission declared the part of Old Havana contained inside the old city walls to be a national monument. This was in keeping with international trends that expanded the concept of historic preservation from isolated monuments to encompass entire building ensembles.[9] Taking advantage of the visit of the UNESCO director general to Old Havana in 1982, the Ministry of Culture decided to expand the area of the historic district. In its application to UNESCO for World Heritage recognition, the ministry included the old walled city as well as a zone of early republican expansion outside the Old City's walls. Apart from these legal enactments and redefinitions of the historic center, what is significant in this period is that the Cuban state committed the first dedicated budget, in two five-year plans, to the restoration of the historic center. Moreover, this money was funneled through the municipal government to two organizations: the UNESCO-financed National Center for Conservation, Restoration, and Museum Science (CENCRM) and the OHCH. Together, they became the institutional embodiment of restoration in the socialist period.

In the aftermath of the collapse of the Soviet Union, the state's interest in generating hard currency through tourism transformed its relationship to Old Havana and the international recognition garnered by the World Heritage designation. Ironically, heritage was now looked at not only as a source of national pride but also as a resource for furthering the imperatives of the socialist project in a radically reorganized world. This shift was captured in an interview with a conservationist about the importance of the UNESCO designation for the country in the post-Soviet context:

> Th[e] concept [of patrimony] today is tied to the local sense of pride and the interests of many cities. I was in Porto (Portugal) two years ago and the mayor had a plan: Porto, World Patrimony! And when Porto was declared World Patrimony, the event was like a party. What's behind all of this? It agrees with the mayor [of Porto] that his city be declared World Patrimony, because this is a type of prestige, a merit, the possibility to attract more tourism, ... to sell more books. [T]his opens the possibility for the University to say, come to Porto

> to study architecture because Porto is World Patrimony. I believe that the World Patrimony [designation] has been converted into a kind of small flag of identity. At the local level, people have begun to make a certain kind of business out of it.[10]

The conservationist's comments show how the world heritage designation extended beyond a limited concern with national identity to encompass the economic concerns of the late socialist state in an age of increasing interurban competition. It also suggests the way the World Heritage designation provided Old Havana with the kind of cultural cache needed to enhance its reputation as an international tourist destination.

In this context, the conservationists initially empowered by the socialist state to conserve the historic center became the conduits needed to transform Old Havana into a global tourist destination. This is because they developed a level of technical and administrative expertise that ultimately made them the only actors capable of carrying out this transformation. To capitalize on Old Havana's global heritage status, the socialist state then engineered the unbundling (Sassen 2000) of Old Havana, creating a new political institutional framework and special regulatory environment in the historic district that would permit a heightened dynamic of investment (*dinámica inversionista*) between the global and the local (Rodríguez Alomá and Ochoa Alomá 1999, p. 34). This uncoupling was carried out through the creation of a new legal regime and system of financial regulation that transferred the location of regulatory functions and territorial administration downward from the central government to a local conservation agency, the OHCH. The latter was granted the unusual powers to self-finance the restoration of the historic center and to regulate its territory on behalf of the socialist state. By shifting the scale of urban governance from the centralized state to this local entity, the socialist leadership sought to enhance its capacity to "mobilize and coordinate transnational capital investment" in Old Havana (Brenner 1998, p. 20).[11] This process of institutional rescaling in turn is tied to the effort to reorganize the space of Old Havana in ways that provide a platform for foreign investment while producing a spatial logic that differs from the rest of the city.[12]

Urban Conservationists and the Production of Local Scale

Though UNESCO scans the globe for heritage objects to add to its network of World Heritage sites, these sites are not merely found. They have to be constructed, cultivated, tailored, and ultimately produced as transcendental cultural landscapes. This work is done not by UNESCO or the state but by local-level actors, who in the case of Old Havana I see as a group of prominent urban conservationists. Urban conservationists are involved on a day-to-day basis in doing the work of heritage. This involves bounding, setting apart, and marking the built environment so that it can be known and recognized as a heritage object. The material with which they work is the built urban form, and the product of their work is what I call a *heritage landscape.* As I hope to show in this section, this process of representing an urban locality as a heritage landscape has the paradoxical effect of turning it into a translocality — a highly internationalized border zone that gets more articulated with "global political, economic and social arenas" than the national context (Little 2004, p. 78). This is evident from the international hotel chains, high-speed computer connections, flows of tourists, and global brand names (e.g., Benetton, Paul & Shark) that increasingly define Old Havana as an urban landscape in stark contrast to the rest of the city.

By *urban conservationists,* I refer to architects, art historians, and social scientists who share an aesthetic interest in preserving historic buildings, architectural styles, and aging inner-city districts (Deckha 2000). As a social class they are rich in cultural capital (Bourdieu 1984) — the skills and abilities acquired from family and educational systems that can be used to enhance a position of power, prestige, and influence (Berger 1986, p. 1446). They have trained at the state's most prominent architectural and liberal arts institutions, have had the privilege of traveling abroad, and under UNESCO's auspices have studied preservation in prestigious European centers such as Rome. In this respect, they are a highly internationalized class. Their access to computers with high-speed Internet communications and exposure to outside heritage specialists keep them abreast of constantly evolving heritage trends, declarations, and charters. On a local level, they sit on local UNESCO commissions and ICOMOS chapters as well as on national and local commissions and planning boards. As a group, they are also a tight-knit class that celebrates one another's architectural accomplishments while memorializing the lives of deceased members in solemn ceremonies.

The work of these conservationists consists of conjuring up a particular type of view of the local as a colonial city center or historic landscape. This is not a small task, since new construction has continuously been superimposed on Old Havana's colonial architecture through a process of building over a four-century period. This raises the question of what constitutes the *colonial,* since the majority of colonial houses up to the early nineteenth century consisted of simple, often crude, single-story structures occupied by the poor and working classes rather than the palatial mansions that today are celebrated as the colonial (cf. Venegas 2002, p. 15). Moreover, these simple artisan houses were subsequently demolished or expanded to accommodate nineteenth-century urban growth, while the palaces were often subdivided for use as *ciudadelas* or *solares* — a form of collective housing for the urban poor with shared sanitary services surrounding an inner courtyard or passageway. The task of recuperating the colonial past is thus complicated by a process of continuous erasure and overwriting that characterizes Old Havana as a kind of urban palimpsest (Schein 1997, p. 662). Against this background, constructing the colonial or historic landscape entails a reorganization of the frame of the viewer so that the built urban form can be perceived as a transcendental entity known as *cultural patrimony.*

To see how this operates in practice, let us return to the Plaza Vieja with which this chapter opened. Reconstructing an image of the colonial in the Plaza Vieja, as suggested earlier, was complicated by a complex history of use and reuse and by republican-era transformations to the appearance of the square: the construction of a modern parking structure that elevated the surface of the square, eclectic and neoclassical republican-era buildings that dramatically altered its morphology, and dilapidated and partially collapsed *ciudadelas* that changed its former elite residential function. In addition to these modern accretions, a further hurdle to restoring the colonial hinged on the relative placelessness of the Plaza Vieja. As one conservationist said to me, "This isn't a Plaza where you had a church, a military fortress, or an important palace." This absence of monumental architecture further complicated efforts to recreate the image of the colonial past in the Plaza Vieja.

In light of these challenges, conservationists set out to restore the Plaza Vieja to its early nineteenth-century form, a golden age prior to the construction of the Cristina Market (1832), a covered market for vendors of meat and produce, considered to have hastened the plaza's decline. This image was reconstructed from the lithographs, engravings, and traveler accounts of European artists — renderings that presented an image of the plaza surrounded by shaded porticos and covered balconies of the resident *hacendado* class. In keeping with these historic allusions, the 1982 proposal for the redevelopment of the Plaza Vieja called for things like the removal of contemporary additions and modifications, the uniform installation of fan-shaped stained-glass windows and original carpentry, and the restoration of balconies, iron work, tile roofs, and original facades. What such growing regulation of "color, form and ornament" (Herzfeld 1991, p. 12) points to is an attempt to overcome the "progressive disarticulation of the urban landscape" as the city grows, replacing it with a uniform idea of the colonial city as a "governing norm" (Geertz 1989, p. 293). This is evident, for instance, in a series of architectural renderings that illustrate how to transform neoclassical facades into colonial surfaces through the introduction of Persian blinds and fan-shaped windows (Capablanca 1983, p. 27). Partially collapsed buildings were also to be reconstructed following these standardized design codes, producing an idea of a colonial landscape that in effect was a contemporary product of the architect's imagination.

But the most dramatic form of local conjuring involved proposals to eliminate the underground parking structure and amphitheater. One of the architects who opposed this action argued that it amounted to trying to turn back the clock to the way the plaza once was. She argued that it was a form of historicism violating a bedrock principle of conservation: modifications to the built environment should not be removed. She compared this proposal to the well-intentioned architects from the 1930s, who in attempting to give Old Havana's most prominent monument, the Palace of the Captains General, a more baroque appearance radically altered its appearance, removing a colorful stucco outer layer to expose the building's underlying gray limestone. Apart from the issue of historicism, a debate surged around the costs of demolishing the parking structure and the possible use of the space for other purposes. After fifteen years, the proponents of the demolition won out over contrary proposals (Galeano and Fornet Gil 1998, p. 11). The eventual demolition of the plaza — a noisy, dusty process that lasted for two years — produced a gaping hole, which was eventually filled with hundreds of truckloads of topsoil and was covered with polished cobblestones. Then in the center of the square, a working fountain made of Italian marble was put in place, encircled by a ten-foot-high iron fence to keep neighborhood youth from bathing in its waters.

Like the colors, ornaments, and design codes used to create an image of the colonial in the Plaza Vieja, features such as the fountain are instrumental in constructing an image of the colonial in the Plaza Vieja. One architect's criticism of the fountain — that it represents only one of many images of the plaza depicted in historical engravings and is thus of questionable patrimonial value — overlooks an important point: The fountain operates together with the other framing devices in the plaza to discipline the field of vision of the viewer. Rather than seeing a landscape of disarticulated building styles (e.g., baroque, eclectic, neoclassical) and references to diverse historical epochs (e.g., colonial, republican, revolutionary), the fountain together with these design codes operates to suture the viewer into a particular symbolic register, relegating those elements that fail to fit into the frame into the background.[13]

In the process of reconstructing the image of the plaza in terms of an idealized colonial square, the plaza is transformed from a lived space — where residents once gathered to listen to music, children rode bikes and played games of pick-up baseball, and the elderly paused to sit and enjoy the breeze from the harbor — to a primarily observed or tourist space. The reorganization of space so that it can be observed from the perspective of an outsider viewer is accomplished by tour guides who quickly usher tourists through the square, showing them what to see while narrating how they should see it. Other techniques include the introduction of many viewing points, like balconies from which tourists can gaze down on the square, and a camera obscura mounted on the roof of the plaza's tallest building, through which tourists are afforded a panorama of the plaza. The panorama operates here as a kind of mirror image of the Panopticon, training the viewer to see the surroundings as part of a "disciplined order of things" (Boyer 1994, p. 253). This disciplining is further supported by a mounted placard at the entrance to the square, depicting enlarged reproductions of the original eighteenth-century engravings of the square by various European traveler-artists and life-sized cutouts of Spanish colonial troupes, dressed in signature red-and-white uniforms and playing fifes and drums. In short, this is a locale in which the image of the colonial is constructed out of codes and practices that instruct the viewer in the art of seeing and knowing urban space.

Conclusion

Over a lunchtime conversation during a 2006 conference on colonial architecture in Old Havana, a group of architects debated the merits of the reproduction of the Colegio Santo Angel that now sits on the exact spot where the dilapidated tenement once sat before its 1993 implosion. One of the architects lamented the fact that an opportunity had been lost in building a replica of the original structure rather than a modern structure, which would have given Cuban architects a chance to design something new. Intellectually, this argument was compelling. But it overlooked the fact that a modern structure would have disrupted the frame of the viewer and the constructed colonial image that has transformed the Plaza Vieja into a tourist square. In building a copy of the Santo Angel, in many respects more perfect than the original, conservationists are doing the work of cultivating a local landscape that meets the expectation of what most tourists come to see — an authentic colonial plaza from the nineteenth century. Ironically, the Colegio and the gated marble fountain are two of the most photographed structures in the Plaza Vieja today, along with the last remaining unrestored tenement that somehow speaks to the visitors' search for the authentic in this highly cultivated landscape.

Over the past decade, geographers have increasingly pointed out that spatial scales are best understood not as static, fixed, or ontological entities that exist in some kind of preordained hierarchical framework but are produced as the "contingent outcome" of the practices of human agents (Marston 2000, p. 220). In exploring this constructivist notion of scale, I have suggested that heritage preservation is one such contingent form of scale making that can be used to understand the operation of the global in peripheral places like late socialist Cuba. Globalization can then be understood as a dynamic and scalar process in which different projects of scale making articulate in the context of particular historical conjunctures — such as the intersection of World Heritage, late socialism, and urban conservation. In this respect, scaling is actively produced in response to changing historical situations. Moreover, it is the conjuncture of multiple interlocking scales that combine to produce the global. Globalization then is not something that takes place in a top-down fashion — by global forces that impact the local — rather, it is the outcome of global projects that link up with projects at other spatial scales to achieve their efficacy. In the case of Old Havana, the outcome of these intersections is determined just as much by local needs as global processes.

I have argued then that urban conservationists are involved in constructing Old Havana as a distinctive type of place. Though this place is connected to UNESCO's global heritage grid through the discourse of World Heritage, it is also produced as a unique landscape, giving it a place-specific advantage over other Caribbean destinations. The process of creating place ironically involves practices of bounding, separating off, and fixing the identity of Old Havana as a space that is distinct from other parts of Havana, as well as masking elements that disrupt the image of the colonial city. If the project of UNESCO and World Heritage then is ultimately about creating a global heritage grid, the project of urban conservationists is about creating a local place that ultimately opens outward to capture global flows. It is the production of this locality, an idealized Spanish colonial town, that is ultimately used to create linkages with the global.

Acknowledgements

Research for this project was made possible by the Social Science Research Council, the Lincoln Institute of Land Policy, the MacArthur and Ford Foundation Cuba Exchange Grants, and the Center for Latin American Studies at the University of Chicago. Thanks to Susan Gal, Claudio Lomnitz, Stephan Palmié, Joseph Scarpaci, and Pablo Fornet Gil for their many insights. Special thanks to Saskia Sassen and Tamara Neuman for comments on multiple drafts of this article. The views expressed here are my own, and not necessarily shared by those who have contributed to this project.

Notes

1. Verdery (1995, p. 75–6) describes *allocative power* as the socialist bureaucracy's drive to maximize its capacity to allocate scarce goods and resources.

2. For a further discussion of the restoration plan and fate of the Colegio's former inhabitants, see Sansen (2000, pt. 2, 66–73).
3. UNESCO (1970, p. 22).
4. For the World Heritage Convention, see http://whc.unesco.org/en/conventiontext/. For the Operational guidelines, see http://whc.unesco.org/en/guidelines.
5. The source of this ambiguity is immediately evident in examining the criteria used by UNESCO's operational guidelines to define outstanding universal value. In the case of cultural heritage properties, these criteria require that a property meet one or more of the following: (1) represent a masterpiece of human creative genius; (2) exhibit an important interchange of human values, over a span of time or within a cultural area of the world, on developments in architecture or technology, monumental arts, town planning, or landscape design; (3) bear a unique or at least exceptional testimony to a cultural tradition or to a civilization, living or disappeared; (4) be an outstanding example of a type of building, architectural or technological ensemble, or landscape that illustrates significant stages in human history; (5) be an outstanding example of a traditional human settlement, land use, or sea use that is representative of a culture (or cultures), or human interaction with the environment especially when it has become vulnerable under the impact of irreversible change; (6) be directly or tangibly associated with events or living traditions, with ideas, or with beliefs, with artistic and literary works of outstanding universal significance (The committee considers that this criterion should preferably be used in conjunction with other criteria). (UNESCO 2005, p. 19).
6. Anonymous informant in Old Havana, interview by author, July 18, 1999.
7. This anti-traditional perspective is also discussed by urbanist Joseph Scarpaci (Scarpaci, Segre, and Coyula 2002, p. 300), who notes, "A growing political class in Cuba consisting of the urban proletariat and farmers gave the Revolution a pragmatic approach — one more concerned about satisfying immediate needs and less about inheriting contaminated bourgeois values, including architectural ones."
8. Anonymous informant in Old Havana, interview by author, May 30, 2006.
9. Significant in this regard was the Charter of Venice (1963). See http://www.icomos.org/venice_charter.html.
10. Anonymous informant in Old Havana, interview by author, July 18, 1999.
11. This shift in the geographical scale of governance is in keeping with studies that tie the globalization of capital with the rescaling of state territorial power in ways that privilege both sub- and supranational forms of territorial organization over the national scale (Brenner 1998; Marston 2000, p. 227).
12. While this revitalization strategy parallels place-based, consumption-driven revitalization schemes in European and North American cities—with their focus on the creation of festival marketplaces, restored waterfront districts, shopping centers, and entertainment complexes (cf. Harvey 1989a, 1989b)—its trajectory is shaped by political factors that are specific to Cuban state socialism.
13. Film critic Kaja Silverman (1983, p. 200) defines *suture* as "that moment when the subject inserts itself into the symbolic register in the guise of the signifier, and in so doing gains meaning at the expense of being." In cine-

matic terms, it is the moment in which the being of the spectator is authored by a frame that is constructed by the other, which in this case are those involved in constructing the tourist gaze.

Works Cited

Asad, Talal. 1987. Are there histories of people without Europe? A review article. *Comparative Studies in Society and History* 29(3):594–607.

Berger, B. 1986. Taste and domination: A review of Bourdieu's distinction. *American Journal of Sociology* 91:1445–53.

Bourdieu, Pierre. 1984. *Distinction: A social critique of the judgment of taste.* Trans. Richard Nice. Cambridge, MA: Harvard University Press.

Boyer, M. Christine. 1994. *City of collective memory: Its historical imagery and architectural elements.* Cambridge, MA: MIT Press.

Brenner, Neil. 1998. Global cities, global states: Global city formation and state territorial restructuring in contemporary Europe. *Review of International Political Economy* 5(1):1–37.

Butterworth, Douglas. 1980. *The people of Buena Ventura: Relocation of slum dwellers in postrevolutionary Cuba.* Urbana: University of Illinois Press.

Capablanaca, Enrique. 1983. La Plaza Vieja. Propuesta de restauración. Arquitectura/Cuba 355–56 (1–2): 22–31.Habana: Ministerio de Cultura.

Cox, Kevin. 1998. Spaces of engagement, spaces of dependence and the politics of scale, or: Looking for local politics. *Political Geography* 17(1):1–23.

Deckha, Nitin. 2000. Repacking the inner city: Historic preservation, community development, and the emergent cultural quarter in London. Ph.D. diss., Rice University, Houston.

Eckstein, Susan. 1981. The debourgeoisement of Cuban cities. In I.L. Horowitz, *Cuban communism,* 4th ed., 119–140. New Brunswick, NJ: Transaction Books.

———. 1994. *Back from the future: Cuba under Castro.* Princeton, NJ: Princeton University Press.

Galeano Mastrángelo, Ivonne, and Pablo Fornet Gil. 1998. La Plaza Vieja, 1982–1997: Una imagen que se transforma. Habana: CENCREM.

Geertz, Clifford. 1989. Toutes directions: Reading the signs in urban sprawl. *International Journal of Middle East Studies* 21:291–306.

Gellner, Ernst. 1983. *Nations and nationalism.* Ithaca, NY: Cornell University Press.

Glancey, Jonathon. 1993. Walls came tumbling down. *Independent,* October 20, Architecture Section, p. 22.

Hardoy, Jorge Enrique, and Maruja Acosta. 1973. *Urban reform in revolutionary Cuba.* Trans. Mal Bochner. New Haven, CT: Antilles Research Program, Yale University.

Harvey, David. 1989a. From managerialism to entrepreneurialism. *Geografiska Annaler. Series B. Human Geography* 71B:3–17.

———. 1989b. *The condition of postmodernity: An enquiry into the origins of cultural change.* Oxford: Blackwell.

Herzfeld, Michael. 1991. *A place in history: Social and monumental time in a Cretan town.* Princeton, NJ: Princeton University Press.

Jones, Katherine T. 1998. Scale as epistemology. *Political Geography* 17(1):25–8.

Kelly, Philip F. 1999. The geographies and politics of globalization. *Progress in Human Geography* 23(3):379–400.

Low, Setha. 1990. The Built Environment and Spatial Form. *Annual Review of Anthropology*. Vol. 19: 453–505.

Little, Walter E. 2004. *Mayas in the marketplace: Tourism, globalization and cultural identity*. Austin: University of Texas Press.

Marston, Sallie A. 2000. The social construction of scale. *Progress in Human Geography* 24(2):219–42.

Pérez, Louis A. 1986. *Cuba under the Platt Amendment, 1902–1934*. Pittsburgh: University of Pittsburgh Press.

Rigol, Isabel and Nancy Gonzalez. 1983. *La Plaza Vieja*. Habana: ECIGRAF.

Rodríguez Alomá, Patricia, and Alina Ochoa Alomá. 1999. *Desafío de una utopía: una estrategia integral para le gestión de salvaguardia de la habana vieja. Ciudad City* Vol. 4. Habana Vieja: Oficina del Historiador de la Ciudad de La Habana.

_____. 1997. *Plan de desarrollo integral avance*. Habana Vieja: Oficina del Historiador de la Ciudad de La Habana.

Sansen, Marjan. 2000. *The renovation process in Old Havana, Cuba: Case-study the Old Square*. M.A. thesis, Catholic University Louvain.

Sassen, Saskia. 2000. Spatialities and temporalities of the global: Elements for a theorization. *Public Culture* 30:215–32.

Scarpaci, Joseph L. 2000. Reshaping Habana Vieja: Revitalization, historic preservation, and restructuring in the socialist city. *Urban Geography* 21(8): 659–69.

Scarpaci, Joseph L., Roberto Segre, and Mario Coyula. 2002. *Havana: Two faces of the Antillean metropolis*. Chapel Hill: University of North Carolina Press.

Schein, Richard. 1997. The place of landscape: A conceptual framework for interpreting the American scene. *Annals of American Geographers* 87(4):660–80.

Scott, James. 1998. *Seeing like a state: How certain schemes to improve the human condition have failed*. New Haven, CT: Yale University Press.

Silverman, Kaja. 1983. *The subject of semiotics*. Oxford: Oxford University Press.

Tsing, Anna. 2000. The global situation. *Cultural Anthropology* 15(3):327–60.

Turtinen, Jan. 2000. *Globalising heritage: On UNESCO and the transnational construction of a world heritage*. Stockholm: Stockholm Center for Organization Research.

UNESCO. 1970. *Protection of mankind's cultural heritage*. Rennes: Imprimeries Oberthur.

———. 1983. *Boletín UNESCO* 91, Comisión Nacional Cubana de la UNESCO. Paris: UNESCO.

———. 2002. The World Heritage Convention, http://www.unesco.org/whc.

_____. 2005. *Operational guidelines for the implementation of the World Heritage Convention*. Intergovernmental Committeee for the Protection of the World and Cultural Natural Heritage. WHC.05/2 (February 2005). Paris: World Heritage Center.

Venegas, Carlos. 2002. La vivienda colonial Habanera. *Arquitectura y Urbanismo*. Habana: Ministerio de Cultura. 23(22):14–31.

Verdery, Katherine. 1991. *National ideology under socialism: Identity and cultural politics in Ceaușescu's Romania*. Berkeley: University of California Press.

Zukin, Sharon. 1995. *The cultures of cities*. Oxford: Blackwell Publishers.

CHAPTER 4

Becoming Global?

Evangelism and Transnational Practices in Russian Society

SARAH BUSSE SPENCER

In a poorly heated room in a dilapidated agricultural college, adults in winter coats stand to give answers to the teacher's questions. Unaltered since the 1970s, the room's walls depict methods of bomb-shelter construction, while a life-sized mannequin in full chemical warfare outfit stands vigilant in the rear of the room. On the wall above the chalkboard is a picture of Vladimir Lenin with the quote, "Every revolution which does not learn to defend itself must fail." The date is November 1999, and Lenin's revolution has been replaced by a very different one: the dissolution of the Soviet empire and the introduction of sweeping market reforms. With diminishing state support, the newly impoverished agricultural college rents this building to an American church, whose missionaries put pictures of Jesus on the walls for Sunday meetings. Against this backdrop, the volunteer teacher asks Soviet-raised adults to think about how the Bible applies in their daily lives.

Globalization has myriad facets, each of which can be approached with multiple lenses. In this chapter, the exploration of becoming global entails examining two changes from the individual point of view: more frequent interaction with the global other and the adoption of foreign behaviors and attitudes through face-to-face contact with outsiders. The first involves the globalization of a person's social networks, while the second involves the adoption of a global habitus. In newly globalizing settings, where foreign contact is recent and rapid, the effects of agents of globalization in this process are particularly visible. As individuals in this local setting are bombarded with recent global influences, they choose whether and to what extent to become global within their historical and cultural context.

This chapter explores the idea of becoming global by drawing on an ethnographic examination of globalization in Novosibirsk, a large city in western Siberia. Of the many sources of globalization in Russia, two are examined: a U.S.-based Christian missionary church and a nongovernmental organization (NGO) support center founded by Americans. Data for this chapter, resulting from a larger project conducted in 1999–2000 and 2002,[1] draw on participant observation in church congregations and observations and interviews in the NGO support center. This chapter examines ways these globalizing agents contribute to the globalization of social networks and habitus. Local reactions include adopting global behaviors while also maintaining traditional local practices or rejecting or resisting globalization, thus avoiding or slowing the process of becoming global.

Globalization through Globalizing Agents

Although much attention has been paid to the role of technology in globalization (Sassen 2004), this chapter focuses on the role of face-to-face interaction in facilitating these processes. Repeated personal contact provides tangible opportunities for locals to integrate foreigners into their social network and to choose whether to adopt foreign practices. Research on sojourners and settlers (Margolis 1995) illustrates that the impact of transnational contact varies with the intended length of stay and motives of the traveler. Outcomes of contact also vary with the aims of sponsoring organizations: Tourists usually have private aims, business travelers represent larger commercial interests, and some noncommercial organizations have specific goals for transnational face-to-face interaction. For example, the Peace Corps originally encouraged volunteers to model "good" American behavior with the explicit goal of "making them like us" (Fischer 1998). Religious organizations have sent emissaries for similarly explicit goals: to preach a doctrine and to convert people to a new way of living. Previous research suggests that the efforts of Christian missions (Dunch 2002) and the spread of religion generally (Robertson 1992) have influenced processes of globalization in various locations. Religions have in turn been influenced by globalization (Robbins 2004), a subject beyond the scope of this chapter.

Advocacy for civil society and procedural democracy may also be seen as evangelism, since many nonprofit organizations seek to introduce new ideology and modify others' behavior toward desired norms. Democracy building, like other development goals, can be seen as part of the globalization project to actively encourage countries to adopt Western norms (McMichael 2004). As with religion, NGOs have had significant impacts on globalization (Fisher 1997) and in turn have been affected by these processes. The international growth of the third sector (Hemment 2004) advances globalization through the circulation of modern managerial practices, which flow through transnational networks of NGOs (Roberts, Jones, and Froehling 2005).

This chapter examines the effect of face-to-face encounters of locals with representatives of two globalizing organizations in Novosibirsk, Russia. Both organizations offer locals the potential for face-to-face interaction with foreign others. Both these organizations evangelize, spreading a message of ideal society and of normative behavior that contrasts with local social norms. Both groups choose representatives devoted to spreading their desired norms and ideals. Because both of these organizations take long-term perspectives and aim to change local norms and local networks, their interaction with locals would be expected to produce greater effect on becoming global than organizations without such explicit aims at globalization.

Contextualizing the Local: Novosibirsk, Capital of Siberia

Settings where contact with the global is both recent and rapid and where locals still vividly perceive the contrast between the foreign and the local, offer unique opportunities for studying the interplay between local and global. When the Soviet Union's former "isolation from the world community owing to ideological boundaries" (Ivanova 2005, p. 72) was shattered with the state's collapse, the resulting openness provided a natural laboratory for studying rapid globalization. For example, consumers who previously were offered only one state brand suddenly are confronted by a wide array of foreign and domestic brands. Some foreign consumption items, such as food, are available more abundantly in cities than rural areas, while foreign television programs are broadcast on national television stations and are thus available across the country. In a process Molchanov describes as catastrophic, globalization "dramatically changed Russia and prompted its return to the global market economy on terms largely dictated by the West" (2005, p. 397). Other research also illustrates that Russians have responded to this sudden exposure to Western culture with less than total enthusiasm. Two thirds of respondents to a survey in 2000 doubted or rejected the Western model of society as appropriate for Russia, and a similar proportion of respondents to a 2002 survey agreed that Western culture has had a negative impact on Russia (Krindatch 2004,

p. 133). Effects of globalization on consumption are new enough that even consumers in Moscow think of products as "ours" and "foreign" (Caldwell 2002) and meet this globalizing process with local patterns of consumption (Jackson 2004).

Unlike Moscow, Novosibirsk is a city primarily of regional significance. As the largest city in Siberia, midway between Moscow and the Far East, Novosibirsk serves as the capital of the Novosibirsk *oblast* (region), as the official seat of the Siberian *okrug* (federal district), and the unofficial commercial capital of Siberia. Like elsewhere in Russia, the social legacy of communism (Millar and Wolchik 1994) is palpable in Novosibirsk, especially with its lack of pre-Soviet history and with an urban landscape characteristic of a typical socialist city (French and Hamilton 1979). The city's geography and its place in the Soviet economic hierarchy have continued to shape the impact of global flows of finance and individuals in this region in the post-Soviet period (Spencer 2004). The socialist legacy also includes dense, multiplex, and closed social networks, with little opportunity for meeting strangers or foreigners, encouraging continued cultural preferences for socializing in small groups of friends (Spencer 2003).

Like other urban areas in Russia, this city of more than 1.5 million inhabitants has its share of winners and losers in the transition to capitalism (Silverman and Yanowitch 1997). Local businesses have benefited from improved economic conditions since 1998, while the unemployed and state salary workers face an increasing struggle to make ends meet. Though Novosibirsk was never a closed city, in the Soviet era flows of foreigners were rare and generally confined to academic exchanges. In the post-Soviet era, international academic exchanges have increased, and though foreign direct investment is significantly less than in the capital, Novosibirsk businesses do include joint ventures and a few foreign businessmen. Other foreign influences in the city come through the German consulate, the Israeli cultural center, and from representatives of the Roman Catholic, Lutheran, and Mormon churches.

Agent of Globalization: Mormon Church

For centuries, processes of globalization have occurred through the influence of world religions (Robertson 1992). As Robertson argues, "the movement which can surely lay claim to being the oldest significant globe-oriented organization — the Roman Catholic Church — has recently become a particularly effective globe-oriented and politically influential actor across most of the world" (p. 81). The Catholic Church in the tenth through twelfth centuries was the unifying force in the creation of modern Europe. Roman Catholic priests and bishops spread their faith to the corners of Europe, seeking to bring every village under diocesan control. Bishops insisted on obedience to the pope, on specific rites, including the use of Latin for church worship, and even on a specific social order based in part on Roman law (Bartlett 1993).

Likewise, the Mormon Church acts as an agent of globalization through promoting the uniformity of Mormon theology and practice in its congregations around the world. The Church of Jesus Christ of Latter-day Saints, with its distinctive theology and behaviors, has been called a new world religion (Givens 2003). With a worldwide membership above 12 million in 2004, this church represents the fifth largest religious group in the United States, yet more than half of its members now live in other countries. Originally, converts were urged to move to the church's center, but in the twentieth century, leaders have urged church members to stay at home rather than to emigrate. The resulting local differences in church life has led the church to become a more global institution (Tullis 1979), but one that is increasingly committed to centralized administration and unified doctrine.

In its global expansion, the Mormon Church seeks not only to disseminate its distinctive doctrines in a uniform manner but also to bring converts into the same structure and social order as members in established congregations. Identical programs and Sunday school lessons help create the experience of a single unified church across national boundaries. Doctrines translated from English into nearly 100 languages are spread around the globe. Members around the world observe and sometimes adopt the practices and social behavior they observe in the missionaries sent from the United States. Unlike evangelistic churches that establish dependent congregations in developing countries, the Mormon Church creates new congregations on the same pattern everywhere, intending that all new outposts become equal congregations under the same central administration. This makes it more like the Catholic Church in an earlier era (Bartlett 1993) and more global than merely transnational.

The Mormon Church began operations in Russia in 1992 (Browning 1997) and by 2000 had expanded to most of the large cities in the country. Since 1994 missionaries have worked in Novosibirsk, which serves as the missionary headquarters for Siberia. In early 2000, there were approximately 200 Russians attending five small congregations in Novosibirsk. By 2002, those units had been consolidated into three somewhat larger congregations with a larger total membership. On average twenty-four Mormon missionaries work in Novosibirsk at a time, though specific missionaries rotate among various cities over their two-year term of volunteer service. Legal and financial matters are handled by a few Russians employees, but following the pattern elsewhere in the world, all ecclesiastical church work is handled by volunteer members since there are no paid clergy. In Russia, the church followed its standard practice of initially authorizing missionaries to establish and lead congregations, while gradually training local members to staff their own congregations. In Novosibirsk in 2000, a few positions were still filled by missionaries, but by 2002 all the congregations were staffed by Russian volunteers. In 2000, many congregations in Siberia still rented space on Sundays such as the group previously described. By 2002, the church had purchased or leased buildings in Novosibirsk and other Siberian cities, which they renovated to suit the church's needs and to match their uniform design style, helping them project an image of a unified worldwide church.

Agent of Globalization: NGO Support Center

In the past fifteen years Western organizations have sent money and advisors to Russia not only to support economic change (Wedel 2001), but also to build democracy by establishing and maintaining NGOs (Henderson 2003), which then look like their Western counterparts. These Western-funded organizations are usually oriented to the priorities of their supporting foundations rather than to local needs. Often they remain dependent on foreign grants and out of touch with local interests (Hemment 2004).

A different type of Western influence on the growth of civil society began in Novosibirsk in 1993. Two Americans arrived with the goal of encouraging democratic change from below by supporting grassroots efforts at organizing in Novosibirsk. From their activities emerged a center, which acts as an incubator to support fledgling NGOs. Beginning with ad hoc work in someone's apartment, they garnered enough stable funding, from a variety of U.S. and European agencies, to rent permanent office space beginning in 1994 (Henderson 2003; SCISC 1999). The Siberian Civic Initiatives Support Center (SCISC) has functioned for a decade as an interregional foundation supporting the development of local NGOs through providing small grants and supporting NGO resource centers across Siberia. The Siberian Center, according to its website, is "dedicated to supporting grassroots democratic development" in Siberia (SCISC 2004). From 1995 to 2004, the center provided grants for local organizations and conducted projects that have included the following objectives: "promoting volunteerism, increasing professionalism of NGOs [and] facilitating cooperation between organizations" (ibid.).

At the beginning of 2000, the Siberian Center employed sixteen full-time local staff and numerous part-time consultants and hosted regular visits from Western donors. Publishing booklets and holding free training seminars, aimed at improving the effectiveness of local organizations, have been integral activities in the Siberian Center's role as a regional resource center and incubator. The Siberian Center follows the advice of its American founders and Western funders in advocating the impersonal, task-oriented interactions, planning, scheduling, and budgeting modeled by the corporate world as best practice for NGOs (Drucker 1990). Most activities I observed provided access to information, offered opportunities for networking, and sought to increase the professionalism of NGOs. While helping local NGO leaders locate and apply for grants from foreign foundations, the Siberian Center has not sought to tie local organizations directly into a global organization but has encouraged local groups to function independently. Although globalization in this context means something quite different from the church setting, the Siberian Center contributes to globalization, as have other NGOs (Roberts, Jones, and Froehling 2005), through advocating and modeling specific behaviors based on global ideas of democratic process and professionalism.

Globalization of Networks: Church Ties

Affiliation with a globalizing organization affects individuals' social network, leading them to have increasingly globalized networks. Russian members, like Mormons everywhere, feel a special connection to the missionaries who introduced them to the church, yet Mormon missionaries are reassigned to different areas every few months. Long-term members become accustomed to this constant turnover of missionaries. This recirculation creates a sense of the "world of flow" characteristic of globalization (Appadurai 1996), which differs radically from the stable social structure of the Soviet era. Russians who accept this rapid turnover find their social networks altered by this flow and learn new behaviors to cope with it.

One effect of personal interaction with global others includes new mental maps, which Russian Mormons develop based on their familiarity with foreign missionaries. Most missionaries serving in Novosibirsk have come from America, though a small number come from other Russian-speaking areas. As missionaries describe their home life, Russians add these mental images of small towns to their impressions of America previously formed only through media images.

In a growing church, flow comes from circuits not only of missionaries but also of members. Church growth leads to the establishment of new congregations, and Mormon Church leaders regularly realign congregation boundaries to accommodate or to facilitate growth. It appeared that some Russians have struggled when new boundaries have interrupted accustomed associations, yet those who stay in the church learn to adapt. Mormon congregation boundaries around the world are defined by residential location, and leaders expect members to attend the congregation to which they are assigned. One Russian woman who moved to a new neighborhood told me that it was "hard to get used to" (*trudno privyknut'*) their new congregation and added that "it is hard to make friends" (*trudno druzhit'sia*). Friendship is traditionally a very strong bond in Russia (Pesmen 2000), but those who remain in this the Mormon Church accept the direction of leaders for where to attend church meetings even if friends attend elsewhere. This represents an instance of becoming global based on adoption of foreign beliefs and regular interpersonal contact with foreigners.

Less Globalization of Networks: NGOs

Just as the aims of these two organizations differ, their activities also result in very different social network patterns. A major goal of the Siberian Center has been to promote the ideas and practice of democracy. The discourse of democracy, including notions of personal freedom and rights, has been fostered worldwide by various international NGOs, possibly representing what Appadurai refers to as a "global ideoscape" of democracy (1996, p. 36).

In the rhetoric of the Siberian Center, as stated on their website, in 1995 very few people "recognized that, perhaps first among the new freedoms they had received, was the freedom to play an active role and take responsibility for building the democratic society that encompassed their hopes for the future" (SCISC 2004). In 2000, I noticed that individuals who worked at the Siberian Center freely used Western concepts about NGOs and civil society, even the term *tretii sektor* (third sector). In contrast, individuals active in NGOs but who spent less time at the center rarely used Western terms, did not discuss their role in building democracy, and were unclear about the concept of *grazhdanskoye obshchestvo* (citizen's society, the Russian translation for civil society). The new terms and ideas presented by the Siberian Center represent global ideas, and the acceptance and use of these terms and concepts represents one aspect of becoming global.

One aim of the Siberian Center has been to promote cooperation among local NGOs as a way to build civil society and to strengthen democracy. To this end, beginning in 1995, the center organized an annual NGO Fair for groups to present their work. In 2000, this was held in the lobby of a Soviet-era *Dom Kul'turi* (house of culture) that was too small for the over 100 displays. Each NGO was represented by several individuals, resulting in a crush of several hundred people in a space designed for far fewer. During the busiest hours, from 12 until 2 p.m., there was an immense crush of individuals, all talking simultaneously, like a room full of televisions all on different channels. This multivocality represents a dramatic change from the Soviet-era centralized control of communication. Though few outsiders were present to witness this dramatic cacophony, participants experienced a truly democratic event which represented a moment of becoming global at the local level.

Modifying Globalization: The *Kollektiv* at Church

As several scholars have noted, processes of globalization have uneven or unequal outcomes around the world (Appadurai 1999). For example, a study in China noted that aspects of globalization are "modified and fashioned by the particular circumstances and choices of local institutions" which may "offset and/or resist the global" (Rui 2003, p. 287). Shevchenko argues that post-Soviet consumption of global product represents not merely a reproduction of Soviet attitudes or simple adoption of Western models, but a "complex fusion of global trends and local cultural patterns" (2002, p. 147). Within a context of globalization, Russians combine global elements with the reproduction of local cultural practices and social structure.

Local culture includes the pervasiveness of the collective, or *kollektiv*, traditionally associated with Soviet schools and workplaces. Though the term was first introduced in the 1930s to identify cells of the Communist Party (Kharkhordin 1999, pp. 81, 85), since the 1970s the term has been used to refer to any "group of people united by common work" (ibid., p. 86) and having "cohesion as a system of relations actively built by participants" (ibid., p. 97). Because most Russians experienced a *kollektiv* in fixed-member groups closed to outsiders, such as school classes, the *kollektiv* is often understood to have distinct boundaries. In contemporary Novosibirsk, the term is often used to describe good relations among a set of colleagues. When people in Novosibirsk do not enjoy positive relations among work colleagues, they often complain about the lack of a *kollektiv*. Some Russians seek an alternate *kollektiv* in other organizations, such as the Mormon Church or an NGO.

In May 2000, I helped some Mormon women in Novosibirsk put together a scrapbook of their congregation, which had average attendance of about thirty at the time. At an evening social, women brought pictures of previous socials or other church events. Judging by the photographs, the size of the congregation seemed remarkably consistent over the prior five years, and most of the faces were familiar, suggesting that the core had remained stable over time. Marina pointed out a particular photo and said, "This is when we met in the music school," a building the church had previously rented for Sunday meetings. Marina explained with nostalgia that it had been so nice and cozy (*uiutno*) to meet there. "But then we had to move," Marina explained, "because the congregation got too big," and the tone in her voice conveyed her sadness at this growth-induced change.

In 2002, the leader of another church congregation invited me to their services by saying, "We have a good *kollektiv*, come and see!" On my visit, I met a group of members interested in maintaining good relations with a fixed group of known others rather than interested in welcoming newcomers; in short, they had created a type of *kollektiv*. This congregation had the lowest growth rate in 2002, a fact both reflected in and affected by the unwillingness of members to be friendly to outsiders. While close friendships adversely affect the growth of church congregations everywhere (Olson 1989), in Russia these close ties take on distinctive patterns based on local expectations of a *kollektiv*. The desire for a *kollektiv* illustrates local cultural resistance to the rational plans of church leaders to induce rapid growth, which would represent becoming global for those who accept it.

Hindering Globalization: Personalistic NGOs

Like the desire for a *kollektiv*, other local habitus can also slow or hinder the outcomes of globalizing organizations' activities at the local level. Despite attempts by the Siberian Center to encourage NGOs to contact each other and work together, most NGOs tend to work in isolation. A page on the Siberian Center website described the situation in 1995 thus: "Groups consisted primarily of one strong leader and a couple of friends. There was no impulse to outreach and expand the number of members, hold elections or work together with other organizations" (SCISC 2004). My experience suggested that, despite efforts of the Siberian Center, this was still a generally accurate description five years later.

From several incidents I witnessed or heard about, it seemed that many NGO leaders were reluctant to cooperate with other groups because of personality conflicts or an unwillingness to share power. Though personal dislikes affect business and nonprofit groups everywhere, personal relations loom large over organizations in Russia, where the professionalism of maintaining working relationships despite personal dislike has not been common practice. First-hand experience suggests that efforts of the Siberian Center staff to encourage Western professionalism have often been undermined by local traditions of personalism (Eisenstadt and Roniger 1984).

Though some events were designed for NGOs to network with each other, in 2000 many groups were not interested in letting strangers join or volunteer for their group. A directory published in 1999 by the Siberian Center listed groups by their target populations, such as troubled youth, invalids, pensioners, the poor, veterans, women, large families, or the homeless (SCISC 1999). Though such targeted groups have the potential to cooperate with other groups to benefit their clients, this potential is not typically realized in grassroots organizations in Novosibirsk. First-hand experience suggested that many of these organizations were actually mutual-aid societies — for example, veterans helping veterans — and were closed to outsiders.

A few local organizations sought to fill a commonly expressed desire for greater chance for socializing (*obshchenie*), but even these were organized around principles like those seen in the *kollektiv*, of small numbers, personal acquaintance, and sitting over tea. Natalia runs a ladies' club, a fixed group of women pensioners who gather each month for a tea social. When I was eventually invited to their social, members were very uncomfortable with a foreigner in their midst. Ludmilla runs a Name Day Tea, where women with the same first name gather on a certain day for an evening tea social. Though the invitees are not initially acquainted, they all know Ludmilla personally. Because of this indirect connection, women who might have ordinarily been distrustful of strangers were able to sit down together for tea. Though closed groups exist in any society, first-hand experience suggests that groups like these perpetuate the type of small, closed, cell-like social groups that had developed in the Soviet era (Spencer 2003). In this regard, grassroots organizations do not represent the open society democracy promoted by the Siberian Center. In creating new groups to continue familiar behaviors of drinking tea, it appears that Russians retain familiar small groups and resist becoming global even within the Western form of an NGO and despite contact with the Siberian Center.

At the NGO Fair, when the mayor walked through with his entourage, it was clear that everyone was there in the hopes of getting an audience with the mayor to ask a favor. Staff members followed the mayor to make note of his promises. Patron–client relations in politics (Eisenstadt and Roniger 1984) have been a feature of Russian society since Tsarist times (Vorozheikina 1994), and currying favor with patrons or rewarding clients continues into the post-socialist era in Russia and other Eastern European countries. In a continuation of the patronage tradition, the mayor's office has recently taken over the management of the fair. Though no longer run by the Siberian Center, the NGO Fair still allows NGOs to network with each other if they choose. However, accounts I heard suggest that the most important aspect of the new format for participants is that it gives them a definite opportunity to petition the mayor or one of his deputies. As some Russians continue patronage-seeking behavior, they resist attempts of the Siberian Center to globalize them into more democratic practices.

Transnational Practices?

Sklair (2002, p. 84) discusses the adoption of transnational practices as part of globalizing processes. Both of the agents of globalization described in this chapter seek to change behavior: the church discourages drinking alcohol and encourages attending church services; the Siberian Center encourages NGOs to be professional and democratic. Insofar as individuals adopt behaviors they would not otherwise have adopted because of their affiliation with these globalizing institutions, these behaviors may be thought of as transnational practices and to some extent an indication of a global habitus (Illouz and John 2003). Yet alongside these transnational practices local practices persist, resulting in a distinctive post-Soviet bricolage of behaviors.

The traditional practice of taking tea (*chaepitie*) has long been an important part of Russian interpersonal habitus. Taking tea involves sitting down together at a single table and sharing food as one group and is the most common form of socializing in Russia (Patico 2002). Russians sit down for tea with families, work groups, or sets of friends for both important and everyday occasions (Spencer 2003). In contrast, in groups with face-to-face interaction with foreigners, new transnational practices regarding food are beginning to emerge alongside the old.

In a Mormon congregation at the end of 1999, members organized an evening of skits and songs, followed by refreshments. Although the food items were similar to taking tea, the behavior was very different. Cake, oranges, candy, and soda were set out on a large table in buffet style, and chairs were set out around other small tables. Several old women, pensioners with small incomes, were the first in line and rapidly took as many pieces of cake as they could carry, leaving little cake for everyone behind them in line. Having consumed one piece, they stuffed several others into their purses to take home. Normally Russians are not reticent about correcting behavior they deem inappropriate, but none of the Russians corrected these women publicly as they would have at a tea event; it seemed that they were unsure of behavioral norms for this new food style of buffet. Only the Americans in attendance seemed to consider this unacceptable behavior and were the only ones who complained about it.

One Russian Mormon explained the contrast between Russian tea and American buffet: "in Russian tradition, everyone sits down at the table and is as one *kollektiv* ... If someone speaks, everyone listens, [then] someone else speaks ... Where two walk off over there, two over there, that's not our tradition ... [here] they all sit at the table; they all conduct themselves like a single person. Everyone listens ... it is a kind of communality (*obshchnost'*), like a commune (*obshchina*)." At tea, there is an emphasis on the primacy of primary group life through the creation of moments in which individuals conduct themselves as one person and thus demonstrate their shared *Gemeinschaft* (Toennies 1957).

In spring 2000, the Siberian Center celebrated its fifth anniversary with speeches and a press conference. At the reception that followed, guests found refreshments on a long table in a narrow room, but no chairs. Stacks of small individual plates and appetizers in trays were crowded along the table with alcohol at the far end. The room quickly filled to beyond its capacity, with people trying to make their way along the table to reach particular food items or the alcohol. Despite the crush, no one left the table, and it seemed that they were following the practice for taking tea, which dictates remaining close to others at the table. Several people were standing uncomfortably crowded in a space between the table and the wall, holding their plates, unsure of themselves. A woman whom I did not know stood next to me, trying to balance a drink and a plate, and complained, "I don't understand buffet (*farshet*). If the purpose is to eat, it fails, and if the purpose is to talk, it also fails." The buffet seemed awkward, or foreign, to many guests because it did not conform to behavioral expectations of tea.

In other ways, however, this Siberian Center celebration included familiar local cultural elements. During the reception, some guests presented gifts and congratulations, and toasts were made to the center and the director. Congratulations were stated in the formal language used for such ritual presentations and invoked the Russian tradition of stating three wishes. In these and other ways, the reception corresponded to local practices associated with birthday gatherings and not merely the adoption of a foreign eating practice.

Global Object, Local Practice

Gifting in many traditional societies marks a social relationship through mutual obligation to receive and later to reciprocate (Mauss 1990). In Russia traditional gifting behavior is an important way of strengthening social ties (Patico 2002). Hence, it is not surprising to see gifting perpetuated in new global settings such as the Mormon Church and NGOs.

Mormon missionaries around the world give away copies of *The Book of Mormon* for anyone interested in reading what they describe as companion scripture to the Bible. American missionaries in Novosibirsk were initially puzzled by local reluctance to accept a free book. The difficulty for Russians was not a lack of curiosity, but a hesitation to accept what they perceived as a gift from someone they did not know. In contrast, once a person had established ties with missionaries and other members, they were ready to accept such a gift. Missionaries adopted the local practice of making a presentation of this book when someone chose to become a member of the church through baptism. Many Russians treat baptism as an occasion like a birthday, to celebrate with visiting, cake, and wishes;

hence, gifts, though not necessary, are socially appropriate as markers of relationships at such times. This example demonstrates ways a global object, *The Book of Mormon*, is incorporated into local webs of meaning through the perpetuation of local habitus.

Local incorporation of global objects was also apparent in NGOs. On one occasion, leaders of an NGO that coordinated youth volunteerism were going to visit a subsidiary in a small town and invited me to come along. Four of us jolted along poorly maintained rural roads for an hour to the small town, bringing expensive office supplies purchased with new grant funds. The local journalist and mayor joined the out-of-town visitors for a tour of the village volunteer center, followed by a reception. Instead of just dropping off the imported office supplies, the city visitors followed traditional gifting behaviors. The city NGO leader held a ream of computer paper, a desk caddy, and other supplies in her outstretched arms and handed them to the waiting outstretched arms of the village representative while making a short speech in a formal style. This formal presentation was posed for photographs and greeted with applause and then a toast. Following the presentation, everyone sat down to take tea together. These local practices were used to incorporate these foreign objects into local shared understandings of appropriate social relations rather than allowing the global objects to transform local social relations.

Multiple Scales

These events and interactions reveal how the local is also multiscalar (Sassen 2003). Like Mormons everywhere, Russian members focus on how to live their new religion in their local lives. Yet they are simultaneously made aware through church magazines and foreign missionaries of Mormons in "multiple other localities around the world engaged in similar localized struggles" (ibid., p. 12). At the Siberian Center, many Russians in client organizations focus only on the support or information they need while Russian employees of the Siberian Center focus on influencing NGO policy in the Novosibirsk *oblast* or at the regional Siberian *okrug* level or even seek representation in Moscow. The Siberian Center provides both clients and employees "multiple networks with other similar organizations" (ibid.) involved in NGO-related activities throughout Siberia, though many local leaders remain focused on the local.

The state is also involved at multiple levels in these interactions, especially in the former Soviet Union. Heir to a totalitarian regime, the Russian Federation continues to monitor flows of foreigners and foreign resources, in particular regarding religion and civil society. Federal law guarantees certain religious freedoms (Davis 1997; Elliott and Corrado 1999), although implementation of federal regulations remains with city officials. Local authorities limit the number of foreign missionaries in Novosibirsk and reserve the right to not permit building rental or construction. Registration of domestic NGOs is more strictly controlled at the federal and local level than in the early 1990s, though the increasingly positive relationship between city officials and local NGO leaders somewhat offsets these increasing federal restrictions. Though the ideologies and actions of the globalizing agents transcend state hierarchies, opportunities for globalizing contact are still affected by local and federal governments' approval or restriction.

Conclusion

In very different ways, the Mormon Church and the Siberian Center act as agents of globalization in Novosibirsk, offering opportunities to local residents to become global through evangelizing new behaviors and presenting Russians with opportunities to incorporate foreigners into their personal networks. When Russians accept the global flow of people at the Mormon Church or the democratic or impersonal relations advocated by the Siberian Center, it can be said that these Russians are becoming global in their attitudes and social relations. These new behaviors appear most often where Russians have incorporated Westerners into their social networks. Thus, becoming global emerges first through changes in social network structure, followed then by adoption of a global habitus.

What this ethnography also illustrates is that these newly adopted global attitudes and social networks emerge in the context of existing Russian social structure and culture, which influence how individuals adopt a global habitus. Russians use local practices of gifting to reappropriate global objects, while tea and cake are consumed in a tea event in some settings but in a buffet style in other settings, suggesting that global practices emerge alongside local practices but do not erase them. Practices among some Russians that encourage patronage and closed groups continue, undermining Western notions of building an open society. Efforts by some Russians to recreate a *kollektiv* hinder church growth and the development of civil society, which slows processes of globalization. Even where the Mormon Church and the Siberian Center have actively evangelized processes of globalization, where one might have expected the most obvious impact, individual transformation has been neither as complete nor as uniform as outsiders might have anticipated. This finding reinforces the importance of acknowledging the impact of unique historical and cultural contexts on the outcomes of processes which present opportunities for becoming global.

Note

1. Research on which this chapter is based was supported in part by a grant from the International Research & Exchanges Board (IREX) with funds provided by the National Endowment for the Humanities; the U.S. Department of State, which administers the Title VIII Program; and the IREX Scholar Support Fund. None of these organizations are responsible for the views expressed.

Works Cited

Appadurai, Arjun. 1996. *Modernity at large: Cultural dimensions of globalization*. Minneapolis: University of Minnesota Press.

———. 1999. Globalization and the research imagination. *International Social Science Journal* 51(160):229–39.

Bartlett, Robert. 1993. *The making of Europe: Conquest, colonization and cultural change, 950–1350*. Princeton, NJ: Princeton University Press.

Browning, Gary. 1997. *Russia and the restored gospel*. Salt Lake City: Deseret Book Company.

Caldwell, Melissa L. 2002. The taste of nationalism: Food politics in postsocialist Moscow. *Ethnos* 67(3):295–319.

Davis, Derek H. 1997. Russia's new law on religion: Progress or regress? *Journal of Church and State* 39(4):645–56.

Drucker, Peter F. 1990. *Managing the non-profit organization*. New York: HarperCollins Publishers.

Dunch, Ryan. 2002. Beyond cultural imperialism: Cultural theory, Christian missions, and global modernity. *History and Theory* 41(3):301–26.

Eisenstadt, S.N., and Luis Roniger. 1984. *Patrons, clients and friends: Interpersonal relations and the structure of trust in society*. Cambridge, UK: Cambridge University Press.

Elliott, Mark, and Sharyl Corrado. 1999. The 1997 Russian law on religion: The impact on Protestants. *Religion, State and Society* 27(1):109–34.

Fischer, Fritz. 1998. *Making them like us: Peace Corps volunteers in 1960s*. Washington, DC: Smithsonian Institution Press.

Fisher, William F. 1997. Doing good? The politics and antipolitics of NGO practices. *Annual Review of Anthropology* 26(1):439–65.

French, R.A., and F.E. Ian Hamilton (eds). 1979. *The socialist city: Spatial structure and urban policy*. Chichester, NY: Wiley and Sons

Givens, Terryl L. 2003. *By the hand of Mormon: The American scripture that launched a new world religion*. New York: Oxford University Press.

Hemment, Julie. 2004. The riddle of the third sector. *Anthropological Quarterly* 77(2):215–41.

Henderson, Sarah L. 2003. *Building democracy in contemporary Russia: Western support for grassroots organizations*. Ithaca, NY: Cornell University Press.

Illouz, Eva, and John Nicholas. 2003. Global habitus, local stratification and symbolic struggles over identity. *American Behavioral Scientist* 47(2):201–29.

Ivanova, N.L. 2005. Social identity under various sociocultural conditions. *Russian Education and Society* 47(11):71–87.

Jackson, Peter. 2004. Local consumption cultures in a globalizing world. *Transactions of the Institute of British Geographers* 29:165–78.

Kharkhordin, Oleg. 1999. *The collective and the individual in Russia: A study of practices*. Berkeley: University of California Press.

Krindatch, Alexey D. 2004. Patterns of religious change in post-Soviet Russia: Major trends from 1998 to 2003. *Religion, State and Society* 32(2):115–36.

Margolis, Maxine L. 1995. Transnationalism and popular culture: The case of Brazilian immigrants in the United States. *Journal of Popular Culture* 29(1):29–41.

Mauss, Marcel. 1990. *The gift: The form and reason for exchange in archaic societies*. New York: W.W. Norton and Company.

McMichael, Philip. 2004. *Development and social change: A global perspective*. Thousand Oaks, CA: Pine Forge Press.

Millar, James R., and Sharon L. Wolchik (eds). 1994. *The social legacy of communism*. Cambridge, UK: Cambridge University Press.

Molchanov, Mikhail A. 2005. Russia and globalization. *Perspectives on Global Development and Technology* 4(3–4):397–429.

Olson, Daniel V.A. 1989. Church friendships: Boon or barrier to church growth? *Journal for the Scientific Study of Religion* 28(4):432–47.

Patico, Jennifer. 2002. Chocolate and cognac: Gifts and recognition of social worlds in post-Soviet Russia. *Ethnos* 67(3):345–68.

Pesmen, Dale. 2000. *Russia and soul: An exploration*. Ithaca, NY: Cornell University Press.

Robbins, Joel. 2004. The globalization of Pentecostal and charismatic Christianity. *Annual Review of Anthropology* 33(1):117–43.

Roberts, Susan, John Paul Jones, and Oliver Froehling. 2005. NGOs and the globalization of managerialism: A research framework. *World Development* 33(11):1845–64.

Robertson, Roland. 1992. *Globalization: Social theory and global culture*. Thousand Oaks, CA: Sage Publications.

Rui, Yang. 2003. Internationalised while provincialized? A case study of South China Normal University. *Compare: A Journal of Comparative Education* 33(3):287–301.

Sassen, Saskia. 2003. Globalization or denationalization? *Review of International Political Economy* 10(1):1–22.

———. 2004. Local actors in global politics. *Current Sociology* 52(4):649–70.

Shevchenko, Olga. 2002. "In case of fire emergency": Consumption, security and the meaning of durables in a transforming society. *Journal of Consumer Culture* 2(2):147–70.

Siberian Civic Initiatives Support Center (SCISC). 1999. *Siberian Civic Initiatives Support Center: Making a difference*. Novosibirsk, Russia: SCISC.

———. 2004. The Siberian Civic Initiatives Support Center: Background and Programs. http://cip.nsk.su/fund/; http://cip.nsk.su/fund/Programs; http://cip.nsk.su/fund/History. Accessed on 1 December 2005.

Silverman, Bertram, and Murray Yanowitch. 1997. *New rich, new poor, new Russia: Winners and losers on the Russian road to capitalism*. Armonk, NY: M.E. Sharpe.

Sklair, Leslie. 2002. *Globalization: Capitalism and its alternatives*. Oxford: Oxford University Press.

Spencer, Sarah Busse. 2003. *Social relations in post-Soviet society: Russian capitalism embedded.* Ph.D. diss., University of Chicago.

———. 2004. Novosibirsk: The globalization of Siberia. In Leo McCann, ed., *Russian transformations: Challenging the global narrative,* 128–47. London: RoutledgeCurzon.

Toennies, Ferdinand. 1957. *Community and society.* East Lansing: Michigan State University Press.

Tullis, F. LaMond (ed). 1979. *Mormonism: A faith for all cultures.* Provo, UT: Brigham Young University Press.

Vorozheikina, Tatiana. 1994. Clientelism and the process of political democratization in Russia. In Luis Roniger and Ayse Gunes-Ayata, eds., *Democracy, clientelism, and civil society,* 105–20. Boulder: Lynne Rienner Publishers.

Wedel, Janine R. 2001. *Collision and collusion: The strange case of Western aid to Eastern Europe.* New York: Palgrave.

CHAPTER 5

Deciphering the Local in a Global Neoliberal Age

Three Favelas in São Paulo, Brazil

SIMONE BUECHLER

Individuals, households, and communities are rarely a focus of the globalization literature. This is the case even when the local scale is a focus, itself still rare. Yet today's global world has brought with it a shift of functions of the nation-state both to supra- and subnational levels. Actors at both levels should therefore be gaining power. However, these shifts have also further added to the complexities of locality, necessitating a deconstruction of the local. Here I deconstruct the local scale into three organizational levels: the individual low-income worker, community associations, and municipal governments. An examination of the interaction of these levels among themselves and with the national and supranational levels shows that, for various reasons, the shift of power from the state to municipalities has rarely improved the ability of individual workers and community associations to confront the degradation of their livelihoods.

Municipal governments are often made up of similar elites as those of national governments. These elites respond to international political and ideological pressures but also often support the global neoliberal agenda in their own self-interest. We cannot therefore assume that because they are local they know the needs of their constituents or that, even if they do, they will act in the latter's interest. Therefore, an examination of the diverse actors and organizations of different social classes within the local matters for analyses of local empowerment. The literature has tended to focus on how local actors enter the global arena, most notably through nongovernmental organizations (NGOs). In contrast, my focus is on local actors working at the local level to address global conditions that affect their local conditions, particularly the level and quality of employment (e.g., Sassen 2004). Individual communities cannot be viewed as bounded, as microcosms of the macrocosm (Leeds 1994), or as completely overpowered by the global with no ability to determine their own destiny or to shape the global. I contend that we need to pay more attention to individual workers and communities because these make visible the specific effects of economic globalization and the neoliberal model. It is also workers and communities that enact and carry out both reactive and proactive economic actions that can influence how global processes play out at the local level. Only by truly understanding both how the global shaping is taking place and its effects will there be possibilities for transformation.

Through a series of microlevel ethnographies of squatter settlements, households, and low-income women workers in the Metropolitan Region of São Paulo (MRSP), I begin to ground globalization and to examine the economic and political strategies of inhabitants and community organizations in three communities and of the municipalities within which they lie. This allows me to focus on whether these workers and communities have been able to influence their own employment situation. This chapter examines whether their strategies fit within the global neoliberal model, fight it, or are strategies of crisis displacement and crisis management. I argue that economic globalization has changed the relationship between employment and location, especially proximity to industry. Few signs of empowerment can be found at the core of the local scale — the workers and communities — as the ability to find and create employment weakens. In spite of supposedly democratic representation, community associations seem weaker than they were under the military government. There are few local resources of power amidst the global. However, as Polanyi (1957) argued, markets are political creations, and therefore we need to question the inevitability attributed to economic globalization and its impact on human conditions. I end my analysis with an example of collaboration between different levels of local organization that may, with further modification, serve as a model for local empowerment.

State Rescaling and the Importance of Location

The perception that state functions are rearticulated downward with globalization has led scholars, policy makers, and industrialists (e.g., Keating

2001; Sassen 2001; Scott 1998; Storper 1997) to renew their interest in examining the role of place as a factor of production. Already ten years ago localities were being represented in the social scientific literature as the arenas where "the apparent opposites of enterprise and community, of efficiency and welfare, of economic means and local ends" might be reconciled (Brenner and Theodore 2002b, p. 341). Focusing on western European and North American cities, Brenner and Theodore (2002a, p. 349) argued that "cities have become strategically crucial geographical arenas in which a variety of neoliberal initiatives — along with closely intertwined strategies of crisis displacement and crisis management — have been articulated." Yet they asked whether the local really serves as a site of empowerment and acknowledged that there is a need for more scholarly attention to other regions with different economic histories such as those with import substitution policies. This chapter explores both the recomposition of local power and the loss of power at different local levels in São Paulo, Brazil, a city that was the site for effective social movements under the military government from 1964 to 1985.

The local labor market is one of the key areas that has been affected greatly by economic globalization and the neoliberal model. It is therefore a key site in which to study the strength of the local. I argue in greater detail elsewhere (e.g., Buechler 2002, 2004, 2006) that the current precarious labor market is not simply a continuation from the past but is the result of new types of interactions between local, national, and global phenomena. Informalization — the rise of sweatshops, homework, and unregistered work; lower salaries; high unemployment; and growing social inequity are not just the impacts of global capitalism and the neoliberal economic model but are a few of its main tenets.[1] Work in both the so-called formal and informal sectors has grown more precarious. Within the formal sector, temporary work and outsourcing is prevalent. Within the informal sector indebtedness of clients is mounting, sources of household income to support informal businesses are diminishing, and competition is dramatically increasing as the numbers of small-scale entrepreneurs escalate with growing unemployment in the formal sector. The supposed downward shift in state functions has not brought an empowerment of localities in relation to labor and employment with growing global competition leading to the precarization of labor and dismantling of worker's rights.

Locational factors take on less and more significance under the neoliberal economic model and with economic globalization depending on geography, employment type, and the actors involved. According to my informants, location in relation to the number and close proximity of industries has not been as closely associated with the ability to obtain and maintain an industrial job or to be employed in related and unrelated employment as might be expected. In contrast, they view location as more significant for gaining informal employment since the remaining factories that do employ workers living nearby mainly employ them informally. Location is, however, important for industries that are moving to avoid strong unions and environmental regulations, enabling them to better compete in the global market. If the neoliberal economic model and economic globalization are able to make previously important variables virtually irrelevant, then can individuals, community leaders, and municipal governmental officials have the power to alter the existing economic model or at least how it plays out in their lives, communities, and cities?

To provide the economic context this chapter first briefly examines the degradation of labor in São Paulo and introduces the communities studied. The focus, however, is on actors at the local scale, a term I will continue to use although recognizing Brenner's (2001) concerns.

São Paulo: An Overview of Its Labor Market and Three of Its Communities

Since the opening of the Brazilian markets and strong adoption of the neoliberal economic model, the Metropolitan Region of São Paulo has suffered significantly in terms of employment, with an unemployment rate of 15.7 percent (19.7 percent female unemployment rate) in 2005 — down from over 19 percent a few years before. Industrial employment decreased by 23 percent from 1985 to 2003 (SEADE/DIEESE, PED 2004, 2006). The ABC industrial region,[2] the location of the municipality of Diadema and one of the communities studied, is undergoing the steepest economic decline of the MRSP. This is due to an increasing divestment of firms in the area because of allegedly increasing negative externalities and diseconomies of scale in the MRSP after almost sixty years of import substitution. Municipal funds have been diminishing since they largely come from the state and are based on the state value-added tax. This decline in funds arrives at a time when municipal governments are expected to take on more of the financial responsibility for services and when there is growing poverty due to increased unemployment and subemployment (Rodríguez-Pose, Tomaney, and Klink 2001, pp. 16–18).

The histories of three communities and their inhabitants studied from 1996 to 2003 showed these statistical trends clearly. Favela Sul and Favela Leste are two squatter settlements, and Jardim Sudoeste has squatters living near the creek going through it; most of the land, however, had originally been bought from real estate speculators.[3] Favela Sul and Jardim Sudoeste are located in the Municipality of São Paulo, and Favela Leste is in Diadema, a municipality in the industrial ABC region of the MRSP.

Favela Sul, the oldest settlement studied, inhabited already in 1960, had 325 houses by 1994 and is surrounded by a few smaller primarily clandestine industries and one major metallurgy factory. Jardim Sudoeste is a neighborhood farther away from most industries but with several of the inhabitants going through many of the same employment trajectories with longer commutes. It was established a few years after Favela Sul. In 2006, Favela Leste had four sections from eight to sixteen years old with an estimated 3,100 to 3,600 households in all the sections. According to neighborhood surveys and interviews conducted in 1998, the level of unemployment ranged from approximately 50 percent of the households having one or more unemployed members in Favela Sul (located near the second greatest number of industries), 60 percent in Jardim Sudoeste (located the farthest from the center and from industries), and 75 percent in Favela Leste (across the street from many factories and in the ABC industrial region). The level of unemployment improved slightly in the latter two communities by 2003.[4] All three communities share the plight of many nearby industrial plant closings, with the remaining outsourcing more production. The number of small informal businesses has also increased substantially in all three communities. From 1996 to 2000 the situation worsened given that even finding sideline economic activities was difficult. When factories closed there was a domino effect with services (e.g., security and secretarial services) no longer needed and unemployed workers no longer able to improve their houses or make many other purchases, thereby hurting other workers. In all of the communities over 50 percent of both male and female workers were unregistered, often working for others. Young men were often involved in selling drugs and, if working for a factory, rarely moved with their firm to the interior of the state of São Paulo. Men who were still employed often worked in construction, security, and small businesses, although in Favela Leste they primarily still worked in factories. There was a bit more variety in the women's economic activities, although in all three communities cleaning was a major activity. They were also involved in many different kinds of unregistered economic activities, including, in 2003, ironing at home, selling food on the streets, and collecting recyclables.

Unlike the other two communities, around Favela Leste there are still many industries, which are all foreign, including Krones, a factory producing compressors for other factories. However, many do not employ the inhabitants of the favela, supposedly for fear that there would be more theft, but perhaps also because this way they can more easily disassociate themselves from being part of the cause for workers to have to live in squatter settlements.[5] In addition, unlike the others, the community association of Favela Sul employs many of its community members.

Employment and unemployment in all three communities fit the pattern that the statistics for the MRSP were showing: a growing precarization of labor with fewer registered jobs that meant fewer people had any kind of benefits. Women and men were forced to self-exploit by working at many low-paying economic activities to support themselves and their families. Variables that presumably should have a positive influence on the level and type of employment did not have as much impact as before the economic crisis, in part spurred by economic globalization. Actors at all organizational levels of the local scale, however, were trying to influence the impact of the economic crisis.

Actors on the Local Scale

Individual Worker's Labor Strategies

If specific characteristics of place, such as proximity to industries and community age, play a small role in the level of unemployment and precarious work, do individual workers have any power over their employment situation? This section examines the economic lives of three women in each of the communities. These women represent women who perhaps are not the average woman. They are particularly intelligent (although had little formal education, like their peers), energetic, and ambitious women who tried everything to support their families and to overcome the trends toward more and more exploitative labor conditions. Their cases do represent, however, the typical range of economic strategies and show the links between the local, national, and global economic scales. A woman living in a favela may often have direct or indirect links with the global economy.

Josefa was a home worker in Favela Sul, indirectly connected to multinational corporations, who had been working three months folding or gluing tags and threading and tying strings through the tags for beauty products and clothing. She had lost her job in a nearby diaper factory's packaging department that was struggling due to increased global competition. Antonia was truly self-employed, running her own daycare center and then growing plants and flowers to sell; however, both failed as more and more neighbors became unemployed. Her husband, however, benefited from a stable government job. Rosa had also worked primarily in the informal sector and always in multiple economic activities including unregistered work in a clothing and shoe store and subsequently in two beauty salons. Her husband had been laid off from an auto parts firm in 1997 when his profession had become computerized so the factory could compete in the global market. To support her family, Rosa then became involved in various sideline activities, including doing manicures, cutting hair, and selling yogurt and lottery tickets. Location near industries had provided her with more informal opportunities. In July 1998, Rosa and her family decided to leave the favela for many reasons, including a homicide right outside her house and an available house of her parents-in-law in Estive Gerbi, in the interior of the state of São Paulo.[6] After more than a year, her husband finally found a factory job with a lower salary and currently has to work the night shift. Rosa tried various economic activities including working in the field, making charcoal in a factory, selling clothes from São Paulo, and cutting neighbor's hair, but none of these worked out. Josefa, Antonia, and Rosa and their families have used different strategies to survive the latest economic crisis in part caused by economic liberalization and globalization and also because of their lack of opportunities since childhood. Rosa and Antonia had in common a vision for the community in which they lived. However, the hope had died for both women.[7]

These women occasionally found spaces for income opportunities within and sometimes created by the neoliberal economic structure. Deregulation — as part of the spreading neoliberal economic model linked to economic globalization — was an asset and was empowering in the sense that my informants could work in their homes: Antonia with her unregistered daycare center, Rosa with her bar and sundry other informal commercial activities, and Josefa with her homework for a graphic company contracted by many multinational corporations. It was, however, primarily exploitative in a variety of ways because it provided no social benefits for these three women (i.e., health insurance, pension, unemployment insurance), no living wage, and no stable income. The women were intertwined with and dependent on the whims of the global economy. Josefa was dependent ultimately on multinational contracts. She was actually on the fourth rung of the production chain, with the principal clients being multinationals such as Levi Strauss and Pierre Cardin, which hired graphic companies to produce clothing tags, which were then outsourced to one woman living in the neighboring community, who then outsourced part of the production to women like Josefa. When I returned in 2000 most graphic companies already had started using machines to do the work Josefa had been doing, and the particular graphic company Josefa had worked for had closed, leaving her unemployed again. Rosa was dependent on the employment of her neighbors who were constantly losing industrial jobs due to global competition. And Antonia was dependent on the ability of her daycare students' parents to pay as more lost their more permanent jobs. They all ended up leaving their homes either for other smaller cities or towns in the state of São Paulo where at least their husbands could find jobs — although with lower salaries and less strong unions — or for another family-owned house in the neighboring community so that they could rent out their house. This, however, was not the usual trend, for many did not have that option. They all were self-employed at a time when self-employment had also become more precarious. For this chapter, self-employment means, as it does in the Brazilian statistics, either owning a business or working for a determined firm or person but not being a registered worker, not having a contractually fixed day and not being under the direct control of the firm including workers who get paid per piece. Although the economy depends on cheap services and goods, self-employment had become more unstable due to the indebtedness of their unemployed clients, the growing competition from their neighbors who were producing or selling the same items, their inability to grow their enterprise because of the lack of a stable income coming in to buy in bulk, and the poverty of their neighbors. The actions of these women were both proactive and reactive but primarily reactive to the consequences of the global and neoliberal economy. The essence of the local scale — the workers — shows few signs of empowerment.

Community Organizations and Politics

Various scholars (e.g., Buechler forthcoming; Ireland 1999, 2001; Jacobi 2005; Leeds 1994) argue that individuals like Josefa, Antonia, and Rosa working together can at least help alter the economic path that globalization and the neoliberal model have followed. However, community organizations have been both weakened and strengthened since their relative strength in the 1970s and 1980s. There has been a rich history of social movements and social struggles for economic, social, and political rights in São Paulo. Many of the social movements in São Paulo in the 1970s and 1980s, before the real opening of the Brazilian market but already the beginning of neoliberalism, were making the connection between the exploitation in the workplace and the economy and their atrocious living conditions. These movements recognized that the partnership between corporations and the government guaranteed the urban infrastructure and services required for the rapid circulation of capital but denied labor collective consumption goods (Kowarick 1985, p. 79; Kowarick and Campanario 1986, p. 168). It was the neighborhood movements, often spurred by the Catholic-based communities (*comunidades eclesiais de base,* or CEBs), working with the labor unions that toppled the military government. In realizing their joint exploitation, they worked together with the strength of organization of the labor unions and their links to the national scale. The church was one of the few spaces in which social movements could operate after the 1964 military coup.[8]

The Societies for the Friends of the Neighborhood (*Sociedades de Amigos do Bairro,* or SABs) created in the 1950s and the CEBs, although still in existence, have declined in power with no equivalent neighborhood organizational system to replace them.[9] The CEBs have virtually disappeared in the urban areas but have created potential leaders and spaces for action (see Buechler forthcoming).[10] Neighborhood associations therefore seem to have been more empowered under the military regime than under the neoliberal and global regimes. And many existing groups do not directly focus on employment but rather are cultural movements or social welfare organizations (Jacobi 2005, p. 31).

There are many sources of power, including the control of material resources, the use of organization, and mobilizable masses of people, often with the three corresponding respectably to the three social classes (Leeds 1994, pp. 219–20). Leeds (1994, pp. 220–1) contends that because of organization, localities enter into various sorts of interrelationships with other supralocal institutions dependent on the various interests of both parties and the social structure of the relationship. He continued that the state and its agencies enter into these relationships because of their two ends: public coordination and maintenance of order and their own private self-maintenance. Yet has the addition and increase in power of institutions — such as the World Trade Organization (WTO) or the International Monetary Fund (IMF) — that are further away and without the ends of public coordination and maintaining order, led to the further loss of power at the local level?[11] This largely has been the case for the community organizations studied that may even have links to global institutions, but these links have given them less and not more power. Favela Leste, for example, has links with national movements of favela inhabitants and municipal governments and even marginally with multinational firms but does not have links with any supranational organizations such as the IMF. Although it had power over Krones, a multinational company, in the sense that they invaded and remained on the land it rented, they were unable to stop the company from destroying houses to bring out their metal containers.[12] Favela Sul's community association, also had strong links with the municipal government, which funded the apartment project Cingapura but had no power to control the destruction of part of the favela because of that project.[13] It had for many years, however, fought both the municipal and state governments to get funding for other housing and infrastructure projects with gradual success. The association, however, failed in its attempts to have more links with international companies to create jobs, especially for their youth, and to compete in the global economy through its bag factory that then had to close. The inhabitants of Jardim Sudoeste had links with multinational corporations indirectly or directly in the case of working for a firm producing for Avon and a chocolate factory owned by a large multinational. However, the inhabitants could do little to prevent both from moving to areas with weaker unions and cheaper taxes supposedly to be able to compete globally. The next section examines more closely the history and level of organization of each of the three communities, demonstrating that even those with high levels of organization have been able to do little about employment and the economic models adopted at all levels.

History of Community Organization in the Three Communities Favela Sul's community organization is still the strongest of the three communities but has lost instead of gained strength with global neoliberal reform. The story of community organization and action in Favela Sul is a story of one strong leader, Sister Isabela, who has lived in the favela for over twenty years organizing the community and pushing the government. The government determines not only the funding for all projects but also the level of popular participation.[14] The community association, unlike the associations in the other communities, has also been directly involved in the area of employment. By entering into partnerships with factories owned by corporations such as Xerox and Avon, the community association tried to obtain youth employment, but with few results. However, the association has been directly employing and professionally training many of the inhabitants. The association used to employ more when it ran a small bag factory, but with the cheap Asian imports the factory could no longer compete. Fifty-two people, primarily women, were however still employed in the day care center and youth center as well as working as stonemasons and drivers in 2000. Sister Isabela wrote letters of recommendation, but because jobs were scarce only a few benefited. With the encouragement of the community association, some of the inhabitants had also tapped into programs such as the minimum income program whereby the city augments workers' salary to the minimum income if their children are kept in school. However, without real institutional and structural changes, the process of participation of the community in municipal politics remains chaotic and reversible with the mayoral changes.

Jardim Sudoeste has far less community action than the other two communities even with the efforts of Antonia, the former daycare teacher, and her husband, André. With little success, they tried to improve the lives of their neighbors in a variety of ways such as through adult literacy classes, youth recreation activities, and a community center in their home. André argued that low-income Brazilians do not get together to fight for their rights because "they are people who did not have an opportunity to study and are accustomed to being exploited. Contrary to what I always dreamed, they don't unite and fight for some objective. When they have something to eat, they eat and forget about others" (Personal communication). According to Antonia the evangelical churches were part of the problem because they blamed the poor for not helping themselves.

There were three other types of community organizations in Jardim Sudoeste, with all being fairly unsuccessful and the last two initiated by outsiders. The neighborhood chapter of the SAB was really only involved in passing out milk from the state. The only real evidence of a community effort to generate employment was a clothing cooperative set up by an NGO, Center of Studies and Research in Education, Culture, and Community Action (CENPEC), in 1998. The cooperative after a slight improvement had virtually closed by 2003.[15] In 1996 a NGO that gave microcredit had been operating in the community, but this also had already ended by 1998.

Due to Favela Leste's separate sections with different histories and organizations, the level and type of community organization varies, but the organizations are also primarily focused on physical infrastructure and land tenure issues. Neighborhood commissions were set up immediately after the invasions, with the members getting to work organizing the size and location of each lot and a road and working on the water and sewer and electrical systems with the municipal government helping the association clandestinely from the beginning despite the inhabitants having illegally invaded the land. The community organizations of the first three sections of the favela are part of the Movement of the Inhabitants (*Movimento dos Moradores*). This movement is part of a national and international organization called the Center of Popular Movements.[16] Unfortunately, the very strong and progressive local leader passed away in 1998. As in Favela Sul, the strength of a local leader has been crucial. As in the other communities, the leaders here thought that they could pressure the municipal governments for basic amenities but could do little to change the employment situation.

The two communities with strong community associations, Favela Leste and Favela Sul, had different abilities to help in the legal employment area, with no ability in Favela Leste and much more in Favela Sul. Community organization also played a part in either diminishing or, in the case of the new section of Favela Leste, supporting highly illegal employment such as drug trafficking.[17] Yet the level of organization in all these communities has not increased but rather has decreased. In part this is a result of the lack of faith in government that had been lobbied for change. One of the reasons for the lack of faith in government to do anything about employment is that government at all levels has used economic globalization as an excuse for inaction, giving rise to the image of the absent state (Roberts and Portes 2006, p. 61).[18]

Municipal Governmental Policies and Programs

At both the individual and community organizational level, local actions have primarily been reactive to the consequences of economic change, but at the municipal governmental level there has been a combination of reactive and proactive actions in part due to the added responsibilities given to this level of government. Decentralization is one of the neoliberal economic models' tenets, but funds to local governments have often decreased. Municipal governments have been encouraged to compete for foreign investment and opportunities offered by the global economy (Brenner 2003; Orum and Chen 2003). Some municipalities of the MRSP have been more successful in obtaining foreign investment but often through methods that have not been advantageous to many workers. Yet others have been active in developing programs to increase income generation of low-income workers through initiating the creation of cooperatives and other forms of economic initiatives and through requalifying workers expelled from the labor market so they can take better advantage of the new employment opportunities (Jacobi 2005, p. 27).

The role, power, and autonomy of the municipal governments in Brazil have increased through the politics of decentralization, resulting both from the global neoliberal model and the move to greater democracy after the fall of the military government.[19] The 1988 constitution specifically called for an acceleration of the decentralization process with municipalities given an independent legal status and both the state and municipal levels gaining greater tax and expenditure functions. The constitution also instituted a system of federal grants to subnational levels of government, based on locally generated value added. With the closure of firms this has presented even more financial problems for municipalities. This has also led to intermunicipal competition for firms with tax subsidies and infrastructure, sometimes in the medium and long run hurting the municipality. However, it was economic liberalization that substantially increased the activity of local and regional governments (Rodríguez-Pose,Tomaney, and Klink 2001).

The involvement of the municipal government in the three communities has varied and has primarily been in infrastructure and housing and more indirectly in employment generating programs. The number of programs trying to deal with the unemployment situation has grown substantially under the Worker's Party, which was in power in both of the municipalities, still in 2006 in Diadema, the location of Favela Leste and until 2005 in the Municipality of São Paulo, the location of Favela Sul and Jardim Sudoeste. The employment programs in Diadema included cooperative projects that can be considered to lie outside the neoliberal model (e.g., training and organizing women in small construction jobs; setting up cooperatives of seamstresses, domestic servants, taxi drivers, and street vendors); a job bank where the municipality tried to match workers with employers; professional training for garbage collectors and street vendors; a cosmetics industrial pole with marketing fairs, credit, technical assistance, and export plans; and microcredit. One of the innovative programs in Diadema was working with informal garbage collectors to organize them into cooperatives, setting up recycling centers that would pay them more if they worked together, and retraining some to be gardeners. Another project, although maybe not completely positive, was removing most street vendors — except those selling bus tickets — off the streets, providing them training in business management and sanitation, encouraging them to buy collectively and providing a space in a shopping center in the middle of town.

Under the Worker's Party, the Municipality of São Paulo also became much more active again in trying to generate employment, but since the end of 2005 when the Worker's Party left, many of the programs seem to have died. The last Worker's Party administration in the Municipality of São Paulo set up not only programs to fit within the neoliberal economic model but also cooperative projects, which like the cooperatives in Diadema can be considered outside the individualistic economic model. Marcio Pochmann, the Secretary of Development, Labor, and Solidarity, set up the Program of Solidarity Opportunity, a cooperative project providing courses on citizenship, self-esteem, and solidarity building as well as technical and management skills (Schwengber 2003; personal communication with Marcio Pochmann).[20] Submunicipal offices were also created in the periphery areas of the Municipality of São Paulo to address issues such as employment through instituting microcredit programs.[21]

The employment programs have diminished in numbers and variety with the new mayors, José Serra and Gilberto Kassab, under a different political party, but there are still many, all fitting within the neoliberal model.[22] The programs provided the opportunity for the creation of four centers to help workers, acting as intermediaries between the unemployed and firms. The centers provide professional education courses and credit lines for small-scale entrepreneurs, and maintain a database linking employers with the unemployed. This administration also created a labor observatory to study where there may be employment possibilities and what skills are needed for these jobs. Beyond individual programs, the municipal governments in Brazil have adopted a participatory budget program, mandatory by federal law in 2001. A certain percentage — only 5 percent in 2002— of the budget is discussed and allocated by civil society in well-organized systems of participation (Rolnik and Cymbalista 2004, p. 5).

Yet individual municipal actions have often failed to empower the local within the global economy. Competing against one another has not brought economic success. Together the municipalities in the ABC industrial region have therefore been strategizing on how to compete for foreign and national industries. Realizing the need to work together the municipal governments have set up both a regional chamber and an agency for economic development made up of municipal and state government officials, unions, businesspeople, and civil society that are working on everything from road and metro construction to an industrial clustering program, export training and information, and governmental industrial policy change.[23] These new metropolitan regional institutions are part of a second wave of globalization strategies and crisis management promoting interlocality cooperation and regional economic development (Brenner 2003, p. 318). The regional scale vis-à-vis the national scale gains a new significance. As individual municipal and community responses are becoming more difficult and unlikely to be effective, local community leaders and governmental officials are dealing with their economic problems more through strategic partnerships aimed at regional revitalization, through the integration of traditionally fragmented and highly sectoral strategies, and through local capacity building (Buechler forthcoming; Rodríguez-Pose, Tomaney, and Klink 2001). All the discussed local levels — the individual workers, community organizations, and municipality governments — are strategizing together as to how to gain benefits from the global economy instead of being its victim. Although the development of the ABC Regional Chamber and the Economic Development Agency has been a municipal strategy to enable the municipalities in the ABC industrial region to compete within the global economy, the chamber and agency also have stressed social equality and environmental protection, not integral components to the neoliberal economic model. These municipal governments working with civil society therefore are trying to alter the model even while working within the given system.

Even though there were many new municipal economic programs in both the municipalities of Diadema and São Paulo, the majority of the inhabitants in the communities studied did not think they were changing their economic situation.[24] Many of the inhabitants blamed economic globalization, as this nebulous international force, for their lack of employment, yet they still looked to their municipal governments for help.

Conclusion

My analysis of three São Paulo neighborhoods confirms the importance of deconstructing the local in assessing the claim that neoliberalism has empowered local communities. All three communities, no matter their location, age, or tenure history, show similar trajectories of precarization and disempowerment. The infrastructure has improved through the hard work of their inhabitants and leaders, but the community leaders have not been able to curtail the degradation of their fellow inhabitants' employment and other opportunities. The deconstruction of the local reveals how this disempowerment evolves as individuals have had to further self-exploit, resulting in an economic domino effect. When industries close, favela inhabitants lose their jobs, curtail expenditures by not buying goods or services from their neighbors, and open small enterprises that then compete. Favela inhabitants may no longer improve their houses, thus not employing self-employed daily construction workers in their community, or may fail to pay their debts to their neighbors who own a store or bar. If they follow capital to cheaper production locations, they continue to be exploited, accepting lower salaries and giving up strong labor union representation. Individual low-income workers have found spaces for income opportunities within the global neoliberal economy (e.g., homework). Yet in the absence of a living wage, social benefits, or stability these opportunities are often exploitative. They are often forced to work outside the so-called formal economy, but hardly outside the global neoliberal economic system making tags for Levi Strauss, selling Dannon yogurt on the streets, and providing services and cheap goods for exploited and unemployed workers. Even when self-employed they are dependent on the system, relying indirectly on contracts from multinational corporations (e.g., homework, selling products from house to house, daily construction work), and directly on employment of neighbors (e.g., offering services and goods in the favelas). They constantly need to think of new strategies to survive, sometimes even moving out of their houses to rent them and often partaking in many different kinds of economic strategies simultaneously or subsequently as yet one more activity fails.

On the community level, leaders such as Rosa and Antonia have virtually given up on attempting to transform the system. Even when community organizations attempt to work within the system, trying, for example, to gain contacts with international industries to employ their youth or to open a factory, they often fail, lacking the power to be heard and the ability to compete with global imports. Communities were better able to enter into relationships with supralocal institutions before globalization since global institutions lack the role of public coordination and maintaining local order. Competing for municipal funds being used to attract capital, community organizations struggle to gain access to funds for basic infrastructure. They no longer work closely with labor unions for better living conditions as they did under the military government, partially due to the diminishing strength of labor unions with greater capital mobility. Is Scott (2001, p. 6) then correct in arguing that "the local level, has become a renewed focus of persistent calls for more radical practices of democratic participation and representation, as ever-widening circles of urban society demands a greater voice in decision-making?" Although communities are often demanding a greater voice with democratization, economic global forces seem even more insurmountable than the military government. In part, communities had more power because middle and lower classes had a joint enemy — the military government — resulting in a greater willingness of municipal governments to cooperate with community organizations.

In contrast, at present, the elites within the municipal government have been co-opted by capital whereas the working class is hardly able to subsist because of the mobility of capital. Municipal governmental elites often will do anything to keep local production since obtaining national and state funds is dependent on it and their own private interests are often at stake. Therefore, they often do not protect the interests of the workers, although at least they are now trying to provide some worker's education programs, microcredit, and job placement services. Most of these municipal programs, however, do not question the model but have tried to prepare workers to work and fit within the global economy and the neoliberal economic model, except for perhaps the cooperative programs that encourage sharing of profits rather than pursuing individual gain. The municipal governments under the Worker's Party have been more progressive than those under other political parties, both working within and outside of the neoliberal model. However, as is most apparent on the national level, even the Worker's Party has very much adopted a neoliberal economic model.

If the actions of the individual worker, community organization, and municipal government are primarily reactive, reduced to trying to ameliorate the worst impacts of globalization and work within the system, can they ever become transformative? At least the case of the ABC Regional Chamber shows that they can be. The chamber's decision to make the region competitive globally by, for example, establishing industrial clusters of small enterprises and providing technical and marketing training and assistance is fully consonant with the neoliberal model. However, all of its projects are carried out within the context of fair labor and environmental protection, two tenets often absent from within the confines of the neoliberal model. By working together, governments and civil society hope to show that there is an alternative pathway to the prevailing race to the bottom. I also contend for São Paulo what Brenner and Theodore (2002a, p. 376) argue for cities in western Europe and North America, that, "it remains to be seen whether the powerful contradictions inherent within the current urbanized formation of roll-out neoliberalism will provide openings for more progressive, radical democratic reappropriations of city space, or whether by contrast, neoliberal agendas will be entrenched still further within the underlying institutional structures of urban governance." Will the municipal governments in São Paulo's industrial region be able to strategize together with other local actors at the individual worker and community levels to chip away at the neoliberal economic model, and develop a new model that will combine economic growth and social and environmental justice? Collective action within and among all levels and scales is crucial for social justice and grassroots empowerment.

Notes

1. See Buechler (2002, 2004, 2006) for details about the precarious conditions of the labor market.
2. The ABC region, the industrial region of the MRSP, is made up of seven of the thirty-eight municipalities comprising the MRSP, with three of them Santo André, São Bernardo do Campo, and São Caetano de Sul giving the name to this region. This area was created by a coherent economic and political import substitution program implemented by President Juscelino Kubischek (1956–1961). From the beginning the municipality of Diadema, situated in this industrial region and the location of one of the favelas studied, was one of the hardest hit.
3. The names of my informants and the communities studied have been changed to ensure anonymity.
4. A survey was conducted in Favela Leste and Jardim Sudoeste in 1998 with a more limited survey in 2003. However, a greater percentage of women were interviewed in Favela Sul. The *unemployed* was defined as people searching for work within the last thirty days and not involved in sideline economic activities, people working irregularly (infrequent sideline activities) but looking for stable work in the last thirty days, and people who stopped looking for work because they are discouraged but were looking for work in the last twelve months. However, many of my informants had set ideas of what it was to be unemployed. Therefore, subsequent questions were asked.
5. In 2006 there were a few new factories that opened nearby.
6. Seven years earlier, her parents-in-law had moved back to the interior. The majority of Estive Gerbi's inhabitants work as agricultural workers, but it also has a few factories.
7. Rosa, always a strong Worker's Party supporter, was more optimistic because she had predicted that President Lula da Silva would get reelected and would be able to improve the situation further.
8. As of 1982, 60,000 to 80,000 CEBs were found in Brazil with a membership of two to three million (Hewitt 1987, p. 142). Burdick (1992, p. 172) argues, however, that the image of CEBs as powerful political mobilizers might be slightly overdrawn.
9. In 2003 there were 550 SABs in the Municipality of São Paulo, with most in low-income neighborhoods (Jacobi 2005, p. 27).
10. Although the CEBs might be in decline in terms of activism, they are not completely dead. In 1997 there were 70,000 CEBs throughout Brazil (Drogus 1999, p. 39). In a survey conducted in 1994, half the urban CEBs reported that they continued to participate in struggles for better living conditions (ibid.).

11. One might argue, however, that organizations such as the WTO and IMF do perhaps have to maintain global order and coordination and therefore are not that different from the nation-state.
12. These metal containers were used as homes. Krones had been renting the land from the same Japanese–Brazilian ex-Coca Cola chief executive officer who owned the rest of the land. He had failed to pay taxes, so the municipal government had confiscated land for its own use and was not exactly helping the owner. The inhabitants, however, were beginning to buy the land after years of negotiation.
13. The apartments did not allow them to operate small stores or other businesses, discouraged social interaction, and did not allow for additions.
14. Under the last Worker's Party mayor, until 2005 Marta Suplicy, funds were made available to continue with the building of the community association's self-help housing program, to enlarge and continue the community association's day care and youth center, and to start a computer center.
15. They kept the machines and space but only did some sewing still.
16. In 1998, this group started to work more closely with the internationally known Landless Movement (*Movimento de Sem Terra*). The difference in political stances caused divisions within the movement. Section four, the last section of the favela to be invaded in 1998, is not part of the *Movimento dos Moradores* because of various conflicts.
17. Favela Sul seemed to have fewer people involved in selling drugs simply because Sister Isabela did not allow it and instead provided the youth with other activities, education, and a place to go when not in school. However, Favela Leste had two different highly organized associations with the newest leaders involved in selling drugs.
18. Although beyond the scope of this chapter, it is important to mention that NGOs have often taken an important intermediary role between grassroots organizations and governments and sometimes work at the global scale (Roberts and Portes 2006). NGOs are more likely to be run by the upper class with more access to power.
19. Although Brazil was constituted in 1891 as a federation, there were few practical and constitutional links between different tiers of government (Rodríguez-Pose, Tomaney, and Klink 2001).
20. In the first phase they had difficulties in terms of duration, lack of entrepreneurial knowledge, and illiteracy, but they worked on these issues (Schwengber 2003).
21. The problems with microcredit programs are numerous given the competition between microenterprises; high interest rates; and the lack of experience of NGOs, banks, and the government.
22. In 2005, José Serra, of the PSDB party (the former Brazilian President Cardoso's party) became mayor, but only until March 31, 2006, when his vice-mayor, Gilberto Kassab, took over so he could run for presidential office.
23. See Buechler (forthcoming) and Rodríguez-Pose, Tomaney, and Klink 2001.
24. In 2003, 70 percent of the inhabitants surveyed in Favela Leste did not think the mayor was helping them.

Works Cited

Brenner, Neil. 2001. The limits to scale? Methodological reflections on scalar structuration. *Progress in Human Geography* 25(4):591–614.

Brenner, Neil. 2003. Metropolitan institutional reform and the rescaling of state space in contemporary western Europe. *European Urban and Regional Studies* 10(4):297–324.

Brenner, Neil, and Nik Theodore. 2002a. Cities and the geographies of "actually existing neoliberalism." *Antipode* 34(3):349–79.

———. 2002b. Preface: From the "new localism" to the spaces of neoliberalism. *Antipode* 34(3):341–7.

Buechler, Simone. 2002. Enacting the global economy in São Paulo, Brazil: The impact of labor market restructuring on low-income women. Ph.D. diss., Department of Urban Planning, Columbia University, New York.

———. 2004. The degradation of work in the global economy: Low-income women and the precarious labor market in São Paulo, Brazil. In Saskia Sassen and Peter Marcotullio, eds., *1.18 Human Resource System Challenge VII: Human Settlement Development*, in *Encyclopedia of Life Support Systems (EOLSS)*, Developed under the auspices of UNESCO. Oxford, UK: EOLSS Publishers. [http://www.eolss.net]

———. 2006. São Paulo: Outsourcing and downgrading of labor in a globalizing city. In Neil Brenner and Roger Keil, eds., *Global city reader*, 238–45. New York: Routledge.

——— (in press). Daring to dream: Social actors fighting for labor rights and social justice in São Paulo, Brazil. In Neil Smith and Ida Susser, eds., *Transformative Cities.*

Burdick, John. 1992. Rethinking the study of social movements: The case of Christian base communities in urban Brazil." In Arturo Escobar and Sonia E. Alvarez, eds., *The making of social movements in Latin America: Identity, strategy, and democracy*, 171–84. Boulder: Westview Press.

Drogus, Carol Ann. 1999. No land of milk and honey: Women CEB activists in post-transition Brazil. *Journal of Interamerican Studies and World Affairs* 41(4):35–51.

Hewitt, Warren Edward. 1987. The influence of social class on activity preferences of comunidades eclesiais de base (CEBs) in the archdiocese of São Paulo. *Journal of Latin American Studies* 19:141–56 (May).

Ireland, Rowan. 1999. Popular religions and the building of democracy in Latin America: Saving the Tocquevillian parallel. *Journal of Interamerican Studies and World Affairs* 4(4):111–36.

———. 2001. Grassroots associations and democracy in Brazil. Presentation at the Bildner Center for Western Hemispheric Studies, City University of New York Graduate Center, November 14, New York.

Jacobi, Pedro Roberto. 2005. Civil society and capacity building in São Paulo. In Simon Raiser and Krister Volkmann, eds., *Bringing the citizen in: Civil society in globalizing cities of the south*, 25-35. Arbeitspapiere des Osteuropa-Instituts der Freien Universität Berlin, Arbeitsbereich Politik und Gesellschaft.

Keating, Michael. 2001. Governing cities and regions: Territorial restructuring in a global age. In Allen J. Scott, ed., *Global city-regions*, 371–90. New York: Oxford University Press.

Kowarick, Lucio. 1985. The pathways to encounter: Reflections on the social struggle in São Paulo. In David Slater, ed., *New social movements and the state in Latin America*, 73–89. Cinnaminson, NJ: CEDLA. Distributed by FORIS Publications USA.

Kowarick, Lúcio, and Milton Campanario. 1994. Industrialized underdevelopment: From economic miracle to economic crisis. In Lúcio Kowarick, ed., *Social struggles and the city: The case of São Paulo*, 45–59. New York: Monthly Review Press.

Kowarick, Lúcio and Milton Campanario. 1986. São Paulo: The price of world city-status. *Development and Change* 17(1):159–174.

Leeds, Anthony. 1994. Locality power in relation to supralocal power institutions. In Roger Sanjek, ed., *Cities, classes and the social order*, 209–31. Ithaca, NY: Cornell University Press.

Orum, Anthony M., and Xiangming Chen. 2003. *The world of cities: Places in comparative and historical perspective.* Malden MA: Blackwell Publishing.

Polanyi, Karl. 1957. *Great transformation.* Boston: Beacon Press.

Roberts, Bryan R., and Alejandro Portes. 2006. Coping with the free market city: Collective action in six Latin American cities at the end of the twentieth century. *Latin American Research Review* 41(2):57–83.

Rodríguez-Pose, Andrés, John Tomaney, and Jeroen Klink. 2001. Local empowerment through economic restructuring in Brazil: The case of the greater ABC region. *Geoforum* 32(4):459–69.

Rolnik, Raquel, and Renato Cymbalista. 2004. Communities and local government: Three case studies in São Paulo, Brazil. Democracy, governance and human rights. Programme Paper 14, November, United Nations Research Institute for Social Development. Geneva, Switzerland.

Sassen, Saskia. 2001. *The global city. Second edition.* Princeton, NJ: Princeton University Press.

———. 2004. Local actors in global politics. *Current sociology* 52(4):649–70.

Schwengber, Angela Maria. 2003. O programa oportunidade solidária. In Marcio Pochmann, ed., *Outra cidade é possível*, 137–66. São Paulo: Cortez Editora.

Scott, Allen J. 1998. *Regions and the world economy: The coming shape of global production, competition, and political order.* Oxford: Oxford University Press.

———. 2001. Introduction. In Allen J. Scott, ed., *Global city-regions*, 1–8. New York: Oxford University Press.

SEADE\DIEESE. (Fundação Sistema Estadual de Análise de Dados -State Foundation for StatisticalAnalysis and Departamento Intersindical de Estatísticas e Estudos Socioeconômicos — The Union Department of Statistics and Socio-Economic Studies). *Pesquisa de Emprego e Desemprego na Região Metropolitana de SP (Study of Employment and Unemployment in the Metropolitan Region of São Paulo) 1985–2005.* São Paulo: SEADE.

Storper, M. 1997. *The regional world: Territorial development in a global economy.* New York: Guilford Press.

PART 2

Translocal Circuits and Their Mobilities

CHAPTER 6

Locating Transnational Activists

The United States Anti-Apartheid Movement and the Confines of the National

EVALYN W. TENNANT

Introduction

> If movements are the social domain which most readily escapes the confines of the inherited, and most perceptibly reveals the manner and locus of the society's self-constructive processes, collective action can become the terrain for exploration of the possible (Melucci 1996, p. 380).

Melucci's (1996) metaphor of escaping the confines is particularly apt for a consideration of the organization of transnational activism. But the relationships — analytical and empirical — between national, transnational, and local aspects and scales of contentious collective action remain far from obvious. Nor are they easily theorized within the methodological nationalist assumptions that continue to pervade research in the field. Anti-apartheid activists in various ways escaped the confines of the inherited. What requires further theorization is whether and how at various points this activism did, and did not, escape the confines of the thick institutional environment of the *national* (Brenner 1999; Sassen 2006).[1]

This variability has implications for how the organizational dynamics and potentials of transnational activism are understood.

Social movements are linked historically to national states: They emerged as a distinctive form of contentious collective claim making in the context of the consolidation of territorial nation-states (Diani 2000; Tarrow 1994, 1996, 1998; Tilly 1984). From the nineteenth to well into the twentieth century, forms of movement embeddedness in national states and institutions were multiple and overdetermined. In recent decades, technosocial and institutional transformations in governance have altered the relationships between national states and movements, enabling new forms of contentious collective action (Bach and Stark 2004; Sassen 2006, chap. 7). However, neither the spatial aspects of these transformations nor the consequences for the ways in which local, "micro" processes are articulated into broader national or transnational movements has received systematic attention. As Sewell (2001, pp. 51–2) notes, the social movement literature has for the most part "treated space as an assumed and unproblematic background, not as a constituent aspect of contentious politics that must be conceptualized explicitly and probed systematically."

Through the mid- and late 1990s, the literature on social movements continued to focus on the efficacy of spatial proximity, homogeneity, and face-to-face interaction for mobilization (McAdam, McCarthy, and Zald 1996; Tarrow 1994). As Miller (2000, chap. 1) observes, the specific effects of space and scale on social movements within national states has generally been neglected; movements seem to take place "on the head of a pin," everywhere but nowhere in particular. The same has not been the case with respect to transnational contention. While the social movement literature was emphasizing the importance of face-to-face interaction and spatial proximity among homogeneous populations for purposes of mobilization, Keck and Sikkink's (1998) path-breaking work on "transnational advocacy networks" demonstrated the efficacy of heterogeneity of actors — groups collaborating from different locations, with different capabilities and resources, and with leverage with respect to different national and/or international authorities — working across borders. The common solution has been to distinguish social movements, understood to be rooted in the social networks constitutive of everyday life, from transnational advocacy networks, understood to be mere "connecting structures" (Diani 2000, p. 395; see also Khagram, Riker, and Sikkink 2002). In keeping with a key proposition organizing this volume — that the national and the transnational not be understood as mutually exclusive — this chapter takes a different approach. It looks both at the national structuring of multiscaled activism and at the forms and practices of translocal circulation that characterize both national and transnational activism (Cox 2002; Herod and Wright

2002; Leitner, Pavlik, and Sheppard 2002; Sassen, this volume). I pursue the question of social movements, networks, and the confines of the national by thinking through examples of U.S.-based anti-apartheid activism from the late 1940s through the 1980s, focusing on the period from the 1960s through the mid-1980s. I then return in the final section to a more general consideration of techniques, technologies, and translocal circulation.

Analytic Framework: Translocally Distributed Collective Action

Though the contentious politics literature has been preoccupied with distinguishing national from transnational, I argue here that a more analytically productive distinction is between located, face-to-face forms of interaction on the one hand, and *translocal,* mediated forms on the other. Both national and transnational movements require translocal as well as face-to-face organization. In fact, nearly all social movements are composed *not* of one or the other form of organization, nor of a national or transnational mass, but rather of a complex configuration of translocally articulated local collective actors. Sometimes, local actors are articulated into a national actor within a single hierarchically structured organization; Skocpol (2002) finds many such examples from the nineteenth- and early twentieth-century United States. However, many recent and contemporary movements are organized across rather than within the nested hierarchies of scale of territorially based governance. Such movements can be more productively understood as effects produced not merely by *collective* action but rather by the translocal collection of *distributed* forms of locally organized collective action.[2] The spatially and organizationally distributed aspect of movements has critical implications for how we understand not only the organization of movements within and across places, but also the multiscalar *capabilities* of contentious collective actors with respect to the national and other constituted scales and authorities.

Attending to the distributed character of movements foregrounds questions of translocal collection relevant to both national and transnational movements. In addition to the growing prevalence since the mid-1990s of forms of transnational contentious collective action, movement scholars have observed broad historical shifts in (national) social movement forms. The analytic focus on distribution and collection enables a more precise account of two of the most significant shifts by reintroducing geographic and technosocial considerations. One shift is in the direction of professionalized, "national" (and "transnational") advocacy organizations without local chapters or locally organized members. Another shift, in this case in the kinds of collective claims being made and the kinds of transformations sought, has been observed by scholars of "new social movements"

(NSMs). On this account, earlier movements sought greater voice and inclusion in the polity and could be understood in terms of "interests," whereas new movements from the 1960s onward have been more focused on issues of "identity." The latter have sought to politicize and "reconstitute a civil society independent from [the] increasing control and intervention" of "representative-bureaucratic institutions" of state and society (Offe 1987, p. 65). Both kinds of shifts — toward professionalization and toward an increasing emphasis on identity and prefigurative practices — imply transformations in the techniques and technologies of collective action, in the associated forms of organization within and across space, and, more broadly, in the relation of movements to national states and to the broader institutional infrastructure of the national.

Both shifts can also usefully be seen as part of a broader shift roughly in what Tilly (1984, p. 308) calls *repertoires*: the historically specific "inventory of available means of collective action." Tilly, from the vantage point of 1980s, maintained that the twentieth century social movement repertoire remained strikingly similar to the forms that had evolved with the nationalization of politics in the nineteenth century (ibid., p. 310). Though he noted changes in technology and the role of mass media, he assessed their importance as relatively minor. However, Tilly's conception of available means focused on visible collective challenges rather than on the far less visible organizational conditions of possibility for producing those public, visible challenges to authorities. Forms of public challenge, in other words, may persist even as the context in which they are performed, the techniques and technologies through which they are produced, and the ends to which they are oriented changes.

If innovations in repertoire and capabilities are taking place largely behind the scenes (to continue with the theatrical metaphor), it is essential to examine how these invisible articulations and coordination are organized. But this project is hindered by unwarranted and misleading assumptions about space, scale, and organization. Three such assumptions are particularly important, and although they have contradictory implications, they frequently coexist. One assumption conflates the local and the national, treating the local — in this case, local collective actors and movement dynamics — as but the micro instantiation of the broader, macro, national. This conflation is often accomplished rhetorically by the use of the ambiguous "domestic," which may refer to either local or national. Though domestic powerfully connotes home and the local, it is also understood in specific opposition to "foreign." The synecdochic slippage between the local and the national shows the rather profound effects of well over a century of nationalist and state-building projects: Even social scientists routinely, if implicitly, treat national social movements as if their dynamics were produced exclusively in face-to-face contexts, without translocal mediation.

The second assumption, logically at odds with the first but often coexisting with it, concerns territoriality and territorial embeddedness. It assumes that people are embedded within local territorial contexts and that their access to the national, let alone the transnational, will be mediated through the nested hierarchical scales into which state territoriality is organized. The third assumption is closely related to the second, but it specifically concerns social networks and has implications of a different sort. This version of the territorial assumption not only embeds people in particular, located social contexts, but also assumes that they are for most intents and purposes stuck there, immobile and without direct ties to others elsewhere. Though at any given time most people's social networks may be composed mainly of others physically proximate to them, such a probabilistic statement means little in social contexts where various forms of translocal, and sometimes transnational, mobility are the norm, and where available technologies of both private communication and mass mediation make conceptions of proximity and distance a matter of far more than simple geography (Latour 1996). In practice, these various, highly problematic assumptions about the relation between local and national are frequently combined, making it impossible to investigate critical aspects of social movement organization that are simultaneously local and national and/or transnational. The more literal-minded approach of investigating the techniques and technologies through which collective action is both distributed and collected yields both empirical and theoretical gains — more adequate explanations of particular mobilizations and outcomes on the one hand, and a more nuanced conceptualization of the complex and changing relationships between collective action and national states on the other.

Anti-Apartheid Activism in the United States

Anti-apartheid and other internationalist solidarity activists engaged in collective projects over the course of the post-World War II period, though their activism never attracted as much visibility as their more recent counterparts' did. From disparate institutional and geographic sites, activists deployed new techniques and tactics that forged both organizational and imaginative connections between "local" and "distant" concerns. The innovative techniques and tactics, versions of which feature prominently in contemporary activists' repertoires, were deployed with respect to multiple targets and scales. They were enabled by new forms of official international organization, particularly United Nations (UN) agencies and instruments. U.S.-based activists, especially when in New York, forged close ties with UN delegates and staff and collaborated actively with the UN Special Committee Against Apartheid, in which the United States did not officially participate.

By focusing on activists in the United States, I attend both to shared national aspects of the institutional environment and to the particularities of the multiple local, face-to-face contexts of activism. National forces constrained and enabled organizing in profound and frequently racially specific ways, especially with respect to Cold War domestic and foreign policies. In the late 1940s U.S. authorities promised progress on domestic civil rights issues in exchange for civil rights leaders' avowed opposition to communism and support of American foreign policy. This not only put an end to the black left and the vibrant black internationalism and Pan-Africanism of the Council on African Affairs but also for the most part disarticulated U.S. and global struggles for racial equality (Anderson 2003; Horne 1986; Plummer 1996; Von Eschen 1997). In the name of anti-communism, U.S. foreign policy supported racist, colonial, and authoritarian regimes that professed anti-communism and were strategically important. Such allies included not only South Africa but also North Atlantic Treaty Organization (NATO) member Portugal, which used NATO weapons to suppress independence movements in its African colonies.

While black activists received powerful incentives to eschew internationalism in favor of purely domestic civil rights issues, avowedly anti-Communist white activists enjoyed greater freedom to pursue internationalist projects. Somewhat ironically, Cold War federal funding of university African studies programs — intended to create area experts for the government — often created enabling local environments for anti-imperialist and anti-apartheid organizing in university communities, and the movement of scholars among these institutions facilitated connections among local organizations in different communities. In these and other ways, specifically national dynamics also produced peculiar divisions — and sometimes divisions of labor — between black and white activists. For example, many black activists rejected African studies programs precisely because of their links to U.S. foreign policy interests and in the late 1960s founded new Black studies and Afro-American studies programs explicitly as alternatives. These newer programs also served as institutional supports to local organizing.

By *anti-apartheid activists,* I mean people and groups whose individual and collective practices were oriented specifically, and in more than a passing way, toward ending apartheid in South Africa. These people and groups identified themselves depending on the time period and political ideology in terms of African liberation, African (or southern African) solidarity, anti-imperialism, black liberation, Pan-Africanism, and civil rights as well as anti-apartheid. At any given point in time, not all groups working on anti-apartheid issues would have known of one another's existence, even in a general rather than particular sense. Though all would have had a sense of participating in a movement with a broader range of others than they knew or knew of directly, not all activists would have included the same others. In particular, especially during the late 1960s and early 1970s, not all black activists would have included white participants as part of the same movement. From the mid-1970s onward, though, as only South Africa, Namibia (administered by South Africa), and Rhodesia continued to be ruled by white minority governments, Africa activists' attention increasingly centered on South Africa. Not only did the struggle for majority rule continue in South Africa, but its highly militarized and Western-supported white minority regime was destabilizing the region (particularly Angola and Mozambique) and preventing other, independent states from prospering.[3]

By activists *in the United States*, I mean people — Americans, Africans, and others — who participated in forms of anti-apartheid activism while in the United States, whether during a visit of a few days or over many years. I focus on activism in the United States to foreground two important spatial and organizational features: the dispersed, local character of organizing and the forms and practices of mobility that articulated the dispersed sites. First, from the mid-1960s until the mid-1980s, activism in the United States was for the most part rooted locally, in face-to-face groups in particular places: Madison, Wisconsin, Chicago, New York City, and the San Francisco Bay area, to take four very important examples, but also in scores of other perhaps less obvious cities and towns, including Greensboro, North Carolina, and Dayton, Ohio. At the same time, however, this distributed activism was never simply local; it was always connected directly or indirectly, through various kinds of media and mediation, to other activists elsewhere inside and outside the United States, although the shape and extent of the translocal connections varied over time.

Some activists traveled, whether for activist or other purposes; other U.S.-based activists rarely or never traveled but regularly acted and interacted with and were influenced by those who did. Students and academics, exiles, missionaries, and others moved among North American, European, and African locations, sometimes staying a day or two for a speaking engagement, a few years to obtain a university degree, a few months for research in the field, or indefinitely, waiting from exile for a time when it would be possible to return home. Further, some U.S.-based activists were also, at different points in time, activists outside the United States: Americans doing academic research while also running into exiles and liberation movement representatives in Dar es Salaam, for example, or working for the World Council of Churches in Geneva; or Africans who found themselves in the United States on the staff of international organizations (IOs) or nongovernmental organizations (NGOs), as students or as exiles. More generally, activists who moved around, or who had moved at some point, mediated their less-mobile fellows' sense of place and of connection to other places, forming bases of solidarity both imagined and, often, enacted concretely in ongoing practical ties to people, organizations, and institutions elsewhere. Thus, U.S. would-be activists living in many communities need never to have traveled, to Africa or to anywhere far from home, in order to come into regular contact with people who had and did.

National organizations, which were national in different ways and to different degrees, played critical roles, although anti-apartheid activism was never organized through a national mass membership organization. The Council on African Affairs (through the immediate post-World War II period), American Committee on Africa (ACOA) (from the early 1950s through the end of apartheid), Washington Office on Africa (WOA) (from the early 1970s through the end of apartheid), TransAfrica (from 1977 through the end of apartheid), and sometimes other organizations undertook roles that could be understood in one way or another as national rather than local. In many cases these involved coordination and collaboration with locally based groups. But through the early 1980s, most U.S.-based activists' relationships to activists and groups outside the United States were mediated by grassroots rather than national organizations.[4] This changed in the mid-1980s, when many of those who entered the movement would likely have been influenced — unlike those who entered earlier, in the absence of much mass media coverage at all — by national mass-media representations in which representatives of groups such as TransAfrica (especially), ACOA, and WOA figured prominently.

Making a Movement National

This section describes the quick, coherent mobilization within the United States around economic sanctions and related forms of economic disengagement from South Africa. I then go back in time to African National Congress (ANC) head and 1960 Nobel Peace Prize winner Albert Lutuli's appeal to Americans, issued jointly with Martin Luther King, Jr., in 1962 through the auspices of ACOA, to urge American support in the UN Security Council for sanctions against South Africa. Finally, I give a few very brief examples of the kinds of translocally and transnationally articulated local practices that over more than two decades produced the organizational conditions of possibility for the mid-1980s mobilization and campaign for sanctions. I focus especially on the ways tactics and rationales for economic disengagement circulated and were innovated, adopted, and adapted to the particularities of various subnational scales and places.

In September 1984, protests against apartheid within South Africa increased, as did their suppression. The violence in South Africa became a major story, well covered by U.S. media outlets and particularly network television news (Nesbitt 1986). The Ronald Reagan administration did not move from its policy of constructive engagement with the South African regime, sometimes refusing even verbal condemnation of unlawful arrests and detentions. In late November, several African American activists in Washington, D.C., staged a protest at the South African Embassy. They hoped some dramatic action might increase public attention and interest, and they invited the media, who captured their arrests on tape. This protest launched the Free South Africa Movement (FSAM) — ongoing protests outside the embassy that spread to consulates around the country. The FSAM was to end only when the activists' demands for an end to apartheid were met or when U.S. foreign policy shifted in a direction to make that happen, that is, when the U.S. Congress imposed economic sanctions restricting the ability of U.S.-based firms to do business with and in South Africa. In combination with the media coverage of escalating protest and violence within South Africa, the FSAM dramatically increased the visibility of apartheid in South Africa and of anti-apartheid efforts within the United States, including local and state efforts that were ongoing when the FSAM was launched. Under these conditions members of Congress, including many of the Republicans then in control of both houses, chose to support sanctions against South Africa despite the Reagan administration's fervent objections. In October 1986, the Comprehensive Anti-Apartheid Act passed, with significant Republican support, over the veto of a popular president.

The huge popular response and quick spread of protests took everyone, including the organizers, by surprise (Counts-Blakey 1995). It seemed to burgeon almost overnight into what *Newsweek* referred to four months later as "a vast and diverse grass-roots crusade" (March 11, 1985, p. 28). Over the course of the next two years, from late 1984 through late 1986, tens of thousands of people in the United States were involved in protests against South Africa's apartheid regime and U.S. and corporate support for the regime. Some 6,000 protesters were arrested in the United States during this wave of activism, including members of Congress and other prominent political figures, well-known actors and entertainers, and labor and civil rights leaders whose arrests themselves might be newsworthy (Baker 1989).

But those arrested, and those marching with them but not arrested, also included greater numbers of longtime anti-apartheid activists than celebrities and greater numbers still of new recruits to the cause. These new recruits were moved to participation by some combination of the push of images on television and the pull of an existing infrastructure of organizations or — where there were no local organizations — contacts, templates, and strategies for local campaigns. Among these longtime activists and new recruits were local union organizers, pastors, students, and educators, for the most part unknown beyond the communities in which they were often deeply involved. Though the celebrity participants attracted media attention, so did the sheer numbers of protest events, anonymous noncelebrity protesters, and locations of protests. The diverse campaigns — not just for federal sanctions but also the ongoing campaigns for local and state divestment, for divestment of university endowments and pension funds from South Africa-related firms — had a common logic as well as a common goal, and these local, state, and nonstate targets were easily assimilated not just by the media but also by many activists into a common, now national, movement. In short, these mid-1980s anti-apartheid protests in the United States involved large numbers of people, self-organized in many different locations and mobilized against multiple targets on the basis of a relatively consistent and coherent set of causal claims about the role of U.S. foreign policy and foreign investment and bank loans in helping to maintain the viability, and thus the injustices, of apartheid.

The anti-apartheid movement in the United States in the mid-1980s looked distinctively American in some of its modes of address, often quite explicitly evoking and invoking U.S. civil rights protests of the early 1960s. These images were resonant and effective, given mass-mediated images from South Africa's townships that evoked other aspects of American civil rights protests, for instance, white police in riot gear beating or setting German shepherds on unarmed black protesters. What might appear rather unproblematically at first as a national social movement turns out to be a bit more complex.

From the Sharpeville to the UN to the FSAM

By the November 1984 FSAM launch, grassroots activists had long since organized themselves in many big cities, state capitals, and university towns, and many were primarily engaged in issues of economic disengagement at subnational scales. The campaigns for economic disengagement deployed claims that diverged rather sharply from accepted mainstream understandings of the role of corporations in American politics and society, as well as from accepted courses of action for citizen and subnational government involvement in foreign policy. In fact, these campaigns provide an indication of the transnational collaborations in which they originated, and in connection with which they developed over the course of the 1960s, 1970s, and into the early 1980s.

Both the decolonization of the African continent and the U.S. civil rights movement were well under way at the time of the Sharpeville massacre in South Africa in March 1960; the Greensboro, North Carolina, lunch-counter sit-ins occurred just a few weeks earlier, launching a wave of similar actions across the southern United States. As decolonization increased African representation in the UN, there was an increasing movement, especially in the General Assembly, to use the organization to oppose apartheid, and in November 1962 the General Assembly called on the Security Council to enact an international boycott and quarantine of South Africa and created the Special Committee Against Apartheid, in which the United States chose not to participate (United Nations 1994). That same month, under the auspices of the American Committee on Africa, Lutuli and King jointly issued an Appeal to Action Against Apartheid directed toward Americans, promulgating the UN General Assembly's call as well as following up on an international campaign begun in 1957. It encouraged Americans to

- Hold meetings and demonstrations on December 10, Human Rights Day
- Urge your church, union, lodge, or club to observe this day as one of protest
- Urge your government to support economic sanctions
- Write to your mission to the United Nations urging adoption of a resolution calling for international isolation of South Africa
- Don't buy South Africa's products
- Don't trade or invest in South Africa
- Translate public opinion into public action by explaining facts to all peoples, to groups to which you belong, and to countries of which you are citizens until an effective international quarantine of apartheid is established (United Nations 1994, pp. 252–3).

The multiplicity of scales and scopes for action, indeed for *collective* action by different types of collectivities, is already clear in the appeal. Multiple targets and points of leverage are mentioned — groups (e.g., churches, unions) and governments as well as individuals — as are multiple varieties of economic action (e.g., boycott, trade, investment, sanctions).

In the early 1960s American attention was much more heavily focused on domestic civil rights struggles, but as the 1960s progressed constituencies within both black and white new-left movements increasingly saw domestic and international struggles for racial equality and against Western imperialism as linked. Though much of this anti-imperialist sentiment was channeled into the antiwar movement, many activists' attention extended to Africa as well. They frequently focused on making connections between U.S.-based multinationals' interests abroad and U.S. foreign policy. From the mid-1960s through the early 1980s, local grassroots anti-apartheid groups coalesced in university communities, state capitals, and large cities, particularly in the North and West, most often where there were large African American communities as well as strong labor organization. They formed spatially and organizationally distributed clusters of activism, in many cases relatively well connected through individual and organizational ties to one another and to anti-apartheid organizations and supporters in Europe and Africa. New York-based groups, from grassroots formations like the Patrice Lumumba Coalition to the multiracial and nationally oriented American Committee on Africa, were deeply shaped and enabled by their proximity to the UN: to delegates, including the main South African liberation movements' observer delegations, staff, and visiting activists and diplomats. New York in this respect constituted a particularly denationalized site of activism.

Calls for economic disengagement emanating from the South African liberation movements and the UN were taken up by groups in the U.S. and beyond. In a process more distributed and iterative than is captured by *diffusion*, activists innovated, elaborated, and circulated variations on themes of economic disengagement for more than two decades. This work took place both in places, in the kind of face-to-face interactions emphasized in the social movement literature, and through mediated communication between people and groups in different places. Activists drew new kinds of connections between "here" and "there," enabling new targets and new tactics at new scales in the process. Groups continually picked up on existing strategies and tactics and adapted them for local use, producing local innovations and variations. These circulated through personal communication, newsletters, and how-to pamphlets, and were continually innovated and adapted while continuing to bear a family resemblance to earlier efforts.

In 1965 Students for a Democratic Society (SDS) launched demonstrations against U.S. banks extending loans to South Africa. The campaign was taken up and adapted by ACOA in conjunction with other student groups in the late 1960s. In 1970, a grassroots group in Madison, Wisconsin, broadened the focus from bank lending to business and foreign policy more generally. They produced a pamphlet asking, "Is Southern Africa Wisconsin's Business?" The group publicized and explored a variety of otherwise invisible connections between Wisconsin firms, people, and interests and the conflicts in South Africa and Mozambique and Angola. Establishing local connections and beneficiaries of apartheid and other Southern African conflicts also established those beneficiaries as potential tactical targets. The pamphlet circulated through the well-connected group's formal and informal translocal networks and provided a template for activist researchers elsewhere who in turn produced versions appropriate to their own localities.

Black radicals in the early 1970s organized African Liberation Support Committees (ALSCs) to support African liberation movements and to bring a common purpose and goal to what had become deeply ideologically divided political organizations. The ALSC organization — with its annual African Liberation Day marches and associated groups like the Greensboro, North Carolina-based Student (later Youth) Organization for Black Unity, which published the *African World* — lasted only a few years, but its effects lasted much longer. Participating activists and groups continued to pursue anti-apartheid and related efforts through other channels, including more official ones. In 1976, the Congressional Black Caucus convened a Black Leadership Conference on Southern Africa. The conference produced an election-year manifesto, disseminated in the widely read *Black Scholar*, demanding U.S. support for UN sanctions and a range of other southern Africa policy changes (Congressional Black Caucus 1977). The conference also created TransAfrica, an African American lobby organization for African and Caribbean issues and one of the most significant and most visible anti-apartheid organizations in the mid-1980s.

In 1980, a Boston-based coalition of former student activists, black community activists, church and labor activists, and other veteran solidarity activists began working with legislators on state divestment legislation. In 1982, they succeeded in getting the Massachusetts legislature to pass the strongest state legislation up to that time over the veto of a conservative Democratic governor. The campaign to "Make it in Massachusetts, not in South Africa" persuaded legislators to support legislation requiring that pension funds divest holdings in South Africa-related corporations and, to the extent possible, to reinvest those funds in firms doing business with or in Massachusetts. As in other campaigns, the question of who was benefiting from investments — the South African state or local communities — was used as a means to connect South African to "local" concerns. In the relative absence of national mass-media coverage, ACOA distributed the MassDivest leaders' account of their successful campaign to anti-apartheid and other organizations around the country. The "Make it in Massachusetts" pamphlet served as a template for both effective mobilization and effective legislation, and focused on coalition-building tactics, the importance of sticking to a demand for total rather than partial divestment, and ways to address issues of fiduciary responsibility (MassDivest 1983).

These few examples merely illustrate the range of forms of U.S.-based activism and translocal and transnational coordination and collaboration prior to the mid-1980s mobilization. What remains almost invisible even here is how South African and other international visitors, especially but not only students, influenced and motivated Americans to act. For example, in 1972, a decade before the MassDivest campaign, South African exile and Harvard divinity student Chris Nteta, along with then-law student and future TransAfrica director Randall Robinson, participated in a takeover of the Harvard president's office to protest the university's investments in Gulf Oil, which was at the time supporting the Portuguese in Angola (Robinson 1998, p. 90).

Over the quarter century following the Lutuli–King appeal, the broad approaches it outlined took on increasingly sophisticated forms, leveraging new sources of influence — institutional investors, especially universities, and state and local governments' own fiscal and financial policies — and making more specific connections between "here," somewhere in the United States, and "there," South Africa. The path from the 1962 appeal to the passage of federal sanctions was hardly direct; in fact, there was no single path, and innovations in tactics were not contained within national borders. Nor were activists contained within national borders, though they did not necessarily move as activists (except in the case of liberation movement representatives), let alone as professional activists moving from one international conference to another.

Activists sought an audience, a public, and public support. They produced and circulated numerous publications in various media, including newsletters, pamphlets, films, and filmstrips. These were not private, let alone secret, communications,[5] but they were also not messages that reached a national, mass public. They reached and circulated among many people and organizations in many places within and outside the United States, but prior to the FSAM nowhere did *most* people, or even most influential people—the public understood as a national, attentive public, as in Habermas's (1989) *public sphere* — read them or attend to their claims. Rather, activists' literature and other media addressed and reached a much smaller counterpublic, neither a bounded audience nor a universal one, but rather one both presumed and constituted by common interest and attention (Warner 2002).

Most activists were embedded, at least temporarily, in places as well as in relational contexts that connected them to, rather than separating them from, other places and activists. Local efforts — whether city council resolutions or university divestments or campaigns to get a bank to curtail loans — were motivated by a conception of relatedness and connection that transcended geographic distance. These efforts were produced not only by local groups but also by the translocal, collaborative practices that themselves reflected distance-bridging connections. Though activists perceived that they were connected to people with whom they identified and understood themselves to be acting, their knowledge of the specifics of those connections and circuits varied greatly. For example, many locally based activists were well versed in economic data, research into firms' South Africa-related activities, and facts on the ground in South Africa from working conditions to political repression. However, only a much smaller number of activists — often long-term activists — had a good sense of the paths by which that circulating information reached them. Fewer still had a historical sense of the collaborative, trial and error process by which particular kinds of data had come to be collected in service of particular kinds of arguments for economic disengagement.

Though the national institutional environment always structured the organizational opportunities afforded to activists in the United States, the national did not orient U.S.-based anti-apartheid activism until the FSAM. The media-friendly strategy pursued by the leaders of the FSAM was effective neither because it mobilized a national constituency *ex nihilo* nor because it merely made more publicly visible initiatives that were already there. Rather, with the mass-media attention the FSAM generated, it both mobilized new constituents to national and existing local campaigns *and* made those existing campaigns visible as something more than local activism, as something all of a piece with one another and with the sanctions campaign. Local campaigns that had long been transnational in significant respects suddenly became part of a national movement as well. With the FSAM and the sanctions campaign, the distributed, translocally articulated forms of anti-apartheid activism were suddenly collected in a new way.

Following the late 1986 passage of federal sanctions legislation, the national movement as such demobilized, defeated by victory and by the South African regime's increasing restrictions on the media. But activism oriented to university, pension fund, state, and local divestment campaigns continued, and new forms of "people-to-people" connections between North American and South African communities emerged. Though much of this activism too dissipated, even before the end of apartheid in 1994, the temporalities were quite different.

That this national social movement was produced as much by the attention of the mass media as by actions of activists is significant. It cautions against mistaking the movement as publicly visible, nationally mass-mediated *effect* for the relatively invisible activism that was the effect's condition of possibility. As Gitlin (1980, p. 22) wrote of Students for a Democratic Society, "It conducted its activities in a social world that recognized it, liked it, and disliked it through media images, media versions of its events and rhetoric." To this he added, "To some extent the movement even recognized itself through mass-mediated images" (ibid.). Many 1980s activists, mobilized through the FSAM and the sanctions campaign, recognized themselves as part of a national movement. Many older and longer-term activists saw things differently. The distributed character of the movement and its long-term relative invisibility are evident in the strikingly different characterizations given by differently positioned participants.

The techniques and technologies available to and deployed by anti-apartheid activists enabled geographic distance to be bridged in ways sufficient to produce transnational collective action. Activists communicated translocally via telephone, telex, cables, snail mail, and, toward the end, fax. The mobility of a relatively small number of people among locales in Africa, Europe, and North America — whether for movement-specific reasons such as speaking tours or personal reasons such as education — contributed to connecting people and places indirectly but often at only one remove. The local character of so much of the organizing within the United States, in other words, was very much shaped by the fact that so many groups had members with direct, personal ties to people and organizations in or from southern Africa. This kind of face-to-face once removed is a powerful subjective world-shrinking device.

Conclusion

The national is a highly complex and elaborated institutional environment not least because national state institutions articulate localities into a broader, translocal political community (Sassen 2006). But state-territorial forms are not the only potential, or actual, translocal organizational forms either within or across territorial borders (Cox 1998; Leitner, Pavlik, and Sheppard 2002). Representative and bureaucratic state institutions articulate localities, at least formally, on the basis of territorial forms based in nested hierarchies of scale. Nonstate institutions including the mass media and much of organizational life reflect this organization, but only partially. Other forms of social life, even those that may in significant respects also be national, need not be organized on a nested territorial basis, although they must exist in relation to the nested territorial scales of the national state (Brenner 1999; Cox 1998; Judd 1998). In other words, even social formations and actors not organized on a nested territorial basis — such as markets and firms but also many social movements — remain (1) subject to the particular enabling and constraining effects of proximity and distance relevant to the processes at hand, and (2) subject to the institutional and legal regime that is organized on a territorial basis (Cox 2002; Sassen 2006).

The enabling and constraining effects of proximity and distance are effects of the institutional environment, which changes over time. Movement organization in relation to national states has changed over time for many reasons, but available techniques and technologies, and innovations in techniques and technologies, play a big part even when they hardly appear high-tech. On the one hand, old techniques and technologies, even quite mundane ones, can be used to new ends: The postal service infrastructure works equally well to deliver international mail (once it arrives in the United States) even though it is an institution of the national state; pamphlets about geographically distant causes get delivered along with those about purely local causes.[6] On the other hand, new technologies may lead to overestimation of transformations. For example, the Web makes contemporary forms of transnational activism visible to participants and nonparticipants *as transnational activism*, whereas earlier forms of transnational activism did not leave such traces. They either remained invisible or appeared to be merely local or national activism on behalf of distant issues. This is not to say that new information and communication technologies make no difference but rather that they make different kinds of differences than those frequently assumed in the literature. The differences they make can be detected far more clearly when the spatial aspects of organization — and the practices relating face-to-face and translocal collection and distribution — are taken into account systematically and made central to the analysis of processes and outcomes. Given the distributed, self-organized character of contentious collective action, the transformations wrought by the development of new techniques utilizing new technologies will include unforeseen ones.

Notes

1. This analysis of U.S.-based anti-apartheid activism is based on research undertaken for my dissertation (Tennant 2006) and draws on interviews and material from the Prexy Nesbitt Papers, Madison Area Committee on Southern Africa Papers, and Students for a Democratic Society correspondence — all at the Wisconsin Historical Society — and the American Committee on Africa archive at the Amistad Center at Tulane University.
2. I mean here to juxtapose the familiar conception of *collective action* with Latour's (2005) quite different conception of processes of collection and assembly within actor networks.

3. So, for that matter, did the attention of independent African states and their representatives in international organizations. Opposition to apartheid and its effects on the southern African region was a main concern of Africa's continental body, the Organization of African Unity (now the African Union), from its creation in 1963. African delegations to the UN, with the support generally of non-aligned movement and other third-world, Nordic, and Eastern bloc states, pushed to keep apartheid on the UN's agenda. The General Assembly created the Special Committee on Apartheid in 1962, through which monitoring and research for the General Assembly was undertaken.
4. Over the years, ACOA in particular arranged or helped arrange many speaking tours for Africans — labor leaders, liberation movement leaders, and others — on visits to the United States, but this was frequently done in conjunction with local, grassroots activists and organizations.
5. There were, of course, both private and clandestine communications. Liberation support involved support of particular movements, movements often involved in insurgencies, and not necessarily the movements that U.S. policy favored and supported. Between FBI agents provocateurs within black radical formations in the U.S., and CIA involvement in conflicts in Africa, some issues were very fraught and had high stakes for participants. But other aspects of liberation support, and especially those related to the development of strategies and tactics for economic disengagement from and isolation of South Africa were less so, at least within the U.S. Within South Africa, advocacy of international sanctions or divestment was treasonous.
6. This example is prompted by Skocpol's (2002, p. 116) discussion of the role of the U.S. postal service in enabling nineteenth-century federated forms of translocal organization.

Works Cited

Anderson, Carol. 2003. *Eyes off the prize: The United Nations and the African American struggle for human rights, 1944–55.* Cambridge, UK: Cambridge University Press.

Bach, Jonathan, and David Stark. 2004. Link, search, interact: The co-evolution of NGOs and interactive technology. *Theory, Culture and Society* 21(3):101–17.

Baker, Pauline H. 1989. *The United States and South Africa: The Reagan years.* New York: Ford Foundation.

Brenner, Neil. 1999. Beyond state-centrism? Space, territoriality and geographical scale in globalization studies. *Theory and Society* 28(2):39–78.

———. 2002. "Globalization," the "regulation approach," and the politics of scale. In A. Herod and M.W. Wright, eds., *Geographies of power: Placing scale*, 85-114. Malden, MA: Blackwell.

Congressional Black Caucus. 1977. The African-American manifesto on southern Africa. *Black Scholar* 8(4):27–32.

Counts-Blakey, Cecelie. 1995. The FSAM story. *Crossroads* 50:14–8 (April).

Cox, Kevin R. 1998. Spaces of dependence, spaces of engagement and the politics of scale, or: Looking for local politics. *Political Geography* 17(1):1–23.

Diani, Mario. 2000. Social movement networks virtual and real. *Information, Communication, and Society* 3(3):386–401.

Gitlin, Todd. 1980. *The whole world is watching.* Berkeley: University of California Press.

Habermas, Juergen. 1989. *The structural transformation of the public sphere.* Trans. T. Burger. Cambridge, MA: MIT Press.

Herod, Andrew, and Melissa W. Wright (eds.). 2002. *Geographies of power: Placing scale.* Malden, MA: Blackwell.

Horne, Gerald. 1986. *Black and red: W.E.B. Du Bois and the Afro-American response to the Cold War.* Albany: State University of New York Press.

Judd, Dennis R. 1998. The case of the missing scales: A commentary on Cox. *Political Geography* 17(1):29–34.

Keck, Margaret E., and Kathryn Sikkink. 1998. *Activists beyond borders: Advocacy networks in international politics.* Ithaca, NY: Cornell University Press.

Khagram, Sanjeev, James V. Riker, and Kathryn Sikkink (eds.). 2002. *Restructuring world politics: Transnational social movements, networks, and norms.* Minneapolis: University of Minnesota Press.

Latour, Bruno. 1996. On actor-network theory: A few clarifications. *Soziale Welt* 47:369–81.

———. 2005. *Reassembling the social: An introduction to actor-network-theory.* New York: Oxford University Press.

Leitner, Helga, Claire Pavlik, and Eric Sheppard. 2002. Networks, governance, and the politics of scale: Inter-urban networks and the European Union. In A. Herod and M. W. Wright, eds., *Geographies of power: Placing scale,* 274-303. Malden, MA: Blackwell.

MassDivest. 1983. *Make it in Massachusetts, not South Africa: How we won divestment legislation.* New York: American Committee on Africa.

McAdam, Doug, John D. McCarthy, and Mayer N. Zald (eds.). 1996. *Comparative perspectives on social movements.* Cambridge, UK: Cambridge University Press.

Melucci, Alberto. 1996. *Challenging codes: Collective action in the information age.* Cambridge, UK: Cambridge University Press.

Miller, Byron A. 2000. *Geography and social movements.* Minneapolis: University of Minnesota Press.

Nesbitt, Prexy. 1986. *Apartheid in our living rooms.* Chicago: Midwest Research.

Offe, Claus. 1987. Challenging the boundaries of institutional politics: Social movements since the 1960s. In C. S. Maier, ed., *Changing boundaries of the political,* 63-105. Cambridge, UK: Cambridge University Press.

Plummer, Brenda Gayle. 1996. *Rising wind: Black Americans and U.S. foreign affairs, 1935–1960.* Chapel Hill: University of North Carolina Press.

Robinson, Randall. 1998. *Defending the spirit: A black life in America.* New York: Dutton.

Rucht, Dieter. 2000. Distant issue movements in Germany: Empirical description and theoretical reflection. In J. Guidry, M.D. Kennedy, and M.N. Zald, eds., *Globalizations and social movements: Culture, power, and the transnational public sphere,* 76-105. Ann Arbor: University of Michigan Press.

Sassen, Saskia. 2006. *Territory, authority, rights: From medieval to global assemblages.* Princeton, NJ: Princeton University Press.

Sewell, William H., Jr. 2001. Space in contentious politics. In R.R. Aminzade, J.A. Goldstone, D. McAdam, et al., eds., *Silence and voice in the study of contentious politics,* 51-88. Cambridge, UK: Cambridge University Press.
Skocpol, Theda. 2002. United States: From membership to advocacy. In R.D. Putnam, ed., *Democracies in flux,* 103-36. Oxford: Oxford University Press.
Tarrow, Sidney. 1994. *Power in movement.* Cambridge, UK: Cambridge University Press.
———. 1996. States and opportunities: The political structuring of social movements. In D. McAdam, J.D. McCarthy, and M.N. Zald, eds., *Comparative perspectives on social movements,* 41-61. Cambridge, UK: Cambridge University Press.
———. 1998. *Power in movement: Social movements and contentious politics*, 2d ed. Cambridge, UK: Cambridge University Press.
Tennant, Evalyn W. 2006. Making a movement national: Scale, structure, and strategy in U.S. anti-apartheid activism. Ph.D. diss., political science, University of Chicago.
Tilly, Charles. 1984. Social movements and national politics. In C. Bright and S. Harding, eds., *Statemaking and social movements,* 297–317. Ann Arbor: University of Michigan Press.
United Nations. 1994. *The United Nations and apartheid, 1948–1984, the United Nations blue book series.* New York: United Nations Department of Public Information.
Von Eschen, Penny M. 1997. *Race against empire: Black Americans and anti-colonialism, 1937–1957.* Ithaca, NY: Cornell University Press.
Warner, Michael. 2002. Publics and counterpublics. *Public Culture* 14(1):49–90.

CHAPTER 7

Deciphering the Space and Scale of Global Nomadism

Subjectivity and Counterculture in a Global Age

ANTHONY D'ANDREA

Studies on globalization have mostly focused on the nature of economic, technological, and sociodemographic transformations and their impact on urban and nation-state systems. When not ignored, the cultural is residually considered as reactive identities and ideologies that adapt to those "infrastructural" transformations. Conversely, it would be a mistake to reverse relations of causality, claiming the primacy of the cultural over the global, by means of an analytical focus on micro-interactions and motivations behind transnational flows and circuits. Beyond the investigation of transnational flows and macro-institutions, more studies about the entwinement between global and cultural processes must be carried out. This chapter seeks to address cultural globalization as a realm where new forms of subjectivity and identity are being developed in a dialectic interplay with major global processes. In this sense, globalization refers to the sheer intensification of processes of mobility, digitalization, multiculturalism, and reflexivity.

As globalization indexes the potential for cultural transformation, I chose to examine the relations of affinity between globalization and countercultures. This choice is methodologically strategic. As I seek to demonstrate, countercultures express and amplify global processes, resulting in sociocultural patterns that are fluidic, metamorphic, and reflexive. More specifically, notwithstanding the general pattern of co-optation by the economic, social, and moral mainstream, countercultures typically uphold aesthetic-hedonistic projects that seek to eschew the colonization of social life. In terms of social register, countercultures are primarily produced and consumed within specific segments of artists, bohemians, and expatriates who typically inhabit peripheral zones of global cities and tourist regions. They employ bodily, social, and symbolic practices identified in a cosmopolitan culture of expressive individualism. These formations have attracted the attention of scholars and business analysts, who have noted that countercultural practices and ideologies gradually diffuse across wider segments of the middle class, even if in fragmented, mitigated, and recoded forms (Brooks 2000; Florida 2002; Lloyd 2006; Stalnaker 2002). More specifically, due to their marginal and hypermobile components, I consider these expressive expatriates as an empirical instance of a global pattern of neo-nomadism (D'Andrea 2007).

This chapter addresses the analytical categories Saskia Sassen proposes in the book introduction, as references in the development of new methodologies of translocality in complex globalization. In the current age, sociocultural formations tend to acquire hypermobile, fluidic, and metamorphic traits, which cannot be properly captured by means of conventional methodologies based on the macro–micro dichotomy alone. It is necessary to develop multiscalar methodologies capable of addressing the mutuality of causes and effects across spatial, subjective, and systemic domains. The following section examines the emergence of Techno and New Age countercultures as examples of how globalization problematizes the nature of the cultural. Afterward, an anthropological analysis is provided of the meanings of global deterritorialization as a mechanism that constitutes contemporary countercultures in their diasporic and nomadologic features. Such deterritorialization begs the question of what happens with these hypermobile formations as they interact with local economies and moralities. Furthermore, such interaction is an example of the logic that underlies complex globalization (Urry 2003, p. 126). Moreover, to specify the transformative nature of cultural globalization, I conceptualize hypermobile countercultures within the perspective of critical theories of modernity proposed by Max Weber and Michel Foucault. As a result, I suggest the concept of neo-nomadism as an ideal type that reflects and anticipates cultural predicaments of globalization: a way of examining and understanding the post-identitarian nature of global hypermobility. In sum, the empirical and conceptual discussion developed here provides resources for the study of how subjectivities, identities, and sociabilities are being reshaped under conditions of globalization.

Cultural Globalization as Cultural Change: The Countercultural Condition

To talk about cultural globalization is to talk about cultural transformation, that is, the dissolution and retooling of traditional and modern ways of life, along with the emergence of new forms of identity that are defined by their fluidic, de-essentialized and reflexive nature. I have thus selected countercultures as a privileged way of analyzing globalization, for they intrinsically refer to the possibility of cultural change in explicit, assertive, and radicalized ways. Countercultures can be briefly defined as cultural projects centered on the aesthetic-erotic experimentation of unconventional forms of subjectivity and community, all of which is coupled with a critique of modernity within modernity. And, as such, countercultures typically manifest cosmopolitan, expressive, and reflexive features that emerge from the very modern dynamics that they criticize.

It is in this context that *subculture, counterculture,* and *alternative culture* can be differentiated. A *subculture* refers to the shared values, symbols, and practices of a group whose members also adhere to and function in wider societies. The notion of *alternative* implies subcultures that seek some level of autonomy from or replacement of major social models. *Alternative* is thus broader and looser than *counterculture.* The latter is characterized by higher levels of dissatisfaction and rejection of Western institutions and moralities, as well as by the cultivation of transgressive practices and lifestyles. A counterculture can be seen as a heteroclite movement of contestation, often taking the form of radicalized subcultures and providing a powerful ideological referent in times of crisis. In the scope of this study, let us turn our attention to alternative formations that uphold countercultural drives and historicities genealogically referring to the sixties' upheaval and, further back, to nineteenth-century romanticism.

We must ask therefore what constitutes a counterculture in a global age. Wallerstein (1989) claims that the late 1960s upheaval crystallized the very first impact of globalization on the cultural. However, a main limitation in the scholarship on countercultures is that it has mostly focused on historical analyses of the 1960s radicalism, the 1970s decline, and the 1980s co-optation, or on sociological typologies of deviant subcultures and cults (Frank 1997; McKay 1996; Roszak 1995; Zellner 1995). The concept virtually disappeared from debates about the nature of cultural politics and modernity. Nevertheless, such presumed decline actually ignores that the 1960s counterculture has fragmented in a variety of single-issue movements and parallel academic studies. In all of these cases exists a shared, basic dissatisfaction with the promises, modes, and rewards of modernity. Contemporarily, Techno and New Age seem to have inherited such countercultural spirit in contexts of globalization, taking multiple forms and modulations, from experimental subcultures into popular movements and mass commodities, and from bohemian districts of global cities and expatriate communities into mass media, shopping malls, and public debate.

Even though studies on Techno and New Age do not usually interface, a careful comparison reveals a common horizon: the shaping of nonconformist lifestyles centered on mobility and marginality, often associated with interstitial, leisurely, and artistic economies; the cultivation of aesthetic and erotic practices with a meaning upholding expressive forms of individualism, practices, and meanings that are powerfully dramatized in collective rituals entailing charismatic experiences of self-transcendence; and their affinity with cosmopolitan interests, shared in self-marginalized communities of bohemians or expatriates in peripheries of global cities and tourist resorts. In consonance with Wallerstein's (1989) claim about the affinity between counterculture and globalization, Techno and New Age practices, lifestyles, and economies have benefited from the acceleration of flows, digital technologies, and multiculturalism as well as from the deleterious effects of neoliberal capitalism on labor and welfare systems. At a political level, countercultures question the nation-state's drive to control the population in a territory, thus resonating with the global crisis of state governance. At a cultural level, neo-nomads have been experimenting with rootlessness, strangeness, and reflexivity much before these tropes became celebrated by media and academia as defining predicaments of contemporary life. The seemingly disparate practices and imaginaries of Techno and New Age tend to coalesce in a digital art religion that arises globally.

Within the scope of global and critical studies, the emergence of global countercultures can be considered in three different ways. First, in the context of globalization, Techno and New Age comprise transnational formations that suffer as well as induce the deterritorializing effects of globalization, which can be understood in abstract terms as the reconfiguration of the relationship between the social and the local or, more precisely, as the disembededness of the former in relation to the latter. More empirically, processes of global hypermobility, digitalization, and reflexivity must be taken into account in the investigation of Techno and New Age. Their cultivation of practices of self-formation and sociality seem to be in tune with pressures and trends of globalization.

Second, in the context of modernity, Techno and New Age reflect the crisis of the modern nation-state. According to Foucault (1976), the state reproduces itself by means of its ability to control and strengthen individual and collective bodies. This is done by a series of institutional ideological devices — known as *biopower* at a macrolevel of population management and as *sexuality* at a microlevel of subjective interiorities — constructing the modern subject of confession and discipline. In this light, the point is to examine to what extent Techno and New Age operate as a counterapparatus centered on an aesthetic-erotic ethos of the self that departs from the modern apparatus of sexuality and biopower. It is thus necessary to analyze the social life, practices, and ideologies of neo-nomads as empirical grounds for assessing the possibility of new subjectivity and sociability forms, hypothesized as instances of globalization in a post-national, post-traditional, and post-sexuality order.

Third, in contrast to postmodern studies that rely on fictional materials, this investigation scrutinizes empirical phenomena that instantiate seminal tropes of postmodernism: the nomad, the cyberpunk, and the neotribe (Deleuze and Guattari 1980; Featherstone and Burrows 1995; Maffesoli 1996). In connection with the previous point, I seek to demonstrate how nomadic, hedonic, and spiritual practices integrate in a counter-apparatus that eschews systemic regimes — of state, market, religion — and enables a field of possible agencies entwined with a new cultural global order.

Scales of Hypermobility: Meanings of Deterritorialization

Considering their globalized nature, it is a methodological challenge to define a proper scale of analysis by which contemporary countercultures can be addressed. Techno and New Age are typically produced and dramatized amid segments of self-marginalized subjects, usually highly mobile postmetropolitan individuals who, disaffected with life conditions in the mainstream society, migrate to marginal areas of global cities or to remote paradises. These places seem to provide better conditions by which they can develop an alternative lifestyle that integrates labor, leisure, and spirituality in a meaningful, holistic manner. They become artists, therapists, exotic traders, and bohemian workers who live and circulate within a global circuit of countercultural practice. While globally interconnecting exotic places, such as Ibiza, Goa, Bali, San Francisco, and Bahia, as well as global cities, they constitute a negative diaspora that rejects the homeland while identified by a cosmopolitan culture of expressive individualism. Their life strategies and wider contexts are dramatized in ritual practices, such as rave parties and spiritual gatherings, which more deeply index a nomadic spirituality: a core category that dramatizes and informs flexible subjectivities navigating neoliberal environments.

For neo-nomads, mobility is more than spatial displacement. In their attempts to eschew state and market regimes, mobility is deployed as a basic component of their economic strategies as well as of their identity modes. In any of the locations they inhabit, when the annual tourist and party season ends, they travel to other nodes of the global countercultural circuit in global cities or tourist resorts. They then rejoin this deterritorialized community of expressive expatriation and continue trading goods and services in hippie markets, exotic boutiques, nightclubs, and spiritual retreats that cater to wealthy residents, tourists, and other global nomads just like themselves. Outlining a geographic triangle, they also visit family members and friends in the original homeland, where they may work — not necessarily in alternative jobs — and update welfare benefits (e.g., pensions, retirements, stipends, aids) that will complement their mostly informal incomes. In any case, it is taken for granted that they will be going somewhere "after the season," if not effectively, at least always potentially. They frequently talk about remote locations where they have been, will return, or know someone. Mobility is second nature to global nomads, as traveling actualizes both the economic and cultural features of their charismatic, exotically self-fashioned lifestyles.

Expressive expatriates confer a special meaning to traveling, signified as a potentially transformative practice of self-formation. Their revisits to alien hinterlands are described as spiritual experiences that touch their inner selves. In this spirit, travel may also include participation in spiritual and party centers (e.g., raves, cathartic therapies, meditation retreats, shamanic sessions), all of which are deemed more powerful when carried out in places of symbolic relevance (and relative laxity of state surveillance). In sum, because spatial displacements entwine with self-shaping practices, mobility is a component of subjectivity formation among global nomads. It both reflects the instability of labor in flexible capitalist contexts as well as the fluidity of identity formation in a globalized postmodern world.

These hypermobile subjects should not be confused with migrants, tourists, and other expatriates. Whereas tourists consume exotic places for short periods and within tightly structured labor and leisure life cycles, neo-nomads assume remote locations as homes for extended periods and within a holistic orientation that seeks to integrate labor, leisure, and spirituality. Though scorning the commodification of experience characteristic of conventional tourism (MacCanell 1989), as global nomads become veteran journeyers they do not enthuse about the local cultures they engage with in alien lands. In other words, neo-nomads rather emulate the skeptical, romantic, and elitist gaze of the post-tourist (Urry 2002).

Likewise, whereas migrants typically display very localized minds, that is, orienting melancholic identities to their homelands, countercultural expatriates pose a radically different picture. They belong to a universe of displaced peoples with *displaced* minds. Drifting away from the center, they nostalgically move toward rustic paradises, as incarnations of a smooth space of desire and experimentation: 'u-topia' as '*non-space*', by definition. In their familiarity with rootlessness, strangeness, and metamorphosis, global nomads engender post-national identities that question the primacy of fixity in sedentary civilization while claiming to embrace the global as a new home and reference. For all of the material and cultural differences, global nomads cannot be conflated with the sedentary citizen, while closely resembling the figure of the expatriate (Hannerz 1996). In Deleuzian terms, tourists and migrants belong to the striatic space of dwellers, whereas countercultural expatriates live by the lines of flight of nomads in a desiring machine.

Spaces of Hypermobility: Economies of Reterritorialization

Considering that transnational flows must reterritorialize in specific locations, space is a crucial dimension of analysis. Because of historical, geographical, and cultural characteristics, places such as Ibiza and Goa have provided favorable material and semiotic references for global countercultures to foster. In addition to being linked by the transnational circulation of countercultural elements, both places are paradoxical paradises with a similar picture: among the wealthiest places in their respective countries, Ibiza and Goa depend on leisure industries that seek to appropriate countercultural spaces, practices, and imaginaries as commodity forms for consumptive capital.

Global countercultures thus have to interact with various national cultures, institutions, and forces at the local level. It is sometimes claimed that Techno and New Age merely express the escapist drives and the exotic consumerist needs of a stressed middle class. It is also claimed that they are ideological expressions for validating the individualist needs of an emerging global middle class. Though not entirely disagreeable, such criticism must be reassessed and better qualified, since factors surrounding the emergence, conditions, and implications of global countercultures are not yet properly understood. Their development may take multifarious forms and directions: social diffusion (from underground to mainstream) and distinction (production of more substyles), transgression and co-option, singularization and commodification, reflexivity and fundamentalism, utopia and dystopia.

Furthermore, by territorializing in semiperipheral zones, global countercultures interfere with local political economies. Historically, the presence of alternative expatriates in remote villages has provided an important source of income for a large segment of the local community (Cerda-Subirachs and Rodriguez-Branchat 1999; Davis 2004; Joan I Mari 1997; New York Times 2004; Odzer 1995; Paul 1937; Ramon-Fajarnes 2000; Rozenberg 1990; Saldanha 2004; Wilson 1997). For example, following the rise of New Age interests, since the early 1970s a relatively rich circuit of spiritual tourism has evolved in India, comprising revamped ashrams and yoga centers that cater to a regular number of Westerners. In the case of Techno dance, in addition to ancillary activities (e.g., taxing, lodging, restaurants), trance parties — improperly named *raves* — have become joint ventures between Indian gangs and Western disc jockeys. Whereas the former aim at profiting through the rental of sound systems, bar sales, and police bribes, the latter seek subcultural prestige by engendering shamanic excitement in the scene.

However, utopian spaces are gradually invaded by tourists and migrants, in a rhythm set by local and global strategies of development. In this scenario, expressive expatriates become objects and indicators, victims and beneficiaries of modernization. As a pattern, leisure economies create economic opportunities for natives and expatriates to make a living, sometimes with an exceptional gain. But such economic symbiosis is unstable, for the gradual commodification of paradisiacal spaces, practices, and imaginaries undermines the sustainability of both traditional and countercultural ways of life. Big hotel chains overtake the scene as main actors in the encroachment of tourism, resulting in environmental problems and social exclusion (Dantas 1999; *Guardian* 2006; Newman 2001; Ramon-Fajarnes 2000; Routledge 2000; Rozenberg 1990; Sen 1999). Inflation, overwork, pollution, surveillance, and urban sprawling compel expressive expatriates to reevaluate their position in such turbulent environments of mainstream labor, law, and morality. Even worse, natives, who initially welcomed them, now tend to turn against expressive expatriates, blaming them for the malaises of untrammeled modernization.

Transnational flows and the resulting circuits and networks therefore are dynamically reshaped through their interaction with a variety of agents, forces, and structures in varyingly volatile arrangements. For example, the repression of rave culture in the United Kingdom in the early 1990s contributed to the rise of corporate clubbing in Britain while also providing a new impetus to the party scenes of Ibiza and Goa. Likewise, the crisis of clubbing in the United Kingdom and Ibiza by the mid-2000s seems to be somehow related to a modest but significant rave renaissance in the United Kingdom. Throughout the 2000s, northern Goans have resented the police repression of the Techno party scene for stifling their main source of income. Every season, authorities in Panaji, the state capital, have to recalibrate their decisions to accommodate diverging interests of business, villages, and urban civil society. In sum, by means of flows and circuits cutting across nations and regions, global countercultures are shaped through attritions and disjunctures among social, political, and economic domains (Appadurai 1996; Hannerz 1996; Urry 2003).

Post-Sexuality: A Theory of Subjectivity Formation in a Post-National Global Age

In a theoretical analysis, the emergence of transnational countercultures must be understood in contexts of complex globalization and post-industrial capitalism. The iron cage of modernity is rapidly becoming the silicon cage of techno-financial capitalism. In it, the human body is reduced to a carbon cage, a map of genes and rights colonized by high-tech engineering, legal intervention, and amoral commodification. At the semiotic level, the fast production and circulation of signs undermine the subject's ability to make sense of reality, forcing them to make dramatic and uneasy decisions (Appadurai 1996; Giddens 1991; Jameson 1991).

On the other hand, while corroding all claims of essential legitimacy by old traditions, globalization engenders post-traditional forms of identity that are predicated on reflexive and cosmopolitan tropes, assuming the form of detachments from provincial identities and strangeness within and outside the self (Cheah and Robbins 1998). The problematization of locality making must be seen as a resource rather than as a barrier for the production of meaning and identity. In this case, the retrieval of reflexive meaning from global chaos can contribute to overcoming the corrosive effects of global commodification (Turner 1994). It is through the interplay between local environs and global processes that such aesthetic hermeneutics may enable a reconfiguration of time–space notions and structures of affection and belonging. As the production of localities and of subjectivities are intrinsically interrelated (Appadurai 1996; Povinelli and Chauncey 1999), the self consequently becomes the new strategic possibility, an open project of reflexive elaboration within a life politics (Foucault and Lotringer 1989; Giddens 1992). The question then becomes to demonstrate how reflexive subjectivities are formed within deterritorialized conditions.

Among neo-nomads, horizontal, or spatial, displacements come along with vertical displacements, or self-identity. Expressive expatriates, New Agers, ravers, and bohemian travelers define their identity in relation to practices of spatial and cultural mobility. In this realm, spiritual, travel, and psychedelic practices deconstruct and recode the modern subject in experiences colloquially referred to as *trips* into and out of the self. Poles of mystic contemplation and ascetic action are reconfigured in hedonist forms of innerworldly redemption (Corsten 1999; Weber 1913). The drive for mobility indexes the drive for extraordinary experiences of self-transformation while also expressing fears and aspirations about the uncertainties and conditions of globalization.

The simultaneity of multinational backgrounds, nomadic practices, and transpersonal experiences is a central feature of the neo-nomadic identity.

By exploring such limit experiences (Foucault 1978; Jay 1993) in transgressive cults of orgiastic sensuality (Weber 1913), Techno and New Age provide liminal sites for the cultivation of cosmopolitan nomadism (i.e., mobility as lifestyle) by which alternative subjects attempt to make sense of their lives in contemporary contexts . The familiarity of countercultures with experiences and predicaments of the global illustrates the richness of Techno and New Age as interesting sites for the investigation and anticipation of emerging realities of globalization.

Hence, theories claiming that alternative subjects are dropped out by neoliberal capitalism are unable to explain why and how they make critical decisions regarding their life strategies. Certainly, material contexts introduce powerful conditions that shape their life choices and conduct. However, away from the alienation, routine, and stress of modern life — whether technocratic or neoliberal — alternative subjects seek to integrate labor, leisure, and spirituality in a meaningful way, irreducible to economic explanation. In other words, global nomads attempt to engender holistic charisma in a fragmented and disenchanted world. Countercultures precede, coexist with, and may survive neoliberalism and are thus better understood in their problematic dialogue with modernity.

By assembling nomadic, digital, and spiritual apparatuses, New Age and Techno constitute a common space of subjectivity formation and social critique. Their pragmatic strategies may diverge: New Agers cultivate the Romantic shaping of the self as inner substance, whereas Techno freaks celebrate the self-shattering shamanism of god-techno-machine. Nevertheless, both movements deploy material-symbolic devices that seek to foster alternative experiences of the self, life strategies, and postcommunities. As long as their lines of flight are kept open, Techno and New Age will remain as potential sites of experience and meaning of post-national and post-sexuality identities.

Spaces and Scales of Complexity: Subjectivity in a Global Age

In this chapter, the notion of neo-nomadism is based on two premises. First, current understandings of globalization — developed on notions of network, diaspora, and cosmopolitanism — are insufficient for addressing emerging trends and possibilities of globalization, notably, the post-identitarian predicament of hypermobility. Second, having assumed self-marginalized, expressive expatriates as an empirical instance of global mobility, this study has sought to address the cultural impact of hypermobility on self-identities and socialities.

The neo-nomad is an ideal type in the Weberian sense, formulated on the productive tension between evidence and concept. On the one hand, it refers to a minority of high-modern renegades involved in hypermobile practices of space and identity whose meanings refer to an attempt to evade mainstream regimes. In fact, these subjects are mobile in varying degrees, as only a few remain permanently on the road — as mistakenly thought about nomads in general. Most expressive expatriates live in one or two foreign places and travel intermittently across exotic and homeland locations in geographic triangulation. They must adhere to a period of rest and refueling as a condition for further displacements. This pattern confirms the claim about the dialectic of mobility and mooring as a key component of complex globalization: "Overall it is the moorings that enable movements. And it is the dialectic of mobility/moorings that produces social complexity" (Urry 2003, p. 126).

One the other hand, the neo-nomad as a concept addresses the fluidic and metamorphic nature of subjectivity under conditions of globalization, specifically regarding the impact of hypermobility on the self. "Nomadism: vertiginous progression toward deconstructing identity; molecularisation of the self" (Braidotti 1994, p. 16). Globalization has a corrosive effect on conventional forms of identity while opening up reflexive and nihilist possibilities (Appadurai 1996; Beck, Giddens, and Lash 1994; Turner 1994). However, by overemphasizing the mapping of flows and networks, the scholarship has largely ignored the empirical analysis of subjectivity and desire under the deterritorializing effects of globalization (Burawoy and Gille 2000; Gille and Riain 2002; Povinelli and Chauncey 1999).

At a level of subjectivity formation, hypermobility is manifested in identity forms that are pragmatic and adverbially temporal (Maffesoli 1996). Neo-nomads migrate through sites of practice and experience in search of excitement and insight into themselves: "Yesterday I was into tai chi, today I am into yoga, and tomorrow I may try Zen." This pattern defines a nomadic spirituality that resonates with ambivalent trends toward reflexive individualism or ephemeral consumerism (Brooks 2000; Carrete and King 2005; Lash 1994; Taylor 1991). In the ethical realm, expressive individualism may crystallize in an aesthetics of existence that eschews the imperialism of science and rebalances the fragmentation of life principles (Foucault 1984; Goldman 1988; Weber 1918). Ironically, the content of neo-nomadic subjectivity is made not of substance but of flows: "The nomad does not stand for homelessness, or compulsive displacement; it is rather a figuration for the kind of subject who has relinquished all idea, desire, or nostalgia for fixity. This figuration expresses the desire for an identity made of transitions, successive shifts, and coordinated changes, without and against an essential unity" (Braidotti 1994, p. 22)

More widely, *nomadology* refers to the possibility of cultural change in a global age. The postidentitarian predicament of hypermobility correlates with a logic of resistance and control that shapes dissent in contemporary societies (Deleuze 1995; Hardt and Negri 2000). At the local level, neo-nomads and sedentary societies interact in a fragile symbiosis. Expressive expatriates have conferred a special charisma to the places they inhabit, whether bohemian districts of global cities or remote tourist-prone regions. Yet, despite fleeing the mainstream, they are soon followed by large numbers of backpackers and tourists as well as by labor migrants and urban developers. As a result, though leisure industries create economic opportunities for natives and expatriates to make a living, the gradual commodification, or gentrification, of alternative venues, practices, and imaginaries undermine the sustainability of neo-nomadic formations. Inflation, overwork, surveillance, and social stress compel these subjects to reevaluate life strategies within proximate contexts and available alternatives. In this sense, "the more [countercultures] capture the feeling of modern alienation and anomie, the better they serve consumptive capital" (Povinelli 2000, p. 521).

How dwellers and tourists are enticed to experiment with a neo-nomadic lifestyle is a question that requires further investigation. Yet in the places that expressive expatriates share with sedentary peoples, it is not uncommon to witness young tourists inquiring about alternative gigs in hippie markets, nightclubs, rave parties, and spiritual resorts and later dropping out to be seen in other nodes of the global countercultural circuit — whether it be for a season or lifetime.

In this connection, a final note reintroduces the issue of space. Ibiza and Goa are as intoxicating as the hedonistic practices they host. On the one hand, it is obvious that limit experiences and countercultures may occur anywhere in the world — and without recourse to intoxicating elements such as music, drugs, dance, or sex. On the other hand, there is a general belief that emphasizes the importance of being there — in India, in Ibiza, in the "Otherland" — for someone to be able to experience life and being in the realm of the ecstatic or sublime. As such, travel talk, spiritual talk, and drug talk endow as much meaning as prestige on those who have been there: to extraordinary places and dimensions. Yet as the world shrinks, places like Goa, Ibiza, and Bali remain as problematic icons for the expression and commodification of alternative lifestyles. Goa parties, New Age Orientalisms, Ibiza-style clubbing, and hippie fashion have become signifiers with a global circulation, standing in close proximity to circuits of consumptive capital. Paradoxically, as noted, the more countercultures capture the desire for charismatic reenchantment, the more they serve consumptive capital (Best 1997; Povinelli 2000). Nevertheless, how countercultures prompt social and cultural change through the very capitalist and national forms that they criticize remains as a critical question.

Works Cited

Appadurai, A. 1996. *Modernity at large: Cultural dimensions of globalization*. Minneapolis: University of Minnesota Press.

Beck, U., A. Giddens, and S. Lash. 1994. *Reflexive modernization: Politics, tradition and aesthetics in the modern social order*. Cambridge, UK: Polity Press in association with Blackwell.

Best, B. 1997. Over-the-counter-culture: Retheorizing resistance in popular culture. In S. Redhead, ed., *The clubcultures reader: Readings in popular cultural studies*, 18–35. Oxford: Blackwell.

Braidotti, R. 1994. *Nomadic subjects: Embodiment and sexual difference in contemporary feminist theory*. New York: Columbia University Press.

Brooks, D. 2000. *Bobos in paradise: The new upper class and how they got there*. New York: Touchstone.

Burawoy, M., and Z. Gille. 2000. *Global ethnography: Forces, connections, and imaginations in a post-modern world*. Berkeley: University of California Press.

Carrete, J., and R. King. 2005. *Selling spirituality: The silent takeover of religion*. London: Routledge.

Cerda-Subirachs, J., and R. Rodriguez-Branchat. 1999. *La repressio franquista del moviment hippy a formentera (1968–1970)*. Eivissa: Res Publica.

Cheah, P., and B. Robbins. 1998. *Cosmopolitics: thinking and feeling beyond the nation, Social Text Collective*, vol. 14. Minneapolis: University of Minnesota Press.

Corsten, M. 1999. Ecstasy as 'this-wordly path to salvation': the techno youth scene as a proto-religious collective. In *Alternative Religions among European Youth* (ed.) L. Tomasi. Aldershot: Ashgate.

D'Andrea, A. 2007. *Global nomads: Techno and New Age as transnational countercultures in Ibiza and Goa*. London: Routledge.

Dantas, N. (ed.). 1999. *The transforming of Goa*. Mapusa, Goa: Other India.

Davis, E. 2004. Hedonic tantra: Golden Goa's trance transmission. In G. Saint-John, ed., *Rave culture and religion*, 256–272. London: Routledge.

Deleuze, G. 1995. Postscript on control societies. In *Negotiations*, 177–182. New York: Columbia University Press.

Deleuze, G., and F. Guattari. 1980. *A thousand plateaus: Capitalism and schizophrenia*, vol. 2. Minneapolis: University of Minnesota.

Featherstone, M., and R. Burrows (eds.). 1995. *Cyberspace, cyberbodies, cyberpunks: Cultures of technological embodiment*. London: Sage.

Florida, R. 2002. *The rise of the creative class: And how it's transforming work, leisure, community and everyday life*: New York: Basic Books.

Foucault, M. 1976. *Histoire de la sexualite I: La volonté de savoir*. Paris: Gallimard.

—. 1978. *Remarks on Marx*. New York: Semiotext(e).

———. 1984. The return of morality. In M. Foucault and S. Lotringer, *Foucault live: Interviews, 1961–1984*, 465–472. New York: Semiotext(e).

Foucault, M., and S. Lotringer. 1989. *Foucault live: Interviews, 1961–1984*. New York: Semiotext(e).

Frank, T. 1997. *The conquest of cool — business culture, counterculture, and the rise of hip consumerism*. Chicago: University of Chicago Press.

Giddens, A. 1991. *Modernity and self-identity: Self and society in the late modern age*. Cambridge, MA: Blackwell.

———. 1992. *The transformation of intimacy: love, sexuality and eroticism in modern societies*. Oxford: Polity Press in association with Basil Blackwell.
Gille, Z., and S. Riain. 2002. Global ethnography. *Annual Review of Sociology* 28:271–95.
Goldman, H. 1988. *Max Weber and Thomas Mann: Calling and the shaping of the self*. Berkeley: University of California Press.
Guardian. February 26, 2006. Ibiza rises up against blight of tourism. http://observer.guardian.co.uk/world/story/0, 1718122,00.html
Hannerz, U. 1996. *Transnational connections: Culture, people, places*. London: Routledge.
Hardt, M., and A. Negri. 2000. *Empire*. Cambridge, MA: Harvard University Press.
Jameson, F. 1991. *Postmodernism, or, the cultural logic of late capitalism*. Durham: Duke University Press.
Jay, M. 1993. The Limits of Limit-Experience: Bataille and Foucault. Berkeley, CA: Center for German and European Studies, University of California.
Joan I Mari, B. 1997. *Historia de Ibiza*. Eivissa: Editorial Mediterrania-Eivissa.
Lash, S. 1994. Reflexivity and its doubles: Structure, aesthetics, community. In U. Beck, A. Giddens, and S. Lash, eds., *Reflexive modernization: Politics, tradition and aesthetics in the modern social order*. Stanford: Stanford University.
Lloyd, R. 2006. *Neo-bohemia: Art and commerce in the postindustrial city*. New York: Routledge.
Maffesoli, M. 1996. *The time of tribes: The decline of individualism in mass society*. London: Sage.
MacCanell, D. 1989. *The tourist: A new theory of the leisure class*. Berkeley: University of California Press.
McKay, G. 1996. *Senseless acts of beauty: Cultures of resistance since the sixties*. London: Verso.
New York Times. March 30, 2004. Aging hippies prospering in lush Bali. www.nytimes.com
Newman, R. 2001. *Of umbrellas, goddesses and dreams: Essays on Goan culture and society*. Mapusa, Goa: Other Indian.
Odzer, C. 1995. *Goa freaks: My hippie years in India*. New York: Blue Moon Books.
Paul, E. 1937. *The life and death of a Spanish town*. New York: Random House.
Povinelli, E. 2000. Consuming *Geist*: Popontology and the spirit of capital in indigenous Australia. *Public Culture: Millenial Capitalism and the Culture of Neoliberalism* 12:501–28.
Povinelli, E., and G. Chauncey. 1999. Thinking sexuality transnationally. *GLQ: A Journal of Gay and Lesbian Studies* 5:1–11.
Ramon-Fajarnes, E. 2000. *Historia del turismo en Ibiza y formentera*. Ibiza: Eivissa: Genial.
Roszak, T. 1995. *The making of a counterculture: Reflections on the technocratic society and its youthful opposition*. Berkeley: University of California Press.
Routledge, P. 2000. Consuming Goa — tourist site as dispensable space. *Economic and Political Weekly* 35:2647–56.
Rozenberg, D. 1990. *Ibiza, una isla para otra vida: inmigrantes utópicos, turismo y cambio cultural* (Colección Monografias; n. 110. Madrid: Centro de Investigaciones Sociológicas: Siglo XXI de España.
Saldanha, A. 2004. Goa trance and trance in Goa: smooth striations. In G. Saint-John, ed., *Rave culture and religion*, 273–286. London: Routledge.

Sassen, Saskia. 2007. Introduction: Deciphering the Global. In Saskia Sassen, ed. *Deciphering the global: Its scales, spaces, and subjects*, 1–18. New York and London: Routledge.

Sen, G. 1999. *Goa under siege*. Magic Lantern Foundation DVD.

Stalnaker, S. 2002. *Hub culture: The next wave of urban consumers*. Singapore: John Wiley & Sons.

Taylor, C. 1991. *The ethics of authenticity*. Cambridge, MA: Harvard Univ. Press.

Turner, B.S. 1994. *Orientalism, postmodernism, and globalism*. London: Routledge.

Urry, J. 2002. *The tourist gaze*, 2d ed. Berkeley: University of California Press.

———. 2003. *Global complexity*. Malden, MA: Blackwell.

Wallerstein, I. 1989. Revolution in the world-system: Theses and queries. *Theory and Society* 18:431–48.

Weber, M. 1913. Religious groups (the sociology of religion). In G. Roth, ed., *Economy and society*, 399–634. Berkeley: University of California Press.

———. 1918. Politics as a vocation. In C. Wright Mills, ed., *From Max Weber: Essays in sociology*, 77–128. New York: Oxford.

Wilson, D. 1997. Strategies for sustainability: Lessons from Goa and the Seychelles. In M.J. Stabler, ed., *Tourism and sustainability: Principles to practice*, 173–198. New York: CAB International.

Zellner, W. 1995. *Countercultures: A sociological analysis*. New York: St. Martin's Press.

CHAPTER 8

Outsourcing Difference

Expatriate Training and the Disciplining of Culture

HEATHER HINDMAN

In Kathmandu, culture is currency. Authenticity is worn on the sleeve of every shopkeeper and street vendor, tourists trade stories of their visits to real Nepali homes, and aid workers worry if their new project is culturally appropriate. Yet there is one culture that is nearly invisible within this arena because it is not recognized as culture. As one Irish woman who had been living in Nepal for four years asked me as we discussed the lives of foreigners, "Why are you talking to us when there is so much culture all around?"[1] For her, Nepalis had culture, Kathmandu had culture, but white Euro-Americans were culture-free. She was baffled that an anthropologist — a professional culture collector — would be interested in her.[2]

There are many reasons why most expatriate residents in Kathmandu consider themselves to lack culture — or at least lack it in a way that might parallel its presence in Nepal. The contemporary research on alterity and otherness highlights the flight from difference (Fabian 2006; Malkki 1992; Todorov 1984; Trouillot 1991), but also struggles with its continuing importance as rhetoric and strategy. For white expatriates living in Nepal, the idea of being culture free takes on new importance through its reinforcement by institutions that give shape to the experience of living abroad. Looking not merely at the everyday lives of expatriates in Kathmandu but also at the disciplining structures that put them there reveals how understandings of difference are produced as a subsidiary effect at this middle level of global engagement (Malkki 1994; Levinas 1998; Joseph

2002). What is at stake, both theoretically and practically, in the delineation of the included and excluded is "...the irreducible urge to objectify *those people*...the selective, exclusionary strategy of projecting a delimited form of difference...that allows a normative center to operate" (Hartigan 2005, p. 3). It is the existence of a space for the putatively normal that expatriates must relearn in the context of a new life as a racial minority, and it is this lesson about the always-escaping but ever-present normal that allows transnational business to occupy the absent center (Lacan 1998; Zizek 2000). Furthermore, through the multiple levels of bureaucracy that insulate the mid-level workers, these ideas about difference are embodied as structured structures, and it is because they do not know how they came to hold these attitudes toward culture "that what they do has more meaning than they know" (Bourdieu 1992, p. 79).

The Elite Outsourced

Membership in the small expatriate community in Kathmandu changes constantly as workers rotate in and out of their three- to five-year postings in Nepal. Yet there is consistency to their behavior that is induced by the institutions that frame the expatriate experience. This chapter uses the compensation, selection, and training of expatriates as a means to explore how culture is codified and constructed within this seemingly cosmopolitan and multicultural population. The continuity of ideas is produced by a newly emergent system of training that is now largely outsourced to agencies that focus on seeking contracts for expatriate support services. It is through the seemingly scientific calculus of degrees of hardship and by lists of necessities and absences that those about to be sent abroad learn to understand their experience. More than the increasing number and mobility of global middlemen, the presence of agencies willing to take on the tasks of expatriate management has brought greater complexity to the field of international human resources management — outsourcing thus creates its own demand through specialization. The need for new specialized services is crafted by the providers, and with this greater complexity more tasks are outsourced, in an ever-increasing spiral, not unlike other developments in the global service industry (Sassen 2001, p. 99). The world crafted for expatriates by the expatriate services industry is one that thinks a great deal about belonging and home but confines difference to a very narrow domain.

For expatriates used to being reposted across the globe, there is stability in motion as they become accustomed to a style of movement rather than a particular place, thus producing an archipelago of expatriate enclaves that all share a sense of familiarity.[3] Expatriate pathways unsettle common notions about global mobilities, as cross-border movements are usually assumed to be unsettling, whereas in this case the pathway defines stability, and to some extent the boundaries, of the group. This stability is embedded in training and compensation practices as well as enduring institutions; thus, those about to move can access an extant grammar that places postings in hierarchical relation and that one can expect to endure. Tuesday is bridge night all over the world. Whether the increasing complexity of the field of expatriation services is a cause or a result of specialized service offerings, governments, nongovernmental organizations, and multinational corporations are all subcontracting compensation and training to external entities who prepare the family to go abroad, without regard to the industry in which they work or their destination. Yet Nepal's position as an "underdeveloped"[4] nation and site of "hardship" for employees situates it at an extreme of the international employment circuit. Nonetheless, the training received by those to be sent to Nepal follows a standard script, one that situates the experience of difference in ways that limit its scope and produce work as outside the domain of culture. These elite expatriates are living in an era where the world is both the marketplace and the labor pool for American business and where the limited space allowed for difference within the international elite labor management industry facilitates a simultaneous understanding of culture-free business and exchangeable culture — and in this recycles the rhetoric of flows first perpetuated by the academic discourse of globalization (Appadurai 1996; Ho 2005).

The limit to flows, rhetorically and practically, is often found in the intervention of the nation-state. The power of both national governments and nation-state thinking is what global employment seeks to overcome and yet is very much at the center of the endeavor; in fact, it is the ongoing importance of the nation-state that underlies why the deployment of expatriate workers is seen as useful. The state is no longer, if it ever was, self-evident and clearly bounded but instead might be found in a "myriad of other state-like institutions and processes that interpellate them [citizens] as individuals and as members of various communities" (Trouillot 2001, p. 133). Yet the worldview perpetuated within much of expatriate training as well as life abroad is one familiar from long-standing statist assumptions, a world of discrete entities in which culture is bound by political borders and exists in a simplistic relation with self-identity. International middlemen and their families physically transcend nation-state borders, yet it is the idea of people who travel as embodiments of their home, as *ex-patris*, that makes their movement necessary. The mission of the expatriate worker is to be loyal to a home nation and a home company where they are not and to act as the embodiment of a presumed organic connection of nation, state, culture, and identity.

The presumption of a one-to-one correlation of individual and nation is concomitant with a correlation of nation and state. Though the philosophical and to a certain degree ethnological and political underpinnings of the nation-state have complex genealogies, the particular form of nation-statist thinking that has the greatest impact on the situation of expatriacy is a presumption of a world of "formal horizontalities and symmetries" (Kelly and Kaplan 2001, p. 4). The United Nations (UN) acts as motivator for and instantiation of this configuration, which in its structure claims a formally equal of actors, yet this is undermined by the inequality of power structured by World War II, the Cold War, and their aftermath. This institution and its frameworks underpin much of the expatriate understanding of the world, particularly in Nepal where the UN is a major employer of expatriates. Within this logic, expatriates are able to act as acultural human beings with a shared diplomatic and developmental mission while wearing a cloak of culture, albeit one that binds them less than others.[5] Making difference fit within a narrowly defined institutional structure enables a shared dialogue wherein difference is merely a flavor. This mode of confining difference to structurally symmetrical categories, into niches, must be seen as a part of larger strategies of seemingly liberal accommodations to culture. If under this rhetoric, *culture* is protected, then all not protected by this mantle is vulnerable to attack. Difference is permitted only within a very narrow realm, and much of what remains is required to be universal.[6] The structuration of expatriate employment is what gives shape to these attitudes, often through implicit messages as much as explicit instruction.

Expatria as Work and Life

The casualization and flexibility of labor impacts these elite global workers as well as those more obviously disempowered by new forms of employment (Sassen 2000, pp. 5–6). The foreign service industry[7] is outsourcing a diverse array of tasks to private companies, and the jobs that career diplomats could once anticipate are increasingly taken over by political appointments or are disappearing entirely into outsourcing. Among international aid organizations, both governmental and private, full-time staff is shrinking as many tasks are bid out to private companies who work as subcontractors for the primary employer, often without receiving security or support from either entity.[8] One result of this shift in forms of employment is seen in the way both workers and employers understand the parameters and security of their jobs. Long hours, frequent travel, and complex compensation packages force expatriate families and their employers to engage in contentious negotiations over the ambiguous limits of work abroad. The worker's life is transformed completely by expatriation; in many ways the job is the most constant element of the mobile lives of families. The company is responsible for the entire life of the employee and his family,[9] — housing, legal status, and finances — thus, they demand that the employee give his entire life. One woman explained, after having to cancel a regular lunch date with a group of other expatriate women, that she had too many required social functions to have a social life. Between helping new arrivals and leading visitors on shopping trips, she felt that even her recreational time was consumed by company responsibilities.[10] This incorporation of the family into the male job responsibilities has reciprocal implications, as employees who give more than mere hours to the company expect the company to be responsible for aspects of their lives beyond work. The division between work and leisure (or lack thereof) in expatriate employment is set forth in the implicit injunctions that can be read from the terms of the contract. Thus, the extra allowance given to families for entertainment costs implies that social events will be an expected part of the job.

Assigned to Paradise

Expatriates complain about the hardships of life abroad to each other and to those outside the circuit. The responses of those outside the community are rarely sympathetic, and many see the laments as baseless. Particularly in Nepal, a setting many tourists and resident foreigners seek out as an appealing destination, the question posed to them is, "if you are so unhappy, why don't you just go home?" Nepal is seen by foreigners there by choice as Shangri-La,[11] and expatriates enjoy many of those paradisiacal elements of beauty and exoticism as well — and do so with servants, hot water, and a steady salary not enjoyed by other visitors. Yet most employees who accept international assignments have limited choice in where they are posted. The result is a perception of Nepal, not as a beautiful country but as a required career stepping stone, one that could have been filled by other countries. One expatriate woman, commenting on tension between expatriates and foreigners residing in Nepal for other reasons, noted that expatriates stay in Nepal for work, whereas the resident foreigners work in order to stay in Nepal.

Accepting an international assignment is frequently a means to "jump rank," meaning quicker promotions or the opportunity to gain job status not available in a home office. A young employee who might not be able to find assignment as a project manager in his home country may be hired at that level for an overseas assignment and then, having attained this rank, will retain it in future jobs. There are also situations in which work abroad is imposed. One reluctant expatriate recounted a conversation with a superior when he was told that unless he accepted his current assignment, he would never again be promoted, as he had turned down earlier international "opportunities." Employees who engage in international assignments as a means to forward their career goals are often quickly confronted with the ways in which the same assignments can be a detriment to their careers. Abroad, workers find that they are "out of sight, out of mind," and this danger of the life away from the central office is one that few anticipate before departure. Mechanisms to keep the internationally posted employee involved in the everyday activities at the home office are limited. The expatriate employee must strike a fine balancing act, for being away from the center permits advancement but being away too long can hurt a worker or even worse can make central office workers question his loyalty and can suggest that someone has "gone native," obviating their value as a expatriate.

Compensation

Money and other forms of compensation are an appropriate place for observing how employers and employees think about the rights and responsibilities of expatriate employment and the role of difference abroad. Financial gain is certainly one of the major reasons employees choose to take on international assignments. Some of the gains are immediate, in the form of raises, bonuses, and future career gains. An equal attraction is found in the potential for expatriate employment to produce intangible benefits, including an anticipated increase in cosmopolitan sophistication — a benefit particularly mentioned in discussions of the ways that children will benefit from international exposure. The immediate financial rewards for the expatriate are the compensation package. *Compensation* is a poignant term, as workers and employers — through the proxy of the subcontractors — negotiate just what the ordeal is that requires recompense and how much is due. Knowing what variables are considered significant in the calculations of salary is central to understanding what is considered normal by the business community and what are divergences for which compensation is required. Conventionally, raises are associated with changes in responsibility, but within the expatriate context, the raise is directed to creating stasis, overcoming the change of physical displacement.

The categories under which supplements and raises are granted to the expatriate worker illustrate how companies think about the nature of international employment and the role of difference. These inducements, including hardship allowances, differential adjustments, and overseas incentives, are widely discussed among expatriate workers and their spouses. A hardship allowance implies that there is hardship to be endured, and expatriate families often learn of the difficulties of living abroad through these compensations before they actually experience life abroad. Future expatriates are not naïve about working abroad, but through the precise nature of how compensation is apportioned they learn more about their new home and its perils. These categories emerge, particularly for the family, as injunctions rather than information. Thus, funds offered in categories such as private schooling or household staff act as strong suggestions that families will need to pursue these things.

The incentive employees are initially most interested in is the salary increase, whether gained as a result of promotion or as a raise given to all expatriate employees. The rhetoric driving the entire compensation structure is the attempt to ensure that the expatriate employee is given the same way of life he would enjoy in his home country. Monetarily, that is usually calculated from a "hardship index" or a "differential allowance." Countries are ranked based on a wide range of criteria designed to assess the disparity in living conditions between a normative home and the new posting. The hardship allowance is the most well-known aspect of supplementary compensation, particularly in Nepal, and often is used to describe the general package of incentives. A ranking is assigned to describe the degree of hardship associated with specific countries and, at times, even specific cities. This paragraph by the U.S. State Department introduces the logic behind and complex calculations that go into hardship pay.

> The government also pays a post differential (commonly called the hardship differential) to employees at those posts where living conditions are extraordinarily difficult, physical hardships are excessive, or conditions are notably unhealthy... The evaluation procedure consists of the collection of information concerning post conditions, primarily from a *Post Differential Questionnaire*, and the rating of the post for 121 specific environmental factors, weighted for relative importance. Depending on the total hardship rating, employees at qualifying posts are paid differentials of 5, 10, 15, 20, or 25 percent of base pay.[12]

A twenty-two page form used to determine the differential percentage is completed each year by a member of the American mission staff in each posting and is updated quarterly in situations where conditions are changing. The staff member is asked to evaluate factors such as the difficulty of reaching emergency medical care, environmental pollution, and availability of goods. These figures are well known by Foreign Service personnel as well as other expatriates whose salary is frequently based on these calculations.[13]

A separate salary adjustment, the cost-of-living allowance, has less impact on the employee posted to Nepal than countries where the cost of buying imported goods is higher, but the complex calculations entailed in its determination reveal the many considerations taken into account by expatriate employers and employees. The cost-of-living calculation is an attempt to analyze the buying power of the employee's spendable income on predetermined types of goods. To again quote from the U.S. State Department, "Indexes of living costs abroad, as computed by the Office of Allowances of the U.S. Department of State, measure the cost in dollars of goods and services (excluding housing and education) purchased by Americans at foreign posts compared with the cost of comparable goods and services purchased in the Washington, D.C. area."[14] Thus, this mode of calculating cost-of-living allowance fixes Washington, D.C., as equivalent to 100, and foreign postings are compared to this benchmark to receive a numerical assignment between 80 and 150,[15] which is thought to correlate to the cost and ability to buy a list of basic household products abroad. The idea behind this is to find ways to make it possible for the expatriate to purchase the same collection of goods abroad they would at home — both officially and casually known as "the market basket." The market basket concept illuminates the ambivalence of global markets in an expatriate world, where the assumption that all goods flow everywhere meets up with the actuality of trying to acquire strawberry Pop Tarts in Kathmandu, not to mention the assumption that such commodities are a desire of expatriates.

Determining exactly what should be included in this list of necessities and how much it would cost to procure them in foreign lands is one function of the larger international human resources industry, which is utlized both by governments and private entities. In the United States, the calculations are often based on the *Retail Price Schedule*, a data set used for other calculations by the Bureau of Labor Statistics that analyzes the cost for 120 different goods and services. These items are chosen for their importance in the life of the presumed average American. When this framework moves abroad, independent survey officers assess the cost and comparability of items on the list at the two most popular locations for expatriate shopping. What is then calculated is an average cost for acquiring a list of goods in a given location — what the average American family shopping abroad is presumed to want to purchase in a given period. The international cost-of-living calculation diverges from this adjusted market basket cost as the expected spending in each category is seen to vary from posting to posting. If entertaining is presumed to be a larger part of life in a given posting, "alcohol and tobacco" may receive a higher weighting as a percentage of the family's overall spending; in Nepal, the importance of household staff means that the "domestic service" category has a higher weighting. From these assessments, expatriate wives take away messages about what is expected of them, about how much they should entertain, and about the importance of buying the same products as the standard market basket. Entailed within this benchmark are presumptions about the correct form of family, spending patterns, and lifestyle. Beyond the financial disparities in needs and supplements, there are the expectations that accompany these figures. Budgets for alcohol and entertaining, recreation, and domestic service suggest that these should be a part of one's life, particularly when they receive greater weighting.

Basing expatriate salaries on a survey of domestic purchasing practices presumes that employees living abroad would wish to buy the same goods they would purchase at home. From the perspective of the employer, using such a standard list of goods enables a statistical comparison that creates numerical ranking of locations, thus facilitating what are perceived as fair remuneration strategies. From my ethnographic analysis it also creates expectations; new families are often overwhelmed by life abroad and unsure of what is expected. Much of the initial talk about a new posting is about compensation packages, often as a way to entice families to work abroad; as a result, much of what a new expatriate wife is told about her future home emerges from these considerations, and the image is of a place where it is necessary to employ security guards. In shifting from the logic behind the statisticians' calculations to the perceptions of the families they are designed to assist, an odd occlusion takes place. Though the structures of expatriate employment seek to facilitate certain activities — to teach families *how* to do particular things, they end up teaching them *what* to do. In granting market basket allowances, expatriates receive messages about what are the right things to buy. Furthermore, given the general level of anxiety about the unknown that is a part of expatriation, there is also little opportunity to question if these are things that the family will actually want or need. What becomes apparent to the expatriate spouse in the compensation structure and training is that it is necessary and appropriate to buy the same goods they would buy at home.

The Generic Expatriate

What is made possible through the market basket and similar compensation structures is the ability to quantify and make comparable diverse experiences of expatriation. The innumerable difficulties and strains of living away from home are transformed into numbers, and the need to comfort one's family in such a situation of displacement is believed to be ameliorated by acquiring Skippy peanut butter and Kellogg's corn flakes.[16] Although lists and quantifications of displacement have a long history among the internationally mobile elite,[17] the importance of such enumerations and quantification has grown with the rise of a new industry centered on creating successful expatriates, regardless of the starting and ending situations. What is emerging is a collection of companies, journals, and professionals devoted to selecting, training, and assessing employees for posting abroad – the field of international human resources management (IHRM). In researching the practices and impact of this new institutional field, I want to highlight the way the expatriate experience is becoming ever more codified. The result is a genericization of difference, a general method that is supposed to deal with cultural and geographical displacement, regardless of the nature of the difference. Thus, all forms of difference must be quantified and compartmentalized in ways that I argue reduce opportunity for cultural variation to arenas that do not interfere with business practices, which are presumed to be culture-free.

In the course of the last ten years, there has been a great increase in consulting services designed to assess the demands of the corporate international employment world. These firms, with names such as Associates for International Research Incorporated and Integrated Resources Group, have grown out of the human resources departments that were once within the structure of individual corporations but that now exist as outside consultants. In the past, expatriate employment support was both local to companies and postings; now the same services are supplied by large consulting organizations with links to various local service-providing entities. The support of expatriates has become a distinct business with a large body of research and specialists, disconnected from the specificity of the type of business, posting, or employee. Expatriate support services have come to resemble the specialized services used elsewhere in global businesses, becoming both more particular and more general. In a related situation, Saskia Sassen (2001, p. 99) describes the rise of outsourced corporate services, noting that "[p]roducing certain highly specialized services inside the firm has become increasing difficult because of the rising level of specialization and the cost of employing in-house specialists full time." A similar strategy is pursued by corporations in dealing with expatriates as companies seek firms that can negotiate the complexities of international regulations on visas, work permits, and benefits. As important as the special knowledge required is the ability to occlude and dispel the complexity of international employment. Though the inability of the home office to understand the difficulties of working and living in a particular location has long been a complaint of the expatriate, outsourcing the task of expatriate support allows the company to outsource awareness and consideration. The result is a situation where the expatriate support service may be conducting a live Internet chat with an employee discussing the importance of accommodating the needs of local employees on the same day the employee receives criticism from the home office for decreased productivity during a local holiday season.

The Successful Expatriate Family

In the selection, training, and compensation of expatriates a key tension can be observed within the mobile life — the shifting of boundaries between work and home, job and family. Although always in the service of the presumed male breadwinner, expatriate compensation is focused on the family unit. Education allowances, accommodations, and moving subsidies all are granted with a focus on a normative family unit.[18] In taking responsibility for the employee's family, the company in various ways expects a return on its investment. Training procedures during the hiring process all stress that the task of the primary employee cannot succeed without family support, and both members of the couple are often screened to assess their suitability to posting abroad. Governments and companies claim the need to evaluate the entire family as a part of insuring that employees obtain emotional and organizational support. Later, expatriates see other motivations for corporate concern about family life in light of the entertainment and service demands place upon women. Similar to the image of the 1950s American housewife, women often find themselves drafted into secretarial service in times of crisis or called upon to organize last-minute dinner parties when unexpected out-of-town guest arrives. The double-edged sword of paternalism becomes the daily company of the expatriate wife who is given support and comfort but at the cost of independence.

The professional expatriate services firm has amplified what has long been the cry of expatriate employers: carefully choosing and training the expatriate and his family before departure is the key to project success. Job needs are usually the first consideration of a company in selecting employees for expatriation, although this focus is frequently dismissed by consulting agencies, as they cite studies showing that "global assignment failure (poor performance or premature return) is generally the result of ineffective cross-cultural adjustment by expatriates and their families, rather than the outcome of inadequate technical or professional skills" (Black, Gregersen, and Mendenhall 1992, p. 56) cf. Forster 1997. Opinions vary widely over what type of selection and training to undertake to ameliorate failure and to ensure adjustment, and conflicting opinions proliferate in the burgeoning research on expatriate management. Since the structure and logic of training as much as the explicit messages of expatriate preparation that shape how difference is understood by families heading abroad, it is necessary to understand the underlying assumptions of the IHRM industry, particularly with regards to success and the role of culture.

It was not until the 1980s that human resources management became a distinct aspect of business training, but it grew quickly from these early days. Stemming from the rise of a professional class of workers focused on the relationship between personnel and organizations, human resources became a focus in and of itself; and, with its placement as a mandatory element of business training in the Harvard MBA program in 1981 it became an accepted part of the corporate infrastructure (Poole 1990, p. 2). Following definitions adopted at Harvard, "...Human Resources Management (HRM) is seen to involve 'all management decisions that affect the nature of the relationship between the organization and employees – its human resources'"(Poole, 1990, p. 2). It is from this field of study that business scholarship on expatriates, considered under the rubric of international human resources management, emerges.

In the mid-1980s, articles addressing the specific concerns of those managing personnel abroad began appearing in journals open to human resources issues such as *Journal of Organizational Behavior, Journal of Business Research,* and *Human Relations.* A critical interest in the concerns of international issues by the human resource field was reached in 1990, and a number of prominent scholars formed what has become the flagship journal for the topic, the *International Journal of Human Resource Management.* This journal, along with articles in similarly youthful periodicals such as *International Journal of Intercultural Relations* and *Journal of World Business,* has begun a small but prolific field of scholarship on the topic of expatriate employment.

With the outsourcing and privatization of IHRM, the stakes of the study of expatriate life were transformed. The focus on measurability of success (Escobar 1995; Scott 1998) manifested in a transformation in subcontractor practice and competition for business. Companies sought to claim that their mode of expatriate management had the best outcomes for the least amount of money, which changed the way companies saw their employees as well as the language of scholarship about expatriate management. What had been money given to expatriates in a concern over their health and happiness — a state of mind presumed to result in success on behalf of the company — changed in nature and became an investment in productivity. Success became more critically evaluated, and cost-balancing the return on investment in expatriates became a concern. Statisticians began calculating the amount companies spent on expatriate employees and sought to determine if each element was a worthwhile expense. The focus that came to overwhelm the business literature on expatriate management was to determine where resources for expatriates could be spent most effectively and how to select and place expatriate employees so that money is well utilized.

Out of this concern, failure became the most important issue for those who manage expatriate employment. As one significant player in the conversation states, "…it has become almost 'traditional' to open an article on expatriate management by stating that expatriate failure rates are (very) high" (Harzing 1995, p. 458). The ubiquity of this rhetoric is associated with the financial costs of international employment, which even ten years ago was around US$300,000 per expatriate per year according to some (Fukuda and Chu 1994), or three to six times the cost of employing the same individual at the home office (Freeman and Cane 1995). This is amplified by the high estimates of the percentage of expatriate employees who fail, where statistics range from single digits to 79 percent (Shilling 1993). Failure is thus an obsession, one that often brings families into the debate; one study finds between 60 and 80 percent of those refusing expatriate assignments claim their family as the reason (Muton and Forster 1990), whereas another calculates that 80 percent of expatriate failure is due to spouse-related issues (Hawley 2001).

The expense and rates of failure expounded upon by these scholars are questioned by those within the field. Nonetheless, the explanations offered in these articles for such problems are picked up by those seeking to post expatriates abroad, particularly the consulting agencies offering solutions to the very problems indicated by IHRM literature. Failure is seen as a problem of particular personnel, not of the system or of expectations. When assessing what is meant by failure, two categories are significant; first, the expatriates' ability to follow an expected career trajectory; and secondly, the employees' success in meeting particular goals for productive action abroad. Career trajectory concerns can include an early return to the home office, not completing the expecting period abroad, or wider issues such as unwillingness to undertake a second overseas assignment or the inability to receive an expected promotion after returning to the home office. Concern over the successful completion of a mission also holds complex definitions, from agreed-upon mission goals not being completed to inefficiency in comparison with central office-based employees or inability to reach particular production targets. What is new about this way of viewing expatriate life is the rise of specialized services and the genericization of the expatriate process that outsourcing necessitates. Failure is not task-dependent but is created as a category that can exist outside the particular jobs of engineers, diplomats, and salesmen. Successful expatriates are made into a unified category regardless of their home country, destination, or duration. Thus, concerns over why a long-term single expatriate posted to France returned to Australia before her contract was over are extrapolated to the training of a first-time expatriate family posted to Nepal. This same process of making expatriation abstract takes place in the consideration of cultural adaptation and how businesses should adapt, if at all, to new localities.

Selecting Expatriates

When specific studies of expatriate performance are adapted to the needs of the company or outsourced support organization, all complexity is erased in favor of more general presumptions about producing good expatriates. There are two basic components to producing expatriates: the selection of the employees and their training to go abroad. How expatriates are selected and trained provides them the framework with which they and their families approach life abroad. The first criterion for expatriate selection put forth by employers is often job skills, despite protests of its irrelevance, with interest in living in a foreign country a quick second. These are also the categories that the IHRM subcontractors can do the least to affect; thus, they are quickly dismissed within the literature. As one organization describes in in an article entitled "Proactive International Human Resources Management,"

> The successful expatriate contract starts with selection. All too often the company has the habit of selecting the employee based on perhaps his technical competence and maybe a recommendation from one line manager or senior executive that he/she is the right person for the job. Two mistakes here… The first mistake is that the selection of the expatriation is not solely about technical competence of what someone who has never been an expatriate recommends but has to be about ensuring that the expatriate has the desired traits/profile required to handle a tough assignment… (Hawley 2001, p. 1)

This suggestion that "traits/profile" should be emphasized over job skills dovetails with the selection services these companies provide. Consultants seek to analyze workers' appropriateness for foreign assignment through interviewing both potential employees and their families and the administration of general-purpose psychological tests such as the Minnesota Multiphasic Personality Inventory (MMPI), Personality Assessment Inventory (PAI), Meyers-Briggs, and Rorschach testing. Particular to the expatriate situation are tests to measure how an individual might relate to a novel "cultural situation," including the Overseas Assignment Inventory (OAI) and the Cross-Cultural Adaptability Inventory (CCAI).

The CCAI is indicative of the non-technical skills consultants seek to measure to determine how an individual will adapt to cultural difference.

"The culture-general approach assumes that individuals adapting to other cultures share common feelings perceptions and experiences. This occurs regardless of the cultural background of the person or the characteristics of the target culture" (Kelly and Meyers 1995, p. 1). The CCAI is arranged to measure four characteristics determined to be pivotal to success in cross-cultural situations: emotional resilience (ER), flexibility/openness (FO), perceptual acuity (PAC), and personal autonomy (PA). Individuals given this test must respond to fifty questions and are given six options, ranging from "Definitely True" to "Definitely Not True." The questions address each of the characteristics in random order, and some are reverse scored, meaning the same characteristic is sometimes defined by the "Definitely True" response and sometimes by "Definitely Not True" response. Questions include:

- I like to try new things. (ER)
- I don't enjoy trying new foods. (ER, reverse scored)
- I like being with all kinds of people. (FO)
- I am not good at understanding people when they are different from me. (FO, reverse scored)
- I have a realistic perception of how others see me. (PAC)
- When I am in a new or strange environment, I keep an open mind. (PAC)
- I believe that all people, of whatever race, are equally valuable. (PA)
- My personal value system is based on my own beliefs, not on conformity to other people's standards. (PA)

The completion of such a test allows organizations to generate a statistical profile of how successful they believe a potential expatriate, or their spouse, will be. This assumption is problematic in part because of the transparency of CCAI and similar tests, meaning that most individuals are able to give the answer that will produce the result they wish.[19] One of the chief benefits of this type of testing from the perspective of both the specialized service providers and the utilizing agencies is that the same test can be applied to all involved and that it generates numerical results, but there are significant costs as well. As Sassen argues in the introduction to this volume, assumptions about scale and boundaries can produce data that are technically correct but illustrate nothing.

Though some promote the idea that cultural sensitivity and experience of diversity is a prime attribute, many organizations deny this assumption. One consultant suggests the following about selection: "If the ability to live in different places and speak other languages, an intellectual curiosity and an interest in different cultures aren't the principal factors for international success, what are? What, for example, enables a couple who have lived their entire lives in small-town Texas to move to northern England and do a terrific job" (Kozloff 1996, p. 2). Thus, despite a battery of testing and scores of interviews with families and workers alike, there is little agreement on what a successful expatriate looks like. Cultural adaptability, personal stability, job skills, family support — all these factors certainly contribute to how an expatriate will experience life and work abroad. Yet how to measure these and what weight to give the results are unclear, even as the system of outsourcing demands surety as part of the competition for business. Two points that receive general agreement among the consulting organizations are that companies are currently not doing a good job of selecting expatriates, a claim that can be proven using a wide variety of available failure statistics, and that the companies need to better assess skills, a statement that often precedes the sales pitch for their organization's services. Thus, in many ways proclamations of failure and the complexity of assessing success feed into demand for the services of the consulting agencies.

Training Expatriates

A similar conundrum is encountered in relation to the next step of the expatriation process, employee training, in the form of both therapy-like support and more concrete services. Expatriates learn about what to expect from the predeparture sessions, both from the conversations and through reading services as injunctions — and these two areas often conflict. For example, one expatriate wife described her cultural training, which emphasized the similarity of the host culture and her home culture and the interesting food that visitors should sample. In another session, she was handed a long list of things to bring abroad and was told about all the health dangers and food problems. She struggled with which one to believe.

Expatriate therapeutic training usually centers on ideas of culture. The starting point of the training is often the employee's test scores that are seen to assess the arenas in which the individual is deficient in his or her cultural adaptability skills. The main activity undertaken under the rubric of training is some form of discussion with a professional counselor or coach. Those being coached are also often given reading material, ranging from publicly available books on culture shock to in-house pamphlets and checklists, which are often immediately tossed in open boxes due to be delivered to Kathmandu in six to ten weeks. From my research, much of the direct training of expatriates and their families consists of the "culture-general" issues highlighted by tests such as the CCAI. Although employees are given written material discussing their specific location of posting, the classes and interactions are of a more general "cultural awareness" nature. Some companies use role-playing as a means of simulating potential moments of cultural conflict and give participants suggested appropriate responses. Many companies lead seminars on the various difficulties they anticipate expatriates will encounter, focusing on the "W" of culture shock, a common description in this literature for the ups and downs of the experience of difference over time.

In speaking to expatriates about their training experiences, some stated that they had not been given any cultural information, while others said they vaguely remember some seminar but were too busy with preparing for departure to focus on the information presented. Families who were part of organizations expatriating larger numbers of people found the most useful element to be meeting with other families going through a similar transition. In informal discussions with women and their husbands about training and what it contributed to their experience abroad, most saw the information presented as fairly obvious and superficial. Some said that merely having the opportunity to reflect on issues was helpful, whereas others saw it as "a total waste of time. I was just so busy with last minute things; I skipped after the first meeting."

Looking beyond the lacunae that might be inherent in such generalized training, this approach to teaching difference allows only certain aspects of culture to be addressed. Expatriates are taught that what they need to know about Nepal is different ethnic groups, religious rituals, and local dress — the same cultural icons that make up popular conceptions of difference — what might be found in a tour book or popular magazine article. They are given few resources for understanding contemporary Nepal and tend to see Nepal as a country continuing to exist in the past.[20] This becomes problematic as expatriate employees and their families meet their new local friends and coworkers, who hold little resemblance to the exotic figures they see in guide books and are likely to have gone to school in Europe and know little about rural ethnic groups in Nepal. As the companies providing outsourced expatriate training rely on the previously discussed "culture-general" approach, they often lack the knowledge and experience necessary to provide information about diversity of a given place. The genericization of expatriate training not only leads to practical difficulties but can also create conflict when new arrivals find complex communities that do not fit the tourist brochure images they anticipated.

Expatriate Difference, or, How Business Becomes Normal

The coaching, training, and counseling of expatriate or soon-to-be expatriated families does far more implicit than explicit work. The system of agencies and companies that hire, train, and employ individuals who are sent to other countries create the space in which the employees are told to understand their encounter. Although expatriates and their families come to the experience of working abroad with their own ideas about other places and peoples, those ideas are restructured by the expatriate system. This distinction is significant in rethinking the naturalization of what an encounter with difference is permitted to look like. This system does not train expatriates; it makes expatriates, and makes them in particular ways. In bringing the issues previously discussed together, I see the production of a domain of expatriate life, a zone which has more in common with other expatriate enclaves than surrounding territory, a space of Expatria, or the Expat Archipelago. In the production of expatriate families, the training of participants frames how they will experience difference, prefiguring their experience abroad and giving them a framework in which to encode their experiences, particularly a distinction between the local/cultural and the international/acultural.

In exploring the expectations placed on employees working abroad and the attendant compensation given to families on international assignment, I see two different assumptions that combine to suggest something about the movement of global capital in the current era. Put quite simply, within this rhetoric, culture is a barrier to capitalism. IHRM professionals appear to be seeking an individual outside culture, unencumbered by national affiliations or attachments to local goods or people.[21] In the system of expatriate compensation, the employer seeks to mitigate the difficulties of cultural displacement, creating a neutral space of home outside the marked space of the posting. Expatriate families pick up these presumptions, seeking to establish their status as acultural, neutral, normal, and modern in opposition to the location to which they are to be posted. Labor and production, in this understanding, exist outside of the realm of culture. Such presumptions are interestingly consistent with the ideology that engages those at the opposite end of the economic spectrum of a global neoliberal economy. The presumptions that enable the outsourcing of sweatshop labor share an ideology with the deculturalization of the expatriate worker, although the outcomes for the participants are very different.

Culture does have a place in this economic system though, one that is particularly salient in Nepal. Within the dimension of consumption, culture is a positive valuation. Difference is marketable, and as a means of sales it is an important tool. This is sometimes the reason given for sending expatriates abroad: to attempt to understand a local situation in order to enable the company to better market itself to local consumers. The presumptions attendant in this mode of thinking about difference also make their way into expatriate training as expatriate families are given a means of encountering difference through consumption. The information those going abroad receive about the local setting focuses largely on ritual, religion, clothing, dress, and food — all dimensions that allow difference to be made safe through embedding it in specific niches and frequently shaping it into consumable forms. Expatriate families find a space for culture and put culture in its place, excluding difference from the "acultural" space of expatriate work through allowing discreet units of "the other" in comfortable form.

What is ultimately at stake in the architecture of Expatria? I suggest that in this phenomenon there is an opportunity to catch a sidelong glance at the workings of global capitalism, through the messages of the system to those middlemen who are trained to be its implementors. The way that companies and governments consider expatriate employees and train them and their families can be read as the implicit curriculum of contemporary international political and business practices. In the approach taken by expatriate specialists to private life, difference, and compensation, a great deal is expressed about how these entities see the world and their place in it. In addition, in looking at the type of space allowed for difference, one is granted access to a conflicted vision of community and culture, in which various forms of "otherness" are constrained to make the rest of the world safe for business. This confinement requires one to look beyond the liberal celebrations of culture, in its song and dance form, to those who gain and lose from its institutional location.

Acknowledgments

This piece has benefited, as have I, from the wonderful community of scholars represented in this book. I must particularly thank Saskia Sassen, Evalyn Tennant, and Anne Bartlett for their unflagging support. Richard Lloyd, Marina Peterson, Giselle Datz, Josh Kaplan, Rachel Harvey, and Matt Hill have been the sort of rigorous and insightful collaborators that should be the norm in academia. Colleagues at various institutions, including Jill Gillespie, Veve Lele, and Robert Oppenheim, have been kind enough to help me forward the ideas here. The women of the United Nations Women's Organization and American/Active Women of Nepal must receive my greatest thanks for their welcoming attitude and interest in my research. All inadequacies and errors are, of course, my own.

Notes

1. The ethnographic material for this article was collected between 1997 and 2000 during eighteen months of field research funded by the Social Science Research Council and the Committee on Southern Asian Studies at the University of Chicago.
2. On anthropology's increasingly problematic relationship with culture and the problems of the culture concept, see Trouillot (2002).

3. This idea of a noncontiguous zone of expatriate enclaves, referred to elsewhere in my work as Expatria, is an attempt to capture the similarity of these various sites despite their spatial separation. The archipelago concept is borrowed from Lyotard's (1988) and Arendt's (1994) extrapolation of Solzhenitsyn (2002).
4. Throughout this work I use terms such as *underdeveloped* and *third world* as they are used by interlocutors in development, diplomacy, and business.
5. Malkki's (1992, p. 28) work with refugees from Burundi highlights the different ways culture is worn or imposed on different polities; in the UN system this creates what she calls following Appadurai (1988, p. 37) "the spatial incarceration of the native," an incarceration that binds expatriates less tightly.
6. Liechty (2003) explores how, in Nepal, that which is marked as culture-free is positively associated with the modern, and his analysis describes well attitudes that pervade throughout the country.
7. As is becoming clear with the U.S. government's contemporary subcontracting of military operations previously deemed too vital or dangerous to be left to nonmilitary hands, the division between government and business is increasingly difficult to find, and a similar process is found in aid agencies and even among businesses — for example, the firms that exclusively subcontract to Wal-Mart, making inside and outside a matter of semantics, albeit legally important semantics. It is in this vein that I use the term *foreign service industry*. This is also gaining importance with the rise of private military forces (cf. Chatterjee 2004; Singer 2003).
8. In Nepal, there is the issue of who should receive government benefits, such as access to mail pouches, national clubs, and tax-free imports, as fewer and fewer workers are direct government employees. One woman commented that the American Club, which was once the center of expatriate life in Nepal, would have to close if the rules for membership were strictly enforced, as there was no one left who was eligible under old employment understandings.
9. In Nepal, the vast majority of expatriate employees are male. This is somewhat less true in other postings, but the rhetoric of the system as a whole presumes a male breadwinner and a nuclear family. The presumptions of a masculine worker made by employers prompt me to mirror their practice and thus not to use gender-neutral language in this context.
10. This idea of the woman who is incorporated into her husband's job responsibilities abroad is explored in Callan and Ardener (1984) and Coles and Fechter (forthcoming).
11. Although elements of the Maoist revolution and other political conflict were in evidence in 2000, they neither predominated nor greatly affected tourism to the region at the time of my research.
12. State Department, "Compensation of American Government Employees in Foreign Countries," January 2002, http://www.state.gov/m/a/als/qtrpt/2002/9248.htm.
13. Kathmandu currently has a 20 percent ranking, which it has held for some time. For context, neighboring India ranges between 15 percent and 25 percent, depending on the city of posting.
14. See State Department, http://www.state.gov/m/a/als/qtrpt/2002/9248.htm.

15. Those working in countries with a cost-of-living allowance percentage below 100 receive neither an increase nor decrease in salary.
16. For a more extensive discussion of expatriate consumption and the challenges of transforming market basket allowances into actual goods, see Hindman (in press).
17. By the late nineteenth century, books and magazine series had been released addressed to British women headed to the colonies that recommended lists of clothing, food, medicine, and housewares needed in India (cf. Platt 1923; Steel and Gardiner 1898; Wilson 1904).
18. This dehistoricization and normalization of family structures has been explored by a number of authors in gender and sexuality studies, perhaps best by Warner (1999).
19. The expressions of will demonstrated by these tests can be interesting in and of themselves. I heard from one tester of a case where the spouse did not wish to go abroad and yet was not willing to say so directly in interviews. Instead, whereas her husband was given a high cultural adaptability rating, hers was quite low, a fact the researcher attributed to her desire to undermine the posting abroad through indirect means.
20. The information expatriates are given about postings has many of the same lacuna as described in Lutz and Collins (1993), including a detemporalization, feminization, and exoticization, or Fabian's (1983) concerns about the denial of coevalness.
21. This is actually the latest trend in expatriate management services and research: the promotion of despatialized workers, or international citizens as described by Freeman and Kane (1995), who would not need compensation for work abroad because it is claimed that they would be equally at home everywhere.

Works Cited

Appadurai, Arjun. 1988. Putting hierarchy in its place. *Cultural Anthropology* 3(1): 36–49.

———. 1996. *Modernity at large*. Minneapolis: University of Minnesota Press.

Arendt, Hannah. 1994. *Eichmann in Jerusalem: A report on the banality of evil.* New York: Penguin Books.

Beer, M., B. Spector, P.R. Lawrence, D.Q. Mills, and R.E. Walton. 1984. *Managing human assets*. New York: Free Press.

Berlant, Lauren. 1997. *The Queen of America goes to Washington City.* Durham: Duke University Press.

Black, J.S., H. Gregersen, and M. Mendenhall. 1992. *Global assignments: Successfully expatriating and repatriating international managers.* San Francisco: Jossey-Bass Publishers.

Bourdieu, Pierre. 1984. *Distinction: A social critique of the judgments of taste.* Cambridge, MA: Harvard University Press.

———. 1992. *Outline of a theory of practice*. Cambridge: Cambridge University Press.

Callan, H., and S. Ardener. 1984. *The incorporated wife*. London: Croom Helm.

Chatterjee, Pratap. 2004. *Iraq, inc.* New York: Seven Stories Press.

Coles, A., and Fechter, A. Forthcoming. *Beyond the "incorporated wife": Gender and social reproduction among mobile professionals.* New York: Routledge.

Escobar, Arturo. 1995. *Encountering development.* Princeton, NJ: Princeton University Press.

Fabian, Johannes. 1983. *Time and the other: How anthropology makes its object.* New York: Columbia University Press.

———. 2006. The other revisited. *Anthropological Theory* 6(2):139–52.

Forster, Nick. 1997. "The persistent myth of high expatriate failure rates": A reappraisal. *International Journal of Human Resource Management* 8(4):414–33.

Freeman, Kimberly, and Jeffrey Kane. 1995. An alternative approach to expatriate allowances: An "international citizen." *International Executive* 37(3):245–59.

Fukuda, K. John, and Priscilla Chu. 1994. Wrestling with expatriate family problems. *International Studies of Management and Organization* 24(3):36–47.

Haraway, Donna. 1989. *Primate visions.* New York: Routledge.

Hartigan, John Jr. 2005. *Odd tribes: Toward a cultural analysis of white people.* Durham, NC: Duke University Press.

Harzing, Anne-Wil K. 1995. The persistent myth of high expatriate failure rates. *International Journal of Human Resource Management* 6(2):457–74.

Hawley, Kevin. 2001. Proactive international human resources management. Available at http://www.expatworld.co.za/journal_article_1.html; Internet.

Hindman, Heather. 2002. The everyday life of American development in Nepal. *Studies in Nepali History and Society* 7(1):99–136.

———. 2007. Shopping in the Bazaar/Bizarre Shopping *Journal of Popular Culture.*

———. Forthcoming, a. Learning fear and the expectation of a Donna Reed home. In Anne Coles and Anne-Meike Fechter, eds., *Beyond the "incorporated wife": Gender and social reproduction among mobile professionals.* New York: Routledge.

Ho, Karen, 2005. Situating global capitalisms. *Cultural Anthropology* 20(1) :68–96.

Joseph, Miranda. 2002. *Against the romance of community.* Minneapolis: University of Minnesota Press.

Kelly, Colleen, and Judith Meyers. 1995. *Cross-cultural adaptability inventory.* Minneapolis: National Computer Systems, Inc.

Kelly, John D., and Martha Kaplan. 2001. *Represented communities.* Chicago: University of Chicago Press.

Kozloff, Barry. 1996. Assessing expatriate selection. *Relocation Journal*, February, available at http://www.relojournal.com/feb96/exsel.htm.

Lacan, Jacques. 1998. *The four fundamental concepts of psychoanalysis.* New York: W.W. Norton.

Lévinas, Emmanuel. 1998. *Entre nous: On thinking-of-the-other.* New York: Columbia University Press.

Liechty, Mark. 2003. *Suitably modern: Making middle-class culture in a new consumer society.* Princeton, NJ: Princeton University Press.

Lutz, C., and J. Collins. 1993. *Reading National Geographic.* Chicago: University of Chicago Press.

Lyotard, J.F. 1988. *The Differend: Phrases in Dispute.* Minneapolis: University of Minnesota Press.

Malkki, Liisa. 1992. *National Geographic*: The rooting of peoples and the territorialization of national identity among scholars and refugees. *Cultural Anthropology* 7(1):24–44.

———. 1994. Citizens of humanity: Internationalism and the imagined community of nations. *Diaspora* 3(1):41–68.

Munton, Anthony, and Nick Forster. 1990. Job relocation: Stress and the role of the family. *Work and Stress* 4(1):75–81.

Platt, Kate. 1923. *The home and health in India and the tropical colonies.* London: Bailiere, Tindal and Cox.

Poole, Michael. 1990. Editorial: Human resource management in an international perspective. *International Journal of Human Resource Management* 1(1):1–15.

Sassen, Saskia. 2006. *Cities in a world economy.* Third edition. Thousand Oaks, CA: Pine Forge Press.

———. 2001. *The global city: New York, London, Tokyo,* 2d ed. Princeton, NJ: Princeton University Press.

Scott, James C. 1998. *Seeing like a state: How certain schemes to improve the human condition have failed.* New Haven, CT: Yale University Press.

Shilling, Marvina. 1993. Avoid expatriate culture shock. *HR Magazine*, July, 58–63.

Singer, P.W. 2003. *Corporate warriors.* Ithaca, NY: Cornell University Press.

Solzhenitsyn, Aleksandr. 2002. *The Gulag archipelago, 1918–1956.* New York: Harper Collins.

Steel, Flora, and G. Gardiner. 1898. *The complete Indian housekeeper and cook.* London: W. Heinemann.

Todorov, Tzvetan. 1984. *The conquest of America: The question of the other.* New York: Harper and Row.

Trouillot, Michel-Rolph. 1991. Anthropology and the savage slot: The poetics and politics of otherness. In Richard Fox, ed., *Recapturing anthropology*, 17–44. Santa Fe: School of American Research Press.

———. 2001. The anthropology of the state in the age of globalization. *Current Anthropology* 42(1):125–38.

———. 2002. Adieu, culture: A new duty arises. In R. Fox and B. King, eds., *Anthropology beyond culture*, 37–60. New York: Berg.

Warner, Michael, 1999. *The trouble with normal.* Cambridge, MA: Harvard University Press.

Willis, Paul. 1981. *Learning to labor.* New York: Columbia University Press.

Wilson, Anne. 1904. *Hints for the first year's residence in India.* Oxford: Clarendon Press.

Zizek, Slavoj. 2000. *The ticklish subject: The absent centre of political ontology.* New York: Verso.

CHAPTER 9

Producing Global Economies from Below

Chinese Immigrant Transnational Entrepreneurship in Japan

GRACIA LIU FARRER

Research about the mobility of capital and labor has largely been the preserve of two distinct scholarships. Contemporary outsourcing of jobs by multinational firms has begun to make connections between these two types of mobilities. Here I argue that immigrants' transnational entrepreneurship is yet another instance that brings both mobilities into a single conceptual framework. However, among immigration scholars, transnational entrepreneurship is conceptualized as a survival strategy immigrants use to circumvent their marginal social and economic situations in the society to which they migrate (Guarnizo and Smith 1998; Portes 1996; Portes, Guarnizo, and Landolt 1999). No connection is made with larger global dynamics. Such entrepreneurship is at best seen as an alternative form of economic adaptation practiced by a small number of immigrants (Portes, Guarnizo, and Haller 2002). Although helpful in explaining immigrant incorporation, such a characterization does not fully express the significance of immigrants' transnational entrepreneurship in a global economic context. It overlooks even the possibility that immigrant entrepreneurs participate in the production not only of transnational survival strategies but also of the global economy.

Using the case of Chinese immigrants' transnational entrepreneurship in Japan, I argue that immigrant transnational entrepreneurial practice is an integral part of the global economy. Armed with cultural and social knowledge of different societies, using their institutional, ethnic, and personal resources, and maneuvering between structural constraints and opportunities in both host and sending societies, Chinese immigrants contribute to the development of the transnational economy between Japan and China. They are not just carving out a livelihood for themselves. Their professional and business skills, multilingual knowledge, and multilocality networks allow them to expand beyond the China–Japan economic circuit and to reach across the Pacific Ocean. Thus, their economic practices not only are facilitated by economic globalization but also actively facilitate its intensification and expansion. At the same time, the contexts of their emergence and their strategies in carving out a niche in the transnational economy show that immigrant entrepreneurs are first of all immigrants and share the constraints and characteristics of immigrant entrepreneurs documented in other national contexts by immigration scholars. Their transnational activities represent grassroots efforts in producing globalization.

This chapter first introduces the theoretical background of this study and concepts that aid in understanding immigrants' transnational entrepreneurship. Then I explain the characteristics of transnational Chinese immigrant entrepreneurs, the political, social, and economic contexts within which they emerge, and the process through which they became transnational entrepreneurs. I then describe the business strategies and resources they use to ensure survival and development. The chapter concludes by highlighting the main findings.

Multiscalar Globalization and Immigrant Transnational Entrepreneurship

In the recent decade, human geographers have been applying the concept of scales to the interpretation of political and economic phenomena in the globalization process, especially in the interpretation of power relations between different localities and different hierarchical orders (Kelly 1999; Mamadouh, Kramsch, and Van Der Velde 2004; Rankin 2003; Swyngedouw 1997). The idea of scales makes it possible to conceptualize the global economy as operating at diverse organizational and geographic levels and involving different types of scalar actors, from individuals to supranational institutions. Combined with sociological network analysis, we can then conceptualize economic globalization as a process connecting individuals, households, firms, industries, states, unions, and other organizations and institutions into multiple specific multiscalar webs of transactions and actors. An emphasis on multiscalar globalization and global actor networks opens up the analysis to a diverse range of actors, activities, and spaces. It makes it possible to conceive immigrants' transnational entrepreneurship as a constitutive element of economic globalization.

The task is to find out how they enter the process. Guarnizo (2003) provides one type of mechanism that links immigrants' transnational practices with economic globalization. He argues that immigrants' demand for goods and services from their home countries becomes a driving force for some industries to expand their production and markets globally. Therefore, "migrants' transnational engagement has significant influences and transforming effects not only on the development of their localities and countries of origin, but also on global macroeconomic process (p. 667)." However, in Guarnizo's conceptual scheme, immigrants affect transnational corporations and global economies mainly as consumers. How do immigrants become active participants in the producing of globalization?

One possible process is through networks. Studies about immigrants' transnational economic practices find that social networks are the most important condition for immigrants' transnational activities. Case studies about Haitians (Basch, Glick-Schiller, and Blanc 1994), Filipinos (Parrenas 2005), El Salvadorans (Bailey et al. 2002; Itzigsohn and Saucedo 2002; Landolt, Autler, and Baires 1999; Mahler 2001), Dominicans (Itzigsohn et al. 1999), and Mexicans (Roberts, Frank, and Lozano-Asencio 1999) in the United States all document that at the base of immigrants' cross-border activities are the densely knitted and widely extended translocal social and community ties linking the home and the host society. In fact, Roberts, Frank, and Lozano-Asencio (1999) argue that because rural Mexican immigrants are more likely than urban migrants to enjoy strong community ties with their native villages, they are also more likely to be engaged in entrepreneurship than urban Mexican migrants. Portes, Guarnizo, and Haller (2002) find that large networks with ties reaching beyond local communities strongly predict the possibility of transnational entrepreneurship. Is it possible that at some points immigrants' social networks intersect with or become incorporated into global business networks? By reaching across the borders, connecting both developed and developing regions, do immigrants' social networks also help incorporate local business practices into the global actor network and therefore help their global reach (Dicken et al. 2001)? The evidence on the global expansion of overseas Chinese businesses shows that the initially spatially and ethnically enclosed Chinese business networks were forced to change their business practices and to globalize their business processes after they intersected with the global actor network (Olds and Yeung 1999; Yeung 2000). As a consequence, what were originally local ethnic Chinese enterprises in some cases have become large multinational corporations (UNCTAD 2005).

A second possible point of entry into the transnational economy is through making connections with existing global institutions. Immigrant studies tend to portray immigrants' transnational entrepreneurship as disparate business efforts, informal and lacking institutional backing (Itzigsohn, et. al. 1999, Landolt, Autler, and Baires 1999). In fact, the very significance of such practices is found in their resistance to the domination of national and global economic regimes. As Guarnizo and Smith (1998) argue, such a portrayal of immigrants' transnationality fails to capture the reality of international migration in the contemporary world. In recent decades, with the intensification of globalization processes, immigrants have become increasingly diverse in class backgrounds and mobility trajectories. We can find Hong Kong big-business people on the Pacific coasts in the United States and Canada (Mitchell 1997; Ong 1999), Taiwanese small entrepreneurs in Canada (Wong and Ng 2002), and Indian information technology (IT) professionals circulating the world (Xiang 2003). In other words, the utility of immigrants in the host economy has changed from simply providing labor power to providing economic capital, transnational social networks and multicultural skills that benefit host countries' economic development regionally and globally. It means that immigrants are not only the products of economic globalization but also active agents in integrating the regional and global economy. In fact, in the field of information technology immigrant entrepreneurs, by mobilizing professional and institutional resources transnationally, have become an important force in the globalization of technological production (Aneesh 2006; Saxenian, Motoyama, and Quan 2002). As the case of Chinese entrepreneurs in Japan shows, both the expansive social networks with different social and institutional origins and immigrants' roots in existing transnational business organizations provide immigrants access and opportunities to engage in globalized economic operations.

The evidence of immigrants' contributions to the making of economic globalization also sheds new light on the connections between global capital and labor migration. The existing scholarship focuses on capital's causal effects on labor migration. Sassen (1988) points out that industrial countries' foreign direct investments and offshore production in the developing regions have produced material and ideological linkages between the north and south and in effect have built bridges for labor in the capital receiving countries to move northward. The practices of the Chinese immigrants' transnational entrepreneurs, however, indicate that the causal effects of capital and labor mobilities work in both directions. Although structural factors such as Japan's direct investment and active recruitment of Chinese students and skilled labor are important driving forces for Chinese people's migration into Japan, Chinese immigrants' grassroots transnational activities are also facilitating capital mobility transnationally and globally.

Chinese Immigrant Transnational Entrepreneurs: Who Are They?

Being self-employed has become an increasingly important economic practice among the Chinese immigrants in Japan, and transnational business is an aspired model of entrepreneurship. In 2004, 1,268 Chinese immigrants registered in Japan as *investor/business managers,* ranking number one among all immigrant nationality groups in Japan (Ministry of Justice 2005)[1]. And this number by no means describes the scope of business ownership among Chinese immigrants. Chinese business owners are also long-term residents, permanent residents, and naturalized immigrants[2]. Among these Chinese business owners in Japan, many are engaged in transnational businesses between Japan and China. Following Portes, Guarnizo, and Haller's (2002) definition of *transnational entrepreneurs,* I limit the subject of analysis to Chinese immigrants who are engaged in transnational entrepreneurship on a regular basis and for whom this is their primary livelihood. It therefore excludes wage labors who are only occasionally engaged in transnational economic activities and immigrants who are formally employed. Moreover, I focus on a group of entrepreneurs who are in businesses involving regular transnational activities and thereby exclude ethnic service businesses catering to the market in the host society.

My study is based on qualitative data gathered in the metropolitan Tokyo area between September 2001 and December 2004. The data set includes in-depth interviews with 123 Chinese immigrants of diverse backgrounds who came to Japan after 1980, as well as 104 personal stories in an autobiographic collection written by Chinese immigrants in Japan in late 1990s (Duan 1998). Of the 123 people I personally interviewed, sixteen were engaged in independent transnational entrepreneurial practices; 19 out of the 104 autobiographies were written by Chinese immigrants who were transnational entrepreneurs. I supplement the qualitative data with official statistics published by the United Nations Conference on Trade and Development (UNCTAD), the Japanese Ministry of Justice, and the Chinese Statistical Yearbook 2004.

The thirty-five Chinese transnational immigrant entrepreneurs in the present sample were mostly well-educated, middle-age, long-term residents in Japan and, more often than not, former employees in corporate Japan. Table 9.1 groups their ages and years of entering Japan. Two people in the autobiographies did not provide their ages and years of entry. Since the influx of large numbers of Chinese immigrants did not start until the

Table 9.1. Entry years of the sampled entrepreneurs

Age	Year of Entry					
	Before 1980	1980–84	1985–89	1990–94	After 1995	Total
50 and above	1	0	3	1	0	5
45–49	0	0	7	1	0	8
40–44	0	0	6	4	0	10
35–39	0	0	0	5	3	8
30–34	0	0	0	2	0	2
Total	1	0	16	13	3	33

mid-1980s, this study's sample matches findings from North America that entrepreneurs are more likely to emerge among long-term residents (Portes, Guarnizo, and Haller 2002).

Among the thirty-five entrepreneurs in the sample, four people — two men and two women — came as spouses to Japanese nationals. Two were contracted technical workers. One moved to Japan because his wife was a Japanese war orphan. One came on a dependent visa as the spouse of a student. The other twenty-seven entered Japan as students. Most went to language school first. Several came as research students — a program designed to prepare college graduates for graduate school. All entrepreneurs except two in the sample went to college and postgraduate programs (Table 9.2). In addition, at least two-thirds of the entrepreneurs in the sample had experience working in corporate Japan.[3] Another two had part-time work experience in corporate Japan during their university years, which gave them the ideas for establishing their own businesses. As the following sections demonstrate, their good educational backgrounds and corporate experience were necessary conditions for the types of transna-

Table 9.2. Levels of education of sampled entrepreneurs

High School or Equivalent	College	Master's[a]	Doctoral[a]
2	14	11	7

[a] *These numbers include people who studied in the programs but did not obtain degrees.*

tional businesses in which they were engaged and the important roles they played in the Japan–China economic circuit.

All companies in the sample started with the minimal investments required by the law: ten million Japanese yen to register as a corporation and three million yen as a limited liability company, except for two individuals who did not register their transnational trading and hospitality service. The majority of the entrepreneurs employed fewer than ten full-time staff, with the two unregistered businesses having no employees. The entrepreneurs who wrote their autobiography in late 1990s were on average older and came to Japan earlier than the entrepreneurs interviewed for this study in 2002 and 2003.

Becoming Transnational Entrepreneurs

Chinese immigrants' decision to become self-employed business persons in Japan and China's transnational economy has to do with the opportunities and constraints in the context of migration from China to Japan. In particular, their high human capital and Japanese corporate know-how, some with experiences working in China as well, are important conditions allowing them to be transnational entrepreneurs.

Coming to Japan to Study and Work

The presence of a large number of Chinese immigrants in Japan with education and professional skills has much to do with Japan's immigration policy since the mid-1980s. To affirm Japan's power position in the region as well as in the world politics, former Prime Minister Yasuhiro Nakasone proposed in 1983 a plan of annually accepting 100,000 foreign students into Japanese higher educational institutions by the early twenty-first century. Under such a guideline, student visas became easily available. Subsequently, language schools in Japan mushroomed and actively recruited students from China, a poor neighboring country with a large population that had just opened its door. To attract more Chinese students, some language schools also sold sponsorships to students to bring out their friends, siblings, and classmates. The easy availability of student visas and the possibility of financial self-sufficiency, coupled with the going abroad fever (*chu guo re*) in Chinese cities from the mid-1980s to the mid-1990s, led to an influx of Chinese students into Japan. Many informants said Japan was not initially their choice of destination for studying abroad. Since student visas to English-speaking countries, such as the United States and Canada, had much more stringent criteria, they ended up coming to Japan when the opportunity arose. In the sample, twenty-seven out of thirty-five cases began their lives in Japan as students. Except for a few who studied Japanese before coming, the majority started their language training in Japan. Since initially there was no age barrier for a student visa, it was common to see Chinese students in their late twenties and thirties on college campuses in Japan. Because of the immense economic gap between China and Japan, many came to Japan to seek opportunities despite their established careers in China. One entrepreneur whom I interviewed enrolled in a Japanese postgraduate program at the age of forty in 1990, after having become a middle-rank cadre in the central government.

In 2003, the goal of recruiting 100,000 foreign students set by Nakasone twenty years before was realized. 110,415 foreign students could be found studying at universities and colleges all over Japan. Among them, 66.8 percent, or 73,795, were from mainland China. In addition, 75.1 percent of the 47,198 language students were Chinese (Japan Immigration Association 2004). In total, Chinese students in Japan reached the number of 109,245, composing over a fourth of legal Chinese immigrant population in Japan in 2003.

Besides the student population, there are also a large number of skilled technical workers in Japan. In the early 1990s, Japanese companies started recruiting software engineers from China. Skilled Chinese workers have come to Japan either through intra-firm transfer by working for Japanese companies' China branches or through personnel agencies who directly contract them to work in Japan. Given the market demand in Japan, these technical workers are relatively free to move. In 2003, there were over 20,000 immigrants in Japan with technical skill visas, and over half of them came from China. This number did not include those who changed their visa status to permanent residency or who became Japanese citizens.

From Corporate Employees to Transnational Entrepreneurs

Immigrants' ethnic entrepreneurship in North America is often regarded as an alternative mobility channel after failing to access white-collar jobs in the host-society labor market because of the lack of language proficiency and proper credentials or because of racial discrimination (Min 1988). Host labor-market constraints also exist for the Chinese immigrants in Japan, although in a different form. Because Chinese immigrants have come to Japan in recent decades mostly as students, the majority who go through the Japanese educational system are legally employable. So, one characteristic of Chinese entrepreneurs is that they often originate from corporate Japan. Several institutional factors make them exit the host-society labor market and choose transnational entrepreneurship.

The first factor is a blocked career path for those whose human capital cannot be transferred into career advancement because of Japan's labor laws, institutional limitations, or other professional barriers. Jianxing An, a TV producer in China, married a Japanese woman and immigrated to Japan. "Initially, I wanted to find a job in a TV station or a TV production company. I tried for three months and contacted over 30 companies. Either they didn't want me or the salary was too low to make a living" (An 1998, p. 3). He then joined a trading firm that had business with China and later became an independent businessman.

The second labor-market constraint for Chinese immigrants in Japan is a lack of job security in Japanese companies. There are two types of insecure situations. One comes from small and medium-size firms' inability to survive in the economy. Small and medium-size firms are the mainstay of the Japanese economy (Sugimoto 1997). As the Ministry of Justice's (2006) records show, 40 percent of the close to 6,000 foreign students who graduated from Japanese universities with doctoral, master's, and bachelor's degrees in 2005 were employed in enterprises of fewer than fifty people. The majority of the entrepreneurs in the sample had worked for small Japanese companies. In the situation of chronic economic recession, these small and medium-size firms are in precarious situations. The other type of job insecurity comes from the institutional discrimination of big businesses toward foreign employees. Big-business corporations have different career tracks for native and foreign employees. Foreign employees are often contract workers of one- or three-year terms and are the first to be laid off during downsizing. Therefore, although foreign immigrants are in white-collar jobs in the primary labor market, they do not have job security. One interviewee, Zhou, was thinking of having his college classmate who worked as an IT person for a large Japanese company join him in his high-tech staffing and training business: "Recently he was telling me that his company had laid off all the Chinese employees, including the government-sent ones. He is the only Chinese person working for the company right now."

Chinese immigrants who can hold on to a corporate job in a Japanese institution have to confront the third kind of labor market constraint: the difficulty in advancing in the internal mobility ladder because of a discriminatory and inflexible career structure. Japanese firms until recently have instituted life-long employment (Ishida, Spilerman, and Su 1997). Companies expect loyalty and a long-term commitment from their employees. This imposed value has first created gendered career tracks for men and women because of the expectation that women would quit their job after marriage (Brinton 1992). Being foreign contract workers also put Chinese immigrant employees in the temporary category. My informants working for Japanese companies often expressed pessimism about the possibility of their promotion in the company. This sentiment was especially strong among Chinese women employees, who saw no hope of being in any leadership role despite their contribution. Two young women entrepreneurs, Yao and Wang, shared that although they became crucial in their companies' business with the Chinese-speaking world, they could never be anything other than an "overseas representative (*kaigaitantou*)." Yao, thirty-two years old, said, "Guess what the men in my company told me — '*Toshi mo soro soro, kekkon mo soro soro deshou* [You are about the age. Get married soon]'!" Yao left the trading firm when she turned thirty and started her own business. Wang quit her job because although she was a chief profit maker in a company of fifty people, she could not be promoted. "One carrot occupies one hole. The company only has several layers of positions — the president (*shachou*), the department leaders (*buchou*), and everybody else. Japanese men would never allow a Chinese woman to be a department leader." She later made a partnership with her former supervisor and started a transnational trading company between China and Japan doing the same business.

Finally, there are Chinese employees who find Japanese corporations' work environment unpleasant and opt for the freedom of self-managing entrepreneurship. Some complain that the strict hierarchical management typical of Japanese companies calls for obedience and suppresses their creativity. Two interviewees specifically mentioned they left their companies because of difficulty dealing with interpersonal relationships.

Though choosing to exit corporate Japan as a result of the constraints they felt, Chinese immigrants have learned specific trade knowledge and skills through working for Japanese companies. They often start their own business continuing in the same trade. The former television producer who imported construction material from China to Japan worked in a trading company for three years, from preparing import and export documents to sales and marketing. He realized that he alone could do the work done by 120 people in that company. He left the company and set up his own business importing construction material. In fact, fifteen entrepreneurs in the study's sample continued the same business after they left their employers. Several others found a niche market when they were working for a Japanese institution. For example, Su, during his student years, worked part-time installing air conditioners for a small company that subcontracted such jobs. He consequently learned the trade and the market. He set up a company with two other Chinese students after graduation. This service-oriented business led to another related business: manufacturing replacement parts in China to sell to Japanese companies in maintenance services.

In fact, corporate experience not only trained the sampled immigrant entrepreneurs in their trade but also provided partners or the first group of employees in some cases. Several entrepreneurs brought their former coworkers — their subordinates or supervisors — with them when they left their former employers.

Producing a Transnational Economy

The transnational Chinese immigrant enterprises described in this study are engaged in different types of businesses from those typically observed among immigrants in the United States. The Salvadoran and Dominican transnational entrepreneurs mostly provide services to co-ethnics in the host country, invest economic resources back into their home society, and supply ethnic and cultural products to a limited niche market beyond the local community (Itzigsohn, Cabral, Medina, and Vazquez 1999; Itzigsohn and Saucedo 2002; Landolt, Autler, and Baires 1999). In comparison, Chinese immigrant transnational businesses such as trading, consulting, information technology, international hospitality, travel, cultural production, shipping, and manufacturing mostly cater to the general market. Although most of the enterprises in the sample were small and many employed fewer than ten people, they were the bridges for the capital investment and facilitators for economic co-operation between Japan and China as well as potential nodes for transnational business networks. Aside from human capital and skills, the ability of these Chinese entrepreneurs to launch such businesses had a lot to do with the market demand arising from Japan's increasing needs for China's market and labor forces, and the rapidly integrating East Asian regional economy.

The Chinese market was not substantially open to the outside world until the 1980s. Two decades later, China has become an increasingly important production site and one of the most important consumer markets for the Japanese business world. Japan is one of the biggest investors in China. In 2002, Japan poured some US$4.2 billion directly into factories and other operations in China (Belson 2004). However, one Chinese immigrant entrepreneur remarked that the Japanese knew very little about China: "They go to China to do business with either a relaxed attitude of visiting a neighbor or an arrogance as if they have the mission to save the Chinese from poverty. They therefore stumble, and then cry about being cheated" (Li 1998, p. 601). As a result, some pioneering entrepreneurial efforts were in educational, hospitality, and consulting services, helping pave the way for business between Japan and China. They published periodicals introducing Chinese economy, organized Japanese company owners to tour China, and introduced Chinese government delegations to the Japanese business world for potential investment. One such company, while publishing a biweekly called *China–Japan News* (*zhong ri xin bao*), from 1992 to 1997, organized 117 Japanese delegations to China to seek business opportunities, and thirty-seven Japanese companies made successful investment in China (Liu 1998).

More common in recent years are companies that take advantage of the complementary markets in China and Japan. Three entrepreneurs from this study invested in factories in China to produce commodities for the Japanese market. Similarly, the enterprises in information technology make use of the relatively cheap human resources in China. They establish partnerships or branches in China to carry out projects contracted in Japan.

Because of the cultural affinity between Japan and China, Chinese medicine and food have long been a part of Japanese daily living. Several immigrant entrepreneurs in the sample traded in exotic Chinese goods such as Chinese diet food or food supplements. Three were art dealers trading in Chinese art.

China and Japan have also become attractive tourist destinations for each other. Since September 2003 Japanese citizens who schedule to visit China for shorter than fifteen days can obtain a visa upon entry. Japan is the first foreign country to enjoy visa exemption. In return, Japan grants group tourist visas to Chinese citizens. Responding to the opportunities, Chinese travel agencies have multiplied in Japan. These travel agencies not only sell discount tickets to the Chinese in Japan but also cooperate with travel agencies in China to arrange Chinese citizens' Japan tours. One recent business opportunity, according to an interviewee in travel business, is organizing Japanese high school students' school trips (*shugakuryoko*) to China.

In short, there is a transnational economic boom between Japan and China. Accompanying the increasingly dense economic links, social and cultural contacts have also increased. Such an economic environment provides a market niche for Chinese immigrant entrepreneurs who claim knowledge of both societies.

Strategies and Practices

The business strategies that ethnic groups adopt reflect both the opportunity structure within which they operate and the particular characteristics of the group (Aldrich and Waldinger 1990). Chinese immigrants have adopted several strategies in their entrepreneurial practices, including self-financing, partnering with or employing natives, networking, and diversifying business. These strategies reflect their immigrant status and relatively marginal socioeconomic positions in Japan. They are responses to the economic opportunities brought by economic regionalization in East Asia. Meanwhile, they actively expand business ties and activities in the region as well as worldwide.

Self-Financing

Like many ethnic business owners in other parts of the world, Chinese immigrant entrepreneurs typically establish their businesses with their personal savings. If one person's saving is not adequate, they pool the money together through partnership. Therefore, Chinese immigrant companies are usually small in the beginning. Some companies start with co-ownerships among friends and colleagues. There are also companies whose sources of initial capital show their crucial positions in transnational economy.

One woman entrepreneur, Chang, had a clever way of obtaining the initial capital. She helped locate machineries in Japan for a Chinese company before she registered her own company. Since she only had to show the Japanese government that she had the initial capital in her bank account, she registered her company by borrowing for a couple of days the money the Chinese company gave her as payment for the machines. Three entrepreneurs in this study's data were sponsored by Chinese private firms. Their businesses in Japan were in fact results of the requests made by their friends in China to expand the market and find suppliers in Japan.

The strategy of self-financing has to do with the near impossibility for foreigners to obtain business loans from Japanese banks. As Chang explained, "You need credit (*zi xin*) to borrow money from the bank. We had none." In fact, the Chinese immigrant entrepreneurs interviewed never tried to borrow money from banks. One entrepreneur who ran a transnational publishing company said he could not even get a loan to buy an apartment, so he did not think it would be possible for him to get a loan for a start-up company.

He Naihe, one of the most successful Chinese immigrant transnational entrepreneurs in high-tech business, started his company in 1996 by putting in all his savings and selling his car. Predicting he would not make any money in the first year, he asked his wife to take up cleaning jobs to feed the family (He 1998, p. 103).

Partnering and Employing Japanese Natives

To gain access to Japanese market and to have a smooth relationship with the Japanese business world, Chinese immigrant firms typically have Japanese advisors, partners, and employees. The Japanese advisors are often nominal. Two of the immigrants who opened consulting firms had their former Japanese teachers of social fame listed as advisors. One partnered with his retired professor.

Some Chinese firms like to have Japanese partners for more practical reasons. Zhou, a high-tech entrepreneur, explained,

> In Japan, in the software industry, there is a phenomenon that Japanese clients don't trust Chinese software companies. There are two reasons for this. First is language. Do you really understand what the client is talking about? In our software people's words, "you said you understood the client's words, but is what you understood what the client meant?" If there were miscommunication, terrible mistakes would occur. Secondly, the Japanese companies were really on guard of spies. So when they saw Chinese people, they couldn't help suspecting you.

One entrepreneur recently partnered with two Japanese businessmen to expand her current business: "I need them to get into the Japanese market, because they are Japanese and have the experience. And through knowing me, they can access the Chinese market."

Most entrepreneurs in trading, consulting, and high-tech business had native Japanese on their payrolls. Yao told me that she was often treated as a secretary to her native Japanese salespersons when they called on Japanese clients. "But it is so much easier to have them make cold calls. After all they are native speakers and know the place well."

Global Networking

Chinese immigrant entrepreneurs in Japan maintain close social ties in China and establish transnational networks largely by using institutional resources such as work-based ties and school and professional ties. As I have explained, many transnational entrepreneurs learn the ropes through working for Japanese institutions and subsequently run an independent business in the same trade, thus maintaining their client networks in both countries. Zhou got in touch with many influential people in the Chinese government when he was assigned to translate in some technical exchange events by his former employer, a big telecommunications company in Japan. These connections proved to be important assets in his later entrepreneurial activities. Aside from work-based ties, this group of immigrant entrepreneurs, because of their relatively high human capital, also has extensive ties with former classmates and friends that are conducive to transnational economic activities. The ages of the transnational entrepreneurs are mostly between early thirties and early fifties. Rapid economic growth since the 1980s in China made many of the classmates and former colleagues of these immigrants' movers and shakers in Chinese economy. The IT entrepreneurs, because of their professional specificity, are particularly inclined to partnering with their former classmates and colleagues in both China and Japan.

There have also been various Chinese associations specifically organized by entrepreneurs, professionals, or high-tech workers in Japan. As soon as entrepreneurs emerged among the Chinese immigrants, an entrepreneur's association in Japan — Chinese Student Entrepreneurs' Salon — came into being in 1991. In 1992 it changed its name to the International Economic and Cultural Cooperation Center. *The Data Book of Chinese in Japan, 1998–99* (Duan 2000) listed 234 nongovernment Chinese organizations, including old overseas Chinese merchant associations, professional associations, hometown associations, Chinese student councils, and alumni associations. Among them, the majority were founded by the new Chinese immigrants in Japan. Zheng, an entrepreneur and cofounder of one of the largest associations, the Association of Chinese Scientists and Engineers in Japan, told me their association aimed to achieve three goals: "One is horizontal connections, meaning internal network, so Chinese professionals, entrepreneurs and technical people could be connected. The second is to be connected with China. The third is to be connected with the Japanese equivalents." He said the first two goals were achieved. The association helped networking and had a good connection with Chinese business and the government. But the third goal was yet to be fulfilled. "You saw the presence of several Japanese–Chinese friendship associations or business associations at the annual conference. I guess they could probably be called the Japanese equivalents." Zheng believed associations were important for the Chinese to gain positive recognition and access in Japan. "In Japan, there are two kinds of power, one is individual prestige, and the other is group power. If one is very famous he can be easily regarded highly and accepted, but if nobody is particularly famous, it is the strength and the size of the group that bring recognition and therefore access."

In addition to uniting the new Chinese immigrants in Japan, some immigrants are also mobilizing ethnic resources and making efforts to connect the new overseas Chinese networks with the older ones. In recent decades, ethnic Chinese businesses have become increasingly global, and several firms entered the list of top 100 transnational corporations (UNCTAD 2005). There have been many discussions about a global ethnic Chinese businesses network and even the emergence of an ethnic Chinese business empire (Hamilton 1996; Ong and Nonini 1997). Three entrepreneurs in the sample mentioned particularly their intention to be connected to the global ethnic Chinese network. One organized a Chinese communication association to unite the old and the new Chinese immigrants in west Japan (Xu 1998, p. 144). One woman entrepreneur, Chang, had already attended two Global Overseas Chinese Conferences and had made connections with the overseas ethnic Chinese business community. She was considering expanding her trading business to Southeast Asia.

Yao, the young woman entrepreneur's transnational business was mainly with Southeast Asia. She was born in a family with overseas Chinese connections. Her firm in Japan imported interior decorative items from Bali and exported Japanese snacks to Jakarta.

Diversifying and Expanding Business

One strategy for survival and development in the competitive transnational market is diversification and expansion of business. There are two kinds of expansion and diversification: (1) establishing branches in Chinese cities and other countries; and (2) adding business divisions to the original company.

The first kind is commonly seen among growing enterprises in IT and trading. Naihe He's PSB Corporation, an IT company, has opened three branches in three Chinese cities. Another software company, which opened in 1994, has one branch in Beijing and one in the United States. This phenomenon indicates a global allocation of high-tech human resources. Saxenian (2002) reports that two-thirds of start-up companies in the Silicon Valley were opened by Asian immigrants, among whom most were Indian and Chinese. Many IT entrepreneurs interviewed in Japan had former classmates and colleagues in similar businesses in China, the United States, and Canada. Since IT businesses require human resources more than material capital, transnational branches expand through alumni and professional networks.

Several trading firms in the sample also opened branches in China and other countries. This was both for a close contact with the local market and to establish an image of transnational corporation to increase their market competitiveness. The sampled multinational corporations in international trading usually employed fewer than ten people, including both full- and part-time employees. One company had altogether seven employees in Japan and two in Shanghai. The owner had recently found some connections in Southeast Asia and was thinking of opening an office in Malaysia to access the market in Southeast Asia.

Small and with little institutional backing, immigrant enterprises are often in precarious situations and have high turnover. On the other hand, the transnational market is vast. Business opportunities emerge constantly. One survival strategy immigrant transnational businesses adopt is to diversify business. In other words, immigrant entrepreneurs do not confine themselves to a specific trade but take up whatever they deem profitable, given opportunities. For example, the two companies in the cultural production business that produced periodicals introducing Chinese business and Chinese culture to the Japanese business world also ran travel agencies and organized group tours both for Japanese clients to tour

China and for Chinese tourists to visit Japan. One travel agency ran an international matchmaking business. The woman art dealer also owned two beauty salons in Tokyo and Beijing. Service-oriented companies set up factories in China to manufacture related items. The oldest entrepreneur in the sample, Lao Hou, who came before 1980s, first opened a hotel and a duty-free store to serve the Chinese who came to Japan for short-term stays and later expanded the business to a shipping company that helped overseas Chinese ship the purchased goods back to China. He also established a trading firm engaged in transnational trading between Japan and China (Hou 1998).

In short, depending on the available resources and market demand, the immigrant transnational entrepreneurs are quick to expand their business geographically or along the production line.

Conclusion: Discerning the Global in Chinese Immigrant Transnational Entrepreneurship in Japan

Though having emerged in the process of immigration, Chinese people's transnational entrepreneurship can no longer be explained through the framework of immigrant adaptation. Treating it as an alternative adaptation pattern does not sufficiently capture the scope, content, and significance of immigrant entrepreneurship. Besides striving to survive and adapt, transnational immigrant entrepreneurs are also active facilitators of transnational economies with the potential to change and develop the global economy. The case of Chinese immigrant entrepreneurship in the Japan–China transnational economy illustrates this well. The concepts of scales and networks help explain the ways immigrants manage not only to participate in global processes but also to contribute to it through their grassroots efforts and often haphazard enterprising. This analysis particularly emphasizes the network mechanisms and immigrants' strategic use of institutional resources.

Chinese immigrant entrepreneurship in Japan has emerged within the expanding transnational economy between Japan and China. They have become entrepreneurs because they have the human capital. They have mostly been former students and skilled immigrants with transnational corporate experiences. They also possess social capital established through educational institutions, professional organizations, corporate businesses, and ethnic associations. In the process of developing their own transnational enterprises to ensure their own survival and prosperity, they help link originally local businesses and organizations from both sides of the East China Sea. They have deepened the interdependence of the Japanese and Chinese economies. Some have even expanded the networks to

Southeast Asia and to North America. Starting as a grassroots effort and as a response to opportunities and constraints in their immigrant context, Chinese immigrant entrepreneurship between Japan and China has scaled up into the economic globalization process.

Chinese immigrant entrepreneurial activities have close relationships with existing transnational corporations and global organizations. In fact, Chinese immigrant entrepreneurs have often been former employees of both large and small transnational corporations. This origin provides immigrants professional competence and allows them to engage in business practices already familiar to them. It also gives them access to existing transnational corporate business networks. Immigrants can then incorporate these business networks into their own cross-border social networks arising out of their participation in academic and professional institutions or out of their ethnic ties. By combining these networks of diverse origins and contents, they manage to build transnational business networks comprising individuals and firms originating in diverse localities and functioning at multiple scales. The network building strategy of transnational immigrant entrepreneurs points to a mechanism allowing certain business enterprises and practices to go transnational.

Acknowledgment

This article is made possible by generous financial supports from the Fulbright-Hays Doctoral Dissertation Research Abroad Fellowship and a dissertation fellowship from the East Asian Studies Center, University of Chicago. Thanks also go to Saskia Sassen, James Farrer, Junko Tajima, Yoshimichi Sato, and two anonymous reviewers for their critical reading and constructive comments.

Notes

1. Only thirty-five Chinese immigrants entered Japan as *investors/ business managers*.
2. Wang (2001) reports that in 2000, there were over 3,000 registered Chinese immigrant enterprises in Japan. They either started their entrepreneurship after they secured residential statuses or obtained permanent residency or naturalization after several years of successful business operation.
3. Several autobiographies do not give a full account of their career mobility in Japan.

Works Cited

Aldrich, Howard E., and Waldinger, Roger. 1990. Ethnicity and entrepreneurship. *Annual Reviews of Sociology* 16:111–35.

An, Jianxing. 1998. Ye cao de zhong zi (The seeds of grass). In Duan Yaozhong (ed.), *Fu ji dong ying xie chun qiu (Writing history in Japan)*, 1–8. Shanghai: Shanghai Education Press.

Aneesh, A. 2006. Virtual migration: The programming of globalization. Durham, NC: Duke University Press.

Bailey, Adrian J., Richard A. Wright, Alison Mountz, and Ines M. Miyares. 2002. (Re)producing Salvadoran transnational geographies. *Annals of the Association of American Geographers* 92(1):125–44.

Basch, Linda, Nina Glick-Schiller, and Cristina Szanton Blanc. 1994. Nations unbound: Transnational projects, postcolonial predicaments, and deterritorialized nation-states. Amsterdam: Gordon and Breach.

Belson, Ken. Japanese capital and jobs flowing to China, *New York Times*, February 17, 2004.

Brinton, Mary C. 1992. *Women and the economic miracle: Gender and work in postwar Japan*. Berkeley: University of California Press.

Dicken, Peter, Philip F. Kelly, Kris Olds, and Henry Wai-Chung Yeung. 2001. Chains and networks, territories and scales: Towards a relational framework for analysing the global economy. *Global Networks* 1(2):89–112.

Duan, Yaozhong.1998. *Fu ji dong ying xie chun qiu (Writing history in Japan)*. Shanghai, China: Shanghai Education Press.

Duan, Yaozhong. 2000. *The data book of Chinese in Japan, 1998–99*. Kawaguchi, Japan: Japanese Overseas Chinese News Press.

Guarnizo, Luis Eduardo. 2003. The economics of transnational living. *International Migration Review* 37(3):666–99.

Guarnizo Luis E., and Michael P. Smith. 1998. The locations of transnationalism. In Michael Peter Smith and Luis E. Guarnizo, eds., *Transnationalism from below*, 3–34. New Brunswick, NJ: Transaction Publishers.

Hamilton, Gary. 1996. Overseas Chinese capitalism. In Tu Wei-ming, ed., *Confucian traditions in the East Asian modernity*, 328–42. Cambridge, MA: Harvard University Press.

He, Naihe. 1998. Zai bing chuang shang ban gong si (Setting up the company in the sickbed). In Duan Yaozhong, ed., *Fu ji dong ying xie chun qiu (Writing history in Japan)*, 102–7. Shanghai: Shanghai Education Press.

Hou, Mingxuan. 1998. Dong du fu sang 20 nian (20 years in Japan). In Duan Yaozhong, ed., *Fu ji dong ying xie chun qiu (Writing history in Japan)*, 225–230. Shanghai: Shanghai Education Press.

Ishida, Hiroshi, Seymour Spilerman, and Kuo-Hsieu Su. 1997. Educational credentials in promotion chances in Japanese and American organizations. *American Sociological Review* 62:866–82.

Itzigsohn, Jose and Silvia Giorguli Saucedo. 2002. Immigrant incorporation and sociocultural transnationalism. *International Migration Review* 36(3):766–98.

Itzigsohn, Jose, Carlos Dore Cabral, Estner Hernandez Medina, and Obed Vazquez. 1999. Mapping Dominican transnationalism; narrow and broad transnational practices. *Ethnic and Racial Studies* 22:316–39.

Japan Immigration Association. 2004. *Statistics on the Foreigners Registered in Japan*. Tokyo, Japan.

Kelly, Philip F. 1999. The geographies and politics of globalization. *Progress in Human Geography* 23:379–400.

Landolt, Patricia, Lilian Autler, and Sonia Baires. 1999. From "hermano lejano" to "hermano mayor": The dialectics of Salvadoran transnationalism. *Ethnic and Racial Studies* 22:290–315.

Li, Niangu. 1998. Dong jing wu meng (Dreamless nights in Tokyo). In Duan Yaozhong, ed., *Fu ji dong ying xie chun qiu (Writing history in Japan*, 597–605. Shanghai: Shanghai Education Press.

Liu, Cheng. 1998. Mai xiang 21 shiji, wan cheng xin shi ming (Forwarding into 21st century; accomplishing new missions). In Duan Yaozhong, ed., *Fu ji dong ying xie chun qiu (Writing history in Japan)*, 629–33. Shanghai: Shanghai Education Press.

Mahler, Sarah J. 2001. Transnational relationships: The struggle to communicate across borders. *Identities* 7(4):583–619.

Mamadouh, Virginie, Olivier Kramsch, and Martin Van Der Velde. 2004. Articulating local and global scales. *Tijdschrift voor Economische en Sociale Geografie* 95(5):455–66.

Min, P.G. 1988. *Ethnic business enterprise: Korean small business in Atlanta*. New York: Center for Migration Studies.

Ministry of Justice. 2005. 2005 Immigration Control, available at http://www.moj.go.jp/NYUKAN/nyukan46-1.pdf.

Ministry of Justice. 2006. About the employment of foreign students who entered Japanese companies in 2005, available at http://www.moj.jp/.

Mitchell, Katharyne. 1997. Transnational subjects: Constituting the cultural citizen in the era of Pacific Rim capital. In Aihwa Ong and Donald Nonini, eds., *Ungrounded empires: The cultural politics of modern Chinese transnationalism*, 228–58. New York: Routledge.

Olds, Kris, and Henry W.C. Yeung. 1999. Reshaping "Chinese" business networks in a globalizing era. *Environment and Planning D: Society and Space* 17:535–55.

Ong, Aihwa. 1999. *Flexible citizenship: the cultural logics of transnationality.* Durham, NC: Duke University Press.

Ong, Aihwa, and Donald Nonini. 1997. Chinese transnationalism as an alternative modernity. In Aihwa Ong and Donald Nonini, eds., *Ungrounded empires: The cultural politics of modern Chinese transnationalism*, 3–36. New York: Routledge.

Parrenas, Rhacel Salazar. 2005. Long distance intimacy: Class, gender and intergenerational relations between mothers and children in Filipino transnational families. *Global Networks* 5(4):317–36.

Portes, Alejandro. 1996. Transnational communities: Their emergence and significance in the contemporary world system." In Roberto Patricio Korzeniewics and William C. Smith, eds., *Latin America in the world economy*, 151–68. Westport, CT: Greenwood Press.

Portes, Alejandro, Luis E. Guarnizo, and William J. Haller. 2002. Transnational entrepreneurs: An alternative form of immigrant adaptation. *American Sociological Review* 67:278–98.

Portes, Alejandro, Luis E. Guarnizo, and Patricia Landolt. 1999. The study of transnationalism: Pitfalls and promise of an emergent research field. *Ethnic and Racial Studies* 22(2):217–37.

Rankin, Katharine N. 2003. Anthropologies and geographies of globalization. *Progress in Human Geography* 27(6):708–34.

Roberts, Brian R., Reanne Frank, and Fernando Lozano-Asencio. 1999. Transnational migrant communities and Mexican migration to the United States. *Ethnic and Racial Studies* 22:238–66.

Sassen, Saskia. 1988. *The mobility of labor and capital: A study in international investment and labor flow.* Cambridge, UK: Cambridge University Press.

Saxenian, Anna Lee. 2002. Silicon Valley's new immigrant high-growth entrepreneurs. *Economic Development Quarterly* 16:20–31.

Saxenian, Anna Lee, Yasuyuki Motoyama, and Xiaohong Quan 2002. *Local and global networks of immigrant professionals in Silicon Valley.* Berkeley, CA: Public Policy Institute of California.

Sugimoto, Yoshio. 1997. *An introduction to Japanese society.* Cambridge, UK: Cambridge University Press.

Swyngedouw, Erik. 1997. Neither global nor local: "Glocalization" and the politics of scales. In K.R. Cox, ed., *Spaces of globalization: Reasserting the power of the local,* 137–66. New York: Gyildord.

United Nations Conference on Trade and Development (UNCTAD). *UNCTAD handbook of statistics 2005. Available online at http://www.unctad.org. Accessed on July 15, 2006.*

Wang Jin. 2001. 1990 nendai iko no zainichichugokujin shushokusha: nihon no gaikokujin seisaku to zainichichugokujin shushokusha no gensho (Chinese workers since 1990s: Japan's immigration policies and the status quo of the Chinese working in Japan). In Takamichi Kajita, ed., *Kokusai imin no shindoukou to gaikokujin seisaku no kadai — kakoku ni okerugenshouto torigumi (New trends in international migration and issues in policies toward foreigners),* 361-95. Japan: Immigration Bureau, Ministry of Justice.

Wong, Lloyd, and Michelle Ng. 2002. The emergence of small transnational enterprise in Vancouver: The case of Chinese entrepreneur immigrants. *International Journal of Urban and Regional Research* 26(3):508–30.

Xiang Biao. 2003. Indian information technology professionals' world system: The nation and the transnation in individuals' migration strategies. In Brenda S.A. Yeoh and Katie Willis, eds., *State/Nation/Transnation*, 161–78. London: Routledge.

Xu, Shichao. 1998. Xin hua qiao xie xin pian — wo yu jiao liu xie hui (New overseas Chinese writing in new page — exchange associations and me. In Duan Yaozhong, ed., *Fu ji dong ying xie chun qiu (Writing history in Japan)*, 142–50. Shanghai: Shanghai Education Press.

Yeung Henry. W.C. 2000. The dynamics of Asian business systems in a globalizing era. *Review of International Political Economy* 7:399–432.

CHAPTER 10

The Subnational Constitution of Global Financial Markets[1]

RACHEL HARVEY

Even the most globalized financial markets are embedded within spatial scales other than the global. Their operation and development, in other words, also occur at the national and subnational scales. This embedded view of global financial markets contrasts with the prevalent representation of these markets. The quintessential global financial market conjures images of the instantaneous transmission of vast sums of digitized money across space, as well as a ceaseless buying and selling that spans the waking and sleeping hours of the globe. Because these global markets are often experienced in the placeless electronic world of computer screens and networks, they are often portrayed as resting outside the domain of nation-states. These restless and nomadic financial flows represent, therefore, the final victory of time over space.

This idealized model of global financial markets is, however, an abstraction. And, as with all abstractions, it ontologically flattens social space.[2] This one-dimensional vision presents global financial markets as operating within the self-contained global scale, which rests comfortably on a spatial hierarchy of bounded scales. A market operating at the global scale precludes, therefore, the possibility of it also operating at national and subnational scales. These global markets are also free, moreover, of the social and cultural processes operating at these other spatial levels.

The institutional matrices and sociocultural milieus within nation-states too often disappear into the assumptions underlying this portrait of global markets.

Yet even markets that closely approximate this ideal abstraction, as in the case of the foreign exchange market, are embedded simultaneously in multiple levels of complex social space. The computer screens are intently monitored by traders working on expansive trading floors of large financial organizations. The organizations that dominate most financial markets are largely located in the world's key financial centers. The material infrastructure for these electronic markets, moreover, is located under the streets of the cities and in the buildings in which these trading floors are positioned. This stratified layering of social and material realities raises the possibility, therefore, that a global financial market can be conditioned by processes operating at the national and subnational scale.

This chapter explores this possibility by focusing on the role of subnational sociocultural processes in the development of a particular global financial market. Between 1950 and the mid-1990s, the London Gold Fix, a market trading 400-ounce bars of gold bullion, emerged as a global market. Despite being a global market in the 1990s, however, it was not located in electronic space. Unlike the ideal typical market just discussed, the Gold Fix set the price of gold twice a day from the offices of one of the market makers in the City of London. The London Gold Fix was constituted, therefore, by a curious overlapping of local, national, and global forms. This multiscalar dimension allows it to act as an analytical lens for the exploraion of the importance of sociocultural processes, operating at various spatial scales, in the development of a global market.

The first section of this chapter briefly reviews how scholars have traditionally treated the transformation of international markets into global markets. Although research exploring the emergence of global financial markets can be divided into two largely oppositional approaches, each conceptualization shares a spatially truncated and overly formalized conception of these markets. The next section then outlines the transition of the London Gold Fix from an international market to a global market. In discussing this transformation, I highlight the importance of events in 1968 as a turning point in the London Gold Fix's transformation into a global market. At this moment subnational sociocultural processes played a crucial role in initiating the emergence of a global outlook in the Gold Fix. Any understanding of this turning point would be incomplete, I argue, if these multiscalar social and cultural processes are not considered.

Understanding the Emergence of Global Financial Markets

Scholars treat the transition from an international system of markets to a global system as a key moment in the globalization process. This transformation of international financial markets to global formations was initially described by hyperglobalist[3] theorists of economic globalization.[4] From their perspective, this transition was marked by a shift from a world in which nation-states, as discrete territorial entities, were the central actors in their economies and in the international arena to a world where global markets and corporations dramatically limited the ability of nation-states to control their own economies (Friedman 1999; O'Brien 1992; Wriston 1997). This analysis highlights the role of technological and communication developments, such as the Internet and financial product innovations — that is, derivatives — as well as market relations in the creation of global financial markets. Within the hyperglobalist framework, the integration of financial markets around the globe through communication and technological innovations places pressure on national regulatory boundaries and national space. In other words, the factors producing global financial markets create a condition in which social space, particularly national space, is increasingly insignificant.

This hyperglobalist conception of the globalization of financial markets has been challenged by theorists who argue that nation-states are relevant to global economic processes.[5] Although these state-focused theorists recognize that the relationship between global financial markets and nation-states is changing, their research indicates that states still play an important role in the creation and operation of these markets.[6] These theorists generally concede, for example, that states are less able to control and direct capital flows today than in the past (Underhill 1991), that the volatility and speed of financial transactions challenge the state's regulatory power (Sassen 2000), that competitive deregulation dynamics engage states in a race to the bottom (Cerny 1991, 1994; Helleiner 1995), and that international markets and new telecommunications media undercut the state's exclusive control over its territory (Helleiner 1999; Hirst and Thompson 1995).

Despite these changes, there is also a consensus that states still play important roles in the production and reproduction of global markets (Cerny 1991, 1994; Helleiner 1995, 1999; Hirst and Thompson 1995; Sassen 1995, 2000, 2003; Underhill 1991, 2000). The global scale — global institutions, processes, and actors — has not eliminated the national scale. Markets need state regulation and a stable political framework for their establishment and functioning.[7] The state, it is argued, remains the ultimate guarantor of the rights of both national and foreign capital (Sassen 1995; Underhill 2000). These theorists also note that ideological shifts to neoliberal policies within nation-states are responsible for policies liberalizing and deregulating financial markets (Helleiner 1995; Walter 2005). This deregulation does not mean, however, that the state necessarily withdraws from market intervention. It often leads, in fact, to reregulation and even to increased state supervision of markets (Cerny 1991, 1994). Together these theorists argue that global markets need nation-states to function, and they reject the notion that states and global economic structures are engaged in a zero-sum relationship. It is in this manner that these theorists have reinserted a particular dimension of social space — that is, the nation-state — into their models.

This reassertion of the state as a factor explaining the globalization of financial markets indicates that the hyperglobalist's position is problematic because states play crucial roles in the development and sustaining of global markets. Despite recognizing this political element in the constitution of markets, this state-based critique of hyperglobalist assumptions is, nonetheless, limited. This focus on the state-market nexus only includes the role of nonstate actors[8] in the globalization of finance when they enter the political domain of the state or the policy-making realm (i.e., through the lobbying efforts of financial interests or the exercise of control through a hegemonic state). Otherwise, nonstate institutions and actors are placed into the residual categories of market relations and technological and institutional change (Cerny 1991, 1994; Helleiner 1995; Hirst and Thompson 1995; Underhill 1991, 2000). The placement of nonstate forces into these two categories inadvertently reinforces the hyperglobalist conception of global markets. As such, markets remain formally empty structures for transferring products, including financial assets. They are not conceptualized as being located in particular places or as supported and serviced by specific actors or infrastructures.[9] Hence, these state-focused critiques' overriding concern with the state leaves the social content of market relations largely unexamined and inadvertently reinforces the hyperglobalist conception of markets.

The perspective on markets offered by the new economic sociology corrects many of the problems associated with this truncated model of markets. This body of scholarly work demonstrates the concrete manner in which markets are embedded in sociocultural milieus and are constituted by historically specific cultures, institutions, and social networks.[10] Once properly framed, global markets can be conceptualized as being produced and reproduced by sociocultural processes operating at the national and subnational scale.

The remainder of this chapter examines how changing financial cultures, and shifts within the social structure of financial firms, played a crucial role during a specific moment in the Gold Fix's transition to a global market. The closing and reopening of the market in 1968 marked a watershed in this market's transition to a global market.[11] After this two-week closure the Gold Fix began to exhibit a global outlook. Although this moment was important in the development of this market as a global formation, the Fix only emerged as a full-fledged global financial market in the mid-1990s. These two weeks in 1968 saw, however, the first steps in this process. Despite the catalytic role of nation-states in reshaping the international monetary order at this moment, their efforts only provide a partial explanation of the arrival of a fresh outlook in this market. Rather, it was the actions of concrete individuals employed at firms in the City of London that laid the seeds for the London Gold Fix's transformation into a global structure.

The London Gold Fix

The London Gold Fix emerged after World War I through the Bank of England's efforts to restore Britain's currency and the City of London to their former international prominence. Prior to World War I, London was the international financial center in matters of trade, commerce, and finance. This dominance fostered London's position as the world's central gold market. This market was located in London and was constituted by bullion firms that were family partnerships. The London Gold Fix, as such, did not exist at this time. A price was set in London prior to World War I, but the bullion brokers did not meet at a specific time and place to carry out these transactions. Since Great Britain did not control or prohibit the export of gold, the London bullion market was considered to be the only free market for gold in the world. Although this free flow of gold was permitted, the actual price was never allowed to fall below £3 17s. 9d. (pounds/shillings/pence) per ounce since the Bank of England was bound by law to buy any amount of gold offered to it at this price.

After World War I Britain emerged as a markedly weakened power, and its position as a financial center was in question. Although Britain's prewar financial dominance was based on the country's position as the world's leading trading and industrial power, after the war many believed that gold was actually the source of Britain's international economic centrality (Ally 1994; Kynaston 1999). According to this view, the world's confidence in sterling was based on its gold convertibility. After the war, as nations attempted to return to the gold standard, statesmen and financiers associated with the Bank of England believed sterling could only be returned to its prewar position as the central international currency if the majority of the world's gold flowed through London. To achieve this end, the Bank of England engineered an agreement with South Africa, the world's largest gold producer, to ship its gold to London in lieu of other international markets (Ally 1994). Hence, with a majority of the world's newly mined gold flowing through London, the bank believed it had engineered sterling's return to its central international prewar position. The London Gold Fix became, therefore, the world's premier gold bullion market.

The actual structure of the market developed over the first two decades of its life. The architects of its initial form were the Bank of England and the partners of N.M. Rothschild & Sons, with the bullion brokers playing a more minor role. Initially, the singular characteristic of this market was the establishment of a single price for gold each day.[13] This single daily price was first established on September 12, 1919, at the first Gold Fixing, when the market members placed bids for the South African gold by phone. After several days the brokers began to meet, however, at the offices of N.M. Rothschild & Sons (Green 1984). Originally there were five participants in the Gold Fix: four bullion brokers — Pixley & Abell (established 1852), Mocatta & Goldsmid (established 1684), Samuel Montagu & Co. (established 1853), and Sharps & Wilkins (1740) — and a principal refiner. The refiner was N.M. Rothschild & Sons (a merchant bank established in 1804 that operated the Royal Mint Refinery) that presided over the market and acted as the agent for the South African gold producers. Later a second refiner, Johnson Matthey & Co. Ltd. (established 1817), was invited to join the Fixing. Almost a decade after the first Gold Fix phones began to be used inside the daily meeting.[14] By the middle of the twentieth century the rituals and practices of this market were largely regularized, and the once-daily fixing continued to operate until its closure in 1939 at the outbreak of World War II.

The market reopened again on March 22, 1954. Based on the customs and traditions established before 1939, the same six firms gathered at N.M. Rothschild & Sons to resume the once-daily fixing on this date in 1954. At precisely 10:30 a.m. on this pleasant spring morning, the representatives of the various firms sat down at a large table. On the table rested six small Union Jacks laying on their sides and a telephone for each representative. This telephone linked the traders to their respective trading rooms, which connected them, in turn, to the banks' customers on the world bullion market. On behalf of their customers, the banks' representatives then negotiated the price of gold bullion by adjusting the price and quantity of gold available for trade. If at any point a trader wanted to halt the trading to adjust their position, they simply called out, "Flag up," and raised their Union Jack. Once the issue was resolved, the flag was lowered, and trading would continue until a single price was reached. On reaching this moment the representative from Rothschild would declare that the price of gold was fixed for the day.

After the London Gold Fix reopened in 1954, it quickly established itself as an international market. By this time the British state increasingly asserted its authority over the market. Due to the post-World War II Bretton Woods Agreement, the Bank of England,[15] along with other central banks, regulated the price, trading, and flows of gold within this market. These activities were accomplished either through specific regulations by nation-states or through cooperative international action — that is, the Gold Pool and maintaining a price floor of US$34.75. The collapse of the Gold Pool in 1968 signaled the twilight of the gold-exchange standard and forced the closure of the London Gold Fix for two weeks.

When the Gold Fix reopened in April 1968 after a two-week closure, the market had changed. To begin with, central banks were no longer permitted to buy and sell gold at the London Gold Fix as they had in the past. This moment in 1968 marked, therefore, the gradual end of this market as an international formation. Besides this important alteration, the structure of the market changed as well. A second fix was added in the afternoon, and there was a shift to quoting the price of gold in U.S. dollars rather than in British sterling. In practice the market had essentially been a dollar market since the U.S. dollar was linked to the price of gold. The switch to quoting in dollars was, in many ways, an act of "discrete window dressing" (Green 1984, p. 129). These changes brought the Gold Fix in line with the shifting economic environment, yet they also marked an important turning point in this market's history. After the closure of the market for these two weeks, a burgeoning global outlook began to emerge among the Fix's participants. This moment signaled the initiation of globally oriented practices within the fix. As one trader noted over a decade later, since 1968 the London Gold Fixing members ceased to think "London anymore"; instead they thought "the world" (Green 1984, p. 131).

After these initial shifts, other changes followed. In the 1970s British firms involved in the fix established a presence in other major gold markets or became part of multidivisional firms in the process of establishing global institutional networks. In 1979 the abolition of exchange controls in the United Kingdom and later the Big Bang in the mid-1980s — a series of state-induced reforms that eventually transformed the British financial system — effectively increased the presence of non-British banks in London. These state policy changes increasingly brought non-U.K. firms into the bullion market. By the mid-1990s Deutsche Bank (Germany), the Republic National Bank of New York (United States), and HSBC (a nineteenth-century colonial bank originally based in Hong Kong), had seats at the Gold Fix. It was this moment in the 1990s that the London Gold Fix emerged as a global market. The dominant participants in this market were not representatives of states but rather of private institutions.

The firms within this market, moreover, were no longer just British firms. These institutions qualified as global or transnational corporations in that they had an integrated network of offices located throughout the world.

Although the Gold Fix was now constituted by global firms, and states became one of many participants in this market, this market was not global in the ideal typical sense. The qualities associated with global markets — electronic trading, speed, twenty-four-hour trading, and market operations occurring at the global scale — appeared to be largely absent from the Gold Fix in the 1990s. The market's meeting place was still the offices of N.M. Rothschild & Sons. The representatives of these firms continued meeting twice a day to set a single price in which all gold offered for sale was captured by the demand. In sum, the traditional practices and rituals originating at the local scale still dominated the structure of the Gold Fix in the 1990s. As such, it was anything but a global market.

Yet despite the dominance of these survivals grounded in the local scale, the Gold Fix was truly a global market in the 1990s. This decidedly local market with its traditional practices established a price used as a global benchmark throughout the world when traders and their firms quoted the price of gold. Although the price was set in a meeting at an office in the City of London, the trading floors with which each firm's representative at the Fix spoke were connected, in turn, to customers located throughout the globe. During the morning Fixing, traders in Asia and Europe would intently wait for the news of the morning Gold Fix. This process would be repeated later in the day when European and American traders turned their gaze to the afternoon Fixing. These characteristics of the London Gold Fix at this moment in the 1990s meant this market was a nodal global market. It was a market located within a national territory and was a node in a global network of firms and institutions that used this trading forum.

As this narrative indicates, in the fifty years following World War II the London Gold Fix was transformed from an international market into a global market. Though nation-states played a crucial role in the Fix's transition, their activities do not entirely explain the emergence of the London Gold Fix as a global structure. Instead, as I explore in the next section, subnational sociocultural processes played a crucial role in this markets development into a global market. Alterations in the City of London's sociocultural milieu and social change within the bullion firms were key factors responsible for the initial emergence of a global outlook within the Gold Fix. Along with the nation-state, sociocultural processes operating at the subnational scale were central in this market's transitioning to a global market.

The Subnational Production of a Global Outlook

As noted earlier, 1968 was a historical turning point in the London Gold Fix's transition to a global formation. Although the Gold Fix was still an international market after its closure and subsequent reopening, it began to exhibit a global orientation. This turning point was clearly the product of the efforts of nation-states to preserve the Bretton Woods Monetary Agreement. This interstate system of fixed exchanges rates using the U.S. gold-backed dollar as its anchor was becoming increasingly unsustainable. Specific actions of nation-states in salvaging this system included the British government's closing of the Gold Fix for two weeks at the request of the U.S. government. When the Gold Fix reopened, the market confronted a state-produced two-tier market: One tier was for central banks and monetary institutions to trade monetary gold, whereas the other was for nonmonetary, or free market, gold. Within the nonmonetary gold market, which included the London Gold Fix, the price of gold would no longer fluctuate in a narrow band around $35.00 per ounce or its sterling equivalent. It would be solely determined by market forces, since under the auspices of the Washington Agreement, central banks could not buy or sell gold in this market. These changes did not include, however, the addition of a second fixing, nor the fixing price being quoted in U.S. dollars. To understand the source of these changes, it is not sufficient to look at state action or technological and communication developments; rather, shifts within the structure of the bullion firms were a crucial factor in this initial moment of the Fix's transition to a global financial market.

In an informal meeting on March 26, 1968, representatives from the five bullion firms (after the merger of Pixley & Abell with Sharps & Wilkins in 1957 there were only five firms in the market) decided to add a second fixing in the afternoon and to quote the price in U.S. dollars to "avoid the attendant foreign exchange difficulties" associated with quoting the price in sterling.[16] A second fixing was added since this was "common practice for most metals" and the "Canadians, Americans, and South Americans" preferred to "see the state of the Market" when they were "awake."[17] After this informal meeting the bullion firms asked the Bank of England for their input on these changes.[18] After the final and formal meeting the decision was made to have the second fixing at 3:00 p.m. London time — as opposed to the original suggestion of 3:30 p.m. — and the commission to be paid by purchasers was set at one-quarter percent, instead of both purchasers and sellers paying one-half percent commission as initially proposed.[19] It is not clear what impact the Bank of England had on these two decisions. One thing, however, is clear. The impetus for these changes emerged from the five firms.

In a situation in which international forces, such as the collapse of Bretton Woods and the maneuvering of nation-states, were shaping the future and fortunes of the gold market, it seems strange that individuals from five firms would have been given such a powerful say in the operation of an international market. The ability of these firms to impact this important international market was undoubtedly based on the small size of the market and the organizational structure of the bullion firms. These firms had been involved in the market and had been interacting with each other for over 100 years by 1968. In 1968 the great majority of these firms were still relatively small with no more than 600 employees apiece.[20] Moreover, the bullion departments within these firms were commonly made up of only five or six dealers. Often there would be a bullion department manager, a head dealer for silver and a head dealer for gold, with each having an assistant. These individuals would be in constant contact throughout the day on the phone with other bullion traders both in London and throughout the world. The size of the firms and their bullion departments were important factors in making this international market a small fraternity (Green 1968). Together the small number of firms in the market, along with the compact organizational characteristics of the firms, created a situation in which a relatively small group of subnational actors could influence market policy and thereby could initiate the transformation of the Gold Fix into a global market.

The changes in the London Gold Fix have an added dimension of complexity. It was not simply a matter of these firms making these changes; rather, the impetus for these changes emerged from specific traders (Green 1984). The traders shaping these alterations in the Gold Fix shared an important characteristic. The two or three traders spearheading these shifts were young men (Green 1984). Given the fact that a majority of the bullion firms were characterized by a very traditional corporate culture, the ability of these young traders to have an impact on policy was unusual to say the least. N.M. Rothschild & Sons was still a family partnership controlled by the Rothschild family, and several of the other firms — Mocatta and Goldsmid; Sharps, Pixley; and Samuel Montagu & Co. — were still governed by members of the founding family. Despite being a wholly-owned subsidiary of Hambros merchant bank, Edward "Jock" Mocatta still presided over Mocatta and Goldsmid, and the firm largely operated out of its traditional offices on Throgmorton Avenue. A similar situation existed with Sharps, Pixley, & Co. In 1966 it was purchased by Kleinwort Benson, but Stewart Pixley, the fourth generation, remained its managing director. Integration with a merchant bank did not necessarily entail great changes within the daily workings of these firms. Decades later, Jack Spall, former deputy chair of Sharps, Pixley, recalled how when he joined the firm in 1970 it was "an autonomous company" with its "own board" and was not "even in the same building (as Kleinworts)" (Courtney and Thompson, 1996, p. 96).

The traditional culture and the hierarchical nature of these firms undoubtedly stemmed from their family partnership structure and control. At the same time, there was a larger, subnational context that conditioned these conservative corporate cultures. Their values and beliefs also resonated with and were reinforced by the hierarchical and conservative working culture in the City of London. The City of London, or the Square Mile or City as it was also and still is called, refers to the financial heart of Britain. London's geographical square mile at one time actually corresponded to Britain's financial sector, although during the 1960s the overlapping of this term with the geographical Square Mile had begun to separate. Despite the diversity of those working within the City (Thrift 1994), the Square Mile was dominated by a working culture grounded in the values of loyalty, duty, and honor. This complex of values and norms permeated the City's leadership and structured their relation with their employees. This "City ethos" fostered a sense of "duty" and "responsibility" in the directors and partners of the firms "to act generously to those who served" in their businesses.[21] Jack Spall, who spent his life working in the City, noted, "When I started off, most companies were paternalistic and there was tremendous loyalty from the people to the employer and the employer to the employee" (Courtney and Thompson 1996, p. 96). This sense of loyalty and duty was also expressed in the lifetime employment practices of many City firms (Courtney and Thompson 1996; Kynaston 1999; Thompson 1997a, 1997b). Michael Verey recalled this gentile quality during his time at the City merchant bank Helbert, Wagg: Employees "practically never resigned," they either "retired or died" (Courtney and Thompson 1996, p. 60).

Together the importance of family influence within these bullion brokers and the working culture of the City helped to foster these gentile values within the firms during the 1960s. Within the bullion firms, issues of succession and advancement were shaped by this hierarchical and traditional ethos. Promotion and movement within each firm were tied to length of time an individual worked within a bullion broker. It was rare to find a bullion dealer — as opposed to an assistant — in the 1960s under the age of thirty, even though many employees working in the City started in their twenties, if not earlier. It often took individuals decades to become the managers of their departments, if they even advanced at all. As in the City, individuals employed by these bullion firms often spent their entire working life in the same firm. Movement in a firm's hierarchy often occurred when a person left the firm or died. It was not until the 1970s that one of the bullion firms employed an individual who had worked within another market-maker's bullion department.

The sociocultural characteristics of these firms meant that major decisions normally originated from a managerial stratum of older gentlemen. Hence, the ability of these young dealers to shape the decisions made during this crucial moment in 1968 indicates that something unusual was occurring within the bullion firms making up the London Gold Fix. In his illuminating work on the gold market, Green (1984, p. 131) describes how the "London houses also benefited at this time from a fresh influx of young traders as several of the old guard, in what had been very conservative family partnerships, retired… London had a younger generation ready to take advantage" of the changes occurring in the Gold Fix. In effect, innovation was possible in the Fix because of cohort shifts within these traditional, hierarchical, and family-dominated firms.

Besides making these changes in the structure of the market, these young traders brought a different ethos to the market. These young dealers began to infuse the Fix with a dealing mentality and different understanding about what type of market the Fix should be. In the minds of the young traders, the pre-1968 Gold Fix was not a true market, but merely a mechanism for dispersing South African gold around the globe (Green 1984). Instead, these traders wanted to transform the post-1968 market into a true trading market that quoted a true two-way market price (Green 1984).

Prior to this shift, the pre-1968 London Gold Fix was a market for brokering South African gold. The representatives were providing a service to their clients by matching up the South African supply of gold with demand from around the world. At one level, the representatives involved in the Fix were acting as salesmen for the marketing of South African gold. Post-1968 the Gold Fix was still a market for brokering gold, yet the price was now free to fluctuate beyond the constraints of the pre-1968 narrow price bands. To these changing market conditions, under which the London Gold Fix was expected to operate, these young traders brought with them a "trading mentality" (Green 1984, p. 131). These young traders who entered the gold market around 1968 had "cut their teeth on foreign-exchange dealing," which contained a greater range of price movements and an increased price volatility despite the exchange controls and fixed exchange rates being imposed by the state apparatus (ibid.). The London Gold Fix became a market that brokered gold, but with an increasing "dealer" mentality quoting a "spirited two-way price" (ibid.). This change in the market ethos was particularly important as prices became increasingly volatile during the 1970s. The traders in the London Gold Fix had a skill set and an ethos that welcomed the increased uncertainty in price movements.

This view of the pre-1968 London Gold Fix as a distribution mechanism for South African gold, as opposed to a two-way price making market, was not reflected in earlier descriptions of this market (Anon 1954; Green 1968). In these descriptions the London Gold Fix was always portrayed as a genuine market as opposed to a channel for distributing South African gold. The pre-1968 Fix was viewed as a two-way market in that demand was always met with adequate supply (Anon 1954).[22] Price movement might have been largely tied to differences in shipping costs, but the process of making the market involved quoting a two-way market price. The Gold Fix was just as much a market before 1968 as it was after 1968. The designation of the post-1968 Fix as a true market reflects, therefore, that a different way of conceptualizing the London Gold Fix was emerging. In other words, these descriptions of the Fix, both before and after 1968, indicate that a shift in the meaning of a two-way market was under way within the market. The younger generation was not simply creating a true two-way market; instead, they expressed a different set of understandings about markets in general. The London Gold Fix had changed, but a different conception of markets was also being increasingly used.

This moment in 1968 represented a turning point in the history of the London Gold Fix. It laid the foundation for the Gold Fix's emergence as a global market by fostering this market's burgeoning global perspective. As one trader noted, "Prior to 1968, London was complacent, it felt the world came to it to buy gold" (Green 1984. p. 131). After 1968, Gold Fix participants focused their sites beyond London and began to view the world as their potential marketplace (ibid.). This shift was clearly due, in part, to the actions of states in shaping the international monetary order at the time. Yet their actions were not sufficient to produce the changes occurring within the Fix; rather, it was cultural and social change at the subnational level that also acted as a catalyst for this market's emergent global outlook.

Conclusion

Through an exploration of changes occurring in the London Gold Fix during 1968, I have tried to demonstrate the crucial roles played by subnational sociocultural processes in an international financial market's transformation into a global market. Regardless of the extent to which financial markets are global, they are also partially located in national and subnational spaces. Consequently, the ideal typical financial market utilized in the scholarship on these markets needs to be modified to incorporate the multiple scales involved in the production and daily reproduction of global financial markets. This is not to say that all global financial markets contain the same type of scalar dynamics as the London Gold Fix.

Rather, it is crucial for further theorization and research to capture the interaction between the fluid mobility and the multiscalar embeddedness of these markets.

Incorporating the multiscalar dynamics involved in the study of global financial markets can help to minimize the ways in which social space is flattened in traditional models of these markets. Yet this alone is insufficient for capturing another crucial characteristic and dynamic of these financial markets. Understandings of global financial markets also need to go beyond the variables normally identified as crucial in the production and reproduction of these markets: the nation-state, technological and communication developments, and market relations. These variables are clearly important, yet they ignore the myriad of sociological factors that might play a role in the development of global financial markets. Rather, as this chapter suggests, sociocultural variables such as firm structure and culture, interfirm dynamics, and working cultures of the various cities where financial firms are located should be considered when explaining the emergence of global financial markets. Without incorporating these sociocultural elements as possible causal forces in this transformation of international markets into global formations, an understanding of these changes would be incomplete.

Notes

1. This chapter is based on research conducted for my dissertation. The findings are based on archival research and interviews. I thank the London Bullion Market Association for its very generous assistance in facilitating this research, and the archival staff at the Bank of England, Hong Kong and Shanghai Banking Corporation (HSBC), the Rothschild Archive, London and the Guildhall Manuscript Section for their assistance and kindness. My research would not have been possible, as well, without the various individuals who took time out of their very busy schedules to speak with me about my project. This chapter reflects their valuable insights, but the conclusions and interpretations with their possible limitations, are my own. Finally, I want to thank Tim Green for his rich and detailed chronicles of the London Gold Market. Without his attention to the subtle nuances of this gold market much of this market's history would be lost.
2. This chapter focuses on making the spatial element of this model more complex. This standard conceptualization of financial markets, however, also flattens social time. These markets also operate across and within different temporal orders (Miyazaki 2003.) This element of temporal stratification needs to be incorporated into the aforementioned abstraction. When the London Gold Fix emerged as a global market in the mid-1990s, it still retained an element of the leisurely and gentlemanly temporal order that once dominated this market and the broader London bullion market.

3. The term *hyperglobalist* refers to arguments regarding economic globalization declaring that nation-states are no longer meaningful economic actors, that standardized products create a world of homogenized tastes and cultures, and that place no longer matters as corporations can move freely across the globe in search of the most profitable production location. The term *first-wave theorists* has also been used to describe this group (Hay and Marsh 2000). Scholars focusing specifically on the globalization of financial markets also describe this group as using a liberal model (Cohen 1996) or engaging in technological determinism (Walter 2005).
4. I understand globalization as a dialectical process in which the acceleration of capital flows through geographic space is dependent on relatively fixed and immobile social structures that do not operate at the global scale (Brenner 1998, 1999; Sassen 2000, 2003, 2005). Within this framework, scales interdigitate in strategic ways through a negotiation between elements of national and subnational scales with global processes (i.e., denationalization).
5. These scholars have been grouped in the general rubric of *second-wave theorists* (Hay and Marsh 2000) since they directly challenge hyperglobalist or first-wave theories of globalization. The term *second wave* does not simply pertain to theorists of the state. Second-wave theorists, in their varied and diverse work, argue that a homogenous global culture does not dominate all other cultural forms, that nation-states are not engaged in a zero-sum relation with global processes, that the hypermobility of capital is greatly exaggerated, and that national economic spaces remain far more intact than hyperglobalists assume.
6. These theoristss are largely working within the tradition of international political economy. These theorists agree that the hyperglobalists, liberal model, or technonogical determists overstate the erosion of state power. Beyond this general agreement, however, different theorists stress various ways that states relate to global financial markets. Cohen (1996) divides these state-based theorists into a realist model, a pluralist model, and a cognitive model. Walter (2005) breaks this group of scholars into hegemonic power approaches and rationalist interest group approaches.
7. Within this literature, states are not treated as having equal power. The power differentials between states of developing and developed countries, both within and without their own territorial borders, are great. When talking about the role of the state, therefore, these theorists largely focused on the states of the most developed countries.
8. Nonstate actors include, for instance, individuals or institutions participating in the daily functioning of global financial markets, as well as industry organizations and trade associations involved in the governance of these global markets.
9. Works by Sassen (1995, 2000, 2003) and Brenner (1998, 1999) begin to address these issues by recognizing that the conditions for the functioning of global markets and institutions are also produced at the subnational, or urban, level. Institutions, processes, and actors at the subnational or local scale also constitute global structures. In other words, local practices and conditions can articulate with global dynamics within national territories (Brenner 1998, 1999; Sassen 1995, 2000, 2003).

10. Although scholars working within the new economic sociology use different types of analysis — cultural, institutional, and network — they can be divided into two schools of thought, each of which makes salient points in relation to the social character of markets. One approach treats markets as bounded entities shaped by sociocultural processes. An example of this is Carruthers's (1996) exploration of how politics shaped the trading behavior of the shareholders of joint-stock companies in late seventeenth- and early eighteenth-century Britain. The second framework considers markets to be constituted by various sociocultural processes. The works of Knorr Cetina and Bruegger (2002), Zaloom (2003), and Salzinger (2003) are examples of this tradition in that they explore how markets are constituted as cultural forms (Knorr Centina and Bruegger 2002; Zaloom 2003) or by cultural forms (Salzinger 2002; Zaloom 2003). Zaloom and Salzinger also pay attention to the role of the trading floor in constructing traders' subjectivities and understandings of the market. Zelizer (2002) contains a brief discussion of these two approaches in the new economic sociology as they relate to markets in general, as opposed to financial markets.
11. This moment constitutes an event (Sewell 1996) in the history of this market. The changes occurring in this market are congruent with Sewell's contention that "events bring about historical changes in part by transforming the very cultural categories that shape and constrain human action" (p. 263).
12. The governor of the Bank of England, Sir Brien Cockayne, and the partners of N.M. Rothschild and Sons were the architects of this market. Bank of England Archives, C40/360/90, Notes on a meeting, August 6, 1919; and Bank of England Archives; C40/360/71, Letter from N. Charles Rothschild to Sir Brien Cokayne, July 28, 1919.
13. The originator of this central structural feature was Cokayne. Bank of England Archives, C40/360/90, Notes on a meeting, August 6, 1919.
14. Bank of England Archives, C43/139, Gold Fixing, November 29, 1933.
15. In 1946, in fact, the Bank of England was nationalized and became an agent of the state.
16. Bank of England Archives, 3A139/1, London Gold Market, March 26, 1968.
17. Bank of England Archives, 3A139/1, Attachment to letter from E.B. Bennett at the Bank of England to A.K. Rawlinson at H.M. Treasury.
18. Bank of England Archives, 3A139/1, London Gold Market, March 26, 1968.
19. Bank of England Archives, 3A139/1, Attachment to letter from E.B. Bennett at the Bank of England to A.K. Rawlinson at H.M. Treasury. Bank of England Archives, 3A139/1, London Gold Market, March 26, 1968
20. Johnson Matthey might have had more employees since they were also an industrial company that refined and marketed many other types of metals as well. Through my research it appears, however, that the structure of their bullion department was similar to the departments of the other bullion-broker firms.
21. Montagu (1913, p. 58-59) provides this description of her father's treatment of his employees.

22. In discussing the importance of the London Gold Fix after its reopening, an article in *The Banker* noted, "Equally important, however, is the fact that the London gold market, unlike so many of the free markets that have flourished in recent years, can claim to be a genuine two-way market— a market to which a large part of the gold production of the world is canalized and where the demand can, therefore, always be met by an adequate supply." (Anon 1954: 266)

Works Cited

Ally, Russell. 1994. *Gold and empire: The Bank of England and South Africa's gold producers 1886-1926.* Johannesburg: Witwatersrand University Press.

Anon. 1954. Is gold staging a come-back?" *The Banker* 102(340):265–70.

Brenner, Neil. 1998. Global cities, glocal states: Global city formation and state territorial restructuring in contemporary Europe. *Review of International Political Economy* 5:1–37.

———. 1999. Beyond state centrism? Space, territoriality, and geographical scale in globalization studies. *Theory and Society* 28:39–78.

Carruthers, Bruce. 1996. *City of capital: Politics and markets in the English financial revolution.* Princeton, NJ: Princeton University Press.

Cerny, Philip G. 1991. The limits of deregulation: Transnational interpenetration and policy change. *European Journal of Political Research* 19:173–96.

———. 1994. The dynamics of financial globalization: Technology, market structure, and polity response. *Policy Sciences* 27:319–42.

Cohen, Benjamin. 1996, Phoenix risen: The resurrection of global finance. *World Polity* 48:268–96.

Courtney, Cathy, and Paul Thompson. 1996. *City lives: The changing voices of British finance.* London: Methuen London.

Friedman, Thomas L. 1999. *The Lexus and the olive tree.* New York: Farrar, Straus, and Giroux.

Green, Timothy. 1968. *The world of gold.* New York: Walker and Company.

———. 1984. *The new world of gold: The inside story of the mines, the markets, the politics, the investors.* New York: Walker and Company.

Hay, Colin, and David Marsh. 2000. Introduction: Demystifying globalization. In Colin Hay and David Marsh, eds., *Demystifying Globalization,* 1–20. New York: St. Martin's Press.

Helleiner, Eric. 1995. Explaining the globalization of financial markets: Bringing states back in. *Review of International Political Economy* 2:315–41.

———. 1999. Sovereignty, territoriality, and the globalization of finance. In David A. Smith, Dorothy J. Solinger, and Steven C. Topik, eds., *States and sovereignty in the global economy,* 138–57. London: Routledge.

Hirst, Paul, and Grahame Thompson. 1995. Globalization and the future of the nation state. *Economy and Society* 24:408–42.

Knorr Cetina, Karin, and Urs Bruegger. 2002. Global microstructures: The virtual societies of financial markets. *American Journal of Sociology* 107:905–50.

Kynaston, David. 1999. *The city of London: Volume III, illusions of gold, 1914–1945.* London: Pimlico.

Miyazaki, Hirokazu. 2003. The temporalities of the market. *American Anthropologist* 105:255–65.

Montagu, Lily H. 1913. *Samuel Montagu, 1st baron Swaythling: A character sketch.* London: Truslove & Hanson.

O'Brien, Richard. 1992. *Global financial integration: The end of geography.* London: Royal Institute of International Affairs.

Salzinger, Leslie. 2003. Market subjects: Traders at work in the dollar/peso market. Presented at American Sociological Association Conference, August 16–19 Atlanta, Georgia.

Sassen, Saskia. 1995. The state and the global city: Notes towards a conception of place-centered governance. *Competition & Change* 1:31–50.

———. 2000. Territory and territoriality in the global economy. *International Sociology* 15:372–93.

———. 2003. Globalization or denationalization. *Review of International Political Economy* 10(1):1–22.

———. 2005. When national territory is home to the global: Old borders to novel borderings. *New Political Economy* 10(4):523–541.

Sewell, William H., Jr. 1996. Three temporalities: Toward an eventful sociology. In Terrance J. McDonald, ed., *The historic turn in the human sciences,* 245–80. Ann Arbor: University of Michigan Press.

Thompson, Paul. 1997a. The pyrrhic victory of gentlemanly capitalism: The financial elite of the City of London, 1945–90. *Journal of Contemporary History* 32(3):283–304.

———. 1997b. The pyrrhic victory of gentlemanly capitalism: The financial elite of the City of London, 1945–90, part 2. *Journal of Contemporary History* 32(4):427–40.

Thrift, Nigel. 1994. On the social and cultural determinants of international financial centers: The case of the City of London. In Stuart Corbridge, Nigel Thrift, and Ron Martin, eds., *Money, power, and space,* 327–55. Oxford: Blackwell.

Underhill, Geoffrey R.D. 1991. Markets beyond politics? The state and the internationalization of financial markets. *European Journal of Political Research* 19:197–225.

———. 2000. State, market and global political economy: Genealogy of an (inter-?) discipline. *International Affairs* 76:805–24.

Walter, Andrew. 2005. Understanding financial globalization in international political economy, LSE Research Online, available at: http://eprints.lse.ac.uk/archive/00000798.

Wriston, Walter B. 1997. Bits, bytes, and diplomacy. *Foreign Affairs* 76:172–82.

Zaloom, Caitlin. 2003. Ambiguous numbers: Trading technologies and interpretation in financial markets. *American Ethnologist* 30:258–72.

Zelizer, Viviana. 2002. Enter culture. In Mauro F. Guillen, Randall Collins, Paula England, and Marshall Meyer, eds., *The new economic sociology: Developments in an emerging field,* 101–25. New York: Russell Sage Foundation.

PART 3

The Political: Shifting Spaces and Subjects

CHAPTER **11**

The City and the Self

The Emergence of New Political Subjects in London

ANNE BARTLETT

September 2003. The phone rang. We were sitting in a café in Notting Hill, London, and it seemed an unlikely place to be speaking to the rebel leader of the Sudanese Liberation Army (SLA). Yet satellite phones change everything. High in the hills of the Jebel Marra mountain range in Darfur he had called Abdul, a member of the Fur tribe,[1] to ask for help with a number of logistical issues. Before I knew what was happening, the phone was thrust into my hand. "Thank you for your support of our people … for your help in London" the rebel commander said so clearly that he could almost be standing next to me. "*Afwan,*"[2] I replied. "How are the people there? How is the situation? This man was, of course, already known to me by reputation. He was a lawyer who had taken up armed struggle to protect members of his tribe from being killed. In common with his colleagues, he had left his home and spent years away from his family trying to defeat militia forces known as the *Janjawiid*[3] and their backers, the government of Sudan. Yet as I talked to him, I couldn't help reflecting on the effectiveness of global communications technology; at the way it could circumvent structures of authority, skip from a volcanic mountain range in Sudan into a café in the west of London. It was almost as if telecommunications technology was able to bring Darfur to London; as if a *microspace* opened up that momentarily linked two places together, crushing distance and time, enabling a war in Africa to be managed by satellite phone from city streets in the West.

Over the following months, these kinds of interactions recurred frequently. Spending time on the streets of West London, helping out in small human-rights offices, and sleeping out on the pavements of the capital to protest against the genocide of people of Darfur, it became clear that the city is a vital space in the emergence of new political practices. As a communications circuit, as a space where rights can be fought for, as a bulwark against authoritarian regimes, London's urban space provides a crucial environment in which political alterity can flourish. In the informal spaces of the city, I was transported into another world, one that made visible the ways in which city space is strategic terrain for those who can navigate the dialectic between everyday and formal political practice in pursuit of their political goals. Inside this world, I saw how refugees and immigrants build their own forms of political meaning and act to redefine themselves as political subjects capable of making change. I also learned how political legibility is produced in contemporary urban space; how new ways of being political are incrementally, yet indelibly, changing the political landscape of the West.

The question of how immigrant groups become political and how the politics of developing countries are brought to life on the streets of Western cities is now critical. With the onset of major international crises, the influx of foreign nationals and the existence of multiple forms of political being, cities now play a pivotal role in producing the conditions of possibility for new types of political action. Since the outcomes can be emancipatory and inclusive on one hand, or reactionary and exclusive on the other, it is now vitally important to understand the drivers behind such processes because they are as important to those involved in politics as those who are not.

Yet these dynamics are staggeringly complex. Starting fieldwork in January 2003, I had no idea of the world I was about to enter. For sure, I had done a lot of background research; I had trained extensively as an ethnographer at the University of Chicago and was no stranger to movement across borders, since I had moved from the United Kingdom to Chicago some years before. But this was not the same — not even close to understanding what it means to be caught up in the whirlwind of political action that *is* an international conflict of this kind. Being involved in forced migration, having to reconstitute networks elsewhere and being politically effective in a system that differs and is in many ways incompatible with one's own, requires a particular kind of engagement with discontinuity and the possibilities it can bring. It is this ability to live life on the margins — and perhaps more importantly to use those margins to effect change

— that marks the shifting parameters of what it means to *be political* in urban centers today.

This chapter analyzes the process through which new types of political subjects emerge in contemporary city space. Using the Darfur crisis as a lens to illuminate changes in the political landscape, it shows how new actors emerge inside existing political fields and how these new political fields are related to host country politics. Changes, borne of disjunctures and contradictions between old and new migration flows; between competing ideologies of nation, region, tribe, and party and between formal and informal ways of doing politics, open up the political landscape and allow new modes of being political to emerge. Deciphering the global means getting into these spaces of contestation — into the cracks that are appearing in the political landscape and watching as new forms, actors, and practices start to make themselves known.

New Subjects, New Spaces

How do we explain the processes at work here? Despite vast amounts of ink that have been spilled analyzing the prevalence of radical political behavior, rather less attention has been focused on the mechanisms that produce new types of political subjects in the first place. In part this is due to the difficulty of doing this kind of work, the necessity of ethnographic involvement, and the access needed to particular communities and their informal political networks in the first place. But it also speaks to the difficulty of tracing out such processes on the ground and the practical difficulties in tracking these exceedingly complex changes as they occur.

Isin (2002) has, however, made some significant strides forward in this direction with interesting results. In his book, *Being Political,* he uses a framework developed from Foucault's work to analyze the means by which strategies and technologies of citizenship are historically re-appropriated and overturned by marginal groups as they seek to make change. His point — that there is an ontological difference between being political and politics — goes to the heart of both contemporary and historical political practice. As he points out, it is only through the ability to constitute oneself as an actor vis-à-vis others over matters of justice, that the conditions for new kinds of politics emerge. And of course, this change does not happen in a vacuum. As he suggests, it is the city — specifically dialogical encounter in the city — that provides the synergy from which new kinds of actors emerge:

> The city is a difference machine insofar as it is understood as that configuration that is constituted by the dialogical encounter of groups formed and generated immanently in the process of taking

> up positions, orienting themselves for and against each other, inventing and assembling strategies and technologies, mobilizing various forms of capital, making claims to a space that is objectified as "the city." Neither groups nor their identities exist before the encounter with the city.[4] (p. 49)

Yet the importance of the city as an incubator of political change has not always received uncritical acceptance. At other times, for example, factories, workplaces, and other sites also played important roles in the emergence of political subjects too. But with the onset of globalization, the institutional mediation of political action has been supplemented by action across a variety of informal spaces shaped anew by new global dynamics. The city is at the heart of this change. As a locus of complexity and difference it makes possible the many acts of demarcating self from other as groups and individuals jostle for position and prestige. As Sassen (Sassen 2006) makes clear, it is in the city, where multiple scales and actors can operate, that local practices are most clearly articulated with global flows.

Changes such as the redrawing of territorial boundaries and the decline of the nation-state as a natural and inevitable[5] container for social, political, and economic processes presage other changes on a subnational scale. In a metropolis such as London, these changes reconfigure the economic structure of the city and also produce new forms of authority, rights, and claim making within its bounds (Sassen 1991). On its streets, flows of legal and illegal immigrants, refugees, and aliens create new milieus: changes in the life and appearance of the city, a poiesis based around consumption, smells, noise, ways of using, of dressing, of marking space and using time — changes that incrementally yet profoundly alter everyday practices of living and being in the area. As a result, new logics emerge to govern the encounter between one group and another. These changes mark a shift in the boundaries between self and other in the city: Boundaries that once delimited nation-state territory are now inside the city, dividing, inscribing, and incubating new ways of action that have the ability to structure everyday life in quite different ways.

Boundaries and the Self

But it is one thing to suggest the emergence of new political actors and claim making and quite another to explain the process through which this is actually happening. This chapter suggests that a return to the simplest unit of analysis, the boundary, is the most helpful way to think about how people become political. As I argue, political selves do not simply emerge in a vacuum; they emerge at the point of encounter with others — at boundaries where identifications are made, communities are constituted and reconstituted and where difference is a marker for particular kinds of association (Glaeser 2000). Boundaries matter in the formation of new types of political being not simply because they are points where different groups and individuals meet, but also because they are the locus of conflict, of political agency, and the place where the choreography of the street and staking of claims is most evident.

Yet in environments where multiple cross-cutting political ties exist, it is extremely difficult — if not impossible — to read off larger changes and the direction political action is moving without attention to micro-level interactions on the ground. Global dynamics, the ebb and flow of enmity and alliance, the radicalization of certain groups become inexplicable unless more is understood about the mechanisms through which such changes are instigated. Such mechanisms, borne of the immigration history of the country concerned, the interaction of informal and formal political groups on the ground and their relation to the politics of the host and sending countries, yield clues as to dynamics of the political terrain. Yet when faced with this almost daunting level of political complexity, it is only at a boundary where new kinds of political tensions make themselves most evident that we can go to work trying understand the dynamics that are involved in driving such change.

If I needed reminding of this fact, my rude awakening came at a refugee center in West London where I started fieldwork as a means to acquaint myself with local Middle Eastern and African communities. The center appeared, at least on the face of things, to be a place where welfare advice was handed out, where people from various ethnic communities could meet, and where the isolation of forced migration could be eased. But it had other functions too. Despite the appearances of a U.K. government-funded community center, it was also a place where the political rivalries from Sudan could be fought out. At the time I was there, the center and its resources were controlled by one of the mainline political parties from Sudan, the Umma Party. Not knowing this at the outset of my research, I had unwittingly struck up friendships with two men, one from the Sudanese Communist Party (SCP) and one from the Sudanese Liberation Army/Movement (SLA/M). These men — particularly one of them — stood in the way of the director of the center and his political ambitions. As I would find out, this was a major problem that would have a significant impact my future research. And, of course, given the speed at which the Darfur crisis was escalating, it wasn't long before events conspired to make these tensions abundantly clear.

On return from a short trip to the United States, I was rather abruptly asked to leave the center. At the time, it was unclear why a cordial atmosphere in which I was an outsider — a researcher who got in the way but who could provide occasional help — should change overnight into an atmosphere in which I was viewed with suspicion. Later reflection and subsequent phone calls from members of the refugee community provided the answer. Almost without exception, the analysis was the same: "You talked to the wrong person." By making contacts and trying to diversify those to whom I could talk, I had symbolically challenged the power of the director and with it the Sudanese Umma party. I had crossed an invisible line or boundary that had been inscribed in the local territory demarcating who could and could not be spoken to. And it was not just any boundary. It marked the old political guard from the new in Darfur. It marked conventional Sudanese party politics from the informal politics of the street which was the domain of the rebel movements. It divided many of the refugee political actors into opposing and ultimately irreconcilable factions.[6] And this boundary was not marked on the war-torn land of Darfur: It was marked on London's city streets.

Boundaries are not a new object of study in the social sciences. From physical boundaries that demarcate one part of the city from another to temporal, linguistic, and politico-organizational boundaries, they are the stuff of everyday interaction and the place where the microprocesses of self-formation take place. Yet there are, of course, ways and ways to think about boundaries. In much of the voluminous literature on boundaries (see, e.g., Barth 1969; Burgiere and Grew 2001; Haaland 1969; Kimmerling 1996; Lamont and Molnar 2002; Ong 1996; Sahlins 1989; Tilly 2003, 2004; Zerubavel 1991), effort is directed toward understanding how boundaries demarcate one group from another: what the criteria are for signaling inclusion and exclusion. In this type of analysis emphasis is often placed on the way that social boundaries define membership, as well as the way ethnic boundaries canalize social life.

But it is also possible to think about boundaries in a different way: as threads of difference that emerge inside groups or fields and how they are linked to minute changes in identities or beliefs on the ground. In a situation where refugees and immigrants inhabit new spaces in Western cities, tensions between groups usually circumscribed by national or regional boundaries now reinsert themselves into urban space, reconfiguring the political character of the city. The key to understanding boundaries in this respect is not to think of them as territorial encasements but as lines of difference that emerge or fade. These lines of difference may produce new spaces within existing political fields or may die fast and quiet without the energy to sustain them. Yet by focusing less on political subjects and spaces as they exist and more on *entities in the making*, it is possible to see how particular conjunctions or disjunctions act to produce, stabilize, and enact certain kinds of spaces and possibilities of being (c.f. Abbott 2001).[7]

At the beginning of the chapter I recounted a situation in which communications from the Jebel Marra in Darfur were funneled through London, thereby creating *microspaces* of representation in West. Conceived as gateways between the developing world and the West, these *microspaces* are eminently dynamic since they emerge from technological innovation together with the ability to navigate changing global events. They are created by actors who, for a variety of reasons consider existing political forms to be inadequate and have stepped outside of the constraints of these structures to create a new political project. Through their ability to utilize resources made available to them either in the West, Africa, or the Middle East, they build a new architecture of political representation inside a political field. But this is not the end of the process. Once inside these spaces, internal logics go to work creating threads of difference that will bring new types of political actors into being. It is these kinds of dynamics that still need elaboration.

By thinking of boundaries as threads of difference or logic within these new zones, *process* can be understood in its rawest sense: how difference, authority, and possibility conjoin to produce more radical political actors. In the case of Darfur, the kinds of actors that emerged in these new spaces were rebel groups such as the Sudanese Liberation Army/Movement (SLA/M), the Justice and Equality Movement (JEM), and more recently the National Redemption Front (NRF). Tired of the inefficacy of political parties, they utilized a syncretic array of ideas and beliefs in order to get the work of rebel insurgency done.[8] Situated in the interstices of the Sudanese and British political fields, these groups had representation on the ground in London as well as on the field of battle in Darfur. Constantly innovating to keep abreast of events they produced a new political energy and force for change, which also underscored the increasing irrelevance of old types of diaspora politics.

The Emergent Political Actor

If these new spaces of contingency allow us to identify areas where innovation might occur, then what is the process that drives changes in subjectivity on the ground? Theoretically and practically, a number of issues should be confronted. Where the theoretical tools are concerned, some of the answers can be traced to Mead (1934) and his discussion of the way selves come into being. His presumption that the self is a social process — that the self comes into being as a result of interaction with others — is key in this regard. Arguing that gestures made within the social act have to be understood not just by the self but also by the other to whom the gesture is being made, Mead concludes that the cornerstone of self-consciousness is shared meaning, and, as such, gestures have to be shared by both parties to the interaction.

But the self is not a static thing. If we are to understand how subjects are changing and how dynamism is introduced into political fields, a basic discussion of self and other simply will not suffice. Here the relation between the *"Me"* and *"I"* components of the self become vital for Mead (1934). The *"Me"* component of the self as the habitual individual must be counterpoised against the *"I,"* which is the locus of the creativity and growth of the self. Therefore, through the *"I"* new plans are constructed, and the self is able to grow and develop in new and innovative ways. Thus, the relationship of the *"Me"* to the *"I"* provides the necessary dialectic between tradition, custom, ethics — the immersion of the self in society — on one hand and the ability to move according the needs of a fluid and ever-changing world on the other.

This is a fairly rudimentary point, but it has a great deal of bearing on the way that refugee political actors operate in London. Mead (1934, p. 154) believed that selves came into being in response to others, and where London is concerned the potentiality for other formation, or influence on the self, is enormous. Inside London's reconfigured political field, the political self that emerges does so in a space that lies at the intersection of British society, in the intersection with crisis, with displacement and other refugee communities, with new forms of interaction based on media such as the Internet, with tribal affiliations and existing party structures. What emerges is a much larger set of permutations and combinations for being political. The political horizon of possibility for self-making is therefore much wider.

Yet the big question is a pragmatic one: how to track changes in belief and action on the ground. Glaeser (2000) provides some clues with his work on identity formation and a process he calls *identification.* In this work he argues that identity is produced through the constant interpretation of self and other. The actual work of identification happens at the point of confrontation — and by inference at a boundary — where connections are made with the other parties to the interaction. Meaning is thus produced by contextualization, by making connections to the other in a particular kind of way. As Glaeser points out, the meaning of self (i.e., identity) is produced "by identifying (i.e., connecting) self with itself at other points in time; with other persons; with beliefs ideas and values; with the world in the widest sense" (p. 9). Through this approach he aims to show how identity formation is in essence hermeneutic and how minute identifications constitute the building blocks through which this process is accomplished.

This process — and process is the key here — takes place across time, giving a provisional identity that is constantly made and remade. And while this process can convey a sense of stability of self it should also be noted that it is not set in stone. For even though a sense of self is open to confirmation in a process such as this, it is also worth pointing out that counter identifications can challenge or subvert the self being created. Overall, however, these minute identifications of self and other provide the best means through which the identity formation process can be physically observed. It is through these identifications — made in the grind of everyday life — that identities are produced and solidified.

Yet everyday life does not just entail interaction in a proximate setting; it also entails situations where the self encounters "other" in all forms. Whether this is another person, a group, an identification made through the Internet, or a discussion held by satellite phone, it has the potential to force us to consider who we are. Consider, for example, media or discursive formations. For someone living in diaspora, identifications made on the Internet, by satellite phone, or by newspaper may provide an invaluable source of self-knowledge about who he or she is relative to others. Daily recourse to newspapers, to Internet sites, or to government propaganda provides an important diet of virtual interaction with the country that has been left. So even though this type of news is not physically embodied in the sense of news given by word of mouth, it nonetheless comes from an "other" elsewhere and has the character of a linguistic and informational boundary that acts in the process of constituting self and subsequent self–other interactions.

These kinds of interactions have become increasingly important over recent years for refugee political actors in diaspora. Unlike the kinds of thin sociality Knorr Cetina (2005) describes in her work on financial markets and the intersubjective domains of traders, access to the Internet for refugees may constitute the only microspace that links back to memories, beliefs, and forms of belonging in the homeland. As political ideas change — and if the actor is not physically situated among other refugees of like mind[9] — the microspace of interaction between self and other on the Internet becomes increasingly important in producing hybrid forms of political being. What gets produced is not therefore simply a reincarnation of tribal loyalties from the homeland carried through a different medium, but a real sense of shifting political terrain and novel ideas that generate new selves and ways of thinking about political action.

How does this actually work? Though face-to-face interaction between political rivals on the street is one way to constitute self in a proximate setting, virtual interaction allows a kind of switching into another set of much more temporally and spatially extended set of relations. When one encounters the other in virtual form on the Internet, the actor is in effect viewing a new social horizon, which links into new microspaces and ways of seeing. This provides an extended set of possibilities for difference production across the diaspora network worldwide. It connects political selves formed in the intersection of Sudanese and other systems of representation, producing new ways to articulate claims and to move political action forward (cf. Glaeser forthcoming).

And so by virtue of this switching into a more productive set of possibilities, actors expand the set of boundaries between themselves and others that can generate self. These boundaries, mediated through virtual formats, are read across the globe and allow the connection of context to context, in a way that local interaction does not. So, for example, a refugee can exist on the street vis-à-vis his or her new society, those who have fled in a similar situation, or those who have been identified through the Internet as belonging to this political faction or that. And in many of the chat rooms inhabited by politicos of all stripes, this process of innuendo and counter-innuendo operates with a force that is almost hard to believe: The virulence of identification leads not just to electronic fist fights in the virtual sphere, but also to confrontation out on the street and new allegiances and rivalries that act to reconfigure political fields. This leap into a vastly expanded set of interaction possibilities allows the alteration of standard temporal and spatial frames; it permits the immediate closing of distance and play of time to achieve certain political ends.

Finally, in addition to this switching into a virtually mediated set of relations, there are also potentialities brought about by communications media such as satellite phones. Here self/other interaction goes on by voice and is a way of extending co-local relations via satellite streams. Yet there is something far more interesting about the way cell and satellite phones are used in the process of forming and maintaining political alliances than was previously the case for land lines. Far from being held hostage to discursive systems, many political activists actively use cell phones to circumvent structures of authority and to update activists in diaspora about movements on the ground inside Sudan. Tribes maintain tribal lines of authority through cell-phone contact suggesting how best to handle intertribal relations in London. Rebel commanders fighting wars, for example, in the Darfur conflict, talk strategy by satellite phone with their compatriots on the ground. Funding needs for communication technology in third-party countries such as Saudi Arabia get negotiated by phone. But satellite phones, particularly those that can fend off interception, can also provide microspaces of representation in the West. They can transport their users into another space from where they can piggy-back on the ideas and resources of others, making their own claims and challenges salient elsewhere.

Street Politics

All of these forms of interaction contribute to the reconfiguration of the political field and anchor new claims into the changing terrain.[10] And on the street, in the cut and thrust of political life, these dynamics start to become clear. It is through the choreography of political life on the street — through the ability to make claims, to have them accepted, to reveal power through language, bodily comportment, and conviction — that changes in the political sphere become most marked.[11] It is those informal talks — those deals cemented with handshakes as men meet on the street, the coffee drinking and chewing the fat[12] — where politics might seem farthest away, yet it is most firmly entrenched. It is through this informal political choreography that attempts are made to wrest political advantage from other parties and groupings and, in doing so, to create opportunity in a political landscape that has been otherwise dominated by other political forms for years.

Demonstrations are a case in point. November 2003, 2 a.m. I find myself squatting on the side of the pavement with a group of young men, recent refugees, from Darfur and talking about their reasons for leaving Sudan. We are on hunger strike outside the offices of the United Nations (UN), Millbank, one of the major thoroughfares in London alongside the bank of the Thames. The crisis in Darfur has been under way since at least 1999, although at this point the mass carnage, the rape of women and children, and the burning and looting of villages are just starting to make their way into the headlines of the West. A group of about 200 to 300 Sudanese and Darfurian men have gathered from all parts of the United Kingdom and Holland to demonstrate and to appeal for action. A letter has been sent to Kofi Annan in New York via the London UN offices. We wait for his reply before deciding whether to continue the hunger strike or, alternatively, if action is promised, to give up and embark on the long journey home.

It is freezing on the side of the river: the sort of cold that permeates right to the bones, forcing you to dig down to your core to feel any warmth at all. We have not eaten for more than twenty-four hours, yet this emptiness only serves to intensify the resolve to get something done. As we sit on the street, time appears to slow down.[13] We talk to forget about the cold, although as we talk our breath empties out into the night air releasing yet more warmth from our bodies. Against the wall others huddle together on top of old rugs wrapped in flags, protest banners, whatever they can lay their hands on. People play songs from Darfur on small cassette players, broadcasting them out into the night air through a handheld megaphone. The songs have a political message:

> Burned villages are a scandal;
>
> the blood and slaughter is forbidden
>
> Farms have turned into thorns;
>
> wild plants have taken over
>
> Schools and mosques are empty;
>
> homes are destroyed
>
> People have been displaced;
>
> living in shelters and tents
>
> This wouldn't have happened if we'd made up our minds…
>
> to live as one.[14]

On the other side of the river, demonstrators walk along the riverbank keeping a brisk pace to ward off tiredness and the cold. Police come by intermittently to ensure that nothing untoward is going on. Passersby ask questions, even in the middle of the night: "Who are you; what are you here for?" We pass out leaflets and do our best to explain.

Demonstrations have a strange facility for making the invisible seem visible, not just in the immediacy of the protest but also in marking out who deals with whom, where the social and linguistic markers are. And there is something about long nights spent on the street — the cold and exhaustion — that breaks down the political front, allowing observers such as myself to see where the political boundaries lie. For many of the young men participating in the hunger strike, narratives of persecution and arrival yield clues to identification categories. For some this amounts to a more generic description of the tensions riven through Darfurian society and why they felt it was no longer safe to remain in a particular area. In these cases, there is often no well-articulated story of what provided the initial impetus to political action, or what it was — except for a cumulative series of events — that stirred them to leave.[15] Yet for most of them, a path of political action has already been tread, a history followed, a trajectory seared into their consciousness and marked on their bodies long before a foot was even placed on British soil. There is the history of oppression, which often starts in the highly politicized world of student life in Sudan, where the seeds of being political and acting on this identity emerge. Many find themselves on the rough end of the security services, many have been tortured, some try to avoid conscription,[16] and some leave the country under threat of what might happen to them if they do not.

Life on the street, life lived in movement, forces these young men to dig deep inside themselves in search of explanation. Though some of them retain their affiliations to long-standing parties operating within Darfur, such as the Umma Party, many others are cynical that parties will ever be able to change the pervasive patterns of racism and marginalization. A large number therefore foreswear politics altogether or join local rebel movements based on tribal affiliations. For these young men, they have lived many lives, moved across borders, and lost everything. Their political subjectivities and identities turn on a quest for recognition, yet recognition does not come easily amid dislocation, lack of familiarity, and constant movement from place to place.

In the demonstration, however, they are at once concentrated; new arrivals from Darfur mingle with government agents and old hands at the practice of opposition. Some young men find friends they had last seen in Darfur and joyfully walk up and down hand in hand explaining how they made the long journey to the United Kingdom. As the day wears on, big names in Darfur politics start to arrive. The popular politicians — those outside the main parameters of Sudanese party politics — draw large crowds. They lean against the wall next to the Thames and give impromptu talks about the current situation, about their thoughts, and about the way forward. Others who are less popular stand with their followers — a loyal

Figure 11.1 Hunger Strike: Night falls on the side of the Thames.

cadre — trying hard not to notice the spatial demarcation of political authenticity. Young men, who are apprentices of political leaders or those thought to be rising stars in particular political milieus, stand around watching the political scene and talking tactics. Others seize the opportunity to report to leaders in Sudan by cell phone, often seeking political advice. Parties such as the Umma Party, the Democratic Unionist Party (DUP), or Communist Party naturally gravitate toward their designated political grouping, while ex-party members look on with disdain. Government sympathizers mingle with the crowd trying to learn what they can yet not succeeding except with neophytes who are unaware of their designs.[17] Power marks itself on the landscape as those who have legitimacy act as nodes around which friends and admirers congregate, those who do not, stand alone. Well-known faces from human rights or other organizations in London, many of whom are Sudanese, arrive and survey the scene, eyeing particular groups with suspicion.

Spatial boundaries say much about the nature of the political terrain, but so do linguistic ones. In Darfur, languages such as Fur, Zaghawa, and Massaliit signal particular forms of belonging or particular circuits, nomadic or otherwise. They have their own kind of currency, which is made clear in the way that such languages are used to mark difference. Tribes switch between the *lingua franca*, Arabic, and their tribal languages frequently to preserve or generate intimacy. This provides an edge, since many political operatives from the center of Sudan and some elites from Darfur cannot speak these languages. The use of different languages permit the ruse of engagement: On one hand there is interaction, the acknowledgement of sameness as Sudanese; on the other is selective disengagement and a Certeauian tactic of talking privately inside the political throng (De Certeau 1984).

Life on the street gives power to the powerless. Ali Mazrui put it aptly when he argued that Sudan is characterized by multiple marginalities. Poised between Arab, African, Muslim, and Christian worlds, perceiving its Arab identity as preeminent over its Africanism yet looking more African than Arab, it is plagued by fundamental contradictions (Deng 1995). These contradictions play out in strange ways on the street. On the face of it at least, tribes from Darfur appear to have less power. They suffer from the sort of allochronism that Joannes Fabian (2002) talks about where through a process of identification, they are displaced into a traditional, African — and by implication — inferior time by those from the center of the country. In theory at least, this produces a hierarchical political ordering where the people in the center of Sudan are identified as more powerful, civilized, and modern and, of course, closer to the Arab world. Yet political relations are far more complex than that. These tribes may lack certain forms of cultural capital, but for all that, they are still politically savvy. In the space of language switching and in the cracks of the political structure there are many opportunities for political tactic and countertactic. It is from these potentialities, from the constant identification and counteridentification, that new subjectivities and ways of doing politics grow. Their politics is rooted in liminality, but it is this liminality that gives them the edge.

Afternoon brings television crews and illustrates just how important media is to cement boundaries between different groups. Leaders of tribes, spokespersons, and those well versed in communication go to prepare press statements and to give interviews. Bunched in groups alongside the river wall, these political spokespersons tape interviews with the BBC World Service about the effect on the region.

Al Jazeera arrives, and things change. The protesters know the power of media, but especially the power of Arab-speaking media that will be screened in areas outside Sudan with significant diaspora concentrations. Arabic media stations unsettle those inside Sudan, most particularly the authorities who have access to satellite and know that information about the genocide is getting out. For any political party, one's power as opposition is marked by one's presence in such demonstrations. As the Al Jazeera cameras pan across the crowd, the urgency becomes obvious. The younger contingent leap up and down, their eyes fixed on the cameras in angry stares. Fists punch the air while they shout, "*Al-Bashir, Al-Bashir, down, down, Al-Bashir!*" in Arabic.

Although not a form of person-to-person interaction, television stations like Al Jazeera produce an exponential increase in Internet and e-mail traffic. Web traffic and newscasts link context to context across a virtual frame. They connect Cairo, Saudi Arabia, Washington, DC, and many other diaspora concentrations worldwide, thereby immediately giving refugees forums in which to identify with or against each other. Outlets such as the BBC with access to world broadcast networks link Western and non-Western worlds together. Information from such broadcasts make the rounds, providing information even to those inside marginalized areas of Sudan, creating resolve and cementing difference. Inside London, groups like the Associate Parliamentary group on Sudan invite those in the know to the Houses of Parliament to discuss latest developments and to contribute to policy discussions. Talking heads emerge — often people who were not professional politicians in Sudan, but those who have leverage and connections across media outside. This in turn affects the existing Sudanese opposition structures in London, as those outside the political mainstream increase their power bases in London and over time are taken more seriously inside Sudan itself.

Changing Political Landscapes?

Though there is not space here to discuss the effects of the production of difference across all these boundaries, the point is simple: The micropolitical climate within cities such as London is changing rapidly. The preceding section looked at interactions within demonstrations and at the role of language switching, spatial demarcation, and the use of information technology to preserve and generate difference. But one could just as easily look at weekly political party meetings, informal meetings in houses (*gaadat*), coffee shops, and encounters on the street to see such dynamics — how existing centers of power are challenged and how new political boundaries emerge.

A critical component of such change is complexity in the urban environment. A particular kind of synergy results from the anonymity of the city, its diverse populations, the agglomeration of certain types of political actors, and the presence of nongovernmental organizations (NGOs) and other institutions. Sassen (1991) writes of changes to the economic structure of cities such as London and of the changing structures of authority, rights, and claim making that emerge as a result of these reconfigured dynamics. She also argues that these changes produce new spaces at the intersection of systems of representation, which require further elaboration and investigation (Sassen, 2006).

In these spaces new kinds of political selves can be generated by direct face-to-face contact with the other. But here I also argue that extended sets of relations generated through the use of Internet and other technologies constitute a different yet equally important moment of production. With exponential increases in email, Internet, and satellite phone traffic, there is a multiplier effect of possibilities and means through which political actors can constitute themselves vis-a-vis others. And these new possibilities for identification, counter-identification, hostility, and alliance create new tensions that do not just reside in the virtual sphere; they collide on the street to produce new ways to do politics and new ways for political actors to think of themselves. Microspaces or gateways for action open up, created by flows and dynamics no longer contained within territorial bounds.

Often in the West we tend to see politics as something circumscribed by action in certain kinds of spheres with particular kinds of actors. Refugee and immigrant groups demonstrate that politics is part and parcel of everyday being — part of the framework of life. In the West, the politically disinterested can ignore politics altogether; it has no necessary salience for their everyday lives. Yet for many immigrants, particularly those who have escaped from tyrants and torturers, politics is a form of memory, of belonging, of, as an informant pointed out, "being something for your country." Doing politics for many immigrant groups is not an optional extra; it is the essential lifeblood of the disapora.

And when these political *weltanschauungs* collide, interesting possibilities emerge. In the chaotic intertwining of boundaries in the city — between old and new, between Africa and the West, between formal and informal, between identities accomplished proximately and with reference to information streams from elsewhere — new types of claim making emerge. More often than not, such claims orient themselves toward recognition, rights, and what the West might see as legitimate grievances. But at other times, as writers such as Body-Gendrot (1993) point out, grievances flare into violence; radical political forms emerge that mark the city indelibly with another kind of message.

The political underbelly of the city is a sphere that is closed off to many and that requires some considerable effort to understand. Yet a new set of logics governs political encounters in this kind of sphere. It is not as simple as saying that immigrants bring their old ways of doing politics and insert them into a Western political matrix. What is happening is very much more complex than that. The fast-moving political terrain of places like London speaks volumes about what politics can be; it brings changes not only to London but also to other nodes worldwide. What we are starting to see is a new kind of informal political architecture which has resonances across many differing groups and countries, but has no necessary connection to the way that politics has been traditionally configured

If we are to understand the political changes in Western cities attention should be paid to incipient political forms not just to existing political structures. Effort must be expended in deciphering not just the macro-level flows, but also those complex and less visible processes by which strategic political actors emerge on the ground. As cities continue to evolve into spaces of diversity and difference; as articulations between the global and local become ever more prevalent, it is vital to think through these spaces of complexity to understand how they incubate new forms of being. And this work means moving away from a familiar terrain into something that is more difficult to decode. Yet this endeavor is now vital if we are to gain an understanding of the nature of contemporary change. For in the final analysis, formal conceptions of politics may still have resonance for a proportion of those inhabiting Western cities today. But for many more who have become embedded in these spaces through design or necessity, politics may, of course, have quite different ontological roots.

Notes

1. The Fur tribe is the largest tribe in Darfur, whose homeland is based in the vicinity of the Jebel Marra volcanic mountain range. This land, which is said to be some of the most fertile in the region, is at the center of the government campaign to remove indigenous black Africans from their *dars* (land)
2. You're welcome.
3. *Janjawiid* has been variously translated as "men on horseback" or "devils on horseback." The word is said to be an amalgam of the Arabic word *jinn*, meaning "devil" or "malevolent spirit"; G3, a rifle; and *jawad*, meaning "horse" (DeWaal 2005).
4. Isin, E, (2002). *Being political.* Minneapolis: University of Minnesota Press, pp49.
5. Of course, there is nothing natural or inevitable about the nation-state as many have recently pointed out, despite the fact it has been the cornerstone of many social science disciplines.
6. In the case of the Sudanese diaspora, these tensions had come to the fore as a result of the layering of different parties, movements, groups, and individuals in the capital. From the 1970s onward, in the face of repeated authoritarian regimes, London became a repository for the people of Sudan: first the southerners and later communists and other intellectuals and politicos fleeing either Jaafar an Nimeiri's regime or the current regime of Omar al-Bashir. Over time, their arrival secured the boundaries of the Sudanese political field demarcating who was legitimately involved in politics and where the political boundaries lay between legitimate opposition groups such as the communists, rebel movements, and Islamist sympathizers. The Darfur crisis changed all this. Although Darfur had once been a stronghold of the Umma Party, its popularity had long since declined due to its inability to deliver any promised development to the region. Starved of cash and resources, Darfur had eschewed involvement in conventional party politics, falling back instead into more conventional tribal loyalties. As the crisis started to unfold, these tribal loyalties migrated to London along with the refugees that carried them. The effect was a displacement of the traditional political field. As the political field fissured, new types of political actors emerged in the interstices of traditional party forms. Instead of a reliance on party lines, these new actors used media outlets in the West and interacted with the parliament and organizations such as Amnesty International. Able to draw attention to the plight of their people in Darfur, they offered testament to the inefficacy of the political parties. New tensions between old and established politicos emerged on the streets of the capital. The political field started to unravel and reconfigure itself instead with an emphasis on pragmatic, informal, fast-moving, street-driven forms of politics.
7. Abbott's point here is that by looking at boundaries in this way we can read temporal sequences front to back. Instead of starting with the entity and looking at how it came into being — that is, running the historical narrative back to front — we should start with the local accidents or structures that initially produce lines of difference and then try to figure out how boundaries and entities actually emerge from them.

8. Some of the groups emerged from tribal affiliations infused with Western philosophical ideas and modern professional practice. Others emerged out a dissatisfaction with the Islamist project in Sudan and the way this was marginalizing the west of Sudan. More recently, the NRF emerged as an amalgam of two rather contradictory groups — The Sudan Democratic Federal Alliance (a broadly liberal group) and JEM (former followers of Al-Turabi — an Islamist). All of these groups had significant representation on the streets of London as well as in Darfur itself.
9. In the case of Sudan, for example, it is perfectly possible to be in the diaspora but not necessarily be close to any others who share the same kinds of ideas on account on the multiple forms of marginality that operate in the country. The virtual sphere becomes a way to meet those that one might share a natural affinity with and to use that medium to launch verbal attacks on others that will be played out elsewhere on the ground.
10. Sudan has witnessed a demise of the legitimacy and salience of its political parties and the growth of more informal forms of politics. This is in part due to their failure to provide an effective challenge to the tyrants and torturers that have ravaged the country since independence in 1956, but it is also due to the deterioration of economic conditions over the periods of authoritarian rule. Many areas of Sudan now consider themselves as marginal vis-à-vis the Arab center. This has led to the increasing importance of tribal affiliations and movements such as the Sudanese People's Liberation Army/Movement (SPLA/M), National Redemption Front (NRF), Justice and Equality Movement (JEM), Sudanese Liberation Movement (SLA/M) and others in preference to a political center that has nothing to offer them.
11. Herzfeld (1988) calls this a *poetics of social interaction*. For him, each performance or encounter is an incident in a struggle toward a particular end. For our purposes here, the end is political advantage, and it is the performance that enables politicians to make their power, wit, and political savvy real, to mark on their opponents their influence, which in turn will direct the course of subsequent interactions.
12. See Wedeen, *Peripheral Visions: Political Identifications in Unified Yemen* (forthcoming) for a consideration of the effect of informal sphere and *khat* (chat) chews on Yemeni identity.
13. Although there is not space to address this issue, there is a strange juxtaposition of slow time versus fast time as a refugee. Life as a refugee, life lived in protest — in the limbo of not having a "normal" life — gives more time than ever before to contemplate the situation. This is juxtaposed against the increased speed of events elsewhere, the exponential increase in the circulation of discourse and images about the situation in the media. There is also an immediacy of these time disjunctures in the lived reality of the speed up of the asylum process, the urgency to reduce the numbers of asylum seekers in the United Kingdom, and measures to put this in place (Cwerner 2004, pp. 71–88).
14. From the songs of Omar Ihsas, Sudanese singer from Darfur, lyrics given to author by Ihsas, London, June 2005.

15. Many of these accounts refer to the stresses of living life in Darfur while the *Janjawiid* and other militia groups are in operation. Often refugees move from village to village as each successive village is burned, family members are killed, and the security situation deteriorates. Ultimately, when they are imprisoned and manage to escape, they realize the situation is hopeless. They subsequently find their way to Port Sudan and from there to an agent who can smuggle them out so that they can make their journey onward to London.
16. Conscription for black Africans in Sudan is tantamount to a death sentence. They are often sent to fight their own people or into situations where they will face certain death. This Sudanese government policy is known as *"aktul al 'Abid bil 'abid"* (kill the slave by the slave).
17. In demonstrations, many of the research subjects that I was working with watched me like a hawk. Government sympathizers often target people such as myself or refugees new to the area to try to glean information. On more than one occasion I was dragged away from someone — in mid-conversation — who was thought to be "on the wrong side."

Works Cited

Abbott, A. 2001. *Time matters.* Chicago: University of Chicago Press.

Barth, F. 1969. *Ethnic groups and boundaries: The social organization of culture difference.* Long Grove, IL: Waveland Press.

Body-Gendrot, S. 1993. *Ville et violence: L'irruption de nouveaux acteurs.* Paris: Presses Universitaires de France.

Burgiere, A., and R. Grew (eds.). 2001. *The construction of minorities: Cases for comparison across time and around the world.* Ann Arbor: University of Michigan Press.

Cwerner, S. 2004. Faster, faster and faster: The time politics of asylum in the U.K. *Time and Society* 13(1):71–88.

De Certeau, Michel. 1984. *The practice of everyday life.* Berkeley: University of California Press.

Deng, F. 1995. *War of visions: Conflict of identities in the Sudan.* Washington, DC: Brookings Institution.

DeWaal, Alex. 2005. Who are the Darfurians? Arab and African identities, violence and external engagement. *Justice Africa*, London, 14.

Fabian, J. 2002. *Time and the other: How anthropology makes its object.* New York: Columbia University Press.

Glaeser, Andreas. 2000. *Divided in unity: Identity Germany and the Berlin police force.* Chicago: University of Chicago Press.

———. Forthcoming. An ontology for the ethnographic analysis of social processes: Extending the extended case method. *Social Analysis.*

Isin, Egin. 2002. *Being political: Genealogies of citizenship.* Minneapolis: University of Minnesota Press.

Haaland, G. 1969. Economic determinants in ethnic processes. In Fredrik Barth, ed. *Ethnic groups and boundaries: The social organization of culture difference,* 58–73. Long Grove, IL: Waveland Press.

Herzfeld, M, 1988, The poetics of manhood: Contest and identity in a Cretan mountain village, Princeton: Princeton University Press

Kimmerling, B. 1996. Changing meanings and boundaries of the political. *Current Sociology* 44:152–76.

Knorr Cetina, K. 2005. How are the global markets global? The architecture of a flow world. In Karin Knorr Cetina and Alex Preda, eds., *The sociology of financial markets,* 38–61. New York: Oxford University Press.

Lamont, M., and Molnar. 2002. The study of boundaries in the social sciences. *American Sociological Review* 28:167–95.

Mead, G.H. 1934. *Mind, self, and society: From the standpoint of a social behaviorist.* Chicago: University of Chicago Press.

Ong, A. 1996. Cultural citizenship as subject making: Immigrants negotiate racial and cultural boundaries in the U.S. *Current Anthropology* 37:737–67.

Sahlins, Peter. 1989. *Boundaries: The making of France and Spain in the Pyrenees.* Berkeley: University of California Press.

Sassen, Saskia. 2001. *The global city: New York, London, Tokyo,* 2d ed. Princeton, NJ: Princeton University Press.

———. 2006. *Territory, authority, rights: From medieval to global assemblages.* Princeton, NJ: Princeton University Press.

Tilly, C. 2003. Political identities in changing polities. *Social Research* 70:1301–1315

——— 2004. Social Boundary Mechanisms. *Philosophy of the Social Sciences* 34:211–36.

Wedeen, L. Forthcoming. *Peripheral visions: Political identification in unified Yemen.*

Zerubavel, E. 1991. *The fine line: Making distinctions in everyday life.* Chicago: University of Chicago Press.

CHAPTER 12
Ghetto Cosmopolitanism
Making Theory at the Margins

RAMI NASHASHIBI

My interest in the contemporary ghetto began in the early 1990s as a community activist observing the development of an urban Muslim aesthetic and culture amid a set of transnational globalizing circuits. Confronting notions of the black ghetto as a space ensconced in hyperisolation and parochialism, Islam's intersection with a legendary black street gang and hip-hop emerged as two poignant illustrations of a larger trend. After a series of interviews, many months of ethnography, and years of community work, I began to assemble an intellectual project that hypothesized the emergence of a global ghetto and ghetto cosmopolitanism as a means to further engage and theorize these discoveries.

The data in this chapter are primarily derived from an ethnographic account of Islam's encounter with two uniquely postindustrial ghetto phenomena: (1) the legacy of one of Chicago's oldest black street gangs, the Black P. Stone Nation (hereafter called the Blackstones); and (2) the rise and rapidly globalizing trends of hip-hop. Using these rich and complex encounters, I posit ghetto cosmopolitanism as one illustration of the contemporary American ghetto gone global.

There is a growing consensus among urban social scientists that a new set of dynamics characterizes the modern ghetto. Citing the late 1960s as its beginning, various terms have been deployed to identify and theorize this distinct space: arguments about the *third ghetto* (Nightingale 2003), the *postindustrial ghetto*, the *excluded ghetto* (Marcuse 1997), and the *hyperghetto* (Wacquant 1998) have all emerged from such a project.

While acknowledging distinct developments in the ghetto over the last thirty-five years, many have yet to extensively theorize the presence of the global through these changes. Sociologist Loic Wacqaunt has written significantly (Wacquant 2002, 1998, 1996) on multiple aspects of the postindustrial ghetto, or what he calls the *hyperghetto*, but cautions restraint when attempting transnational comparisons of race-based American ghetto institutions with those multiethnic class-based ghettos of the Parisian suburbs, for instance. Nightingale (2003, p. 257) uses the term *global ghetto* to explore historical processes that position the U.S. ghetto as "fundamentally immersed in... a century of world-spanning political conflict (p. 262)." In this work, he posits a historical analysis of the globalization of the ghetto talk and provides a basis for thinking about the ghetto's contemporary evolution in respect to the effects of twentieth-century global–political conflicts on the world economy and race.

My notion of a global ghetto is, in part, a continuing argument about a multilayered space anchored within the periphery of today's global city. Globalization theorists like Saskia Sassen have persuasively suggested that such a site can be understood as part of a larger "geography of centrality and marginality" (Sassen 1998, p. XV). Geographies of marginality provide the theoretical framework to begin probing the multidimensional and peripheral spaces of the global command centers. Yet Sassen and others hesitate to read this new conditionality as something uniformly or pervasively inscribed on urban space: Not everything in these spaces is a manifestation of the global. Rather, it is more instructive and revealing to identify and research the complicated instances within which facets of the global get produced: I rely on these insights to posit the counterintuitive notion of ghetto cosmopolitanism as one such instance. In considering aspects of contemporary ghetto space the most unlikely source for alternative notions of cosmopolitanism, this chapter expands on work that deciphers the global within local and seemingly very provincial spaces.

The chapter begins by briefly reviewing the current literature's capacity to frame the exploration of ghetto cosmopolitanism. Next the chapter takes an abridged historical and ethnographic look at the Blackstones and hip-hop's postindustrial ghetto encounters with Islam. Finally, the last part of the chapter is reserved for consideration of the theoretical and sociological implications of ghetto cosmopolitan virtue in relationship to Bryan Turner's construction of this concept (Turner 2000).

The Literature

Immanuel Kant is regularly cited as a seminal force in shaping modern Western and liberal notions of *cosmopolitanism*. Centuries later the term has become part of a larger globalization discourse with various normative formulations deployed to advocate for global civility. It is in this spirit that Mignolo (2002) defines *globalization* as a set of designs to manage the world and cosmopolitanism as a set of projects towards planetary conviviality and alternative global citizenship (p.157).

For Turner (Turner 2000, 2002), Georg Simmel laid the foundation of cosmopolitanism while detailing the dynamics of blaze attitude in "The Metropolis and Mental Life" (Simmel 1903). Deploying what he attributes to Durkheimian notions of *cool loyalties* and *thin solidarities*, Turner posits cosmopolitan virtue as the antidote to a range of totalitarian possibilities associated with the residual connections to the nation-state. For Turner, these virtues emerge from the global city and enable the individuals in possession of them with practical ability to navigate the terrain of the postemotional city.

Criticism that Turner's (2002) formulations of *cosmopolitan virtue* retain an underlying colonial discourse of neoliberalism or exude an elitism that marginalizes working class and urban poor are partly acknowledged by Turner himself. Turner's response is to categorize this large segment of the population as bounded by poverty and other variables that render such virtue elusive. So as opposed to the aforementioned cool loyalties and thin solidarities, he suggests that "the working class, ethnic minorities and the under classes may in fact continue to have hot loyalties and thick patterns of solidarity" (p. 142). This elitist construction of cosmopolitan virtue reflects the disparities associated with economic globalization and the profoundly uneven spatial geography of today's global city.

A growing number of social scientists have engaged some of these Eurocentric and elitist notions of cosmopolitanism and global civil society.[1] Oddly enough, not many ethnographers have picked up on intuitions that Chicago School sociologist Harvey Warren Zorbaugh posited more than seventy years ago. It was in the late 1920s when Zorbaugh described the Near North Side slum as one of "the most cosmopolitan areas in a distinctively cosmopolitan city" (Zorbaugh 1929, p. 151), a claim even more counterintuitive for today's ghetto than it was when Zorbaugh wrote it. The postindustrial ghetto or slum is commonly described as a hyperisolated and an intensely parochial space, but I am inclined to hypothesize that Zorbaugh's observations about a slum- or ghetto-based cosmopolitanism have reemerged in a form associated with globalization and the transnational flow of culture, capital, and people in the contemporary era. Zorbaugh argued that that the slum was the most cosmopolitan of spaces decades before cosmopolitanism discourse surfaced within the ever-growing and popular globalization framework (p. 153). The contention that the slum produces cosmopolitan sensibilities not only confronts some of the presuppositions of Zorbaugh's early Chicago School contemporaries but also challenges modern notions of cosmopolitanism that associate valorized ideals like *cosmopolitan virtue* with the *gold coasts* of today's world cities.

Roy (2002) points to some of what she characterizes as key limitations with urban-space theories when exploring notions of alternative cosmopolitanism or hybrid identities. Roy argues that theories about urban space have been developed in intimate connection to specific urban centers over the last 100 years and that little attention has been given to the effect some of these same global forces have had on non-Western European cities. Roy contends that "locating global history or urban materiality in the Third World, I believe, yields not simply a new repertoire of cities but also a new repertoire of theory" (p. 7). Roy calls this "making theory at the margins" (ibid.), and I suggest that finding significant ways to connect America's urban ghettos to broad globalizing processes could challenge the way we theorize the contemporary ghetto and the way we understand the questions of global scaling

Islam and the Postindustrial Ghetto Encounter Part 1: The Blackstones

The Blackstone story is as fascinating as it is long and complicated.[2] The purpose here is to focus on how this story helps to illuminate one facet of ghetto cosmopolitanism. It is not to outline a definitive history of this legendary street organization. Yet in writing about the Blackstones as active agents of ghetto cosmopolitanism and as individuals emerging from a history of racial exclusion, I do attempt to extricate them from the confining parameters of gang literature and criminological studies. To appreciate the extent to which the Blackstones' encounter with Islam is an instance of ghetto cosmopolitanism, they must be understood as part of a larger story of how blacks, particularly young and highly criminalized black men, developed a cosmopolitan narrative while embedded in the racially and economically provincial borders of the modern postindustrial ghetto.

Wacquant (1998) cogently describes the postindustrial ghetto as a *hyperghetto* that bears the brunt of deindustrialization with the ever-marginalized ghetto residents subjected to a range of criminalizing policies. One devastating consequence is the alarmingly high and disproportionate incarceration rate of young black men in places like Chicago's South Side.[3]

The hyperghetto often perpetuates a hyperisolation where poor communities of color are further marginalized from resources and one another. The reluctance to discuss the Blackstones within this context is partly due to an overwhelmingly criminological bias imposed on the sociological study of young black men. The gang easily becomes the pretext through which a slew of age-old stereotypes and biases get resurrected. Conquergood (1990, p. 12) poignantly critiques this tendency in an essay on gangs and the power of symbols:

> The gang member is our urban savage, an all-purpose devil figure into which we project our deepest fears about social disorder and demographic change. The stereotypical gang member is a young minority male from the impoverished inner city, the "breeding ground" of drugs, violence and depravity, and our contemporary "heart of darkness"… "gangs" functions as cover and camouflage for a vitriolic language of racism and revulsion that would not be tolerated without the codeword.

Throughout their forty-year-history those associated with the Blackstones have been persistently depicted in the media through such language. Unfortunately, academic analysis of the Blackstones often validates rather than challenges these tendentious oversimplifications. This chapter aims to provide a more nuanced look at the Blackstone legacy in relationship to Islam and alternative notions of cosmopolitanism.

The Blackstone Story

Under the leadership of Jeff Fort and Eugene Hairston, the Blackstones began in Chicago more than forty years ago as the Blackstone Rangers and developed in the late 1960s into the Black P. Stone Nation. Possibly one of the oldest black street gangs in America, the Blackstones have been many things to many people. At one point the *Chicago Tribune* dubbed the infamous and legendary Blackstone leader Fort the most feared man in Chicago. In the mid-1970s, Fort, then referred to as Chief Malik, became associated with Moorish Americans while in prison and, on his release, introduced the first significant wave of Islamic teachings to the organization. As part of this Islamization of the structure, Fort transformed the Black P. Stone Nation into the El Rukns, an Arabic word referring to *pillar*. Yet the shift to the El Rukns required enormous structural and personal changes, which many of the Black P. Stone Nation members, including Chief Bull, were not prepared to make, and for some time both the Black P. Stone Nation and the El Rukns existed simultaneously. Though members of both entities claimed partial or total loyalty to Chief Malik, other gangs as well as the police still considered both groups to be one entity under his leadership.

The El Rukn transformation was the most notable in terms of ideological and structural change and was crucial in the sense that it set the tone for a developmental process that swept through all facets of the organization. For instance, the body members were now referred to as *majleeks,* in reference to the Islamic governmental terms known as *majlis.* Generals became *amirs* and officers became *officer muftis.*[4] Dramatic changes also occurred in the strict codes and protocol gradually introduced into the Blackstones after this point.

It was during this era that the transformation of the El Rukns also extended to the way they inhabited and thought about physical space. After Fort's release from prison in 1975, he, along with high-ranking members in his organization, formed the El Pyramid Maintenance and Management Corporation. In the later part of 1978, El Pyramid, then incorporated under Fort, bought the building at 3947 South Drexel and initially listed it as the El Rukn Grand Major Temple of America, but it quickly became know as simply The Fort.

In 1982 the El Rukns dropped their affiliation with the Moorish Science Temple and moved closer toward a more orthodox understanding of Sunni Islam. In keeping with Muslims throughout the globe, *Jummah* prayer was now held at noon. Instructions in Arabic were taken very seriously, and El Rukns had to meet once a week outside their *Jummah* meetings to focus on learning the language. In addition to *Jummah* prayers many El Rukns, particularly the women, also attended what was termed the *Magreb* meeting on Sunday at sundown.[5] El Rukns learned how to make the five daily prayers but followed the practice of making communal prayer during the appointed *Jummah* and *Magreb* times. Ramadan, the Islamic month of fasting from sunrise to sundown, also became a mandatory observation for all El Rukns. When the El Rukns adopted more of an overtly Islamic character in the mid-seventies and -eighties, they not only memorized and attempted to apply a set of lessons from the Moorish Koran but also sought to convey an explicitly Muslim effect through dress and other symbols. Turbans, fezes, and mandallions with pyramids on them became part of urbanized Islamic hipster apparel that drew envy and respect from many in the community.

A well-publicized federal crackdown charging the El Rukns with, among other things, conspiring with Libyan terrorists dismembered the El Rukn infrastructure and eventually resulted in Fort's incarceration.[6] In the wake of this dissolution, those remaining loyal to the El Rukns, whether in prison or in the community, now referred to themselves as *abdullahs* (servants of God), attempting to signify a more refined understanding of

Islam. A younger generation of the Black P. Stone Nation reemerged in the early nineties, scattered throughout Chicago. This generation was still claiming Chief Malik as their leader and still using an amalgamation of Islamic lessons, symbols, and culture developed throughout the different periods of the Blackstones' history.

Mo Town and the Reign of Young Prince Keetah

After the destruction of The Fort in 1989 and the ensuing federal indictment of the El Rukns, much of the larger El Rukn infrastructure, along with its leadership, was systematically dismembered. The El Rukns lost all of their buildings, and though Chief Malik remained the undisputed chief of the nation, a younger group of Blackstones less organized but still committed to upholding the memory of the organization emerged in what would become Mo Town. Young Prince Keetah, Fort's son who was mentored and raised by older El Rukns, emerged as the individual to impose a legendary level of order and discipline in Mo Town and would help to make Mo Town one of the largest and most intimidating stretches of gang territory on Chicago's South Side.

Keetah's presence and name is still ubiquitous throughout portions of Mo Town. Young children swear on his name, and many of the Blackstones who were considered Keetah's right-hand men went so far as to tattoo YCK (Young Chief Keetah) on their foreheads and fingertips. When listening to different residents of the three- or four-block radius of Mo Town talk about those days, it is common to hear a striking level of admiration for Keetah's ability not only to produce cohesion in Mo Town but also to infuse the Blackstones with a sense of purpose.

Within a relatively short period of time the Blackstones memorialized Keetah's role in shaping and leading a new entity in Mo Town. Since Keetah has been incarcerated he has repeatedly requested that the Blackstones continue to consult the Qur'an and to attempt to follow the teachings of Islam. Keetah was also diligent in establishing relationships with Palestinian Blackstones while he was running Mo Town. In fact, many of the Palestinian Mos, as they were once called, spoke of being afforded a tremendous amount of respect by other Blackstones who seriously sought their assistance in pronouncing the many Arabic words in the Blackstones' literature. Other Palestinians, especially those who had spent time incarcerated, were also elevated as teachers of the Qur'an, even though in many cases second-generation Palestinians growing up on Chicago's South Side had just as much, if not less knowledge or interest in Islam than the average Blackstone. Keetah's appreciation for and emphasis on Islamic principles and teachings simply underscored what he was taught as a young Blackstone by older El Rukns and from what he read in his father's teachings.

There arose a narrative of nostalgia in Mo Town suggesting that the arrest of Keetah and the loss of a sincere approach to Islam has been in part the reason for the community's downfall. Such recurring sentiments are held by the young and old and by many who were not even around during the El Rukn era and are hardly old enough to recall Mo Town's good old days under Keetah. Many Blackstones with whom I spoke often interpreted the disarray and underlying sense of weakness that had crept over Mo Town with this departure from an organizational and spiritual discipline that once held the Blackstones together.

Such nostalgia has made many Blackstones across Chicago more receptive and accommodating of Muslim immigrants than most other communities. In fact, there were sentiments among some Blackstones that in effect rendered places like Mo Town an indigenous part of the Muslim world. Such sentiments and their capacity to generate a form of interracial and cross-ethnic empathy can further be appreciated by considering the larger history of racial and ethnic segregation on Chicago's South Side. The Blackstones are not the only street organization in Chicago with a long and complicated encounter with Islam. The Vicelords, the Four Corner Hustlers, and even the Latin Kings have all incorporated some facets of Islamic teachings into their structures and literature over the last several decades.

Sensationalized media coverage of Islam's incorporation into black or urban gang culture often fuels fears of a homegrown Islamic fundamentalism or local terror networks.[7] Yet not only are these mostly baseless reports sensational; they also obscure the fact that a small percentage of those members have transformed themselves into strict adherents of the faith. What the encounter with Islam has more commonly produced, even for the more nominally practicing, is a vast repository of terms and practices that render the most stigmatized segments of urban society some of the most tolerant and informed of American citizens when it comes to understanding Islamic practices and embracing Muslim immigrants. For instance, in the course of my interviews I have come across a significant number of men associated with the Blackstone legacy who have traveled to parts of the Muslim world for the Hajj, religious study, or even marriage. Many others have become culturally fluent in the etiquettes, religious symbols, customs, and transnational networks of first and second generation Southeast Asians and Arab Muslim immigrants. Such discursive knowledge gets infused into the everyday ghetto interactions between those connected to the Blackstones and other Muslims who may happen to work, live, or pass through these spaces.

One of my earlier set of ethnographic notes in Mo Town captures an aspect of these interactions. This encounter took place while Nader, a younger Palestinian Blackstone, and I were returning a ladder to CC, a middle-aged man who had been part of the El Rukns and who was a considered one of the Blackstone leaders in Mo Town.

> CC greeted both me and Nader very warmly and asked us to wait with CC's younger cousin, a Blackstone who grew up and spent most of his life in Mo Town. CC promptly returned with a framed picture of the Kabah and everyone was very absorbed in the moment as CC delicately handed it to me. We all looked at it for several seconds when CC finally broke the awkward silence saying, "A beautiful brother from Palestine gave that to me." Nader spurted out he couldn't wait to make the Hajj one day. CC looked at his younger cousin pointed at the picture and confidently confirmed, "Now that's the real Blackstone." The young Blackstone immediately replied saying, "I know what that is, what do you think? Chief been there a bunch of times." CC responded, "of course he's been there, all Muslim got to go there once."[13]

Whether Jeff Fort has ever been to Mecca is highly unlikely, but what is clear is that this image occupies a sacred and vivid space in the imagination of many associated with the Blackstones. Moreover, the young Palestinian who has probably seen the same picture on the wall of his grandparents' home a thousand times gazed at the frame in an entirely different context. In that moment, the Kabbah and Mecca became part of a series of symbols and meanings belonging to a more universal ghetto identity. For CC the picture was simultaneously a reaffirmation of his association with the legacy of the Blackstones as well as his intimate connection to a global Muslim community.

This facet of the Blackstone legacy challenges assumptions concerning cosmopolitan identity and values while confronting conventional perceptions of the ghetto as a space incapable of generating such sentiments. The contention that sociospatial aspects of the contemporary ghetto experience enabled such an interaction speaks to the idea that ghetto cosmopolitanism facilitates a type of agency typically denied to the contemporary dwellers of marginal space across the globe. The only more cogent illustration of this phenomenon is in the postindustrial ghetto encounter of Islam and hip-hop, an equally complicated history also simplified for the purposes of this chapter.

Islam and the Postindustrial Ghetto Encounter Part 2: Hip-Hop

Two enduring images of Malcolm X poignantly embody the most appealing and persistent images of Islam among a wide array of hip-hop artists over the last thirty years. The first image is of Malcolm looking pensively into the camera with his chin elegantly resting in the crevice between his thumb and index fingers. It is the contemplative presence of Islam interwoven within hip-hop's appreciation for alternative forms of knowledge and spirituality outside the dominant paradigm that resonate so deeply with this image. It is not coincidental that Mos Def, one of hip-hop's most politicized and socially conscious lyricists and Muslim personalities in the music industry, produced a similar photo of himself in clear homage to this legacy of Malcolm.

The second ubiquitous image is of a more militant Malcolm, armed with an assault rifle; he is peering outside his windows through his home curtains, a man prepared to meet a violent death for his ideas and principles. Again, it is not coincidental that this image of Malcolm has become a part of the spatial and ideational landscape of the ghetto. This image also invokes an instance of unbridled black masculinity and power, which spoke to the romanticized longing to unapologetically confront white supremacy and racism in society. Memorialized in Spike Lee's "Malcolm X," this message of Malcolm's life is emotionally captured in the moment in which he leads hundreds of Nation of Islam members through the streets to the police station. One of the many references to such instances in rap was in the critically acclaimed Fugees album, *The Score,* where one of the emcees announces, "like those Islam brothers/We march through your hood with a million motherfuckers" (Fugees: The Score, "Comboys," Ruffhouse/Columbia, 1996).

The two photos and what they represent speak to the enduring legacy of Malcolm and Islam on hip-hop. From the socially conscious, contemplative, and metaphysical lyrics of Mos Def to the more militant and thuggish beats and presence of the Outlawz's Napoleon and Freeway, Islam claims an eclectic group of hip-hop artists who see their Islamic identities in relationship with the essence of hip-hop. In fact, in suggesting continuity between themselves and Malcolm these artists may often go a step farther to suggest that Islam and Muslims have helped to shape the very foundation of hip-hop and that this culture's corruption is often interpreted as its alienation from purer and more righteous roots.

Sunni Muslim rappers like Napoleon or Freeway may often distinguish themselves from the predominantly Nation of Islam or Five-Percent Muslim articulation of Islam that initially found its way into countless rap lyrics. Yet as it relates to the argument about a particular type of urban ghetto cosmopolitanism, these distinctions are not as significant. Most major African American ghettos often have a space identified with a Muslim presence established through a mosque, gang, or movement associated with the principles and teachings of Islam. Though very clear and nuanced to many Muslims, these theological differences are often overlooked by the large numbers of ghetto residents who characterize that presence more monolithically.

Moreover, though there has undoubtedly been a great number of rappers and hip-hop artists associated with the various manifestations of the Five-Percent Nation, a significant number of extremely visible and influential rap groups also publicly associate with Sunni or more orthodox expression of Islam. Tribe Called Quest, Jurassic Five, Freeway, Benny Segal, Napoleon, Everlast, Lupe Fiasco, and Mos Def are among many of these artists who overtly identity themselves as Sunni Muslims and make numerous references in their jacket covers, lyrics, and interviews to their relationship with the global Muslim community.

Among these rappers are those whose social consciousness and often complex lyrical construction could be seen as marginal to growing commercialism and formulaic sounds of mainstream rap. Muslims associated with the aforementioned groups continue to embody the very pensive dimensions of Malcolm's broader appeal, yet they also all seem to wrestle with the potential consequences of marginality, which may emerge from their socially conscious and often politicized lyrics. Though certainly consistent with a particular dimension of rap's Muslim legacy, such messages have undoubtedly become less prominent within mainstream and commercial articulations of American hip-hop.

Again, the more militant and highly masculine image of Malcolm with an assault rifle peering out a window or leading hundreds of fellow Muslims to the police station is often the image invoked here, and it assists Muslim rappers like Mos Def and Q-Tip from Tribe Called Quest to connect with an authentic and militant black presence in the ghetto. Yet what has emerged in reference to this highly nationalist black discourse since the nineties is a much more hybrid black nationalism with subtleties and nuances that transcend the rigidity of a more dogmatic appeal to racial solidarity: It is a black consciousness infused with an Islamic humanism that often generates great empathy from urban ghetto residents over the world. These sets of hybrid references are strikingly evident on Mos Def's solo CD unequivocally titled *Black on Both Sides,* which nevertheless begins with "*Bisminallh Allah ur Rahamn Rahmeem,*" (In the Name of God, Most Merciful, Most Gracious (Rawkus Records, 1999.).

Many of these Muslim rappers often engage in contemplative and critical commentaries on hip-hop: A critique posited from the position of an intimate insider providing a heartfelt and occasionally scathing assessment of the culture. It is a form of Turner's (2002) ironic distance that is present in such critiques, which among other things also target the broader and more destructive process of economic globalization.

Again, Mos Def has critically engaged the multifaceted process through which the ghetto is becoming an indelible part of a global landscape. On a track about hip-hop, Mos Def describes an urban landscape commercially sensationalized and packaged for worldwide consumption. This transnational commerce, particularly of the most violent and sexual elements of rap, is done through a process that glorifies facets of the ghetto while imprisoning its residents in yet another exploitative relationship with the urban and global elite.

> Blues people got the blue chip stock option/ Invisible man, got the whole world watching/...Don't gas yourself ock/ The industry just a better built cellblock / Hip-hop is prosecution evidence/ The out of court settlement/ Ad space for liquor /Sick without benefits/ Luxury tenements choking the skyline/ Hip-hop went from selling crack to smoking it/ Medicine for loneliness/ Remind me of Thelonius and Dizzy/ Poppers to B-Boys getting busy /The war-time snap shot /The working man's jack-pot /A two dollar snack box /Sold beneath the crack spot/ Olympic sponsor of the black glock/...From the sovereign state of the have-nots.[8]

Mos Def's play on the issue of globalized hypervisibility is provocatively juxtaposed with Ralph Ellison's monumental novel *The Invisible Man.* (Ralph Ellison, *Invisible Man,* Vintage Books, 1947) Whereas Ellison begins his novel with the black ghetto protagonist offering a powerful treatise about his invisibility, Mos Def muses on today's ghetto residents' global hypervisibility. Yet this critique of globalization suggests that marginalized ghetto residents' hypervisibility still renders him insignificant and ultimately invisible to those that benefit from economic globalization.

Globalization has elevated hip-hop to a transnational trend that provides a global venue and voice for the traditionally voiceless margins while reproducing exploitative patterns — mainly the appropriation and commodification of black culture. It has also become a medium that has catapulted the level of urban-ghetto Islamic consciousness to unparalleled heights. Rappers like Mos Def have both celebrated and critiqued this space in complicated and sophisticated ways, suggesting the range of possible options and outcomes.

Mos Def, The Roots, and Jurassic Five are widely celebrated as pioneers in the industry and have often helped to provide narratives that paint ghetto landscapes infused with a Muslim presence. On a track titled "Water," The Roots conjure up one such image:

> Yo, I want you all to understand I come from South Philly/And when I walk the street is like a pharmacy...For my ghetto legend/ Known from Lil' shyst running/ Cop codeine by the courts and keep comin'/ You burnin' both sides of the rope and keep pullin'/Tuggin,' in

> between Islam and straight thuggin'/ Laying everyday around the way and doin' nothin'. (The Roots: Phrenology, "Water," MCA, 2002).

The reference to South Philadelphia is already a significant connection to ghetto space highly infused with Islamic consciousness and presence through an older generation of black activists, performers, and organizers like leading Muslim community developer and former music mogul Kenny Gamble. The Roots also capture the often contradictory but very prevalent tensions between more austere and orthodox expressions of Islam and "straight thuggin." This tension develops a narrative that is instantiated in urban space through the ubiquitous presence of a Muslim-informed thug aesthetic prevalent in the urban spaces of Philadelphia.

Islam, the Ghetto, and the Thug

Hip-hop artists associated with the more cerebral or underground have to struggle to remain connected and relevant to those residing in contemporary ghetto space. Other highly successful and visible Muslim rappers have less difficulty trying to make that claim due to their more visceral personification of a perceived ghetto identity. Napoleon from Tupac's group The Outlawz and Freeway from Jay-Z's Rock-A-Fella Records are two such rappers.

Born to a Muslim family, Napoleon grew up most of his life distanced and unassociated with Islam but after the death of Tupac Shakur found himself redirected toward spirituality and in 2002 traveled to Mecca for the *Hajj*, or Islamic pilgrimage. In describing the appeal Islam had on his and other rappers' lives, he suggests that the tales of street violence and urban grit seem to have strengthened the respect street soldiers have always had for Islam. While conducting an interview over lunch with Napoleon, his wife (also a hip-hop performer and recent convert to Islam), and a second-generation American Libyan video producer, I asked Napoleon to identify some reasons various rappers have found Islam an appealing expression of spirituality over other traditions. Napoleon instinctively returned to the ghetto and the space that has shaped it to formulate a response:

> I don't know man. I guess a lot of us ghetto kids, Allah always put something in our heart to know the truth. I know in my 'hood they were never really like, even if they say they was Christians, they never really ran with it but they always respected Islam. Because half of the OGs [Old Gangsters] from my neighborhood went to jail came home Muslim…They changed themselves, you know what I mean? You know that's how it is in the 'hood; we love the truth man, you know what I mean? Allah blessed the ghetto.[9]

The transformative appeal of Islam, once again so dramatically embodied through the example of Malcolm X, continues to define the respect Islamic expressions of spirituality convey in the 'hood. Rappers like Napoleon, who derive much of their identity from the thuggish and rough elements of street masculinity can clearly cite many instances of the hardest ghetto thug coming back from prison changed by Islam while maintaining the street toughness and credibility of a solider. Yet though highly ensconced in the local dynamics of this space, rappers like Napoleon also touched on the other immediate connection that Islam provides with Muslims all over the world. While touring with Tupac in Germany and before he publicly embraced Islam, Napoleon spoke of the connection crowds of young Germans Turks made with him because of random references to Islam in his lyrics.

Freeway is credited by many on the streets in Philadelphia with popularizing a hybrid Islamic hip-hop aesthetic that, along with the baggy jeans, Timberland boots, and hooded sweatshirts, came to feature a fist-length beard in deference to Muslim prophetic tradition. The visceral connection to the harsh street realities provides rappers like Freeway with some latitude not necessarily to preach but to instruct. Again, rappers like Freeway do not seem to have strayed far from the example of Malcolm, who was often presented and interpreted to have such great social resonance because of his ability to draw off his experience as a thug and criminal. The ability for Malcolm to be as utterly transformed from this background through Islam while retaining the unflinching street credibility has become part of Islam's larger appeal in the global ghetto.

The educated or spiritually enlightened thug is a motif that resonates deeply among other Muslim rappers influenced by the sound and style of rappers like Freeway or Napoleon. Young second-generation Pakistani and Palestinian American men growing up in cites like Chicago and Los Angeles often find the ability to identify Islam with what Freeway refers to as an educated thuggery,[10] providing a highly masculine and hip vehicle to negotiate the often tortuous terrain of race and ethnicity in the contemporary ghetto. The Web site images of these young second-generation Muslim hip-hop artists in front of graffiti-ridden walls and dilapidated subway stops while posing with hands upward, in the stance of traditional Muslim supplication, capture this synergetic blend of Islamic spirituality with ghetto harshness. The often difficult and violent upbringing of life in these ghetto spaces lends these young rappers legitimacy in the eyes of other hip-hop aficionados across the globe. Narratives that accentuate such struggles are often integral to the lyrics and literature of such groups, who once again use these experiences as a basis for broader spiritual instruction, which are directed not only to the individual fan but to hip-hop culture.

Again, the encounter of Islam with hip-hop in the postindustrial ghetto has helped to produce a forum through which young Muslim hip-hop artists and activists can find meaningful validation for their new urban hybrid identities. While couching this exploration in an earlier articulation of Muslim sensibilities among hip-hop pioneers, the young artists also draw from the already eclectic and diverse sensibilities that leading Muslim hip-hop personalities and activities exude.

Leading underground hip-hop Chicago personality Capital D from the group All Natural is an example of an emcee using his leverage as hip-hop artist and producer to mobilize other groups around the city to create a fluid synthesis between expressions of Islam and cutting-edge urban social issues. In doing this, he has often stated that he is simply celebrating in a strand and element of hip-hop that originally attracted him to Islam. In 2003 Capital D partnered with Muslim and Latino community organizations to initiate a project titled Hip-Hop 101. The project brought more than thirty Latino, African American, Palestinian, and white youth from the across the city to be a part of fifteen-week workshop that culminated in the production of a CD titled *Street Journals*. On one of those days, the youth gathered in a community center on the southwest side and began the normal routine of breaking up into groups to write and rehearse their rhymes. A young group of Latinos explored and celebrated an ancient Aztec civilization on a track that synthesized old Spanish beats with a contemporary hip-hop sound in the genre of currently popular Reggaeton. The young men spoke eloquently and creatively about their links to this indigenous Indian tradition. A Jewish American youth from one of Chicago's northwest suburbs who had grown up listening to hip-hop and identifying with black urban culture wrote about the anxiety that such identity produces. Young Muslim women wrote and performed a track about the multiple impositions men in and out of the Muslim community impose on the significance of the headdress, the *hijab*. On one particular occasion I observed the group practicing with one another to perfect and refine their delivery and critiquing each other's lyrics. As time for the last afternoon prayer came, a group of the young African American and Palestinian Muslims, led by Capital D, went to the corner of the room to offer their prayers while the rest of the group respectfully turned down the music and continued to write. One of the young Palestinian Americans fondly recalls such moments in the project:

> When it was time to pray Cap D would get up, I would get up, my brother would get up, and all the other Muslimeen would get up and pray and all the other non-Muslimeen would respect it. That's how much love we had in that room. There was no hostility it was all love.[11]

On another occasion Pop Master Fable, an internationally renowned member of the legendary Rock Steady Crew, hip-hop's original and premier break-dancing group, interacted with an intimate group of young Latino, African American, and Arab youth. The gathering was facilitated through a local Muslim community organization and nonprofit entity known as the University of Hip-Hop. Pop Master Fable demonstrated moves while providing youth with a dynamic multimedia presentation about the transnational origins of various dance forms. Some were traced back to the heart of Spanish Harlem in the seventies during which Fable provided a fascinating account of the African, Arab, and Spanish origins of those rhythms. In other instances, he connected the moves directly to African American black traditions of spiritual and cultural resistance. Fable spent time with the youth going through the moves; then he closed his presentation by talking about his increasingly hybrid identity as something embraced and encouraged by the founding ethos of hip-hop:

> I'm not only vice-president of the International Rock Steady Crew but long time member of the international Zulu Nation," says Pop Master Fable, a leading Spanish Harlem Puerto Rican Muslim. "'I was born and raised in New York City. I'm what they a call a New Yorican; both my parents raised in Puerto Rico — I'm straight Puerto Rican, no doubt. I embraced Islam in August of 1989 — I was raised in New York, and I was raised with hip-hop.[12]

Illustrations of Muslim hip-hop artists like Fable and Capital D facilitating and embracing a ghetto cosmopolitanism framework may be confined as a more limited example of an underground hip-hop culture, but there are also more commercially successful instances of such a phenomenon that poignantly speak to the issue. In Chicago, for instance, we have seen a tendency in even the most successful hip-hop artists to espouse a form of ghetto-informed ecumenicalism that once again speaks to the type of alternative cosmopolitanism emerging from this space. Moreover, much of this expression remains grounded in, or at the very least alludes to, the identities and culture inscribed into postindustrial ghetto space through the legacy of groups like the Blackstones and Four Corner Hustlers. Chicago hip-hop sensations Kanye West, Common, Lupe Fiasco, and Rhymefest all capture an element of this experience while referencing Islam in either its more spiritual context or as an appendage to a broader ghetto identity.

Kanye West, who is credited with drawing renewed international attention to Chicago's hip-hop scene, makes multiple references to the Blackstones and Mo Town and in one of his singles invokes the phrase *Allahu Akbar* (God is Greater) as he mentions Nation of Islam minister Louis

Farakhan. Meanwhile, Common, another well-known Chicago hip-hop personality, begins his 2005 single "On the Corner" — an homage to the trials, tribulations, and cultural evolution of the corner in black communities — with *Memories of Corners with the Fours and the Mos* (Common: Be "The Corner," Geffen Records, 2005). The Fours and Mos are street abbreviations for the Four Corner Hustlers and the Blackstones, both widely known for incorporating a great deal of Islamic symbolism and teachings into their literature. Moreover, the chorus for "On the Corner" is provided by the The Last Poets, an assembly of Muslim and other sixties street poets partly credited with popularizing the spoken-word art form that later evolved into rap. Though not always associated with Islam, Common has made multiple overtures to an Islamic sensibility over the years; in David Chappelle's *Block Party*, a hip-hop documentary, Common opens the event with an ecumenical prayer referencing Allah, Jesus, and Yahweh (Dave Chappelle's Block Party, Rogue Pictures, 2005).

The last two artists, Lupe Fiasco and Rhymefest, also associated with the success of Kanye West, are two of the four who openly identify as Sunni Muslims. On a track titled "Muhammed Walks," Lupe Fiasco offers a rendition of Kanye West's Grammy-winning "Jesus Walks," and espouses an urban ecumenicalism as one important facet of ghetto cosmopolitanism:

> Same God, different beliefs / Hijabs, Sunday clothes, yamika. Kufis/ Same mission beneath/ We all tryin' to get to where the suffering ends/ In front of the Most High being judged for our sins. ("Muhammed Walks," Lupe Fiasco www.nobodysmiling.com)

Though Lupe Fiasco's creative twist on the immensely popular "Jesus Walks" quickly spread on the Web throughout the Muslim community in the United States and across the globe, many Muslims and others were surprised to discover that the original hit was partly written by another Chicago Muslim emcee known as Rhymefest. After Rhymefest received a Grammy for cowriting "Jesus Walks," he released his 2006 CD titled *Blue Collar*, dedicated to the everyday ghetto narratives of working-class or working poor people. This ghetto cosmopolitanism tradition is evident in one of the first tracks of the CD, where Rhymefest mentions owning a Torah, Bible, and a Qur'an, something he proves inside his CD jacket cover by extracting a quote from each of the holy texts referencing the toils and struggles of "blue-collar" people (Rhymefest, Blue Collar, Allido/J Records: 2006)

Discussion: Ghetto Cosmopolitan Virtue at Work in the Global Ghetto

Many of Turner's (2002, 2000) observations and theoretical insights concerning cosmopolitan virtue and marginal ghettos and slums significantly contradict Zorbaugh's (1929) understanding of such a space more than seventy years ago. Throughout this chapter it has been suggested that in today's global ghetto, cross-cultural and transnational interactions have produced hybrid identities open to accepting and occasionally embracing diverse expressions of faith, culture, and belief. For many it is as counterintuitive to suggest that these alternative cosmopolitanisms have been produced in the contemporary American ghetto as it is to illustrate this phenomenon through the role of Islam's unique intersection with localized processes.

Turner's (2000) notion of ironic distance as a necessary value in embracing and sustaining cosmopolitan virtue is not typically associated with the type of critical and reflective analysis illustrated through Islam's encounter with the Blackstone legacy and hip-hop. Yet as urban black gang culture clashed and collided with Muslim teachings and practice, different generations of Blackstones and hip-hop artists regularly grappled with questions surrounding the multiple implications of Islam's relationship to various hybrid identities. For instance, the Blackstones demonstrated a great degree of reflexivity while debating one another over the theological parameters of Muslim identity, particularly when attempting to reconcile life on the corner with a rigorous set of devotional and spiritual practices associated with Islam. Such interactions became even more nuanced when considering the range of discussions with young Palestinian Blackstones or storeowners about the multiple contradictions of being Muslim in such a space.

Similarly, the constant analysis of Muslim identity within the larger culture of hip-hop among the many Muslim hip-hop artists, activists, and fans lends itself to a dynamic process of critical self examination, as can be seen in many instances throughout Islam's multifaceted encounter with hip-hop. Incorporating, studying, debating, and internalizing facets of a Muslim cultural identity necessitated some distance from preexisting cultural values. It also encouraged and challenged young people of color to examine and question the presuppositions and assumptions of multiple grand narratives. In short, Turner's (2002) ideas of ironic distance abound, as seen vividly through the appreciation, tolerance, and celebration of hybrid identities emerging from these complicated intersections. For example, it is among these circuits and within this space that being a proud Puerto Rican, Zulu Nation vice president, Rock Steady crew member, and Muslim community activist is seen as part of a unified articulation of one dynamic identity.

Turner's (2002) formulation of cosmopolitan virtue also implies that ghetto residents are incapable of exuding such virtues because of perceived immobility. Yet again, the intersection of Islam with the Blackstone legacy and hip-hop in the contemporary globalizing ghetto uncovers many instances of tremendous mobility on both national and global levels. Among the Blackstones, I have encountered a significant number of individuals who have traveled internationally with a Muslim spiritual order to study Islam or to make the pilgrimage. With as much emphasis that had been placed on symbolic spaces in remote parts of the Muslim world and with an original connection to Libya made by the El Rukns in the eighties, it is no surprise to find many associated with the Blackstone legacy to have traveled extensively. Finally, with a generation of transnational Palestinian Muslims emerging in the mid-nineties, ideas and notions of the Blackstones' synthesis of urban street culture with Islam developed an additional layer of global complexity as these youth traveled back and forth between the streets of Chicago's South Side and the West Bank.

Transnational mobility becomes even more pronounced when examining the intersection of Islam and hip-hop. Many of the same youth with whom I talked were also involved in attending international hip-hop conferences and tournaments in Buenos Aires, Paris, and other parts of Europe. Artists like Capital D, Pop Master Fable, and Napoleon talked about their many international trips and their abilities to connect with local Muslim populations in those places. Given the degree of hybridity and mobility generated through such a larger process, one could imagine the degree of tolerance and spirit of ecumenical dialogue at the heart of these interactions. This reality leads to a categorical disagreement with Turner's (2002, p. 61) idea that cosmopolitanism is inherently elitist because "slum dwellers" cannot afford to be tolerant while people in "Beverly Hills mansions" can.

Conclusion

The contention throughout this chapter has been that Islam's encounter with hip-hop and the Blackstone legacy lends partial clarity to the argument underlying the proposition of a global ghetto. This space, as Sassen (2007) reminds, may only be constitutive of a particular global scaling: a scaling I posit comes into sharp relief through the exploration of ghetto cosmopolitanism. As evidenced through the work of Zorbaugh (1929), this is not the first time someone has argued that ghetto and slum space enables a nuanced form of cosmopolitanism. Yet I posit that today's ghetto cosmopolitanism is idiosyncratic of a specific reconfiguration of urban space. This new sociospatial architecture is informed by a range of transnational circuits and provides another lens through which the multiscalar work of the global is made visible in even the most peripheral and hyperisolated spaces.

Certainly, not every encounter of Islam with hip-hop or the Blackstone legacy has produced what can be argued as an instance of ghetto cosmopolitanism. In fact, it could be argued contemporary manifestations of Islam in ghetto and other spaces across the United States illustrate a new global provincialism and this is most likely the case for other normative conceptions of cosmopolitanism. In other words, it would be difficult to cogently argue that all — or even most — jet-setting transnational corporate elites espouse what Turner (2002) constitutes as cosmopolitanism virtue. Rather, as stated earlier, these are moments or instances of localized and small-scale processes that make legible larger circuits and flows: Ghetto cosmopolitanism is one interstitial moment within contemporary ghetto space that reveals such a process. It is on such a scale that Roy's (2002) alternative theory-making practices can acquire enough empirical traction to advance new and provocative conceptions of globalization and civil society implicit in a notion like ghetto cosmopolitanism.

Notes

1. These studies include a range of authors who have used the notions of Saskia Sassen's *noncosmopolitan globalities* to challenge the dominant discourse on this subject (Sassen 2006, chap. 6).
2. One potential point of confusion in referencing the larger Blackstone legacy is the many names associated with the Blackstones: the Blackstone Rangers, Black P. Stone Nation, and El Rukns all refer to different stages in the Blackstones' ideological and cultural development. To simplify I use the term *Blackstones* in referring to all these stages.
3. Human Rights Watch (2000) reports that Illinois has a higher black–white discrepancy of African Americans incarcerated for drug offenses than any other state in the union. The report states that the black–white ratio for such arrests and prosecution is fifty-seven to one.
4. *Amir* best translates as a Muslim leader, and a *muftis* also can be a political leader but refers more specifically to a man of great Islamic learning; both terms are widely used and understood throughout the Islamic world.
5. *Magreb* in Islamic terminology refers to the fourth of five daily prayers and takes place at sundown.
6. Every former EL Rukn with whom I spoke adamantly insists that the government set the organization up at a time when the Libyan government was prepared to give them money to establish legitimate financial security in the city.
7. The case with Jose Padilla precipitated a series of recycled stories in the media tapping into such fears. The summer 2006 story of seven men arrested and charged with conspiracy to blow up the Chicago Sears Tower and Federal Bureau of Investigation (FBI) Florida offices again serves to reinforce some of these stereotypes.
8. From Mos Def's "Hip Hop" (Rawkus Records, 1999).

9. Interview recorded in Arabic Restaurant on Chicago's southwest side August 2004.
10. The notion of "educated thuggery" is taken from Freeway's biography on the Rock A Fella website: www.rocafella.com/Artist.
11. Acquired through an interview with one of the Arab Muslim youth participants in May 2005.
12. Recorded during an interview and presentation by Fable at the Southwest Youth Collaborative on Chicago's Southwest Side on January 29, 2005.
13. This encounter was derived from a set of ethnographic notes I recorded between the fall 1997 and winter 1998 for Leslie Salzinger's ethnography practicum at the University of Chicago.

Works Cited

Conquergood, Dwight. 1990. One city, *Chicago Council on Urban Affairs*, 11–17.

Drake, St. Clair and R. Horace Cayton. 1945. *Black metropolis*. Chicago: University of Chicago Press.

Human Rights Watch. May 2000. "Punishment and Prejudice: Racial Disparities in the War on Drugs."

Marcuse, Peter. 1997. The ghetto of exclusion and the fortified enclave. *American Behavioral Scientist* 41(3):311–26.

Mignolo, D. Walter. 2002. The many faces of cosmo-polis: Border thinking and critical cosmopolitanism. In Carol A. Breckenridge, Sheldon Pollock, Home K. Bhahba, and Dipesh Chakrabarty, eds., *Cosmopolitanism (millenial quartet)*, 157-187. Durham, NC: Duke University Press.

Nightingale, Carl H. 2003. A tale of three global ghettos: How Arnold Hirsch helps us internationalize U.S. urban history. *Journal of Urban History* 29(3):257–71.

Roy, Ananya. 2002. Global histories: A new repertoire of cities. In E. Morss, ed., *New global history and the city*, New Global History Press. Retrieved from http:// www.journalinks.nl/Mijn%20webs/Global%20Histories.doc

Sassen, Saskia. 2006. *Cities in a world economy. 3rd Ed.* Thousand Oaks, CA: Pine Forge Press.

———. 1998. *Globalization and its discontents*. New York: New Press.

———. 2006. *Territory, authority, rights: From medieval to global assemblages*. Princeton, NJ: Princeton University Press.

Simmel, Georg. 1903. The Metropolis and Mental Life. In Donald Levine, ed. *Georg Simmel on individuality and social forms*. 324–339 Chicago: University of Chicago Press.

Suttles, Gerald. 1968. *The social order of the slum*. Chicago: University of Chicago Press.

Turner, Bryan. 2000. Cosmopolitan virtue: Loyalty and the city. In Engin F. Isin, ed., *Democracy, citizenship and the global city*, 130-147. London: Routledge.

———. 2002. Cosmopolitan virtue, globalization and patriotism. *Theory, Culture and Society* 19:45–63.

Wacquant, Loic. 1996. Red belt, black belt: Racial division, class inequality, and the state in the French urban periphery and the American ghetto. In Enzo Mingione, ed., *Urban poverty and the "underclass": A reader,* 234–74. Oxford: Basil Blackwell.
———. 1998. Deadly symbiosis: When ghetto and prison meet and mesh. *Punishment and Society* 3(1): 95–134 (Winter).
———. 2002. From slavery to mass incarceration: rethinking the 'race question' in the U.S. *New Left Review* 13: 41-60 (Jan/Feb).
Zorbaugh, H.W. 1929. *The gold coast and the slum.* Chicago: University of Chicago Press.

CHAPTER 13

Deregulating Markets, Reregulating Crime

Extralegal Policing and the Penal State in Mexico

JENNIFER L. JOHNSON

In recent years, scholars engaged in scalar analyses of state transformation have asked what happens to institutions and practices foundational to liberal democracy when the market becomes "the preferred mechanism for addressing social issues" (Sassen 2005, p. 83.) One compelling thesis emerging from this scholarship is that economic globalization is deeply implicated in the development of a new penal state (McClennan 2001; Peck 2003; Wacquant 2001). Citing rising rates of incarceration, the expansion of prison facilities and personnel, increasingly punitive sentencing laws, and more intrusive correctional practices, some have characterized this process as the retreat of the state from economic regulation and its retrenchment in the sphere of crime control and punishment. This, in the words of Loïc Wacquant, is "a Darwinian state which withdraws into its kingly functions of 'law and order' themselves hypertrophied" (Peck 2003, p. 225).

This chapter proposes a modest amendment to this thesis: Concurrent to the overarching expansion of state regulatory power in the penal realm, the global ascendancy of the market paradigm has set in motion countervailing forces that erode the national state's monopoly on the legitimate means of coercion. More precisely, under certain conditions economic restructuring engenders new subnational forms of political community that effectively claim the right to make and enforce penal law over and against opposition from recognized state institutions. To the extent that these subnational configurations displace the national state as the fulcrum for penal claim making, state transformation is occurring, though in a radically different way than the penal state literature suggests.

I examine this possibility through ethnographic analysis of an extralegal community policing movement in Mexico. This movement crystallized in 1995 when several thousand small-scale coffee farmers in Guerrero state formed policing brigades to patrol the roadways and footpaths that crisscross a mountainous area stretching over nearly 1,600 square miles, a territory the size of Delaware. At its outset, the movement detained criminal suspects and turned them over to the state justice system for prosecution. Ultimately, however, it ceased to operate in tandem with mainstream legal institutions and embarked on a more transformative political project aimed at administering justice locally. Why and how this movement gained popular legitimacy as an alternative to state-sanctioned penal practices is the central question addressed here.

This analysis and its theoretical implications are divided into three parts. The first part suggests how the existence of extralegal community policing in Mexico calls for an understanding of contemporary state transformation that builds on but gestures beyond scalar perspectives on globalization. The second part situates the origins of this movement in the structural conditions created by market deregulation for coffee and discusses how deregulation spurred an economic cooperative movement that became the medium for more concerted and contentious political struggles. Employing ethnographic materials, the third part traces the transformation of this collective endeavor from a pragmatic effort to compensate for state deficiencies into a principled quest to supplant state institutions. As this ethnography demonstrates, transnational rights discourses and activism played a pivotal role in shifting the locus of legitimate law enforcement from the centralized state to village-based institutions reconstituted in the name of indigenous autonomy.

Conceptualizing Contemporary State Transformation

Through its focus on scale, the conceptual architecture constructed in this volume provides an excellent starting point for theorizing extralegal policing and justice administration in relation to the state. If, as Sassen (2007, p. 5) proposes, "the history of the modern state can be read as the work of rendering national just about all crucial features of society," then scrutinizing processes that rescale, denationalize, or otherwise unbundle and rebundle this package of state functions is critical to the study of contemporary state transformation. Seminal work on globalization has demonstrated how the supranational scaling of capital accumulation has shifted statecraft to subnational scales as manifest, for example, in the rise of public-private regulatory experiments in urban governance (Brenner 1999, 2004; Brenner and Theodore 2005; Swyngedouw 2004). Applying a similar logic, this chapter asks whether and how the reregulation of agricultural commodity markets at a global scale engendered subnational modes of crime control in Mexico in the late 1990s.

In its early stages, the movement analyzed here operated as a partnership between state police and citizen patrols, an arrangement akin to the public-private regulatory experiments proliferating in urban areas in advanced industrial societies. Within a few years, however, this initiative became — from the perspective of state authorities — a subnational experiment in policing gone awry. Far from fortifying the state, community policing evolved into a practice that undermined the state's legitimacy and eclipsed its very presence in the penal realm. Put differently, rescaling the state through legally sanctioned collaborative policing opened the door for redefining crime control as the collective right and duty of citizens outside the state's purview.

In rural Mexico, state-making in the second half of the twentieth century relied heavily on systematic intervention in cash-crop markets to incorporate peripheral populations into the national economy, territory, and imaginary. Thus, as late as the 1990s some isolated rural regions remained tied to the state largely through the thread of populist state-owned economic enterprises. The next section offers a description of how this partial and uneven mode of state-making facilitated extralegal state transformation from below when market deregulation attenuated these ties.

Market Deregulation and the Creation of Political Spaces in Rural Mexico

As in much of the developing world, the 1990s in Mexico witnessed the dismantling of a highly interventionist public sector in accord with the dictates of structural adjustment. In the Mexican countryside, this reform agenda entailed the elimination of public enterprises that had for decades regulated markets for key agricultural commodities (MacLeod 2004; Teichman 1995). In southern Mexico, where coffee dominates, the liquidation of the National Coffee Institute (INMECAFE) marked a turning point in this transition from economic populism to neoliberalism.

The federal government established INMECAFE in 1958 to explore the viability of coffee as a crucial source of foreign exchange for state-led import-substitution industrialization. Responding to market trends sustained by the International Coffee Organization (ICO),[1] the agency's mandate expanded rapidly. Social unrest in rural Guerrero in the 1960s and 1970s accelerated this expansion, and by 1973 INMECAFE had begun to purchase, process, and market coffee harvests from small farmers as a means to shore up regime legitimacy (Dicum and Luttinger 1999; Snyder 2001). The Organisation for Economic Co-operation and Development (OECD) estimates that between 1973 and 1993 INMECAFE purchased and exported 30 to 40 percent of total domestic coffee production, mostly from farmers with fewer than five hectares of land in coffee (OECD 1997, p. 68). The agency returned profits to producers and covered operational losses with government transfers. By the outset of the 1990s, more than two million Mexicans[2] — many of them small farmers and their families — had come to rely on coffee, and annual government transfers to INMECAFE had reached US$112 million.[3]

In Guerrero's remote mountain region, INMECAFE collected coffee from local producers by sending buyers into villages where they weighed, sacked, and transported raw beans to warehouses and processing plants elsewhere. In 1985, with INMECAFE's demise on the horizon, several thousand small-scale coffee farmers in the region formed a marketing cooperative — *La Unión de Ejidos Luz de la Montaña* (Light of the Mountain) — to collaborate with and ultimately to supplant this government agency. With administrators and technicians trained by INMECAFE but without INMECAFE's direct intervention, in 1989, Light of the Mountain sold forty-eight tons of member-produced coffee to Nestlé buyers near Mexico City (García 2000).

The state and federal governments rewarded Light of the Mountain's efforts to take over INMECAFE's role in the region with grants and loans (Ravelo Lecuona and Avila Arévalo 1994). In the early 1990s, however, the ICO dissolved and market prices for coffee plummeted. Light of the Mountain's marketing enterprise — in spite of its impressive advances — struggled to stay afloat financially. Without the luxury of drawing on government transfers to cover short-term operating losses, as well as, the long-term capital investments that INMECAFE had enjoyed, the cooperative plunged into debt.

Thus, deregulation of coffee in Mexico entailed at its core a reshuffling of responsibilities for entrepreneurial success or failure from public to private actors. Much of southern Mexico became integrated into world markets precisely because of intense public-sector efforts to subsidize export-oriented coffee production in the 1970s. By the 1990s, however, state agents had extracted themselves from the role of buffering producers from the economic shocks generated by international market fluctuations. In the case of peasant producers, the burden of absorbing these shocks often fell squarely on the shoulders of grassroots cooperatives such as Light of the Mountain.

In the wake of deregulation, many of these cooperatives became sites of political contention that extended well beyond their initial economic mandate. In Chiapas, some coffee cooperatives became organizational foci for the Zapatista rebellion (Harvey 1998; Rubin 2002). Guerrero's largest coffee cooperative mobilized militant postelectoral protests in support of left-leaning opposition candidates in the upper coastal region. And Light of the Mountain launched a regional policing movement in Guerrero's Sierra Madre del Sur that would, by the end of the decade, become a vehicle for a nascent struggle for indigenous self-governance.

An Ethnography of Extralegal Community Policing in Guerrero, Mexico

Part 1: The Tenuous Ties that Bind

"No tickets to Marquelia. Only to Cruz Grande." No one flinched when the agent at the Acapulco bus station refused to sell tickets to Marquelia, the lone point of access into Guerrero's mountain region from the stretch of the Pan-American highway that winds down Mexico's Pacific Coast. No one except me. With bus service suspended at Cruz Grande, I wondered how I would ever arrive at Light of the Mountain's headquarters in the sleepy marketing town of San Luis Acatlán by sundown. Doña Licha showed me how.

When the bus from Acapulco stopped abruptly at its final destination on the outskirts of Cruz Grande, Doña Licha guided me along the expanse of steamy highway where torrential rains had washed out a bridge the night before, severing southern Guerrero's only coastal transport route in two. Army troops escorted pedestrians across the flooded riverbed, and a young entrepreneur with a wheelbarrow carted our suitcases and backpacks for a small fee. We hitchhiked to the fishing town of Marquelia and then boarded the Volkswagen minibus that would transport us up the rolling foothills of Mexico's Sierra Madre del Sur to San Luis Acatlán. The same rains that had cut the Pan-American Highway had swollen a river along this paved, two-lane roadway as well. As we clung to the fenders of the John Deere tractor that ferried us to the other side of the river, Doña Licha touched my arm and told me that we were about to enter her native land. "*Ay güera,*" she whispered, "*ya llegamos a mi tierra.*"

For nearly a decade now, the Light of the Mountain cooperative had operated a milling facility and warehouse located a few miles into the mountains just beyond Doña Licha's hometown, San Luis Acatlán. During an earlier era of booming international coffee markets and state support for coffee farming, the federal government had paved the highway from Marquelia to San Luis Acatlán, a *mestizo* commercial center at the entrance to the mountains. Rumor had it that government reports listed the road beyond San Luis Acatlán as paved as well and that state-level politicians pocketed the yearly sums allocated for maintenance of this public works project. But as I traversed the last leg of my journey to Light of the Mountain headquarters on foot, this highway turned from cobblestones to dust as it exited San Luis's town square and snaked into the highlands. Clearly, government benevolence — and bankroll — had run out before reaching the indigenous villages that comprised the heart of Guerrero's coffee-producing mountain region.

If the gradual disintegration of the roadways from Acapulco inland dramatized the dissipation of the populist political will with the global ascendancy of neoliberalism, it also exposed the irony that, in spite of decades of state intervention to promote coffee export, Guerrero's mountain region still lacked the basic physical infrastructure required for getting goods to market. In the dry season, the road connecting the coffee-growing mountain communities to San Luis Acatlán presented precipitous inclines, hairpin curves, and deep ruts that sent even the sturdiest vehicles careening and made travel both rough and risky. In the rainy season, mud and rockslides frequently halted vehicular traffic altogether. The physical barriers I encountered traveling into the mountains for the first time in the company of Doña Licha had seemed formidable, but they paled in comparison to the challenges of transporting coffee beans — millions of pounds of them each year — out to marketplaces and beyond.

My first field stint with Light of the Mountain commenced in fall 1998, during the cool, dry days preceding the peak coffee harvest season in January and February. It was months before I could observe for myself how Light of the Mountain confronted the obstacles — physical and otherwise — that loomed large between mountain coffee growers and the global market. The sunny afternoons that unfolded before me during this preharvest lull, however, provided ample opportunity for learning of the events that had propelled the cooperative forward thus far.

"My father gave me his plot of land in '78," Oscar commented as we whiled away one such afternoon inside the gated complex surrounding Light of the Mountain's warehouse. "And I've sold my entire crop to the organization just about ever since." When the elders from his indigenous Tlapanec coffee-growing community requested that he serve Light of the Mountain on the village's behalf, Oscar became more active in the cooperative's affairs. With his solid secondary education and some technical training in the use of video equipment, Oscar had since become the cooperative's unofficial historian. If I wanted to know more about the organization's background, he would be more than happy to oblige.

We climbed the concrete steps to the warehouse's second-floor offices, and Oscar explained that Light of the Mountain had videotaped all of its major events since 1990 after participating in an extensive training course on video production sponsored by the government's National Indigenist Institute (INI). He scanned the gray metal bookshelf lined with video cassettes now in front of us and then rested his finger on a jacket labeled "A Living Experience: The 1990–1991 Harvest." The 1990–1991 cycle marked the first growing season that INMECAFE relied on Light of the Mountain to buy up the local harvest and then to resell it to the agency in bulk. As the audio played on in the Tlapanec language accompanied by Spanish subtitles, the visual depicted Light of the Mountain members paying growers, weighing 130-pound burlap sacks, loading them onto flatbed trucks, drying and sorting raw beans at the warehouse facility, and then reweighing and packing them.[4] It then cut to a member of Light of the Mountain's marketing committee who exhibited receipts for payment of coffee shipments to INMECAFE and a breakdown of the quantities of coffee the organization had turned around each year since its inception. According to the figures that flashed before me, Light of the Mountain had handled ten tons in 1990–1991, an estimated 63 percent of the total coffee cultivated in the region that year.

An hour's worth of footage on the milestone 1990–1991 harvest wound to an end, and I wondered out loud about the course of events that had led Light of the Mountain to that historical juncture. "It all began in 1981," Oscar offered. "Back then, INMECAFE paid a decent price...and it showed us how to sell coffee. Before that, we hauled our sacks of coffee on beasts of burden as far as San Luis Acatlán where merchants would send 'coyotes' to force us to barter or sell our coffee for a pittance. Sometimes they would simply steal it." And local law enforcement officials — in collusion with the coyotes — turned a blind eye to these abuses. Working together, INMECAFE and the committees that would coalesce into Light of the Mountain put private middlemen in San Luis Acatlán out of business, and the threat of theft along the road to market subsided.

By the 1990s, however, the same government corruption and neglect that perpetuated the sorry state of regional roadways that had appalled me on my first visit had allowed crime against coffee growers traveling these roads to reach crisis proportions. In the thick of the economic crisis that had impacted tens of thousands of local coffee growers and their families since the beginning of the decade, the incidence of violent crime along these roads spiked dramatically. As an organization, Light of the Mountain initially addressed this problem by hiring private security guards to protect both its warehouse and vehicles. But the 5,000 farmers who formed the collective's rank and file remained vulnerable. These villagers repeatedly suffered insults, theft, and even rape perpetrated by common criminals but also by the state police that investigated and purportedly prevented these crimes. By mid-decade, Light of the Mountain adopted a new strategy for redressing this deep-seated and unresolved grievance. In 1995, the cooperative convened a council of village elders from forty-two communities to consider lawlessness in the region and to propose solutions. In 1996, this regional council mobilized 500 patrolmen and thirty-six commanders from their communities to supplement official law enforcement efforts.

"Robberies happened every day. And rapes." Don Macario spoke softly but deliberately into my tape recorder as I conducted our first and only formal interview in December 1998. I first met Don Macario in his capacity as a leader of Light of the Mountain but had since discovered that he commanded a policing brigade from his community. Through his eyes, I began to see how peasants became policemen in Guerrero's mountain region.

Don Macario began our interview by recalling INMECAFE's work in the region, continued with an account of his participation in Light of the Mountain, and then veered onto the topic of the cooperative's policing initiative. "And the people grew tired because…[t]hey raped your wife and your daughter along the roadside…and they beat you. And we had to report all of these incidents to the district attorney's office so that they could issue warrants. But the government never listened."

Repeated trips to the state capital to request support for their local fight on crime did in fact yield the intervention of state judicial police. "[But] when they came," Don Macario told me, "they came to harass innocent people. They emptied our sacks along the roadside and searched us. They didn't pursue the criminals." Petitioning official law enforcement agents to impose the rule of law in the region had resulted in a combination of insults and inaction, and villagers resolved to adopt a more proactive stance. In the words of Don Macario, "we decided that if the government couldn't protect us we would protect ourselves."

One evening I found myself in the company of Don Macario and a half-dozen police commanders after a Light of the Mountain assembly held in a highland community. We made our way down treacherous roads to San Luis Acatlán in the back of a pickup truck equipped with a CB radio. An arc of white letters painted on the doors to the cab declared the vehicle property of *La Policía Comunitaria, San Luis Acatlán, Gro.* For two years now, brigades like this one had patrolled these desolate thoroughfares in search of criminal suspects. With an unsurpassed familiarity with the region and personal commitment to ridding it of crime, these brigades had proven extraordinarily effective, and my companions expressed pride over this accomplishment. As we traversed a craggy pass, one pointed to the spot where his brigade had uncovered the stash of a local ring of thieves.

The booty had consisted of canned goods and cigarettes heisted at gunpoint from delivery trucks en route into the mountains. These goods had stocked local mom-and-pop concessions until the community police had caught on to the scheme. My companion boasted that only someone with intimate knowledge of this inhospitable terrain could have succeeded in capturing those crooks. Glancing again at the cliffs and crevices towering above us, I agreed.

Stymied by this topography and other challenges to imposing law and order in this remote mountain region, the executive branch of Guerrero's state government had collaborated with this self-help policing initiative at its outset. The governor donated a truck and twenty low-caliber firearms to augment the fleet of vehicles and equipment supplied by village and municipal authorities or provided by rank-and-file community police officers themselves. Licensing officials in the state capital extended permits to carry arms and other necessary *acreditaciones* to individuals who identified themselves as community police, with no questions asked. And with the tacit approval of the governor, federal troops stationed in Guerrero trained the movement's brigades in the efficient use of these weapons.

By 1998, however, relations between Guerrero state government and the region's community police had soured. Community policing commanders complained bitterly to me that even when their brigades apprehended offenders *con las manos en la masa* (red-handed), the district attorney released detainees on bail without punishment, and the offenders would return to the villages to take revenge. "If the law won't punish them," Don Macario asked rhetorically, "who will?"

For its part, the regional district attorney's office contended that the community police were illegal and sent representatives to movement assemblies to publicly threaten commanders with imprisonment. The state attorney general employed similar scare tactics. Movement members also claimed that unnamed government sources had tried to discredit the community police by leaking false information to an Acapulco newspaper alleging links to Maoist guerillas. All the while, state judicial police conducted periodic arms sweeps in villages actively involved in the movement in attempts to forcibly disarm local brigades.

"And so our regional council of elders decided that we needed to make our own laws," Don Macario stated as our interview drew to a close. "Now, we imprison whomever we catch in the act and re-educate them in our communities." As cooperation from prosecutors deteriorated and retaliation from these and other state agents heightened, the community police had indeed ceased to turn detainees over to state authorities, opting instead to adjudicate and sentence offenders on their own. In fact, in the weeks just before my arrival, the regional council had met repeatedly to hammer out written guidelines for these procedures and to deliberate on the fate of the handful of individuals it now held in custody. "But to apply justice in the region, to our prisoners," Don Macario added, "we needed to know our rights. We wanted to know what rights we have as indigenous peoples."

In 1990, Mexico ratified the International Labor Organization's (ILO) Convention 169 concerning Indigenous and Tribal Peoples in Independent Countries, and through the INI the federal government launched a campaign to inform the nation's fifteen million indigenous peoples about the rights that this legislation guaranteed. Don Macario and others in Guerrero's mountain region recalled INI booklets and courses on the topic. "But they only told us a half truth," he alleged. "They told us that indigenous peoples had the same rights as everyone else."

In the context of government hostility, Light of the Mountain leaders became more receptive to ideologically diverse perspectives on the question of indigenous rights and, in 1998 and 1999, hosted a series of rights workshops conducted by extralocal activists. In the crucible of events like these, rank-and-file movement members began to fashion new understandings of identity, citizenship, and state from the fabric of transnational rights discourse. Grounded in these cognitive shifts, extralegal policing ultimately became deeply embedded in Mexico's nascent movement for indigenous autonomy and self-governance.

Part 2: Rights and the Appropriation of the Rule of Law

In the wee hours of a brisk December morning, Angel navigated a lumbering Light of the Mountain cargo vehicle through the roughly paved streets of San Luis Acatlán and halted in front of the guesthouse where I resided. Charged with collecting passengers from a dozen villages en route to our final destination in the uppermost reaches of the mountains before daybreak, he ushered me hurriedly into the front seat. As I slid into the cab, I greeted Oscar, who would spend a good deal of the next several days behind the lens of a video camera filming the upcoming event, and he passed me a television monitor for safekeeping against the bumps that would jar us mercilessly on our journey ahead. I dozed in and out of consciousness for hours, cradling this precious load on my lap until the silhouette of San Miguel El Progreso appeared on the horizon.

For nearly two generations, virtually everyone in San Miguel had cultivated coffee for a living, and, for the past decade, most everyone had marketed their harvests through Light of the Mountain. Over the years, this Tlapanec village had produced many dedicated cooperative movement leaders and had hosted countless assemblies where representatives from throughout the region met to determine the course of their own collective efforts at coffee marketing. On this day, however, San Miguel would witness the inauguration of an event that seemed out of sync with Light of the Mountain's traditional emphasis on coffee: a three-day workshop on human rights. "This business about human rights is a bit out of our area," Light of the Mountain's president announced apologetically to the scores of coffee farmers and cooperative members gathered for the workshop. "Still, we think it's important."

The course that commenced at noon formed part of year-long series organized by Light of the Mountain and imparted by a team of popular educators from Mexico City. Talented human rights lawyers devoted to the indigenous cause and impassioned by developments in Chiapas, José and Elena, headed up this team. José had first come to the region to help the cooperative extricate an export permit application that had become mired in bureaucratic red tape. He had performed similar pro bono work for other indigenous coffee cooperatives in Oaxaca and Chiapas and came highly recommended by them. Now, months later, he had returned to Guerrero with his wife, Elena, and three bright-eyed youth apprentices — Ana Luisa, Angélica, and Magda — to initiate a five-part training event titled "The Rights of the Tlapanec and Mixtec Peoples."

I caught up with José and his associates that morning in the adobe dwelling where participants would take their meals together for the next several days. Over bowls of steaming hominy soup, they discussed the pending event. The course in San Miguel would examine how indigenous peoples (*pueblos indígenas*) in Mexico had demanded state and federal legislation that guaranteed their rights: the right to education in their own language, the right to land, the right to their own forms of political representation. "The government didn't just sit down and decide that it wanted to benefit indigenous peoples," Elena stated. "Indigenous peoples themselves had to take up this struggle." In fact, the next day we would view a documentary on indigenous groups around the hemisphere that had mobilized to support the International Labor Organization's Convention 169. José chimed in to say that with clips from tapes of the Light of the Mountain workshops, he hoped to produce a video of the struggle that the people here had undertaken to inform and inspire yet other *pueblos indígenas.*

Hours later, a village elder inaugurated the Light of the Mountain affair with words of welcome uttered in broken Spanish. One of José and Elena's assistants then took the floor and requested that everyone state aloud his or her name and *pueblo indígena* as an introduction. "Your *pueblo indígena* is the same as the language you speak," Elena objected when the first to speak claimed his *pueblo indígena* to be San Miguel. José added that every *pueblo indígena* had the right to name themselves as they pleased but that the Spaniards had systematically violated this right. "You call yourselves the Mee'pa people," he asserted emphatically, "but the Spaniards called you *tlapanecos*, which means people with dirty faces." "My name is Sylvia," the next participant to introduce herself volunteered, "and I come from the Mee'pa people."

The nongovernmental organization (NGO) that José and Elena ran from their home in Mexico City had obtained funds from the Mexican INI and the Canadian Embassy to prepare didactic material for each of the workshops it held with Light of the Mountain. As stacks of workbooks made their way around the expansive semicircle of participants, Elena explained that many Mexican states in recent years had passed legislation on indigenous rights. Bound with a canary yellow cover adorned with folk art depicting the coffee harvest, the workbooks for the San Miguel session contained the text of the Chihuahua and Oaxaca state laws on indigenous rights. We would study examples of these laws in the next three days. The workshop then broke into small groups to pore over articles from Chihuahua's indigenous law.

When we reconvened, our instructors pointed out flaws in this legislation. "It presumes to protect indigenous peoples' right to their own land," Ana Luisa noted, "but this contradicts Article 27 of the Mexican Constitution that says that all land belongs to the federal government." Likewise, Chihuahua's law guarantees access to bilingual education, but this guarantee also corresponds to the federal government. Only by amending the Mexican Constitution could indigenous peoples gain respect for these rights. The following day, Angélica led a comparable discussion on Oaxaca's indigenous law. As she concluded her analysis, an air of dissent seemed to take hold of the Light of the Mountain members assembled in San Miguel. "These laws deceive us!" someone interjected angrily. "They're empty gestures, crumbs the government throws us to keep us happy." Another participant exclaimed in frustration, "They've always fed us gruel from their fingertips." Others remarked that the situation in Guerrero seemed especially backward compared to other parts of the country. "We're just barely waking up from our ignorance and lack of information," a woman I had come to know quite well commented. "But," she added with a militancy that caught me off guard, "if we need to shed blood for change, we will."

After the San Miguel event, I reflected on how the interactions I had witnessed belied a certain discontinuity between extant notions of identity, collectivity, and governance, and novel forms of conceptualizing these and their interrelationship. If the people of Guerrero's mountain region had once deployed the language of *pueblo indígena* to denote their village of origin, extralocal activists had prepared the terrain for an emergent sense of *pueblo indígena* as a meaningful collective category grounded in a shared ethnic identity. Moreover, the proliferation of state laws on the rights of indigenous peoples stood as a vivid testimony to how state actors validated this category as a basis for unique legal claims. Inscribed in state legislation but devoid of legal substance, the collective rights of indigenous peoples had become a rallying cry for the Mexican indigenous rights movement at large. In San Miguel, this contradiction — refracted through the rhetoric of popular educators and rights activists from Mexico City — spurred a propensity to interpret long-standing grievances centering on government neglect through the lens of indigenous rights.

In November 1998, Light of the Mountain held its second indigenous rights workshop in Tierra Colorada, a Tlapanec village with a spectacular view of the peaks and valleys that separate Guerrero's coffee-growing highlands from the Pacific Ocean. Observations in the first workshop suggested that indigenous rights had emerged as a meaningful collective category for Light of the Mountain coffee farmers. Events in Tierra Colorada would reveal how this transformation shaped the trajectory of extralegal policing.

"Use them like the tools that you use to ensure your everyday survival," José exhorted us as he raised a copy of the workbook for the session in Tierra Colorada in one hand and a small purple handbook in the other. "Like a hand mill to grind corn for tortillas or a machete to clear the fields." The handbook contained the full text of ILO Convention 169 with commentary. I opened my copy of the workbook and perused its contents as well: excerpts from the United Nations (UN) International Pact on Economic, Social and Cultural Rights; the UN International Convention on the Elimination of All Forms of Racial Discrimination; and the Organization of the American States (OAS) Declaration of the Rights of Indigenous Peoples. "Sometimes marches, demonstrations, and hunger strikes aren't enough to achieve your demands," José added with a dramatic air. "Indigenous peoples need to protect themselves with the law."

The fifty or so Light of the Mountain members gathered that morning had traveled to Tierra Colorada to attend a workshop titled "International Instruments on Human Rights and the Rights of Indigenous Peoples." Some of them, like the sizeable contingent of community police officers interspersed among the crowd, had done so on foot. Visible from a distance as they marched single file up a footpath toward our meeting place, the group had caught my eye from the very outset of the event. "This workshop is for everyone who belongs to Light of the Mountain," José explained to me as I watched the group uniformed in navy t-shirts and caps with hunting rifles slung across their shoulders, "but we especially encouraged community policemen and village elders to attend."

On that first morning, José divided the assembly into small groups and assigned each an international instrument to read and reflect on. No one in my group spoke Spanish as a first language, and few had more than a grade-school education. But a bilingual schoolteacher among us volunteered to read slowly and deliberately from Article 1 of the UN Pact on Economic, Social and Cultural Rights on the right to self-determination. "All peoples have the right to self-determination. Under no circumstance can anyone deprive a people of their own means of subsistence." Ana Luisa approached our group, taped a large sheet of newsprint to a nearby brick wall, and instructed us to jot down our thoughts on this elusive right to self-determination. An uncomfortable silence settled over the group until someone quipped that it was getting late and that depriving him of lunch constituted a violation of his human rights. A young boy who had come to seek out his mother listened intently to the ensuing light-hearted banter and then piped up with the rejoinder, "And I have the right to go play now."

In the afternoon, vague but humorous invocations of rights turned serious when José reconvened the larger assembly and revisited the topic of self-determination with the active participation of the community police officers in our midst. What did the right to self-determination guaranteed by the international laws and conventions we had studied mean to those individuals? "The right to apply our own laws to punish guilty people for their crimes" someone asserted. "That the authorities from outside recognize our internal laws."

On the final day of the workshop, José and his helpers taught us how to appeal to international governmental organizations like the OAS when Mexican government officials violated this right to self-determination. Dividing us into small groups once again, he instructed us to fill out a sample complaint form addressed to the Inter-American Human Rights Commission based on a real-life experience. Natalio brimmed with excitement as he rehashed for our group how Mexican government officials had barged into a recent meeting of the Regional Council of Village Elders (*la asamblea regional de autoridades indígenas*) as they discussed matters pertaining to community policing. "They told us we had no legal right to operate as policemen," he recalled. "Some of us had copies of 169 with us. We waved it in their faces and told them to go brush up on the law." The sample complaint form we filled out that afternoon began, "Name of Victim: Regional Council of Village Elders. Age: Three years…"

I returned from Tierra Colorada that evening huddled under a plastic tarp with José, Ana Luisa, Angélica, and Magda in the flatbed of a Light of the Mountain truck. Unseasonably heavy rains pelted our flimsy shelter as we gripped the truck's rickety wooden rails that stood between us and the rocky ravines inching by below. I lamented my chilled, miserable existence at that moment, but José's young charges waxed warm with nostalgia as they reminisced about their work with him and contemplated the prospects for bringing justice to indigenous peoples throughout Mexico. They had met one another through a Zapatista solidarity group (*un comité del frente zapatista*) in Mexico City. "We're working to circulate information on the San Andrés Accords through the church. There's a new parish priest in the neighborhood, and he supports us," Magda explained enthusiastically. "It's really not all that organized," Ana Luisa added modestly. "Mostly young people." José had attended meetings and invited them to get involved in his organization. He and Elena had taken them to participatory rights workshops in Mexico City and in Chiapas. Now Ana Luisa, Angélica, and Magda had the chance to become rights advocates among indigenous peoples in Guerrero.

In Tierra Colorada and San Miguel, I witnessed how these advocates helped transform a pragmatic issue of self-defense into a principled issue regarding who has the right to govern. In the 1980s and 1990s, the neoliberal state devolved the economic functions of financing, processing, and marketing coffee to the private and civil society sectors. But in Guerrero's mountain region, the state also devolved, *de facto* if not *de jure*, the responsibility for public security to those individuals and collectivities most affected by its absence. Inspired by extralocal indigenous rights activists, Light of the Mountain's move to fill this void engendered a process of consciousness raising that challenged orthodox notions of who makes and enforces penal law. Light of the Mountain's struggle to appropriate the productive process had expanded to include the appropriation of the legitimate bases of law making and enforcement. Community policing had become, in short, an arena for appropriating the rule of law.

Part 3: Postscript

In the following years, the growing awareness of *rights, indigeneity,* and the *law* fomented in situ by extralocal activists took on more palpable political expression linked to the broader movement for indigenous autonomy. When the Guerrero state congress deliberated over President Vicente Fox's proposed constitutional amendment on indigenous rights in summer 2001, the community police joined other grassroots organizations of indigenous peoples statewide to occupy the congressional building in protest of the legislation's exclusion of constitutional guarantees for indigenous self-governance. These events sparked unprecedented media interest in this parochial struggle for self-defense that in turn linked the movement to a wider circle of extralocal indigenous rights advocates. In the fall, the Zapatistas commemorated Guerrero's extralegal policing movement's sixth anniversary on their official Web site (http://www.fzln.org.mx), and the Chicago-based Chiapas Media Project initiated the production of a video featuring "the Indigenous Community Police movement of Guerrero…one of the most dynamic grassroots movements in Mexico today."[5]

In September 2002, an email notice titled "Indigenous Rights/Community Police Tour" found its way onto my virtual desk. Posted to the Mexico Solidarity Network subscribers list, the message sought "community, church and university-based sponsors" in the Midwest United States to screen this new video and to host the "indigenous video maker" who directed it.[5] From my vantage point at a computer terminal in Chicago, I marveled at how the relatively obscure grassroots movement I had researched in the heart of Guerrero's mountain region just years earlier had achieved a remarkable degree of recognition within transnational rights networks. Through the mass media as well as concrete working relationships with NGOs in Mexico and abroad, Guerrero's extralegal community police had become a symbol of national and international struggles for indigenous autonomy and self-governance.

Conclusion

This chapter traced the emergence and gradual institutionalization of community policing and justice administration as an extralegal penal practice among indigenous coffee farmers in the southern Mexican highlands during the 1990s. At its inception, community policing operated as a simple extension of the state justice system. By late decade, however, the movement had reconstituted a body of law grounded in indigenous custom and had begun meting out justice according to these laws.

Viewed in ethnographic detail, the trajectory of this movement reveals that core assumptions about what states owe citizens in exchange for their continued complicity in the national state-making project changed as deregulation progressed in the Mexican countryside. At its outset, community policing upheld conventional understandings of state agents and institutions as the sole legitimate arbiters of justice. Moreover, the movement's collaboration with the official justice system reinforced the state-propagated view of citizens as partners in governance in a neoliberal era, an ideology assiduously cultivated by Mexico's ruling elite in the 1990s. Parallel to the private sector's acceptance of greater responsibility for social service delivery in advanced industrial nations, the community police in Mexico symbolized increased citizen willingness to help the state enact the rule of law.

Over time, however, this practice evolved into a crucible for redefining the rights and duties of citizens and states, respectively, as participants came to perceive the task of making and enforcing penal law as a collective right and duty of indigenous peoples. Manifested in the crystallization of a regional council of village elders to oversee and arbitrate within an extralegal criminal justice system, the penal center of gravity in this region shifted from state institutions to a form of political community counterposed to the state. Put differently, this transformation entailed not only the denationalization and subnational scaling of statehood in the penal realm but also the invention of subnational penal institutions and practices located outside and in tension with the overarching framework of the modern state.

Thus, empirical analysis of extralegal policing in Mexico complicates the imagery of contemporary penal institutions and practices as the site of concentrated state power, a bastion to which the modern state has retreated under the pressures of global capitalism. Surely, processes that contribute to the configuration of a penal state in Mexico are at work, as evidenced by the adoption of recent tough on crime measures in Mexico City. As this chapter suggests, however, multiple, concurrent, and competing trends are unfolding in unexpected places and among some of the most historically marginalized sectors of Mexican society. These testify to the vulnerability of modern state forms within the penal realm and the complexity of contemporary state transformation writ large.

Notes

1. The International Coffee Organization was a price-setting cartel that brokered multilateral export quota agreements. This regulatory regime benefited roasting companies by guaranteeing stable supplies and friendly relations with producer countries but also generated economic rents for producer countries (Talbot 1997).
2. Estimates range from 2 million (Snyder 2001, p. 29) to 2.5 million (Carbot 1988, p. 97).
3. These increased from US$31 million in 1979 to US$112 million in 1989 (OECD 1997, p. 68).
4. Each burlap sack holds approximately 130 pounds of coffee. Trailers typically transport 100 or more sacks — over 100,000 pounds of coffee — at a time.
5. This message was sent from list-owner@mexicosolidarity.org on September 11, 2002.

Works Cited

Brenner, Neil. 1999. "Beyond state-centrism? Space, territoriality, and geographical scale in globalization studies." *Theory and Society* 28: 39–78.

———. 2004. New state spaces: Urban governance and the rescaling of statehood. New York: Oxford University Press.

Brenner, Neil, and Nik Theodore. 2005. Neo-liberalism and the urban condition. *City* 9(1):101–7.

Carbot, Alberto. 1988. *Fausto Peña Cantú: Café para todos.* Mexico City: Editorial Grijalbo.

Dicum, Gregory, and Nina Luttinger. 1999. *The coffee book: The anatomy of an industry from crop to the last drop.* New York: New Press.

García, Carlos. 2000. De la costa a la montaña. In Armando Bartra, ed., *Crónicas del sur: Utopías campesinas en Guerrero*, 275–320. Mexico City: Era.

Harvey, Neil. 1998. *The Chiapas rebellion: The struggle for land and democracy.* Durham, NC: Duke University Press.

MacLeod, Dag. 2004. *Downsizing the state: Privatization and the limits of neoliberal reform in Mexico.* University Park: Pennsylvania State University Press.

McClennan, Rebecca. 2001. The new penal state: Globalization, history, and American criminal justice, c. 2000. *Inter-Asia Cultural Studies* 2(3):407–19.

Organisation for Economic Co-operation and Development (OECD). 1997. *Review of agricultural policies in Mexico, National policies and agricultural trade series.* Paris: OECD.

Peck, Jamie. 2003. Geography and public policy: Mapping the penal state. *Progress in Human Geography* 27(2):222–32.

Ravelo Lecuona, Renato and José O. Avila Arévalo. 1994. *Luz de la Montaña: Una historia viva.* Mexico City: National Indigenist Institute.

Rubin, Jeffrey W. 2002. From Che to Marcos: The changing grassroots Left in Latin America, Summer, 39–47.

Sassen, Saskia. 2005. The repositioning of citizenship and alienage: Emergent subjects and spaces for politics. *Globalizations* 2(1):79–94.

———. 2007. Introduction: Deciphering the Global. In Saskia Sassen, ed. *Deciphering the Global: Its Scales, Spaces, and Subjects*, 1–18. New York and London: Routledge.

Snyder, Richard. 2001. *Politics after neo-liberalism: Reregulation in Mexico.* New York: Cambridge University Press.

Swyngedouw, Erik. 2004. *Social power and the urbanization of water: Flows of power.* Oxford: Oxford University Press.

Talbot, John M. 1997. Where does your coffee dollar go? The division of income and surplus along the coffee commodity chain. *Studies in Comparative International Development* 32(1):56–102.

Teichman, Judith A. 1995. *Privatization and political change in Mexico.* Pittsburgh: University of Pittsburgh Press.

Wacquant, Loïc. 2001. The advent of the penal state is not a destiny. *Social Justice: A Journal of Crime, Conflict and World Order* 28(3):81–7.

CHAPTER 14

The Transnational Human Rights Movement and States of Emergency in Israel/Palestine

JOSH KAPLAN

It is widely held that the Israeli state, much like other states, has undergone an extensive transformation in the face of globalization (Shafir and Peled 2000, 2002). In this view, the state is neither as strong nor as large as it used to be, the once-dominant Labor Party has fallen into decline, bourgeois individualism and individual rights are on the rise, many of the founding myths of the state have been challenged, and there has been increasingly vocal resistance and advocacy coming from, and on behalf of, the Palestinian minority. However, despite these transformations, and notwithstanding premature obituaries, a powerful logic of the state persists and that logic has great bearing on both the practice of human rights and the extent to which it can be claimed that the state has been transformed. If globalization helped bring the nation-state into question, global terrorism has brought its enduring elements back into focus. In Israel and elsewhere, whatever challenges the state has faced by globalization seem to have been effaced — both at the level of popular consciousness and political practice — by a return to more traditional notions of "stateness." Perhaps most salient among these is the apparently commonsensical notion that a state faced with an emergency — a perceived threat to its very existence — should do whatever is in its power to defend itself.

In the face of the proliferation of intrastate violence and terrorism, states are increasingly finding themselves in a position of having to make choices about self-defense that could entail severe limitations on human rights. Emergencies can seem to justify, and to legally ground, a range of action for governments that would otherwise be considered inexcusable, morally reprehensible, and extreme, not to mention illegal and contrary to human rights; such actions are carried out in the name of the security, or survival, of the state. Though international human rights law provides various restrictions on state action, it leaves wide latitude in practice for states to take defensive measures in the face of existential threat. This is enabled in part because the concept of existential threat — the thinking behind the primary international legal basis for a state to derogate or suspend its human rights obligations — is a perceptual category. And in emergencies the presence of existential threat is widely presumed.

States of emergency are not new; neither is their link to dictatorship-like modifications to democracies and suspensions of constitutions; indeed, they are provided for in many constitutions. As Agamben (2005) explains, they are part of a broader phenomenon of states of exception that were characteristic of World War I, World War II, and the U.S. Civil War. What is new, and what Agamben glosses over, is the regulatory machinery and moral landscape in which they can be invoked — and the dynamism of media and advocacy groups that can pressure the state to alter its behavior — all of which might be called *global*. While the determination of an emergency, whether *de facto* or *de jure*, continues to carry considerable implications for the enjoyment of human rights, conditions have changed such that human rights advocates, the media, and other actors can contribute to altering state behavior, even in emergencies. Moreover, state policies are formulated in this environment in the first place, that is, in anticipation of possible criticism and pressure.

States of emergency bring to light how a particular instantiation of a global process, the human rights movement, comes up against certain quite durable limits in practice. Whatever dynamic exists between the logic of the state and the human rights movement is far more difficult to see in an emergency. At the same time, we can observe a slight relaxation of these limits over time. To illustrate this argument, this chapter turns to the particular case of emergency, human rights, and the state found in, and in relation, to Israel/Palestine. The apparently extreme example of the Israeli case — a continuous state of emergency in place since before the founding of the state in 1948, a widespread tendency to perceive existential threat, and the ongoing conflict between Israel and its neighbors — is not simply exceptional; it is also characteristic of an exceptionalist logic of the state that tends to hold sway in emergencies. Moreover, the focus on a particular example helps to reveal a subtle interplay between apparent state entrenchment in the name of security and survival and judicial and policy decision making sensitive to human rights concerns and human rights advocacy.

To fully appreciate the case, several points framing the issue more generally must first be understood. The first section therefore briefly introduces the concept of state survival in international law before turning in the second section to discuss human rights law in emergencies and the state survivalist formulation at its heart. The following section introduces some of the more salient characteristics of the Israeli case, including entrenched domestic emergency laws, the Israeli Jewish predisposition to perceive existential threat (i.e., the trigger for exceptions to human rights law), and the philosophy of jurisprudence of the former president of the Israeli High Court, Aaron Barak. The next sections discuss how these characteristics influence judicial decision making in the Israeli High Court, particularly with respect to Palestinian rights. Against this cultural and jurisprudential background, the final section examines the limits and possibilities of human rights advocacy.

A Note on Sovereignty and the Survival of the State

This chapter presupposes a particular understanding of the meaning of *the state;* the concern here is not just with the political and administrative body but also with dominant ideas about how it does — and should — work. These ideas also obviously exist outside the state. One dominant idea is that survival, or self-perpetuation, is at the core of what it means to be a state (cf. Foucault 1991; Heathcote 1998). A central goal of the state is then to ensure its survival or self-preservation, especially in the face of various threats.

It follows, therefore, that issues thought to be directly tied to preserving the existence of the state are typically argued by states to be part of the *domain reservé*: outside the purview of international law and subject only to domestic jurisdiction. In line with Hobbes's (1996) formulation that self-preservation is *the* natural right, classical thinking on the state often took state survival to be a fundamental right: In a conflict between international law and a state's existence, the right to existence would trump the law (cf. Heathcote 1998, p. 25; Tuck 1999).

State survival is rarely referenced explicitly in international law; neither is self-preservation. The International Court of Justice's (ICJ) Nuclear Weapons Opinion of 1996 is one of the few instances in contemporary international law in which the issue of state survival is directly addressed. But, despite the best wishes of some international lawyers (e.g., Kohen 1999), it is by no means the only instance in which state survival, or self-preservation, comes into play in international law, much less in contemporary affairs. Particularly in the context of the various wars on terror, the concept is now routinely resurfacing. What is most striking about the nuclear weapons opinion is the reading it allows: In situations in which the survival of the state is at stake, virtually anything goes. Specifically, the court wrote that it could not decide, finally, if the threat or use of nuclear weapons would be legal in a situation in which the survival of the state was at stake. As there is currently no more extreme act in which a state could engage than the use of nuclear weapons, the court effectively suggests that anything is possible under such circumstances.[1]

If a judicial body as important to international legal thinking as the ICJ reaches such a conclusion, it would seem, therefore, of the utmost importance how we arrive at a situation in which the survival of the state is at stake. I strongly suggest that in most cases such a situation is triggered by the perception of existential threat; indeed, it may be impossible to conceive of a situation in which that is not the case. What this means, then, for international law — and therefore also for human rights — is that a great deal hinges on a single perception: existential threat. It is clear, of course, that such perceptions are not made in a vacuum; they must fit pre-existing categories of danger and safety, threat and promise, and so on; and they must be largely supported by popular opinion and the media. As the next section demonstrates, the notion that exceptional threat can justify extraordinary measures underlies the key formulation for exceptions to human rights law: the derogation clause.

Sovereignty and Emergency in International Law

The derogation clause provides a possibility for states to suspend, or more properly, to legally alter, their human rights obligations in the face of exceptional threat. Marks and Clapham (2004) rightly note that the clause is subject to certain qualifications, among them: (1) certain nonderogable rights are protected at all times; (2) the measures taken to counter the threat must be necessary and proportionate to the threat at hand; (3) the state must notify appropriate international bodies; and (4) the state must act in a manner consistent with its other obligations in international law (cf. Fitzpatrick 1994). However, the combination of the actual wording of the texts, the complexity of many situations of emergency, and the typically deferential attitude of national and international review bodies — particularly with regard to determining emergencies in the first place — gives states wide latitude in practice in a situation of emergency.

The details of the relevant international standards concerning human rights in states of emergency are readily available. The most interesting question here is the threshold for derogation, that is, when a situation becomes sufficiently pressing as to merit the suspension of a state's obligation to respect certain human rights. For example, Article 15 of the European Convention on Human Rights contains an especially pithy formulation for the threshold for derogation: a "public emergency threatening the life of the nation" (1950); the International Covenant on Civil and Political Rights (1966) — what is sometimes considered a key text in the "international bill of rights" — provides a similar formulation. It may be observed that the scope of the concept of the life of the nation is not self-evident (cf. Fitzpatrick 1994, p. 55); for example, does it concern threats to the self-conception of the nation or its demographic balance? Put another way, the most basic element in deciding the threshold for derogation is determining what constitutes an existential threat.

I suggest, then, that the principal obstacle to the success of human rights monitoring and compliance in emergencies is neither access to sufficient level of detail in a particular case, lack of financial resources, insufficient staffing of monitoring bodies, nor, indeed, any of the usual arguments. It is, rather, the difficulty in evaluating the severity of the perceived threat at hand invoked to justify the state of emergency in the first place. And added to this is the typical unwillingness of legal bodies to treat this issue; the focus is nearly always on actions taken, not on the determination of emergency in the first place. The existence of an emergency is simply assumed.[2] Court attitudes toward the issue of the exception in states of emergency underscore the point that the threshold for determining the threat or emergency — in other words, the threshold for derogation or exception — remains largely in the domain of the state.

The legal position and practice contributes to laying the groundwork for what might in any case become a *de facto* state of emergency. Once it is established that there is a state of emergency, the notion that exceptional measures should be taken to combat the exceptional threat posed by said emergency seems to go without saying. The situation is, then, both reflective and productive of an atmosphere in which it seems obvious that exceptional measures must be taken, and often against, or in response to, certain categories of people who seem to constitute a threat almost by definition (cf. Pandey 2006); in Israel, this group is obviously the Palestinians. This is not to suggest, of course, that criticism cannot subsequently alter the direction of actions taken, nor is it to suggest that the thinking behind the original actions taken does not take moral or legal concerns into account; it is simply to suggest that the order of priority tends to shift in thinking through these issues.

Israeliness, the Predisposition to Perceive Existential Threat, and the Naturalization of Emergency

In discussing emergencies, the distinction must be made between a state of emergency in international law and emergency powers or an emergency government. In Israel both states of emergency exist simultaneously. The most significant aspect of emergency legislation in Israel is that it has become permanent and naturalized to the point that many Israelis are not even aware of its existence (cf. Bailin 2000). Israel has been in a continuous, official state of emergency since before its founding in 1948. Six decades later, there are no demonstrations, no flags, and no political movements calling for an end to this state of affairs. Even the Israeli human rights organizations have largely neglected to take up the state of emergency as a campaign issue. In fact, few Israelis are even aware of its formal existence. This state of emergency affects — or potentially affects — the entire body of laws dealing with individual rights in Israel (Hofnung 1996). Moreover, the fact that a vast amount of subsequent legislation has been based on the emergency legislation has had the result of making the state of emergency less likely to be repealed (ibid., p. 50).

When emergency laws are enacted domestically, the state can suspend rights and liberties in the name of security at any time (cf. Agamben 2005). In this case, it is the domestic law that provides for the exception and international bodies may or may not concur with the legality of actions taken. The fact that such laws were kept in place even during the more optimistic Oslo period of the mid-1990s provides an indication of the sort of defensive ethos at play in Israel.

Much can be said about this last point, but here I would like simply to emphasize how a milieu of presumed existential threat, now heightened in the context of the second *Intifada*, forms the starting point to judicial decision making in the Israeli High Court, particularly in cases concerning Palestinian human rights. In its recent jurisprudence, the court has made several notable decisions standing up to the state on actions taken in the name of countering the threat of terrorism. Much has been made of these cases, particularly one in which torture was rejected as a means of interrogation of suspected terrorists. What is remarkable for the discussion here is that in all of these cases, including of course those in which the court sided with the state, the court presumes that it is deciding in a situation in which the existence of the state is in peril. What the court challenges, if anything at all, is the permissibility of certain measures, usually their necessity and proportionality.

It is in these conditions — with the widespread and deep-rooted conviction among Jewish Israelis that military activities in defense of terrorism are a must — that the High Court attempts to strike a balance between what it thinks of as might and right or between self-defense and the human rights of the other. This can be quickly gleaned in the philosophy of jurisprudence of former High Court President Aaron Barak. In an autobiographical speech delivered in 2001, Barak says it outright: His experience of the Holocaust forms the basis of his view on human rights and the state.[3] This view is worth quoting at length:

> These two lessons — on the one hand, the importance of human rights, and on the other hand the importance of the state — are frequently in a state of tension, on a collision course. What we are required to do, and this is my lesson from my personal experience, is not to prefer the one above the other. I noted in several judgments that a constitution is not a recipe for national destruction and human rights are not a platform for suicide. We need to create solutions in which we recognize both human rights and the state as the solution to the problem of the Jewish people.

Thus, Barak has learned two lessons: the importance of the individual (read human rights) and the importance of the state (read security, collectivity). Though he claims one should not be preferred above the other, the language of his next sentence seems to suggest otherwise: "A constitution is not a recipe for national destruction and human rights are not a platform for suicide." Here he explicitly links the question of human rights to existential threat; in fact, in this phrasing it seems as though if issues placed before him are not balanced properly — that is, with sufficient attention to protecting the life and values of the nation-state — a High Court judge could perform a sort of assisted state suicide.

The Israeli High Court and the Jurisprudence of Emergency

Having discussed some of the context in which the Israeli High Court operates — entrenched domestic emergency and emergency laws, the widespread presumption that terrorism is an existential threat, and a philosophy of jurisprudence attuned to how even human rights can pose an existential threat to the state — we can now turn to see how this context plays out in the court's decision making.

The High Court is widely regarded in Israel, on both the political right and left, as an activist court. Under High Court President Barak, the court has taken a lead in the area of individual rights, and recent innovations in Israeli law (e.g., the 1992 Basic Law on Human Dignity and Liberty) have been hailed as particularly significant to the advancement of human rights (cf. Barak 1992). Indeed, the High Court made some of its most notably favorable rulings in the area of Palestinian rights following the introduction of the Basic Laws and in response to considerable pressure exercised by human rights groups. The concern in this section, however, is how, in the High Court, the values of security and human rights come head to head, particularly in the area of Palestinian rights in the Occupied Territories. Indeed, the apparent advancement of Palestinian human rights in the Israeli High Court was seriously compromised following the outbreak of the second *Intifada*.

Part of the explanation for this lies in the fact that national institutions, including supreme courts, tend to become far more deferential to executive authority and far more tolerant of human and civil rights abuses during times of emergency or perceived emergency. Though the Israeli High Court has examined, and occasionally challenged, the procedure and proportionality of specific state actions taken in the name of national security, it has rarely challenged the legitimacy of the actions themselves (cf. Benvenisti 1993; Kretzmer 2002). Thus, for example, the court has not outlawed house demolitions but rather restricts state action to certain types of demolition following certain procedures and, in so doing, effectively sanctions house demolitions in general.[4]

Let us look for a moment at the High Court's argumentation regarding house demolitions. This will also frame the following discussion on how human rights advocacy groups have approached the same issue. As with other cases in which the court has been asked to review state actions taken in the name of security, the existence of a serious threat to security (terrorism) is presumed.

The case against punitive house demolitions has a strong basis in international humanitarian law; house demolitions are expressly forbidden in the Geneva Conventions of 1949. The Israeli government, however, has put forward an interpretation of the Geneva Conventions that effectively sanctions the military administration's use of house demolitions as punishment (cf. B'Tselem 2004; Dinstein 2000; Kretzmer 2002; Shehadeh 1985).

Then attorney general and later High Court President Meir Shamgar first laid out the official position in an influential article in 1971. In addition to noting the basis for house demolitions in Israeli national law in the Emergency Defense Regulations, Shamgar notes that the Geneva Conventions provide for house demolitions in certain exceptions, "where such destruction is rendered absolutely necessary by military operations" (Shamgar 1971, p. 264). Shamgar then suggests that punitive demolition of houses is both necessary for military operations and serves as a deterrent for future terror attacks. Neither of these arguments fits the official Red Cross commentary on the Geneva Conventions, which calls for a much stricter interpretation of the terms *necessary* and *military operations* (cf.

Shehedah 1985). Nevertheless, on the basis of Shamgar's position, the High Court has consistently upheld the right of the military administration to demolish houses as punishment (B'Tselem 2004; Dinstein 2000; Kretzmer 2002; Shehadeh 1985). Indeed, for more than thirty years, the government's official position continued to take the same lines as the original Shamgar argument.[5] So resilient was this argument and its variants that only the Israel Defense Forces (IDF) was able to break through it. And it did so not so much for considerations of human rights and humanitarian law, but because a study commissioned by the chief of staff found that house demolitions were not, in fact, effective as a deterrent; they stir up more hatred than fear. Yet even this study seems to have done little to affect the momentum of the practice.

A few points are worth underlining before proceeding. A key presumption at work in the High Court's decision making on Palestinian human rights issues is that terrorism poses a grave threat to security and defensive actions can and must be taken in response. The rationale for these actions is extensively documented by the IDF and the High Court in the language of international law. Moreover, the court sometimes limits state action also on the basis of international law. It would seem, therefore, that both government bodies are highly aware of the context in which they work — with human rights organizations, the media, and the so-called international community watching over.

The High Court in Crisis and Calm

Thus far it may appear that there is very little room for the human rights movement to influence the High Court's decision making in cases thought to be linked to security concerns. However, certain qualifications need to be made. This section discusses two of these: (1) whether the case is thought to be an "internal" or "external" dispute; and (2) the timing of the decision. There are other qualifications as well. One was particularly crucial in the landmark case against torture discussed later: pressure from international observers and connections. Another is the concern just mentioned to ground national court decisions and IDF policy in international law.

One crucial factor affecting the High Court's decision making is whether the court believes it is adjudicating between the state and an external party or in a domestic matter between a government agency and an individual (Kretzmer 2002). The significance of this distinction lies in the fact that judges' role as state actors generally fades into the background in internal matters (i.e., when state survival is not perceived to be at stake); when faced with an external matter thought to threaten the authority or very existence of the state, the court often takes on another role: that of protecting the state, even at the expense of individual rights (ibid., pp. 191–2). As Kretzmer points out, against the backdrop of the second *Intifada,* the Israeli High Court is very likely to perceive petitions regarding challenges to military authorities by Palestinians in the Occupied Territories as external disputes between the government and its enemies — that is, threatening to the very authority and existence of the state — and not domestic disputes between the government and an individual (ibid., p. 193). This prediction is strengthened by the fact that, even outside of the two *Intifadas,* the court has tended to uphold state actions when reasons of security or military necessity are invoked. It would appear, therefore, that even in the absence of active war, the court, like most of Israeli society, has tended to perceive the situation between Israel and many of its neighbors (e.g., Syria, Lebanon, Iraq) and certainly the West Bank and Gaza, as one of constant threat of war.

It might be tempting to think that this tendency renders meaningless the distinction between the court's behavior before and after the *Intifadas.* This is not the case. The most obviously significant achievements of the human rights movement — those occurring at the level of the court — have generally occurred in moments when there is no active violent conflict. Indeed, the court made two very important decisions positively affecting Palestinian human rights in the year and a half immediately preceding the second *Intifada*: one on torture and another on access to land for Palestinians. These decisions were no doubt facilitated by the perception among many Jewish Israelis at the time that peace might be imminent.

It is clearly not always a straightforward matter to determine whether a case is, in fact, a challenge to the legitimacy of the state or whether the matter at hand is external or internal; but, following Kretzmer (2002, p. 192), one factor will always be dominant: whether a society perceives itself to be under threat. This insight notwithstanding, Kretzmer does not sufficiently emphasize two key factors that bear on the perception of threat: dominant cultural dispositions and the timing of the situation in question. Actors are not generally universally threatening, that is, for all courts, and peoples, at all times. This may seem a trite observation, but it allows us to make a more fundamental one: Threats may be considered existential at one moment and relatively insignificant in another (e.g., terrorism was not widely thought to be a global problem before September 11, 2001, while after five decades of attention the Soviet nuclear threat on the United States has completely vanished from discussion); the same can be said for cultural setting (e.g., Palestinians may be frequently viewed as a threat in Israel, particularly during the second *Intifada,* but this tends not to be the case in Iraq or Jordan). And this allows us to make a further observation about threat perception: It can shift over time.[6] This means that the space available for judicial or human rights advocacy can shift as well.

The Human Rights Movement in Israel

The human rights movement in Israel is both part of, and facilitated by, the ongoing transformation of the Israeli state in various spheres. Funding from philanthropies abroad geared toward expanding Israeli civil society coupled with new realities faced in an era of globalization (e.g., the increasing class divide, privatization, the rise of liberalism) and an emergent post-Zionist (i.e., post-Israeli nationalist) sensibility, in some ways both arising from and contributing to state transformation, have facilitated the emergence of thousands of nongovernmental organizations (NGOs) in Israel, though those focused explicitly on Palestinian rights remain few in number. The human rights movement is both reflective and productive of this emergent liberal atmosphere in Israel.

Despite this process of liberalization, in Israel even human rights advocacy may be perceived to be an "enemy," in the sense of its potential threat to the very existence of the state. Barak's (2002) comments on the potential for a state to commit human rights suicide illustrate this perception.[7] In many cases, human rights organizations and activists are involved in an attempt to redefine the state by emphasizing its democratic (state of its citizens) as opposed to its Jewish (state of the Jews) character. This, along with their association with "defending the enemy," puts human rights activists effectively in the same camp as Palestinians: in the enemy camp. Besides this rather limiting perception, Israeli human rights activists and organizations, dedicated as they typically are, have their own limits to the sort of advocacy they undertake, especially with regard to Palestinian rights. Consequently, there are certain issues that an Israeli human rights organization will generally not touch — such as the right of return for Palestinian refugees — and these issues tend to be tied to what are seen as blatant threats to security or threats to the self-conception of the state.[8]

The decision by *Israeli* rights organizations to avoid certain human rights issues has a significant effect on the possibilities for activism in Israel. This is the case because among Jewish Israelis these organizations are generally seen to have the most legitimacy of all the human rights organizations that work on Palestinian rights. Both Palestinian and international human rights organizations are often taken to be biased against Israel. In contrast, because of their Israeliness, Israeli organizations are presumed at bottom to have some interest in preserving their own state.[9]

With these concerns in mind I turn now to two advocacy campaigns that highlight the efficacy and limits of the human rights movement in

Israel: the first against house demolitions and the second against torture. In their campaign against house demolitions Israeli human rights advocacy groups have focused primarily on *administrative* house demolitions, that is, typically those resulting from lack of proper building permits.[10] Despite the fact that the case against them has a strong basis in international human rights law, punitive house demolitions are seen by many Israelis as just retribution for a grievous wrong against Israeli society (terrorism). Administrative house demolitions, on the other hand, are often seen as cruel and excessive punishment, at least by moderate and left-wing Israelis and certainly by sympathetic foreigners abroad.

Before the outbreak of the second *Intifada*, when asked what they would describe as their greatest success, several different NGOs cited the campaign against house demolitions. The presumed success of the campaign is based on three results: considerable media attention, including multiple appearances on CNN and BBC World News; gaining the attention of Madeleine Albright, who for a time as U.S. secretary of state was said to have made it her pet issue in the Middle East; and dramatically reduced numbers of demolished houses in a period of about three years. Whether human rights activists would continue to view this campaign as a success is uncertain. House demolitions, of both the administrative and the punitive variety, have been on the rise in the second *Intifada* (B'Tselem 2004); indeed, the IDF recently invented, and executed, a new policy category of demolition of property: clearing large stretches of agricultural land.

The campaign against torture represents a contrast to the campaign against house demolitions in several respects. Perhaps the most crucial of these is the fact that, like punitive house demolitions, torture is clearly tied to the perceived threat of terrorism. At issue in the 1999 landmark High Court ruling against torture was the power of the security services to decide when the imminent danger of terror faced by the state may justify employing certain physical methods in the interrogation of a detainee. From the point of view of many Israelis, the possibility of saving a school bus full of children overrides any potential harm inflicted on a terror suspect. Though these people may oppose torture in general in the abstract, they view the absolute ban as naive and potentially unjust.

In contrast to most other human rights laws, the prohibition on torture is absolute. As stated in Article 2(2) of the Convention Against Torture, "No exceptional circumstances whatsoever, whether a state of war or a threat of war, internal political instability or any other public emergency, may be invoked as a justification of torture" (United Nations 1984). This absolute prohibition provided human rights NGOs with moral ammunition unavailable in their campaign against house demolitions.

What officially introduced the practice of moderate physical pressure in interrogations was the government's Landau Commission Report. By making a case for exceptional circumstances such as what became known as the ticking time bomb scenario, the report injected ambiguity into the absolute prohibition in international human rights law. The result — combined with protracted violent conflict and the sort of predisposition to perceive existential threat described above— was broad desensitization to force in interrogations. What was initially argued by the Landau Commission as acceptable only in situations of absolute necessity became widely used by the security services.[11]

In considering the role of the human rights movement in advancing the case against torture, it is worth bearing in mind that the landmark Israeli High Court ruling on torture took during place during the Oslo peace process, before the outbreak of the second *Intifada* and before September 11. Even at the time, the decision was unpopular among Jewish Israelis, and the High Court had stalled for more than ten years, facing numerous petitions on the issue before making what it viewed to be possibly the most difficult substantive decision in its history. If the case had been decided later, it is quite possible the court would have decided otherwise.

That the High Court ruled against torture is especially significant given that it represents a privileging of an international norm — the prohibition against torture — over arguments put forward by the General Security Services (GSS) that the methods in question could in fact prevent terror attacks in certain exceptional circumstances. To make this decision, the court had to rule against Israeli popular opinion, the specific concern about the threat of terror, and its own tendency with respect to security considerations. Barak (2000) later admitted to having many sleepless nights worrying about the consequences of his decision.

What seemed to push Barak over the edge in making this decision was the fact that just prior to the hearing his reputation was put on the line in front of prestigious international colleagues (Pacheco 2000). During his regular visiting appointment at Yale Law School, he was met with angry protesters; this happened again at a lecture at the University of Michigan just before the hearing.[12] Much of the initial research and activism on torture in Israel was conducted by local NGOs; this formed the basis for what also became an international campaign. Indeed, Allegra Pacheco, the lead lawyer for the case and staff attorney for the Public Committee Against Torture in Israel, gave a lecture tour in the United States in the months preceding the case.

Aside from the issue of derogability, the effect and limits of the human rights movement in Israel are influenced by several key variables, among them: (1) timing (e.g., whether the case or campaign in question occurs during a period of relative calm or of acute conflict); (2) especially if it is a moment of conflict, whether the issue has some bearing on the physical security of the state; and (3) whether or not the issue itself is seen to pose a threat to the Jewishness of the state, such as the right of return for Palestinian refugees. Clearly, the third conclusion could also be applied more broadly by substituting the variable of the Jewishness of the state with perceived threats to the national character of the state in question. To these must be added the general climate in which the human rights movement, and the High Court, operate: entrenched emergency laws, widespread presumption of existential threat, and a widespread understanding of Jewish history, including very recent history, as one of ongoing threats to the very existence of the people and the state.

Conclusion

States may formally have the power to declare states of emergency — and with arguably little international legal oversight — but actions following from the declaration, whether that declaration is *de facto* or *de jure*, can be challenged, even if the emergency tends to be presumed. This is an indication of how what is arguably one of the most durable aspects of stateness — the right to self-preservation or defense in the face of existential threat — though rarely challenged directly and frequently reasserted, is both not unlimited and subject to various indirect challenges. And many, if not most, of these challenges are based on some sort of nonnational, nonstatist understanding of right and good that is arguably connected with human rights.

Though considered only briefly here, if we look to national courts, we can observe a series of shifts in stance regarding the presumption of human rights or deference to the state or executive. Part of the explanation for these shifts has to do with the broader context in which national courts operate, which is at once domestic and global. The prevailing understanding has been that national courts are more deferential in crisis, more likely to be critical in calm, and this does generally appear to be the case. But conditions can shift within moments of perceived crisis, such that the state is challenged even then (cf. Benvenisti 2004). Yet even in the face of such challenges, there is a certain starting point that holds: the presumption of an emergency in the first place. That is, once a determination of emergency has taken place — whether *de jure* or *de facto* — courts, including international courts, are very unlikely to challenge it. They may challenge what follows, that is, specific measures taken in the name of emergency, but not the emergency itself. This is significant in a number of respects; I mention two of them here: First, it forms the background lens through which what is normal, possible, and acceptable are evaluated, and, second, it therefore limits the space of possibility for human rights advocacy, since the starting presumption is that an emergency, in fact, exists.

Thus, what shifts in jurisprudential and state policy stance that do occur are very much tied to the way sensitivity to public opinion limits the apparent breadth of state discretion in emergencies. The fact that states are sensitive to criticism, both external and internal, and sometimes even update their policies in response to such criticism has more than one implication. First, the broad discretion allowed the executive in war or emergency is, in practice, always limited or checked by both domestic and international public opinion — and in both of which human rights advocates can play a significant part. Second, policies are therefore clearly drafted in the first place with this in mind and may be adjusted, if necessary, which is to say that policies are influenced by human rights concerns from the beginning and not just after being subject to criticism by human rights advocates. The first point suggests as well that the extent to which public opinion supports the linked notions of grave threat and any means necessary to combat them — that is, to what extent they support the presumption of emergency and exceptional measures to deflect it — will shape the margin of discretion the executive has in practice to act. It also means that given that such opinions can change over time, especially when not supported by regular infusions of threat — or when undermined by sustained public criticism — the way this context shapes the latitude for defensive action, and therefore also possibilities for advocacy, can also change.

None of this undermines the larger point that the determination of a state of emergency can make a tremendous difference in the presumed starting point for thinking, or evaluating, what is possible, necessary, legal, or even moral when combating that emergency. It is clear that this determination or decision is not, however, exclusively in the hands of one person, the sovereign (*pace* Schmitt 1985), but rather requires the support of a wide swath of the local population, other government officials, and so on. The fact that the global war on terror is supported — or at least not challenged in basic terms — by a large number of states, the UN Security Council, and international review bodies serves to reinforce the basic and widespread understanding that there is a grave threat and that it must be countered.

Turning more broadly to the study of "the global," I suggest that we need an understanding of core concepts, particularly those central to, or apparently in tension with, global processes — states, state survival, nationalism, Zionism — to be in a position to make claims about whether these things have changed or are in the process of doing so. The very use of these concepts — including, admittedly, in this chapter — often seems to underline the notion that nothing has changed, yet transformation can occur gradually, subtly; it need not be radical or revolutionary in a particular moment. We must therefore take care in analyzing such concepts not to assume that simply because they seem to continue to hold no change has, in fact, taken place. A crucial analytic question is how to represent that change, for this, or more properly, the dynamic, is ultimately the analytic object, not the specific changes visible in a particular moment. Marx (1993) famously recognized the difficulty of this task in his *Grundrisse*. Written description, he suggested, is necessarily restricted to snapshots of particular moments. Since the only constant is in fact movement, or historical process, the written representation is what it would look like if the system could be frozen in time into a moment of rest. States of emergency are a particular sort of snapshot that can lead the observer to believe there is little room for movement.

Notes

1. In light of this, the prevailing assumption that the state is the primary violator, and therefore the primary obstacle, to the enjoyment of human rights is perhaps not surprising. Though this assumption does sometimes hold, Kaplan (2006) suggests that the relationship between the state and human rights advocacy is considerably more complex.
2. Consider, for example, the European Court of Human Rights, the international review body with the most case law on states of emergency. As it is not a national court, the court spends little time emphasizing the gravity of threat a given state party faces in an emergency. Neither does it challenge the existence of such a threat. Indeed, the court has invented, and stuck to, a striking doctrine for this stance: the margin of appreciation. This essentially means that, "by means of their direct and continuous contact with the pressing needs of the moment," a state's own leaders are in a better position to determine the existence of an emergency than judges sitting in Strasbourg (Ireland v. UK, 1978).
3. This speech also reflects a point made in Kaplan (2006) about how a certain reading or, indeed, experience of Jewish history — as one of ongoing threats to the very existence of the Jewish people — shapes Israeli stances toward human rights issues, including in the High Court.
4. This is a subtle point, and overstating it can understate the power of review the court nevertheless maintains. Challenges to procedure, necessity, and proportionality can, indeed, be significant, and several recent cases concerning Palestinian rights have made sophisticated use of this (cf. Kaplan 2005).

5. In 2005, several human rights organizations submitted a petition to the Israeli High Court challenging the use of the "absolute military necessity" exception to IHL to justify the military's policy of house demolitions. On the basis of military officials' claim that they would refrain from demolitions, the court dismissed the petition but noted that this dismissal did not constitute a rejection of any of the petitioners' arguments. For our purposes here, the significance of this statement is that the original justification for house demolitions remains effectively in place. (H.C. 4969/04, *Adalah, et al. v. IDF Major General, Central Command, Moshe Kaplinski, et. al.*, 2005)
6. In explaining these developments, it is also important to consider the difference between the tendency of the court's judgments concerning the Occupied Territories and its judgments concerning Israel proper. In Israel proper, many Palestinians have Israeli citizenship and are thus in theory protected by the Basic Laws and the state's presumed democratic character; moreover, the court is more likely to consider petitions regarding Palestinian citizens as internal disputes. In contrast to the court's stance toward Palestinians in the Occupied Territories, many of the most significant decisions regarding human rights in recent years have concerned human rights in Israel proper (Kretzmer 2002).
7. As do the actions of the Israeli intelligence agency, the *Shin-beth*, which has long followed the potentially subversive activities of left-wing organizations, including human rights NGOs, despite its suspicion that these organizations had virtually no impact on Israeli society (Gillon 2000).
8. This is not to say that human rights workers make these choices solely on the basis of concerns about potential threat to Israel. They also make these decisions on the basis of what sorts of campaigns are judged to be viable in Israeli society and which are perceived to have little chance of success.
9. They may want to change the state in certain respects. However, most do not want to see it annihilated, nor do they wish to engage in activities that may threaten its continued existence. Moreover, despite their fight for human rights, certain aspects of the Jewish character of the state, in particular the notion that Israel is a safe haven for Jews, and that this safety depends on maintaining a Jewish majority, are deeply ingrained even among many Israeli human rights activists.
10. In later years, when punitive house demolitions dramatically increased in number, some Israeli human rights organizations, notably B'Tselem, turned their attention to these as well.
11. A prominent Israeli human rights organization described the situation in the following terms: Based on official sources, human rights organizations, and attorneys, B'Tselem (1998) estimates that the GSS annually interrogates between 1,000 and 1,500 Palestinians. Some 85 percent of them — at least 850 persons a year — are tortured during interrogation.
12. I do not mean to suggest that Barak was susceptible to these criticisms only out of self-interest. His own conflicted views about balancing human rights and state security surely affected him (cf. 2000, p. 122).

Works Cited

Agamben, G. 2005. *State of exception*. Chicago: University of Chicago Press.

Bailin, Y. 2000. Keynote address, Conference: Legal Aspects of Emergency Regimes, Tel Aviv University Law Faculty, December 21.

Barak, A. 1992. A constitutional revolution: Israel's Basic Laws, speech delivered at University of Haifa, May 18.

———. 2000. Comments delivered at the closing panel of the Conference: Legal Aspects of Emergency Regimes, Tel Aviv University Law Faculty, December 21.

———. 2001. Speech delivered in honor of High Court Justice Haim Cohen's birthday, Association for Civil Rights in Israel, Jerusalem., June 21.

Benvenisti, E. 1993. *The international law of occupation*. Princeton, NJ: Princeton University Press.

———. 2004. National courts in the war on terrorism. In A. Bianchi, ed., *Enforcing international law norms against terrorism*, 307–330. Oxford: Hart Publishing.

B'Tselem. 1998. *Routine torture: Interrogation methods of the General Security Service*. Jerusalem: B'Tselem.

———. 2004. *Through no fault of their own: Punitive house demolitions in the al-Aksa Intifada*. Jerusalem: B'Tselem.

Council of Europe. 1950. Convention for the Protection of Human Rights and Fundamental Freedoms. Rome.

Dinstein, Y. 2000. The Israel Supreme Court and the law of belligerent occupation: Demolitions and sealing off of houses. *Israel Yearbook on Human Rights*, Vol 29: 285–296.

Fitzpatrick, J. 1994. *Human rights in crisis: The international system for protecting rights during states of emergency*. Philadelphia: University of Pennsylvania Press.

Foucault, M. 1991. Governmentality. In G. Burchell, C. Gordon., P. Miller, eds., *The Foucault effect: Studies in governmentality*, 87–104. Chicago: University of Chicago Press.

Gillon, C. 2000. *Shin-Beth between the schisms*. Tel Aviv: Yediot Ahronoth Books and Chemed Books [in Hebrew].

Heathcote, Sarah. 1998. *State survival and international law: The background*. Mémoire de DES, Genève: Institut universitaire de hautes études internationales.

Hobbes, T. 1996. *Leviathan*. Ed. and introduction by J.C.A. Gaskin. Oxford: Oxford University Press.

Hofnung, M. 1996. *Democracy, law, and national security in Israel*. Brookfield, VT: Dartmouth Publishing.

International Court of Justice. 1996. *Legality of the threat or use of nuclear weapons*. Hague: Advisory Opinion.

Kaplan, J. 2005. Two takes on the wall: Human rights, "self-preservation," and the "survival of the state." *Anthropology News*, 46(8): 54–55, November.

———. 2006. The transnational human rights movement and the logic of the state in Israel/Palestine. Ph.D. diss., University of Chicago.

Kohen, M. 1999. The notion of 'state survival' in international law. In L. Boisson de Chazournes and P. Sands, eds., *International law, the International Court of Justice and nuclear weapons*, 293–314. Cambridge, UK: Cambridge University Press.

Kretzmer, D. 2002. *The occupation of justice: The Supreme Court of Israel and the Occupied Territories*. Albany: State University of New York Press.

Marks, S., and A. Clapham. 2004. *International human rights lexicon*. Oxford: Oxford University Press.

Marx, K. 1993. *Grundrisse*. London: Penguin.

Pacheco, A. 2000. Personal interview with the author, Bethlehem, August.

Pandey, G. 2006. *Routine violence*. Stanford: Stanford University Press.

Schmitt, C. 1985. *Political theology: Four concepts on the concept of sovereignty*. Trans. G. Schwab. Cambridge, MA: MIT Press.

Shafir, G., and Y. Peled (eds.). 2000. *The New Israel: Peacemaking and liberalization*. Boulder: Westview Press.

———. 2002. *Being Israeli: The dynamics of multiple citizenship*. Cambridge, UK: Cambridge University Press.

Shamgar, M. 1971. The observance of international law in the administered territories. *Israel yearbook on human rights*, vol. 1: 262–277.

Shehadeh, R. 1985. *Occupier's law: Israel and the West Bank*. Washington, DC: Institute for Palestine Studies.

Tuck, R. 1999. *The rights of war and peace: Political thought and the international order from Grotius to Kant*. Oxford: Oxford University Press.

United Nations General Assembly. 1966. International Covenant on Civil and Political Rights. New York: United Nations.

———. 1984. Convention against Torture and Other Cruel, Inhuman or Degrading Treatment or Punishment. New York: United Nations.

CHAPTER 15
Illegal Immigrants as Citizens in Malaysia[1]

KAMAL SADIQ

Citizenship is a privilege the state bestows on people within its borders, or so the theories of citizenship and immigration assert. Traditional understandings of citizenship continue to assume that only legal immigrants — not illegal immigrants — are eligible for naturalization and thereafter the privileges of national citizenship such as voting. This is for the simple reason that national and state-level voting has always been thought to be the most protected privilege of citizenship in the post-World War II international system — a privilege illegal immigrants by definition cannot enjoy.[2]

The purpose of this chapter is to demonstrate that the conventional wisdom, insofar as it purports to apply to developing countries, is wrong. The common assumption of scholars that all democratic states protect the privilege of national and state-level voting for their citizens cannot be sustained in the face of empirical evidence from the developing world. This evidence demonstrates that illegal immigrants in developing states are voting in large numbers because, for various reasons described here, they are able to illegally procure documents that allow them to enjoy all the privileges of citizenship. Moreover, many of these states lack the surveillance capacities to combat document fraud and have not even developed the administrative systems necessary to properly document nationality in the first place. Citizenship ceases to be a clear-cut, well-defined category in an era of globalization. Citizenship in these states cannot be viewed as a sealed container of rights and duties. Globalization is redefining the subjects of the nation-state by embodying individual identification in documents, whether paper or plastic. Mapping the complexities of citizenship in a time of globalization is therefore urgently needed.

Weak documentation systems leave states open not only to illegal entry of economic migrants, terrorists, and other criminals via document fraud, but also to massive electoral fraud, which has serious implications for the conduct of democratic politics. By acquiring and possessing seemingly legal documents that prove juridical membership in a state, a noncitizen[3] can easily acquire citizenship status. I call this process through which citizenship status is ascribed to a noncitizen *documentary citizenship.* Documentary citizenship is a central feature of globalization as states increasingly depend on standardized documentation to distinguish the identities of individuals. Illegal immigrants, refugees, and varieties of noncitizens embed themselves locally and gain native status through documentary citizenship.

This process has important implications for understanding international security. Since September 11, 2001, there has been an intensification of border controls and a tightening of visa regulations. The prospect of a worldwide trend of increasing documentary citizenship thus raises serious security concerns regarding flows of people as tourists, travelers, illegal workers, businesspersons, and students. Localized identification schemes have now become globalized. If, as this chapter demonstrates, illegal Filipinos can easily acquire Malaysian citizenship documents, then what prevents al-Qaeda terrorists from doing the same? Foreign terrorist groups in neutral states such as India, Malaysia, Thailand, and the Philippines could fraudulently acquire the paperwork for the citizenship of these states and then could get legitimate visas to enter the United States or any other target country. Alternatively, they could use documents from neutral states to enter other neutral states — such as those in Eastern Europe or Central and Latin America — before making an attempt to enter the United States or any other target country. In fact, cities such as Delhi and Bangkok are major centers for fraudulent passports and other paperwork that enable illegal immigrants to enter the restricted borders of Western European or North American states. Therefore, what are the implications of documentary citizenship for the war on terrorism and on the increasing human mobility that is part and parcel of globalization?

Through a detailed case study of immigration into Malaysia, this chapter describes and explains the emergence of documentary citizenship, a growing reality in many developing countries in which illegal immigrants acquire citizenship documents that many of the native[4] rural poor lack. Even more striking is that in the Malaysian case, not only does documentary citizenship enfranchise illegal immigrants, but the political participation of these individuals alters political outcomes in favor of governments that enable illegal immigrants to acquire proofs of citizenship and the ability to vote.[5] Documentary citizenship clearly shows how globalization is reconfiguring the conception of the national.

The fact that illegal immigrants in Malaysia receive the same privileges as citizens[6] adds a new dimension to the literature on citizenship focusing on the social, political, and economic rights of citizens (Kymlicka 1995; Marshall and Bottomore 1996), which highlights gradations of immigrant membership (Joppke 1999; Koslowski 2000; Schuck and Smith 1985), and the literature viewing the erosion of the state due to global processes as creating a new form of membership not tied to the nation-state (Jacobson 1997; Sassen 1998; Soysal 1994). Neither of these literature deals with documentary citizenship. Moreover, local Malay authorities were constantly being accused of encouraging illegal immigration from the southern Philippines and Indonesia to Sabah, a region in East Malaysia.[7] At a time when both the European Union and North America were erecting immigration barriers, Malaysia was facilitating the entry of illegal immigrants.[8] Taken as a whole, these practices contradict the conventional wisdom about immigration, especially illegal immigration (Stalker 1994).

The analysis provided in this chapter is divided into the following sections. First, the illegal immigration to Sabah, Malaysia is outlined, highlighting the visibility of the phenomenon and discussing its impact on the state's changing ethnic composition. Next, an analysis is given of the lack of institutionalization of citizenship that makes possible the incorporation of illegal immigrants through varieties of documents. Importantly, *documentary citizenship* denotes the process by which illegal immigrants are incorporated into the state, get on the electoral rolls, and gain access to the rights of citizens. The increasing reliance on documentation to represent identity is a feature of globalization, which illegal immigrants use to their advantage. They subvert a global system of divided sovereignties by acquiring local citizenship documents. As a consequence, these *suffraged noncitizens* wind up being privileged over native, *nonsuffraged citizens*. This is followed by focusing on electoral politics and scrutinizing the effect of illegal immigration and documentary citizenship on the political process. The use of illegal immigrants as voters advantages certain political parties, thus giving insight into why the manipulation of migratory flows takes place. The chapter concludes by examining whether Malaysia is a unique case or an outlier on the graph of immigrant incorporation. This case is shown to be generalizable, indicating that it requires rethinking globalization's impact on citizenship.

Illegal Immigration to Sabah

How visible is the presence of illegal immigrants in Sabah? Worried locals had this to say in a letter to the editor: "Ours must be the only place in the world where illegals have the courage to walk about in the streets with impunity, commit crimes, use our over stretched government hospitals, steal our water, attend our schools and milk us of our resources in numerous ways" (*Daily Express* 1999a). Migration from the Sulu Archipelago in the Philippines to Sabah has a long history. Barter trade existed as early as the ninth century; today it is the cornerstone of a regional economic trade forum called the Brunei, Indonesia, Malaysia, Philippines East Asian Growth Area (BIMP-EAGA). The first migrants to Sabah from the Sulu Archipelago arrived in the late fifteenth century when the Spanish began pushing southward toward Sulu and Tawi-Tawi in the southern Philippines. As a result, members of ethnic groups such as the Suluk and the Bajau came to straddle the modern boundaries of Sabah, Malaysia, and the southern Philippines. The second wave of migration is associated with the Mindanao insurgency in the Philippines; many refugees migrated to Sabah during 1970–1977. Thousands of Suluk and Bajau women, men, and children took small wooden boats (*kumpits*) to flee the war-torn southern provinces of the Philippines for the relative safety of Sabah. This wave of political refugees arrived on the east coast of Sabah and settled in towns such as Sandakan, Tawau, and Lahad Datu. However, the number of 1970s refugees is small compared to the number of migrants since 1978.

Today it is commonly known among Sabahans that the coastal town of Sandakan, in the eastern part of Sabah, is overwhelmingly Filipino, whereas Indonesians comprise the majority of residents in Tawau, a Sabah town bordering Indonesia. According to illegal immigrants in Sabah, it takes approximately two days by boat to reach Kota Kinabalu, the capital of Sabah, from the Philippines. In fact, one of the landing points is just below the Yayasan Sabah, a skyscraper housing the chief minister's office and other key Sabah ministries dealing with immigration or security.[9] For example, Catherine, an illegal immigrant from the Philippines, came to Sabah twelve years ago after spending two nights on a boat.[10] She landed at Yayasan Sabah and later married a Muslim Filipino, who was a legal worker, nominally converting to Islam. She says many Christian Filipino women convert to Islam, as conversion makes it easier to become Sabahan. After a few years she legalized her presence through her husband's networks and is now a legal worker. So it is probable that her achievement of legal status did not preclude extralegal means to that end.

It is common for immigrants to become seemingly legal through fake documents. Labor operators (*towkays*), for example, help to facilitate this semblance of legality. Most of these *towkays* who transport Filipino immigrants to Sabah are paid in Philippine pesos. The boats anchor in the night near the shore, and immigrants carry their modest belongings — only small bags are allowed — on their heads while wading to the shore. Most immigrants already know of friends and relatives in the region; thus, these connections enable recent immigrants to establish themselves in safe houses from where they are directed to possible employers. The *towkays* receive part of the initial earnings of new immigrants as payment for their services.

Local circuits enable Indonesians and Filipinos to become natives through the acquisition of documents. As immigrants settle, they move inward and toward big towns on the west coast. Both Indonesian and Filipino migrants have physical and cultural features similar to those of the Malays; the Indonesian language, Bahasa Indonesia,[11] is almost the same as Bahasa Malaysia, whereas southern Filipinos speak dialects that have commonalties with Bahasa Malaysia. In major towns of Sabah, there are very visible pockets of illegal immigrant settlements such as Kampung BDC in Sandakan, Kampung Panji in Lahad Datu, Kampung Ice Box in Tawau, and Kampung Pondo at Pulau Gaya, Kota Kinabalu. According to some legislators, these settlements are security threats to Malaysia (*Daily Express* 2000b).

The public perception in Sabah is that an initial trickle of refugees has now turned into a torrent of immigrants. A range of figures is quoted on the number of illegal immigrants in the state. According to unpublished data for 1997 obtained from the state immigration department by Kassim (1998, pp. 282–5), there were only 120,719 registered alien workers in Sabah. According to the Malaysian census, between 1970 and 1980 the net immigration from Indonesia and the Philippines to Sabah was 45,000 Indonesians and 36,000 Filipinos (Department of Statistics 1983, pp. 58–9, table 5.3). The total immigration to Sabah for the same period, after counting immigrants from other countries, was only 127,000 persons out of a total population of 950,000 (ibid., table 5.2, p. 258). The 1991 census in Sabah identified 207,366 persons born in Indonesia and 161,533 persons born in the Philippines out of a total of 383,076 people born outside Malaysia (Department of Statistics 1995, p. 144, table 4.1). However, this is a distortion in at least one way: The Filipinos are a significant presence in Sabah now, whereas the official figures present the reverse picture.

Recognizing the problems of underestimation in state data, Kassim (1998, p. 285) cites a former chief minister as estimating illegal immigrant numbers to be in the range of 400,000 to 500,000. Most leaders of the main opposition party, the Parti Bersatu Sabah (PBS),[12] give the figure of one million foreigners out of a current Sabah population of about 2.8 million.[13] Leaders of the Filipino community in the Philippines give similar estimates; their numbers in Sabah have passed the one million mark, making them the "biggest concentration of Filipino illegals in any part of the world" (*Philippine Daily Inquirer* 1999). This means that almost one in every three residents of Sabah may be a foreigner, composed of both illegal migrants and legal workers.

What complicates the estimation issue further is that very often during regularization programs many illegal immigrants get regularized and therefore change their illegal status.[14] Over the years many have already made the transition from illegal status to legal citizenship. Many deported illegal immigrants have been known to return to Sabah within a few months, if not weeks or days. For example, Mustali, a recently arrested twenty-eight-year-old Filipino, had lived in Sabah since the age of eight (*Borneo Post* 1999c). Since then, he traveled between Malaysia and the Philippines with impunity, visiting his family several times in the Philippines. He has four children with him in Sabah; his wife returned to the Philippines to look after their older children who were being schooled in Jolo, Philippines. The judge ordered that Mustali, as an illegal immigrant, be jailed because he "had no respect for the laws of the country by going in and out of the country as though the Philippines and Malaysia were two different states in one country" (*Borneo Post* 1999c; *Philippine Daily Inquirer* 1999).

Illegal immigration is changing the ethnic makeup of Sabah in significant ways (Table 15.1). At the beginning of the twentieth century, Kadazandusuns were the dominant ethnic group, comprising about 42 percent of the state population. They fell to 32 percent by the 1960 census, 29.9 percent by 1970, and then by 1990, to their alarm, they had fallen to 19.6 percent (Table 15.1). Similarly, Muruts have seen their share decline from 4.9 percent in 1960 to 2.9 percent in 1990. Both of these non-Muslim groups overwhelmingly support the non-Muslim, non-Malay regional party, the PBS, which opposes the migration and settlement of illegal immigrants in Sabah.

In contrast, the United Malays National Organisation (UMNO), which derives its support from Muslim groups, has seen the ethnic makeup of Sabah change in its favor. The Muslim Malays have risen from just 0.4 percent of the population in 1960 to 6.2 percent of the population in 1990; the Indonesians have risen substantially from only 5.5 percent of the population in 1960 to 21.3 percent in 1990; and the Filipinos, who had a negligible presence until 1960 (1.6 percent), represented 8.2 percent of Sabah's total population by the 1990 census. Continuing Filipino and Indonesian illegal immigration further increases the stock of various Muslim ethnic groups (e.g., Bajau, Bugis, other Muslims, Suluks), whereas non-Muslim groups such as the Kadazandusuns, Muruts, or the Chinese are declining into demographic and political insignificance. The incorporation of illegal

Table 15.1 Political Affiliation and Ethnic Group Representation in Sabah[a]

Census	Political Party	Ethnic Group	Years			
			1960	1970	1980[b]	1991
Regional	PBS	Kadazandusun	32.0	29.9		19.6
		Murut	4.9	4.8		2.9
National	UMNO	Malay	0.4	2.8		6.2
		Bajau	13.1	11.8		11.7
		Other Muslims	15.8	13.5		13.6
		Indonesian	5.5	6.1		21.3
		Filipino	1.6	3.1		8.2
National	MCA	Chinese	23.0	21.4		11.5

Source: Tomiyuki (2000, p. 37).

[a]*PBS, Parti Bersatu Sabah; UMNO, United Malays National Organisation; MCA, Malaysian Chinese Association.*

[b]*The 1980 census collapsed all those who were not Chinese or Indians into a single category called Pribumi, thus making it impossible to obtain data for individual ethnic groups.*

immigrants as citizens is critical to the changing ethnic demography and subsequent political map of Sabah. To understand the large-scale incorporation of illegal immigrants, the crucial role documents play in making citizens must be examined.

Documentary Citizenship

This section demonstrates the nature of documentary citizenship, where the weakly institutionalized character of citizenship in developing states facilitates the entry of illegal immigrants and allows them to bypass naturalization and gain citizenship rights.[15] Documentary citizenship is an informal device — a back channel — to many of the benefits associated with the narrower and more difficult path to legal citizenship. It expands and accelerates the incorporation of illegal immigrants into the citizenry of a state. More importantly, it allows many illegal immigrants access to political suffrage. Political suffrage, as we know it, is closely linked to legal citizenship since it opens the door to many protected domains of state activity such as the legislature and other public offices involved in defense, foreign, and security policy making. By transforming illegal immigrants into citizens, documents challenge the traditional view of the relationship between immigrants and the state.

Malaysia's effort to define and restrict citizenship is problematic because a large section of its population, as in so many developing countries, does not possess birth certificates or passports. Weakly institutionalized citizenship in Malaysia is the condition whereby some legally eligible natives have no documentary proof of citizenship whereas others have multiple documents proving citizenship — issued by multiple state agencies. Since many natives do not have a standardized document such as the passport, a birth certificate, or a national identity card, the state will not insist on a standard document for the exercise of an individual's civil, political, economic, or social rights. Another important aspect of weakly institutionalized citizenship is that some services provided by the government that require standardized documentation are unavailable to these sections of the population. This is especially true for urban areas. In as much as illegal immigrants do, or hope to, gravitate toward urban areas, they are likely to have a greater incentive to acquire documents that prove their citizenship than are long-time inhabitants of difficult-to-reach areas, such as the interior of West Malaysia or the many islands of Sabah. On the other hand, since natives are accustomed to other natives either not possessing documents or, alternatively, having multiple documents, the distinction between legal and illegal is hazy. Coherent legality depends on monitoring, surveillance, and maintenance of certain state-established standard rules and regulations. However, given (1) the absence of proof of citizenship in some regions and (2) the varying nature of documentation in their other parts, it becomes impossible to firmly establish these rules and regulations under the condition of weakly institutionalized citizenship. It is difficult, based on paperwork, for authorities in developing states to monitor and distinguish those who are legal citizens from those who are not.

This brings up an important question: Why is the weakly institutionalized character of citizenship in Malaysia important? Theories of immigration and citizenship assume that the receiving state has standardized documentation for its population, which permits citizens to be distinguished from immigrants, legal or illegal. In the real world, however, illegal immigrants are not so easily distinguishable from those locals who do not carry any documents in many developing states. The forces of globalization fuse this distinction even further. Even network analysis explaining the process of immigration by illuminating how social and personal networks enable entry and settlement of immigrants ignores the lack of standardized citizenship in countries like Malaysia. Additionally, illegal immigrants know that the local population in some parts of Malaysia has no documents and that settlement will therefore not likely be a major hurdle. Information flowing through networks of family, kin, or fellow villagers ensures that illegal immigrants have reliable knowledge about their future host state. Illegal immigrants' confidence of not being detected during residence because the local population is also in a similarly weakly institutionalized condition facilitates their settlement.

In April 1999, an official of the National Registration Department (NRD) in Sabah complained that over two million people residing there did not possess birth certificates (*Sun* 1999). This is significant considering the total population of Sabah is estimated to be about 2.8 million (Government of Sabah 1998).[16] Many Sabah residents are born at home in villages or on remote islands and not in hospitals or maternity clinics, where birth certificates can be provided. Ignorance of the law, which requires registration certificates of birth and death, also causes the absence of citizenship-related documents. According to the NRD's director general, any birth must be reported at a National Registration Department office within fourteen days; in case of problems, parents are allowed to register their child within forty-two days (*Borneo Post* 1999a). After that, the NRD requires evidence and has to interview parents to determine the child's citizenship. This is obviously a difficult process for natives living in the interior as well as the poor living in remote areas or on islands. The result was that almost 10,000 out of 500,000 babies born each year in Malaysia were not registered within the stipulated period (ibid.). Before April 1987, no birth certificates were required for a Malaysian identity card, and the records show most people did not possess birth certificates. Since then, however, the birth certificate has become an essential document for acquiring a Malaysian citizenship identity card. It is an offense to fail to obtain a Malaysian identity card after the age of twelve. There were 39,120 applications for identity cards in 1998 from twelve-year-olds alone throughout Sabah (*Sun* 1999). Therefore, it may take as many as two to three years before an identity card is issued.

The NRD is worried about the possibility of people using other persons' birth certificates to acquire Malaysian identity cards as well as the problem of forged identity cards (*Sun* 1999). Immigrants say that it is quite easy to get an identity card. A blue card is for citizens only, but migrants can get a fake one for as little as ten Ringgit (US$2.63) (*Borneo Post* 1999b). The NRD seeks the help of community leaders, village chiefs, and other agencies to verify or register people in remote areas who may not have birth certificates and, therefore, no identity cards. However, the verification process can be corrupted with bribery and collusion of native chiefs and other local community leaders responsible for verification, thus resulting in issuance of real cards for illegal immigrants. Complicating the issue of identity cards is the problem of unclaimed Malaysian cards. Malaysia has shifted to a new high-security identity card, and as of February 1999 there were 52,320 new unclaimed cards which had been applied for since the beginning of 1991 (*Sun* 1999). There were 9,344 cards from Kota Kinabalu, the capital of Sabah; 7,143 from Sandakan, an east-coast town bordering the Philippines; 8,371 from Tawau, an east-coast town bordering Indonesia; and 4,709 from Lahad Datu, a west-coast town.

The nonpossession of birth certificates or identity cards by many natives, the slow process of acquiring birth certificates, the registration for ever-changing new high-security identity cards, the conversion from old cards to new, the many cases of forged cards, and the wrongful acquisition of cards based on someone else's birth certificate all create a citizenship card mess allowing illegal immigrants and various sections in Sabah to misuse the citizenship system for their own electoral benefit. Since it is difficult to physically distinguish a Malaysian Bajau from a Filipino Bajau or a Malaysian Bugis from an Indonesian Bugis — the language, physical features, and food habits are all the same — it can be surmised that many illegal Bajau and Bugi immigrants possess one or more of these documents, which makes them eligible to vote in Malaysian elections. Otherwise, they can make use of fake papers since state agencies on the street cannot distinguish between fake and real documents. Recall the influence of local ethnic circuits through which such documentation is easily attainable. A central feature of globalization is the ways local networks strengthen national and global trends.

Suffraged Noncitizens

This section explains why the incorporation of illegal immigrants through citizenship documents occurs and how this incorporation is connected to the electoral politics of Sabah. Legalizing illegal immigrants becomes the preferred strategy of the dominant Malay parties when overt Malayization — through, for example, conversion or internal migration — does not proceed quickly enough.[17] The goal of the Malays, who dominate the federal government, is to change the demographic and political character of Sabah so that it becomes Malay Muslim dominated, and due to cultural–religious commonalties these immigrant Indonesians and Filipinos can easily be Malayized over time, after which they will support Malay Muslim parties.

The tacit support of fraudulent activities by sections in the federal government and by Malay elements in the state government produces a very insidious politics from within: A section within the state is trying to undermine the political rights of the major ethnic groups in a regional state through migration. According to Luping (1994, p. 444), a former attorney general of Sabah, "the popular belief amongst Sabahans, of course, was that both UMNO and USNO leaders wanted these people [illegal immigrants] to stay in Sabah and become citizens so that they could swell the votes for their Muslim-based party." Contrary to the experience of other countries, it seems that the decision as to who will be the ruling government in Sabah is now being determined by the crucial illegal immigrant vote. What is lost is the distinction between citizens and immigrants.

It appears to Kadazandusuns and other natives that there is active involvement of some state officials in the process of legalizing illegal immigrants.[18] In a 1999 court case — *Harris Mohd Salleh v. Ismail bin Majin* — the petitioner, Dr. Chong, told the court how a number of senior UMNO members from Sabah were detained under the Internal Security Act (ISA) for their involvement in the falsification of identity cards (*Borneo Post* 1999d; *Daily Express* 1999b).[19] The list included UMNO deputy chief of Tawau, Shamsul Alang, as well as Datu Akjan, Jabar Khan, and Dandy Pilo, among others. Some NRD officers and businesspersons were also detained under the ISA for their part in this operation. According to Hassnar, a former ISA detainee and a participant in this operation who like many people in Malaysia only goes by one name, a total of 130,000 illegal foreigners were issued blue identity cards in 1985 alone (*Borneo Post* 1999d).[20] Hassnar testified in court that he played a leading role in the operation, which was aimed at increasing the Muslim population in Sabah. He further alleged that this endeavor involved foreigners, government officers, and members of the ruling Barisan Nasional (BN) party.

Making citizens out of noncitizens has become a major industry in the state. With a potential market of 400,000 foreigners, the illegal identity card business can be very lucrative (*Daily Express* 1998).[21] Jeffrey Kitingan, a prominent Kadazandusun leader who was incarcerated under the ISA, says he was "privileged to meet fellow ISA [Internal Security Act] detainees…who were directly involved in the project IC (identity cards) — businessmen, government servants and Indonesians" (Kitingan 1997, p. 23). A local daily reported the arrest of seven officials from the NRD under the ISA for their involvement in the issuance of fake identity cards to foreigners (Kurus, Goddos, and Koh 1998, p. 174).

Though the fake documentation business is partly driven by sheer profit motives, many non-Muslim natives allege that these are indicators of a deliberate political strategy of demographic change. For example, these officials are not put on trial because that would involve media and publicity, which risk the possibility of all the details of the identity card project being made public in a court hearing. The ISA, under which these persons are interned conveniently, permits the government to hold these officials without trial and then to release them after a few years. Current juridical practice permits the government to refrain from releasing reports or figures on these internments, as would be the case if these officials were charged in a court of law. Taken as a whole, these appear to be face-saving forms of support for a well-functioning citizenship-card-making machinery. Kitingan (1997, pp. 23–4) alleges, "What the Malaysian Schemers are doing is tantamount to selling out our birth rights to aliens."

Many Kadazandusuns and other natives feel that this deliberate strategy is a way of demographically overwhelming them. The largely Muslim makeup of this illegal immigration into Sabah is viewed as an instrument for changing the voting pattern of Sabah to benefit Malay parties such as UMNO — the ruling Malay party of peninsular Malaysia. The motive is to increase the UMNO's vote banks. The UMNO's obvious goal is to override the Kadazandusuns and Muruts in favor of a coalition of Muslims groups represented and led by UMNO. Just before the state elections, PBS submitted a list of 49,270 illegal immigrants who had been issued identity cards, enabling them to vote. Mutalib's (1999) best-selling book about illegal immigrants identifies hundreds of illegal immigrants who have fake identity cards and may have voted in recent elections. It lists their identity card numbers and their affiliation to UMNO, provides the photographs of these individuals, and in some cases even lists their foreign passports (ibid.).

These false-document-holding illegals who vote are called phantom voters in Sabah. I use the term suffraged noncitizens to capture the contradiction of noncitizens' voting. There are three kinds of suffraged noncitizens in Sabah according to the main opposition party (Borneo Post 1999b; Daily Express 1999c): Foreigners who were (1) illegally issued identification cards and receipts and were registered as voters in Sabah; (2) issued fake identity cards or receipts bearing the names of others who appear on the electoral rolls; or (3) illegally issued fake identification cards and receipts bearing the name of dead voters whose names are still in the electoral rolls. What motivates these illegal immigrants to vote? Do they have rational, self-interested reasons to exercise the franchise? Though UMNO benefits, what is the benefit for them? Besides gaining material benefits such as the distribution of water tanks, rice, money, and fishing nets of various sizes — many Filipino immigrants are excellent fishermen — an issue well covered by various local dailies during the elections (*Daily Express* 1999d), there is the additional lure of access to better living conditions in Sabah if a Malaysian identity card can be secured. The card comes with the expectation that these immigrants will vote for their benefactors, which in Sabah happens to be the ruling Malay party, UMNO. Some of these illegal voters earn lucrative pay by such activities as working for the ruling party during elections, making billboards, mounting posters, and distributing pamphlets.[22] Also, connections with powerful UMNO members and other officials bring with them other privileges for these illegal immigrants. It is quite beneficial for these illegal immigrants to be involved in the Sabah elections.

In response to this involvement, former chief minister of Sabah Datuk Pairin urged the government to stop allowing holders of temporary identity documents such as forms JPN 1/9, 1/11, and 1/22 to vote in elections (*Borneo Post* 1999f). JPN 1/9 is a document issued to new applicants of identity cards, JPN 1/11 is issued to those who report a loss of identity card, and JPN 1/22 is given to those who change their blue identity card to the new *Bunga Raya* card (*Daily Express* 1999e). All are temporary documents, yet persons with such documents are allowed to vote. Dr. Chong, a PBS candidate from the Likas constituency, submitted evidence alleging misuse of these temporary documents (*Borneo Post* 1999g),[23] which anonymous individuals surrendered to him after the Sabah state elections in March 1999. In *Harris Mohd Salleh v. Ismail bin Majin* — a historic decision on the petition Dr. Chong filed — the High Court declared the election result of the Likas constituency null and void, ruling that "noncitizens had cast their votes in the polls" (*Daily Express* 2001). Accepting Dr. Chong's submission that the 1998 electoral rolls of the N13 Likas electoral seat were illegal since they contained names of illegal immigrants and persons who had been convicted for possession of fraudulent identity cards, Judge Awang of the High Court wrote, "The instances of noncitizens and phantom voters in the electoral roll as disclosed during the trial may well be the tip of the iceberg …It is common knowledge that an influx of illegal immigrants has plagued Sabah for some years. It is a well-known fact as it had appeared in the local dailies too frequently…" (ibid.) The judge noted in his decision how people convicted of possessing fake identity cards in 1996 continued on the electoral rolls of Likas constituency in 1998.[24] Therefore, it can be assumed that there are cases of Indonesian immigrants who have voted both in Sabah as well as in the elections in Indonesia when considering that an estimated 1.4 million Indonesian immigrants voted in the 1996 Indonesian elections while still living in Malaysia (Kassim 1998, p. 285).

The Malaysian experience this chapter documents highlights three remarkable features of international migration: (1) illegal immigrants can vote; (2) documents enable their political participation as citizens; and (3) parties and immigrants both have an interest in preserving the irregularities of documentation and collaborate to that end. Leading scholars of the mobility of labor and capital have pointed out the global character of such flows but have ignored the critical role that documents play in enabling the mobility and incorporation of labor (Sassen 1998). In actual practice, voting and political participation are not products of some abstract group membership but rather are products of the documents an individual holds — documents that are plentiful wherever there is illegal immigration. Around the world, documents, fake as well as real, are facilitating the incorporation and absorption of illegal immigrants into the state. This is only possible because documents have become the embodiment of individual identity in an era of globalization.

Conclusion

According to most studies of immigration politics, documentary citizenship should not be occurring, because the presumption is made that when it comes to national and state voting the lines between citizen and immigrant are sharply drawn. One has political suffrage; the other does not. The national state is assumed to be a sealed container of membership and loyalties that constitute citizenship. But driving this process of documentary citizenship is globalization, an all-encompassing feature of not only Western states but also developing nations. With increasing mobility due to rural dislocation and improvements in travel technology, identifying individuals has become a central feature of the state. Malaysia, like most developing countries, has only recently begun to control migration and certify identity. Many developing states with large rural populations are thin on documentation of any aspect of identity: There are no birth, marriage, or death certificates. The distinctions between citizens and immigrants do not matter for sections within the state that seek to change the ethnic composition of the region by using the features of globalization such as documentary citizenship. By acquiring documentary citizenship, illegal immigrants can and do become a part of the electoral process in the host state, a right that, according to the laws of the state, should be restricted to real citizens.

The breach of national citizenship through documentary citizenship reveals the local–global circuit as a key node of globalization (see Introduction by Saskia Sassen, this volume). Let me clarify three features of this circuit:

i.) Local circuits are directly connected to the global and represent an actual practiced localization of the global. They are not national circuits even when functioning within the thick environment of the national state. In fact, the sole purpose of these local–global circuits is to bypass national regulation, which has been the obsession of the Westphalian state since the late nineteenth century. In effect, the same circuits that make it possible for illegal immigrants from Indonesia and the Philippines to get absorbed in Malaysia will point them to alternate circuits for future travel to Singapore, Australia, and member countries of the European Union.

ii.) These circuits are invisible, so even as the national state increases its surveillance capacity through national identity cards and biometric measures there is an invisible absorption of immigrant communities through the power of global circuits placed locally. Invisibility firmly embeds the global in local networks, thus making them invisible to any national surveillance schemes.

iii.) Since surveillance has been a nation-state obsession, an increasing recognition of documentary citizenship will lead to a simultaneous rise in surveillance at the global and the local level. Evidence of the former can be found in the current activities of Interpol creating a global database for lost or stolen passports. Simultaneously, urgent funds are being directed through the United Nations Children's Fund (UNICEF) and international nongovernmental organizations (NGOs), for example Plan International, to improve the birth registration coverage of developing countries, especially in their neglected regions. Post 9/11, such schemes have been launched in Malaysia, India, Bangladesh, Pakistan, Afghanistan, and Indonesia, along with many other developing countries. Birth registration is only the beginning of identity documentation in these states. Parallel to this is the effort to create centralized national databases of citizens in Malaysia, India, Pakistan, and Indonesia.

Clearly, the national state is confronting the power of thick social environments where the global is localized efficiently, made invisible, while bypassing national surveillance efforts. What is unseen cannot be controlled or monitored. Documentary citizenship allows illegal immigrants the status of citizens. In such circumstances, the notion of the national interest and the state's pursuit of it are thrown into crisis. The reality of both citizens and illegal immigrants competing on an equal footing to set the policies of states requires major rethinking of the role of illegal immigration in a time of globalization.

Notes

1. This chapter is a modified and abridged version of Sadiq (2005). I gratefully acknowledge the support of Shamsul A.B. of the Universiti Kebangsaan Malaysia during my year-long stay in Malaysia.
2. See, inter alia, Marshall and Bottomore (1996), Brubaker (1992), and Smith (1997). Citizenship has always been safeguarded such that all outsiders, of whatever sort, were denied the right to vote until the middle of the twentieth century. For example, women and certain classes of people were denied the franchise in many developed states, notably the United States, at the turn of the twentieth century, as Smith (1997) brilliantly documents. The right to vote at the national level is, according to Tiburcio (2001, p. 190), "granted only to citizens, that is nationals with full political rights, and aliens are left outside the electoral process entirely." She cites the constitutions of indi-

vidual states to show that only citizens can vote in national elections in, among many others, Austria, Belgium, Brazil, Canada, Denmark, Greece, Hungary, Israel, Monaco, Norway, Poland, Portugal, Switzerland, Turkey, Thailand, the United Kingdom, and the United States (ibid., 189–90).

3. Non-citizen includes the following categories: legal immigrant, illegal immigrant, refugee, and tourist.
4. *Natives* are individuals whose ancestors were born in the country.
5. An anonymous reviewer drew a parallel between what is happening today in Malaysia and the United States during the nineteenth century: Some illegal European immigrants to America during this period stepped off the boats and were immediately permitted to vote by ethnic political machines. This occurred even as indigenous populations — Native Americans — were denied basic citizenship rights. The parallel is illuminating; however, the distinction between citizen and immigrant — and regulatory structures for dealing with these two categories — only became deeply institutionalized after World War II. This chapter covers the period from the 1970s until September 11, 2001.
6. Illegal immigrants, mainly from Indonesia, are exercising social, economic, and even political rights in West Malaysia (Kassim 1998). A leading scholar of immigration into Malaysia, Kassim (ibid., p. 285) says that "estimates on illegals in the *Peninsula* vary from between 300,000 to one million," indicating the difficulty in measurement. Over the years, illegal immigrants have gained access to Malaysian citizenship; in fact, Malaysian authorities have accused many Indonesian immigrants of being politically active in radical Islamic groups.
7. West Malaysia is over 1,000 miles from Sabah, a regional state in East Malaysia, and is separated from it by the South China Sea. It takes about two and a half hours to reach Sabah from West Malaysia by airplane.
8. Now it is true that, after September 11, 2001, the Malaysian authorities cracked down on illegal immigration after Malaysia became a partner in the war on terrorism (*New York Times*, 2002). But this transitory focus on deportation of immigrants was not at odds with the purpose of encouraging illegal immigration from the 1970s until September 11, because the ruling Malay-dominated parties had already achieved their demographic goals: Many illegal immigrants had already become citizens. Furthermore, Sabah's geographic position and traditional immigrant networks are such that deported Indonesian and Filipino illegal immigrants can return to Sabah within days and acquire citizenship documents easily. Public shows of deportation of Muslim illegal immigrants from West or East Malaysia conceals the fact that these illegal immigrants can and do return very soon and that their networks ensure their access to citizenship.
9. Based on the author's conversations with Filipino immigrants.
10. Due to the sensitive nature of this research, the names of some of my interviewees have been changed to protect their identities.
11. The word *Bahasa* is Indian in origin and means "language" in Sanskrit.
12. PBS is the main Kadazandusun and Murut party. A confidential and comprehensive, almost census-like, project was done on these illegal immigrants when PBS was in power from 1985 to 1994: the *Transient Population Study* undertaken by the Chief Ministers' Department, Kota Kinabalu, 1988. The

study covers statistics regarding immigration until the period 1988 to 1989 (the author's personal copy).

13. Interviews with Henrynus Amin, a prominent legislator of the native PBS and their spokesperson and other members of the party during my stay in Sabah in 1999.
14 Interview with Maximus Ongkilli, vice president, PBS. July 9, 1999.
15. As a status, documentary citizenship is distinguished from Tomas Hammar's "denizen" concept by the fact that "documentary citizens" acquire national level suffrage, whereas Hammar's denizens do not (Hammar, 83-84).
16. The mid-year population estimate for 1998 was 2,812,000 persons.
17. I thank Herman Luping, a former deputy chief minister as well as a former attorney general of Sabah, for this information (Luping 1994, pp. 530–5, 564–7).
18. In fact, Article 159 of the Constitution speaks of the responsibility of the state "to safeguard the special position of the Malays and the natives of the states of Sabah and Sarawak."
19. I was present in Sabah for a period when the court hearings on this matter took place. Dr. Chong went on to win part of his petition, and the Likas constituency election result was nullified by the order of the judge on June 8, 2001. The judicial decision by the High Court judge was delivered despite pressure on him from "sources" to dismiss the petition (*Daily Express* 2001).
20. Hassnar was a former district native chief in Sandakan.
21. Statement by Joseph Sitin Saang, vice president of Parti Democratic Sabah (PDS).
22. Author's conversation with an illegal immigrant. It is not easy to get an illegal immigrant to acknowledge that she/he is illegal and voting.
23. Copy in the author's possession. The evidence includes eighteen pairs of receipts; each pair of receipts has the same photographs of a person bearing two different names and corresponding NRD numbers that also appear on the electoral rolls. Among these thirty-six JPN receipts, three names with the corresponding identity card numbers appear twice but with different photographs, addresses, and dates of birth. The news reports covering this issue are (1) *Borneo Post* (1999g); (2) "Petitioner alleges illegality," *Borneo Post*, September 22, 1999, A5; (3) "Sanctity of electoral rolls challenged," *Borneo Post*, September 23, 1999, A4; (4) "Phantom voters influenced election," *Borneo Post*, September 29, 1999, A1; and (5) *Borneo Post* (1999f).
24. These immigrants were (*Harris Mohd Salleh v. Ismail bin Majin*) Kassim Bin Ali, identity card H0508335; Anwar, identity card H0512235; and Kadir Labak, identity card H0454652.

Works Cited

Borneo Post (Kota Kinabalu). 1999a. September 29, A4.

———. 1999c. Illegal jailed after entering state since 1979. October 6, A3.

———. 1999d. Conspiracy in issuing ICs to foreigners. November 12, A4.

———. 1999e. August 21, A2.

———. 1999f. Flush out fake voters: Pairin to BN. September 23, A2.
———. 1999g. Police report on fake documents. September 22, A5.
Brubaker, R. 1992. *Citizenship and nationhood in France and Germany.* Cambridge, MA: Harvard University Press.
Daily Express (Kota Kinabalu). 1998. May 20, available at http://www.dailyexpress.com.my.
———. 1999a. Letter to the editor, August 1, 20.
———. 1999b. Foreigners voted BN claim, September 29, 1.
———. 1999c. Three categories of phantom voters: PBS, August 21, 3.
———. 1999d. November 17, 2.
———. 1999e. Future generations will not forgive, October 8, 4.
———. 2000. October 25, available at http://www.dailyexpress.com.my.
———. 2000b. 10 hi-tech fake ICs seized daily, July 17, available at http://www.dailyexpress.com.my.
———. 2001. Its by-poll for Likas, June 9, available at http://www.dailyexpress.com.my.
Department of Statistics (Malaysia). 1995. *Population and housing census 1991, state population report: Sabah,* March 1995.
Department of Statistics (Malaysia) 1983 *Population and Housing Census of Malaysia, Vol. 1* January.
Government of Sabah. 1998. *Buku Tahunan Perangkaan.* Cawangan Sabah: Jabatan Perangkaan Malaysia.
Hammar, T. 1989. State, nation, and dual citizenship. In William Rogers Brubaker, ed., *Immigration and the politics of citizenship in Europe and North America*,. Lanham, MD: University Press of America.
Harris Mohd Salleh v. Ismail bin Majin. 1999. Returning Officer, Election Petition k5, k11, High Court (Kota Kinabalu), 2001–3 MLJ 433; 2001
Jacobson, D. 1997. *Rights across borders: Immigration and the decline of citizenship.* Baltimore: Johns Hopkins University Press.
Joppke, C. 1999. *Immigration and the nation-state: The United States, Germany, and Great Britain.* New York: Oxford University Press.
Kassim, A. 1998. International migration and its impact on Malaysia. In M.J. Hassan, ed., *A Pacific peace: Issues and responses*, 273–305. Kuala Lumpur: Institute of Strategic and International Studies.
Kitingan, J. 1997. *The Sabah problem.* Kota Kinabalu: KDI Publications.
Koslowski, R. 2000. *Migrants and citizens: Demographic change in the European state system.* Ithaca, NY: Cornell University Press.
Kurus, B., R. Goddos, and R. Koh. 1998. Migrant labor flows in the East Asian region: Prospects and challenges. *Borneo Review* 9(2):156–86.
Kymlicka, W. 1995. *Multicultural citizenship: A liberal theory of minority rights.* Oxford: Clarendon Press.
Luping, H. 1994. *Sabah's dilemma: The political history of Sabah, 1960–1994.* Kuala Lumpur: Magnus Books.
Marshall, T.H., and T. Bottomore. 1996. *Citizenship and social class.* London: Pluto Press.
Mutalib, M.D. 1999. *IC Palsu: Merampas Hak Anak Sabah.* Lahad Datu: Sabah
New York Times. 2002. Malaysia deporting Indonesian and Philippine workers. August 30, A3.

Philippine Daily Inquirer (Manila). 1999. Filipino illegals swell in Sabah. October 30, available at http://www.thefilipino.com/frames/philinq.htm.

Sadiq, Kamal. 2005. When states prefer non-citizens over citizens: Conflict over illegal immigration into Malaysia. *International Studies Quarterly* 49(1):101–122 (March).

Sassen, S. 1998. *Globalization and its discontents.* New York: New Press.

Schuck, P.H., and R.M. Smith. 1985. *Citizenship without consent: Illegal aliens in the American polity.* New Haven, CT: Yale University Press.

Smith, R. 1997. *Civic ideals: Conflicting visions of citizenship in U.S. history.* New Haven, CT: Yale University Press.

Soysal, Y. 1994. *Limits of citizenship: Migrants and postnational membership in Europe.* Chicago: University of Chicago Press.

Stalker, P. 1994. *The work of strangers: A survey of international labour migration.* Geneva: International Labor Office.

Sun (Kuala Lumpur). 1999. Officially, these folks don't exist. April 19, A12.

Tiburcio, C. 2001. *The human rights of aliens under international and comparative law.* Hague: Kluwer Law International.

Tomiyuki, U. 2000. Migration and ethnic categorization at international frontier: A case of Sabah, East Malaysia. In Abe Ken-ichi and Ishii Masako, eds., *Population movement in Southeast Asia: Changing identities and strategies for survival,* 33-55. Osaka: JCAS Symposium Series 10, Japan Center for Area Studies, National Museum of Ethnology.

CHAPTER 16

Global–National Interactions and Sovereign Debt Restructuring Outcomes

GISELLE DATZ

A prevalent view in early studies of financial globalization was that international capital mobility sharply restricted policy autonomy, both fiscal and monetary, in developed countries (Andrews 1994; Gill and Law 1989). Though some of these countries countries were recognized as diverging from this pattern (Porter 2001), through state co-optation, collaboration, and competition (Cerny 1993; Dombrowski 1998; Pauly 1997), convergence was said to prevail in emerging economies. Here the story was that domestic policy not aligned with financial markets was severely constrained in these emerging economies (Armijo 2001; Mosley 2003; Phillips 1998). Yet I contend that this view of a widespread lack of policy autonomy is at odds with the fact that sovereign defaults were a common practice in the 1990s and early 2000s. One can hardly think of a policy stance more divergent from financial market preferences than the suspension of payments on debt (default)[1] owed to private creditors who purchase government bonds both domestically and internationally.[2]

Efforts to understand the interactions of states and financial markets have much to gain from recognizing the enormous variability across countries in terms of the incorporation, negotiation, or resistance to globalization (Sassen 2003), as well as analyzing instances in which convergence and divergence happen together in a process of "diversity *within* convergence" (Cerny, Mens, and Soederberg 2005, emphasis in original). That is, within a framework of promarket reform, we can spot critical instances of government policy that do not abide by the constraints supposedly imposed by investors and financial traders on emerging economies typically in need of international capital inflows. This chapter's interest in such instances is not merely as a divergent trend in a promarket landscape, but especially as cases that reveal how even when challenging market preferences, daring policy stances may remain embedded in the circuit of financial market operations rather than be excluded from them. In this sense I see the global economy as a realm where there prevails much more adaptability of financial strategies than the assumption of unequivocally punitive markets allows to be seen. It is in this realm of private adaptability that some policy autonomy not only can emerge but also can count on the support of the markets to prosper in the short to medium term.

In fact, a central challenge in theorizing the impact of economic globalization on policy making in developing countries is to avoid explaining the outcomes of globalization for these countries as a more severely confining version of what happens in developed countries. I argue that an apt differentiation of the impact of economic globalization on policy autonomy in developed versus middle-income countries is not simply a matter of degree but of dynamics that reveal ad hoc modes of engagement between emerging market governments and financial markets. Because of such ad hoc modes of engagement rather than formal institutionalized reactions, understanding the actual structural alignments in place becomes less evident. Seeing these alignments requires a closer understanding of institutional incentives within the financial industry.

This chapter examines how markets react to sovereign default in emerging market economies, challenging the notion that they punish defaulters with a severe credit restriction. Instead, I argue that debt restructuring outcomes following defaults are determined by lending cycles and the prevailing market sentiment in the sovereign bond industry, as well as by the primarily short-term strategies of scattered and often sophisticated private investors.

The remainder of this chapter first discusses the conceptual map on which my analysis of global–national interactions is based, with an empirical emphasis on debt restructuring outcomes. Second, it addresses the puzzle of assuming constraints on policy leeway in developing countries given the evidence of successful debt restructurings for debtor countries notwithstanding recurrent defaults. Then a discussion is given of the macro–micro approach I have developed for understanding debt restructuring outcomes in middle-income countries[3]. Finally are discussed the implications of this approach for credit relations in the 1990s and early 2000s through a brief analysis of the cases of the Ecuadorian, Russian, and Argentine sovereign default and debt restructurings.

Deciphering Global–National Interactions: A Conceptual Map

In analyzing the specific dynamics between states and financial markets that mark debt restructuring outcomes, I engage with Sassen's research agenda on "the meaning of the national today" and on "rescaling" interactions between the national and the global (see Sassen, Introduction, this volume) in two key ways. First, her understanding that the global and the national are not mutually exclusive entities finds one application in an inquiry about the extent to which global actors and logics have taken over national policy. Through an empirical analysis of sovereign debt restructurings, I find that state–financial markets interactions in emerging market economies are not a zero-sum game. This holds even at times of debt negotiation, when the threat of a credit crunch can be seen as punishment to sovereign defaulters. At different stages of a debt restructuring both debtors and some more sophisticated creditors can enjoy gains. Debtors can strike deals with private creditors that entail significant reductions in debt repayment — as in the case of Argentina — without losing access to credit markets in an enduring way. In turn, some creditors, such as hedge funds, may find it highly profitable to buy the defaulted bonds of retail, or individual, investors for an extremely low price at the time of the debt restructuring, to join the deal, and to end up with new bonds that value a lot more than at the time of purchase.

The second way this analysis contributes to a renewed effort at deciphering the global originates in Sassen's (this volume) invitation for a reassessment of scales. Beyond a consideration of local-subnational, national, and global categorizations, I suggest that to understand how economic and financial processes in the global economy affect policymaking demands a closer look at the ways micro- and macroeconomic scales interact constantly, producing opportunities and constraints to both state and nonstate actors domestically and globally. As Alexander, Dhumale, and Eatwell (2006) contend, insofar as financial factors determine the ability of individuals, firms, and governments to spend, they also determine liquidity levels and hence overall economic performance. Thus, an understanding of economic performance (i.e., the macrolevel) cannot be disassociated from a microeconomic understanding of financial markets. Indeed, the approach I suggest to analyzing the outcome of debt-restructuring processes combines, at the macrolevel, an understanding of lending cycles with the microeconomic sociology of financial markets, as suggested by Santiso (2003). Based on evidence from the three sovereign defaults in the late 1990s and early 2000s — that of Ecuador, Russia, and Argentina — it is clear that with low interest rates in financial centers, investors' appetite for high return had them seeking riskier securities, and demand for emerging market bonds increased markedly (World Bank 2006). Hence, as long as international liquidity remains high and bond traders have every incentive to perform better than, or at least compatibly with, their competitors, there is no reason for defaulters to be punished with a severe credit crunch by bondholders, who are their key creditors in this era of global finance. That is to say, market punishments to defaulting countries in the 1990s and early 2000s were more a threatening myth than a financial reality.

In analyzing debt-restructuring outcomes in the current era of bond finance — rather than credit from commercial bank loans — empirical evidence reveals that the complexities brought to the default-restructuring scenario by the diversity and dispersion of bondholders as the main creditors of sovereign debt since 1989 helped rather than hindered favorable restructuring outcomes from the point of view of debtor countries. To understand how this happens demands an empirical dissecting of what are ultimately ad hoc modes of engagement between financial markets and emerging markets' governments. To be sure, debt restructurings are formalized procedures, embedded in an often thick web of legalities. However, the dynamics preceding and following restructurings are what I understand to be determined in an ad hoc fashion and leading to counterintuitively positive responses from market players. The complex global–national negotiation that characterized debt restructurings postdefault in the 1990s and early 2000s ended up inciting the support of markets for its resolution. This is a significantly counterintuitive outcome not yet systematically tackled by the vast theoretical literature on sovereign debt in economics or by the compliance literature in political science.

Market Punishments or Discretionary Autonomy in Emerging Market Economies?

The international political economy literature has been keen to stress that finance has become the lifeblood of the current international economy. Within this context, developing countries in particular are tied by binding economic policy commitments that are favored by international investors, whose eagerness for high yields have led to much temporary optimism in emerging markets in times of lending booms but whose herd-driven and panic-prone behavior have also brought much instability to international financial markets with drastic repercussions in some developing countries. Therefore, the behavior of foreign capital in response to perceived sovereign risk in developing countries suggests that there is a very narrow range of options within which these countries can maneuver (Mosley 2003). Hence, for developing countries the costs of nonconformity imposed by the tyranny of bond traders were often described as unaffordable (Armijo 2001, p. 33; Phillips 1998).

However, when the evidence is analyzed, we run into a puzzle regarding sovereign defaults. Despite conventional wisdom about the lack of policy autonomy available to developing countries, defaults — the extreme cases of nonconformity with financial market expectations — were still common practice in the 1990s,[4] and in 2001 the Argentine default marked the largest such episode in history to date. It is interesting to note that despite the complexities added to the default and restructuring scenarios due to the presence of scattered private creditors, rather than to a limited group of commercial banks, the cases of debt restructurings involving Ecuador (1999), Pakistan (1999), Ukraine (2000), and Uruguay (2003)[5] show that debt principal or interest reduction or maturities extensions are viable and that protracted negotiations can in fact be avoided (IMF 2002). Moreover, in all these recent cases debt restructuring resolutions were arrived at in less than a year and a half, and economic recovery was resumed right after (Marx, 2003).

Defaults and debt restructurings are not an automatic outcome of economic chaos and indeed reveal great variation from country to country, especially in the last decade. This holds even if default occurrences can be seen to result from the pressures on developing countries' governments to pursue unsustainable policies that signal credibility to international financial markets. This was the case with the Convertibility Law in Argentina during the 1990s. It is worth noting that the outcomes of debt-restructuring negotiations stand in stark empirical contrast to a popular approach for explaining repayment of sovereign debt: reputational theory (Eaton and Gersovitz 1981; Tomz 2001; Wright 2002). Reputational explanations for debt repayment state that a country in default on its debts acquires a bad reputation in credit markets and is punished for suspending debt payments either via a severe credit crunch or a high premium charge on future loans, or — more likely — both.[6] To avoid these punishments, countries repay their debts.[7] Second-generation default models state that reputations do not simply damage credit relationships but that negative effects may spill over to other international negotiations, such as those involving trade agreements (Cole and Kehoe 1997; Rose 2001). Yet these mostly formal models seldom mention empirical cases or test their premises against current data sets, disaggregating the source of credit — for example, if from commercial bank loans or private purchase of sovereign bonds.[8]

In fact, reputational explanations for repayment in periods past were largely dismissed by detailed work on the 1930s debt crisis. Eichengreen and Portes (1989) report that, historically, remarkably little evidence was found to prove that defaulting countries had acquired reputations for unwillingness to pay, which in turn hindered their ability to borrow. Moreover, Jorgensen and Sachs's (1989) study of five Latin American countries

— Argentina, the only nondefaulter, Bolivia, Chile, Peru, and Colombia — in the critical decade of the 1930s concludes that from the borrower's perspective the cost of default involving the indirect component of reputation effects on future credit access were "low, so low as to be negative" (ibid., p. 78).

When countries returned to international capital markets in the 1950s, no apparent systematic difference between defaulters and nondefaulters was perceived. Eichengreen (1991) found that interwar defaults had essentially no impact on the relative ease with which countries secured private portfolio inflows during the immediate postwar years as well as in the lending boom of 1976 to 1979 (ibid., p. 147).

The evidence for restructurings in the post-1980s period also contradicts theories of reputational or market punishments. Gelos, Sahay, and Sandleris (2004) conducted a rare statistical study including 1990s data and concluded that, contrary to predictions from reputational theories, the probability of market access is not strongly influenced by a default in the previous year. Indeed, in the 1990s, on average countries that defaulted did not experience protracted interruptions in market access. In addition, these authors were "unable to detect a strong punishment effect of defaulting countries by credit markets" for a period between 1982, the onset of the 1980s debt crisis, until 2000 (ibid., p. 4).[9]

Using both macro- and microeconomic variables, this chapter maps out a contextual scenario that explains postdefault credit access. This provides yet more evidence that reputational punishments may have weight as a rhetorical stigma only; in practice these punishments carry no weight. Hence, sovereign defaulters have some significant room to maneuver, allowing them the opportunity to take a tougher stance in debt restructurings than is often assumed when financial volatility is emphasized as a constant threat of capital exit from emerging economies.

Explaining Policy Leeway at Bargaining Times

To understand what determines the design and high level of acceptance of debt restructurings as well as economic performance after restructuring, two key parameters are identified here. The first considers boom and bust lending cycles as playing a key role in the availability of credit to defaulting countries during the default and after the restructuring. Since the focus here is on post-1980s restructuring — or post-Brady Plan of 1989 — the second parameter focuses on the investment incentives specific to the bond industry.

Boom and Bust Cycles in Foreign Lending

Research on lending cycles has shown that domestic political considerations are not the central factor determining substantive inflows of capital to emerging economies. Rather, these are significantly linked to economic booms in financial centers (Gourinchas, Valdés, and Landerretche 2001; Pettis 2001). Fernandez-Arias's (1996) study of portfolio flows to thirteen developing countries from 1988 to 1995 reveals that international interest rates have a larger impact than country creditworthiness in explaining the flows — both in terms of equity and bond purchases. More recently, Pettis's (2001, p. 51) analysis of lending cycles concluded that "global capital flows are less a function of local growth prospect and more a function of independent expansions and contractions in underlying liquidity in rich-country financial centers," which in turn decreases risk aversion at times of lending booms.

Lending busts do not necessarily amount to debt crises. Yet these crises are linked to so-called sudden stops in capital inflows. That is, episodes of a sharp contraction of international capital flows may trigger a domestic eruption, even when local economic fundamentals are well in place (Calvo, Izquierdo, and Talvi 2003). Indeed, the intense financial volatility marking the current era of globalization affects debt management in a particular way that diverges from past debt crises. The sovereign bond market is more affected by changes in market sentiment than in domestic macroeconomic fundamentals in emerging markets, such as fiscal discipline and output growth, among other variables[10] (Eichengreeen and Mody 1998; Mauro, Sussman, and Yafeh 2002).

During periods of high liquidity in financial centers, foreign investors turn to emerging markets in search of high returns. Consequently, credit access, as intrinsically linked to the macroeconomic context in which it is embedded, cannot be thought of as mainly a product of reputational records (i.e., a history of nondefault). The latter is not a negligible factor, as it certainly is present in the estimations of country risk[11] produced by international investors and analysts. However, repayment records are not central to understanding emerging markets' access to credit.

Industry-Specific Incentives and Time Horizons of Sovereign Debt Bondholders

Given that portfolio allocations are chosen based primarily on the risk tolerance and investment goals of investors, it is crucial to understand what determines these portfolio allocations, once international factors point favorably to emerging markets as promising investment harbors — even if only temporarily. Hence, an industry-specific view of the bond market and its players is in order. It reveals how decision making in financial markets is bounded by the bonus granting, index following, and behavior mimicking specific to the financial industry, which in turn ultimately determine the demand for an increasing variety of securities (Calvo and Mendoza 2000; Santiso 2003).

A common practice in institutional money management is to measure performance against benchmarks, usually equity or bond indexes. This approach has become standard in emerging markets, with many fund managers' performances measured against the J.P. Morgan Emerging Market Bond Index. This index tracks on a daily basis the prices and yield of bonds issued by various emerging market countries, which rise and fall based on new developments and interest rate trends. Each country in the index has a percentage weighting — for example, 10 percent for Russia, 15 percent for Argentina, 4 percent for Venezuela — that depends largely on the number of bonds it has issued compared with the total issued by all the countries combined. The index serves the purpose of providing a means through which funds' clients can evaluate managers' performances, which are measured against the index on a quarterly basis or even more frequently in many cases. What is problematic about the index is its potential to feed a vicious cycle in sovereign lending. By relying on the Emerging Market Bond Index, investors are encouraged to lend to the most heavily indebted countries — at times, unsustainably so. Despite dissatisfaction with this trend, investors admit that they have to follow the index because "the contracts of clients frequently specify such benchmarks" (Santiso 2003, p. 75). Structurally critical is that index following and benchmark imperatives contribute to herd behavior in financial markets, playing a crucial role also in explaining contagion effects at times of financial crises (Calvo and Mendoza 2000).

Mosley (2003, p. 42) explains that since clients cannot directly observe the performance of fund managers — that is, "they do not know what information they are collecting or how they are using this information, and they cannot distinguish between managers' abilities and managers' luck — they can use relative performance outcomes to get some sense of individual market participants' efforts and abilities." In turn, fund managers respond to relative performance evaluation in a variety of ways but most commonly by looking at similar indicators and fundamentals.[12] Aware that they will be judged relative to the market-leading analyst, fund managers become prone to mimicking the recommendation of the market leader (Graham 1999).

Moreover, time horizons for asset managers are mostly constrained by frequent performance monitoring. Even if institutional clients — like pension funds and insurance companies — do not generally ask for strategic shifts in allocations during a single quarter, fund managers tend to adopt strategies dominated by short-term horizons (Blustein 2005; Lachaman 2004; Santiso 2003). Also, because bonuses — the part of remuneration based on performance and risk-taking behavior — are more important than salary for actors in the financial industry, they tend to focus attention on short-term gains with a maximum temporal horizon of one year (Santiso 2003, p. 109).

These considerations point to how crucial it is to understand the microeconomics of the sovereign debt market to come up with a theory of sovereign debt restructurings that is finally consistent with a plethora of, so far, disputing evidence.

Debt Restructurings and Credit Access: Ecuador, Russia, and Argentina

How do the parameters outlined here fare against evidence of the three most notable defaults of the 1990s and early 2000s, that of Ecuador, Russia, and Argentina? Was credit access severely constrained by their defaulting records? The evidence does not point to the existence of severe or enduring market punishments. The three cases are very different, especially when it comes to the type of debt defaulted on and its amount. Nevertheless, a brief analysis of each case makes it clear that credit access postdefault is not unequivocally restricted by market punishments. None of the defaulters had to wait long to receive upgrades in their credit ratings and to attract further demand for their sovereign bonds.

Ecuador

The Ecuadorian default in August 1999 was the first in Latin America since the debt crisis of the 1980s and the first default on international sovereign bonds since the 1930s.[13] In addition, Ecuador set the precedent of the first default on the restructured debt of the 1980s, called Brady bonds. With the support of the International Monetary Fund (IMF), on July 27, 2000, Ecuador launched its successful debt restructuring on all of its defaulted Brady bonds and Eurobonds with total face value of US$6.5 billion.[14]

Ecuador's medium-term sustainability is still an open question. Also, the country's public debt-to-gross domestic product (GDP) ratio has fallen, which may be more a product of inflation leading to a real overvaluation rather than to lower debt stock. Yet it is interesting that in March 2004, Moody's Investors Service (2005) upgraded Ecuadorian sovereign debt, citing an improvement in the management of the government's fiscal accounts. The country ceiling for foreign-currency debt was raised one notch (seven notches below investment grade), with the rating for foreign-currency sovereign debt upgraded similarly. The rating agency reported that it expected the country's debt position to continue improving, as Ecuador was then registering surpluses on its nonfinancial public-sector balances. Among the other major rating agencies, both Fitch and Standard & Poor's altered their outlook on long-term sovereign debt to stable from positive in September 2003. More recently, in its "2005 Outlook," Fitch upgraded Ecuador's ratings due to "sound macro policy frameworks and improved economic performance" (*Dow Jones Newswire*, February 1, 2005).

Despite severe economic turmoil, Ecuador was not subjected to an immediate downgrade in its credit rating early in 2005, as volatility was offset by high oil prices (*Dow Jones Newswires*, April 18, 2005) — a sign that international macroeconomic considerations and their impact on the country's balance of payments was more sound a parameter for investors than turbulent domestic politics.[15] In May, a rumor started that Ecuador was in risk of another default as a new president took office (*Bloomberg*, May 31, 2005). Still, compared to 2004, the spreads on Ecuadorian bonds narrowed considerably in the second quarter of 2005, showing that the difference investors demanded for holding these bonds instead of U.S. Treasury notes — the benchmark in the industry — was reduced, a proof of confidence in Ecuador as an investment choice for bond traders (*Bloomberg*, July 11, 2005). High liquidity in the sovereign-debt market, along with high oil prices, presented an extremely beneficial setting for Ecuador. Despite domestic imbalances, the IMF reported that the country's short-term economic outlook was positive (*Reuters*, October 1, 2005). Such statements by the IMF are known to produce positive investment responses in the debt market.

Russia

The Russian default differed markedly from the Ecuadorian case in that it was not fully anticipated by financial players and that the majority of Russia's creditors were banks, not private bondholders. With Russian stock, bond, and currency markets weakened as a result of investor fears of devaluation by August 13, 1998, on August 17 the Russian government devalued the ruble, defaulted on the domestic debt (US$14 billion) and on Soviet-era dollar debt (US$32 billion), and declared a ninety-day moratorium on payment to foreign creditors. At that time, annual yields on ruble-denominated bonds were more than 200 percent[16] (Chiodo and Owyang 2002).

In fact, the Russian default was filled with eccentricities. It was the only case in which the defaulter was able to exclude a significant share of its external debt — its Russian-era Eurobonds — from a comprehensive restructuring. It became clear that Russia wished to preserve its Russian-era Eurobonds to facilitate new borrowing. However, according to Roubini and Setser (2004), Russia was able to carry out this strategy only because its London Club debt (i.e., debt owed to commercial banks) was technically an obligation of a Soviet-era state bank, Vnesheconombank, not the Russian federation. Also, some of the same creditors owned Russian-era Eurobonds and Soviet-era London Club debt, reducing the incentive for the holders of the Soviet-era debt to broaden the restructuring to include Russian-era debt (ibid., p. 172).

On August 25, 1998, the government made its first restructuring offer on its ruble-denominated GKOs, or treasury bills, which was rejected by market participants. The GKOs were restructured in 1999, whereas other debts were restructured into Eurobonds in 2000. Indeed, Russia managed to count on a debt reduction of 35 percent on average. This operation was referred to on Wall Street as *scalping*. Yet none of the foreign banks with operations in Russia before 1998 left the country (Sinyagina-Woodruff 2003).

Did the default and restructuring compromise Russia's credit access? The first postdefault GKO auction in February 2000 counted on a large demand. In fact, Russia's Eurobond due in 2003, which was trading at 20 cents in October 1998, rose to 95.8 cents in 2000. In both 1999 and 2000, the J.P. Morgan's Emerging Market Benchmark Index featured Russia as "the world's best-performing fixed income market" (Sinyagina-Woodruff 2003, p. 544). In July 2005, Standard & Poor's raised Russia's long-term foreign-credit rating to its lowest investment grade so far (i.e., lowest default risk), citing the country's improved ability to pay debt. The upgrade followed similar action by the other two top rating agencies in the global bond market: Fitch in November 2004 and Moody's in October 2003 (*Bloomberg*, July 11, 2005).

In September 2005, it was reported that "Russia is afloat on a sea of cash" due to high liquidity and from record high oil prices, an export commodity for the country. Most importantly, "[I]t is all a far cry from the dark days of 1998, and the achievement is not just due to oil." Years of fiscal austerity and economic growth led the country to accumulate a sizable budget surplus: 8 percent of GDP as of September 2005 (*Financial Times*, September 16, 2005).

Argentina

The Argentine default, in turn, was mostly predicted by bond investors and set the record of not only the largest suspension of debt payments in history to date but also the largest reduction in repayment at the time of the debt restructuring.

After a decade of pouring international capital inflows, Argentina was a time bomb by the end of the 1990s. The Convertibility Law that fixed the peso at a rate of one to one with the dollar became clearly unsustainable.

The costs of keeping the parity had augmented considerably after the many external shocks of the 1990s, notably the financial crises of Asia and Russia with their spillover to Brazil. No longer could the country count on the substantial income it had raised from privatizations in the past decade. On the contrary, the program for pension privatization started at the same time brought high transition costs to the federal budget. The government did not feel the relief of pension payments that had shifted to the private system in the short term but immediately felt the deprivation of a large amount of tax revenue, which had to be compensated via new borrowing.

As a result of mounting fiscal burdens, Argentina's consolidated public debt rose from less than 33 percent of GDP in the early 1990s to more than 41 percent in 1998. Much of the debt had to be serviced in foreign currency, which was made more difficult by Argentina's low export-to-GDP ratio, a product of an overvalued currency. The country's total foreign-currency debt was around five times the size of its foreign currency receipts from exports of goods and services by the end of 2001 (Krueger 2002).

On December 23, 2001, interim President Adolfo Rodrigues Saá officially announced that Argentina would suspend debt payments of approximately US$155 billion, of which approximately US$88 billion was owed to private bondholders, excluding interest.

Debt restructuring in this case was to become the most complex operation of its kind ever; the variety of legislations and types of debt instruments were broader than in any other case of default in the past. Of the total bonds in default, 61 percent were denominated in dollars, 3 percent in Argentine pesos, 21 percent in Euros, 4 percent in yen, and 12 percent in other currencies (Marx 2003). Of the total debt in default residents held approximately 50 percent, a large part of which was held by local pension funds. This established an even more complex political dynamic underlining the debt restructuring process (Datz 2004b).

Although the official debt restructuring of Argentine defaulted bonds was started in 2005, it was only the last phase of a piecemeal process that the government articulated strategically and that allowed it to deal with domestic bondholders — especially pension funds — differently than international creditors. This was a political move to offer a sweeter deal to pension funds given the way the government abruptly tapped into their resources when foreign credit had dried up by the end of 2001.

On January 14, 2005, Argentina's official debt exchange was opened. With it the government hoped to count on a majority of bondholders to swap approximately 150 types of bonds into only three new types of bonds. Despite involving a deep reduction in repayment, the debt restructuring counted on 76 percent of creditors' acceptance. This was far lower a level than that of other restructurings in the 1990s but was a sound outcome given that this process involved the largest repayment reduction so far — that is, a repayment of about thirty cents on every one dollar of debt.

Only two weeks after the official swap was announced, 30 to 40 percent of retail investors had sold their bonds (*Reuters*, February 2, 2005). While the official exchange was still in its first week, Standard & Poor's announced that it would upgrade the credit rating of the swapped Argentine bonds, which injected more confidence into the restructuring process (*La Nación*, February 3, 2005). More strikingly, in October 2005 not only was Argentina receiving better credit ratings, but its country risk was raised to a level very close to that of Brazil — a country that despite having faced severe currency crises in 1999 and 2002, never defaulted on its large debt.[17]

In September 2005, Argentina recorded its thirty-seventh consecutive month of positive growth. The economy grew at an impressive rate of 10 percent in the second quarter of 2005 alone. In fact, Argentina grew at an approximate rate of 9 percent a year since 2003 (*Financial Times*, September 21, 2005). Most agree that the extremely benign global environment has a lot to do with it. Not only was high liquidity — due to low interest rates abroad — a factor in allowing for such record growth rates, but, with high global demand, Argentine agricultural commodities also found a broad demand. Moreover, then Minister of the Economy Roberto Lavagna stuck with a policy of fiscal austerity, leading the country to also register record highs in terms of primary fiscal surplus, which makes investment in Argentina more attractive to foreign investors.

Debt Restructurings as Ad Hoc Engagements Between the National and the Global

In all three cases of default and debt restructuring outlined here, it is important to understand that bond prices and overall economic performance are still contingent on fragile economic structures and volatile financial flows. The benign environment for emerging market bonds may turn with the increase in interest rates in the United States, Europe, and Japan.[18] Emerging markets are likely to be more discriminated by foreign investors on the basis of fiscal soundness and growth prospects in the event of a liquidity drought. Nonetheless, what the evidence presented stresses is the fact that at the time of debt restructurings, most defaulting governments had the leeway and ability to craft and pass favorable deals for their countries, a product of the confirmation of the two parameters spelled out here. In an external environment marked by high-yield appetite on the part of international investors, most of them had the industry-specific incentive to reinvest in bonds of defaulting countries rather than to punish these countries for having suspended debt payments.

An important implication of this analysis is that defaulters are not simply serial contract breakers (Reinhart, Rogoff, and Savastano 2003); they are also players in a debt game that, albeit increasingly challenging, does present opportunities and not only constraints. The interaction between the national and the global in these instances of debt restructurings reveal ad hoc or improvised agendas since the menu of negotiating maneuvers available to defaulting governments may indeed increase with the complexity of debt restructurings. Although restructuring outcomes cannot be predicted from the beginning — as much in economic and financial interactions — this bargaining process is far from a realm of self-defeat to the government in default.

In fact, the sophisticated realm of engagement between emerging markets' governments and international markets that configure debt restructurings does not amount to a zero-sum game. A default is not an overall loss for markets participants who have much to gain at different stages of the process. Gains and losses depend on where one stands and holding which kind of security, at what time, facing what external liquidity conditions. For example, in the Argentine debt restructurings in 2001, large fees were paid to creditor committees' representatives, and "almost all the investment arms of leading Wall Street firms made lucrative deals" (Santiso 2003, p. 193). Indeed, even when Argentine economic fundamentals pointed clearly to the problem of unsustainable debt, Wall Street fund managers and analysts refrained from spelling out their concerns in investment reports, limiting them to private conversations. Blustein (2005) reports that analysts from Salomon (now Citigroup), the fifth largest investment bank to sell Argentine bonds during the 1990s,[19] were bringing in large sums of cash to their firm out of the sale of Argentine sovereign bonds. These market players faced an explicit conflict of interest in making comments that could reduce demand on these same bonds (ibid., pp. 62–3). Salomon was hardly alone in this scheme. Enjoying high fees from assisting Argentina with the selling of its bonds in financial markets, other banks were equally disinclined to issue negative reports on the country, deepening its indebtedness process.[20] There is no doubt that the Argentine crisis proved lucrative for several investment banks (Bonelli 2004).

Also, hedge funds that joined the Argentine restructuring in 2005 at the last minute, having bought defaulted bonds at very low prices from less experienced retail investors especially in Italy, made huge profits with the debt swap (Gelpern 2005b). Even local pension funds that got to finance the Argentine government in late 2001 when international sources of credit were all but gone were offered a deal at the time of the restructuring that was customized to fit their long-term investment strategies. Today, they have reason to believe that the default and restructuring was far from the catastrophic outcome many analysts had predicted.[21]

Far from anecdotal references, this kind of information reveals that more than an institutionalized or interdependent relationship exists between the national and the global, or, in particular, between states and financial markets. What prevail are ad hoc modes of engagement, hardly generalizable across countries and time periods. These modes of engagement are highly adaptable and determined primarily by global liquidity conditions at the macroscale and by financial incentives on the part of different bondholders following their own specific strategies at the microscale.

Conclusion

States still retain a substantial degree of policy autonomy despite the heightened financial volatility that has marked the 1990s and early 2000s. Indeed, despite conventional wisdom about the lack of room to maneuver on the part of developing countries when it comes to contradicting market preferences, what the evidence from the latest defaults and debt restructurings reveals is that debtors were able to impose severe repayment reductions on their creditors without losing access to credit markets in a significant way. More room to maneuver in these cases was a product of a benign context where lending was booming due to higher liquidity in financial centers, as well as to the incentives of investors to remain active in the lucrative sovereign bond market, given their short-term strategies and the competition within their industry.

A fuller picture of the consequences of financial volatility and policy-making autonomy is then captured when political economy and the idiosyncrisies of markets are integrated with attention to rescalings, not only from the global to the national but also from the macroeconomic level to the microeconomic dynamics of the financial industry. The constraints and opportunities available to states in emerging economies are revealed when these scales are continuously unpacked and their connections exposed. What emerges are not only formal or institutionalized relations but also ad hoc modes of engagement that determine what could be seen as improvised agendas ultimately more nuanced than simple zero-sum games between the national and the global.

Notes

1. *Default* is defined here as the failure to make required debt payments on a timely basis or to comply with other conditions of an obligation or agreement. This definition is the same used by Standard and Poor's, one of the most influential credit rating agencies. Since here my focus is on defaults

in the 1990s, where credit to developing countries takes predominantly the form of international bond purchases of sovereign debt, I use the definition as a benchmark for international investment decisions.

2. Given my focus on state–financial market interactions, I analyze only middle-income countries that are issuers of debt in the form of sovereign bonds, largely traded in international financial markets. Left out, then, are the highly indebted poor countries (HIPC) more dependent on credit from multilateral institutions and country-to-country loans, as well as eventual — if still scarce — debt relief or cancellation.
3. For a detailed study with emphasis on the recent Argentine debt restructuring, see Datz (2007).
4. An estimated 19 percent of all sovereigns have defaulted on their debts since the beginning of the 1990s. This represents one of the highest records in the last 180 years. Higher average default rates were only registered in the 1830s when thirty-one of sovereign countries defaulted on their obligations, in the 1980s when the rate was 22 percent and in the depression of the 1930s when the rate was 21 percent (Beers and Chambers 2002).
5. The only defaulter in the group was Ecuador. The other countries restructured their debts prior to an official default, an instance of what some analysts term a *quasi default.*
6. Rarely do authors provide a definition for *reputation* in economic studies. When that is the case implicit in the definition is the idea of learning over time from observed past behavior.
7. The second common explanation for repayment is the risk of direct sanctions following a default (Bulow and Rogoff 1989). The evidence for the enforcement of sanctions as a punishment following default is, however, not significant (Tomz 2004). A particularly apt study conducted by Martinez and Sandleris (2004) finds evidence of a decline in trade for the defaulting country postdefault. However, the authors find no relevant effect on bilateral trade between the defaulting country and the creditors that suffered the default. Also, when examining trade with a large group of creditors — not only the ones affected by default — they find that trade seems to decline more markedly with creditors not affected by the default than with those affected by it or with noncreditor countries. Hence, they find evidence to reject the argument that trade sanctions are a severe punishment to defaulting countries and, consequently, function as the underlining logic for why countries repay their debts — a very popular assumption in economic models. For Martinez and Sandleris, the reason why trade declines for a defaulting country after its decision to suspend debt payments remains "an important open question" (p. 19).
8. An example of such a study is Rose (2001). To check for default's detrimental spillover effects on trade, the author looks at data from 1948 to 1977. Despite being a relatively recent study, it is surprising that the data set used to make a contemporary argument — to be applicable to debt theory today — deals with data that do not encompass any one of the three key phases of sovereign indebtedness and defaults: the 1930s, the 1980s, and the 1990s and early 2000s. Another example focusing on a possible collusion of creditor banks is found in Wright (2002).

9. Importantly, this periodization includes the severe financial crises of the 1990s and only leaves out the Argentine default of December 2001.
10. Eichengreen and Mody (1998) study a sample of 1,300 developing country bonds launched in the years 1991–1997. When it comes to Latin American bonds in particular, they find that correlation coefficients between the Latin American countries in their sample for the period between December 1997 and September 2000 indicate that although markets have some capacity to differentiate among Latin American countries on the basis of policies and fundamentals, they also perceive Latin American countries as a group when assigning risk. This practice is conducive to market volatility and indicates that market sentiment is indeed a key component in the determination of spreads — that is, the difference in the price of sovereign debt bonds and that of an alternative risk-free security, U.S. Treasury bills.
11. For a discussion of the rhetorical property of risk as operationalized in country ratings, see Datz (2004a).
12. The logic underlining this idea is that a poor investment decision affects absolute performance dramatically, but if all actors take similar action, it affects relative performance negligibly.
13. Technically, the first Latin American default of the 1990s was that of Venezuela on domestic currency bonds totaling US$270 million in July 1998. However, this default was cured within a short period of time.
14. Brady bonds are the bonds emergent from the restructurings of debt defaulted on in the 1980s by most Latin American countries.
15. The political turmoil was not a minor misgiving. In April 2005, President Lucio Gutierrez declared a state of emergency and dissolved the Supreme Court, alleging the unpopular magistrates were the cause of the street protests in Quito. His allies in Congress had appointed the judges in December in a process widely viewed as violating Ecuador's constitution (*Dow Jones Newswires*, April 18, 2005).
16. *Domestic debt* means domestic-law, domestic-currency debt — in particular, the GKOs (short-term treasury bills) and OFZs (federal bonds). Russia also defaulted on interest arrears notes (Ians), restructured principal notes (Prins), and past-due interest bonds (PDIs).
17. It is also important to note that Brazil received large loans from the IMF, especially in the 2002 debacle preceding the presidential election of Lula da Silva.
18. The last week of May 2006 was plagued by severe downturns in emerging markets, amid fears of incremental increases in interest rates in financial centers (*Wall Street Journal*, May 2006; *Financial Times*, May 28, 2006). Emerging markets' bonds suffered less than the currency and equities markets. A new bond issuance by Argentina in July 2005 met with eager demand.
19. Salomon sold US$5 billion worth of bonds in the 1990s, for which the firm earned US$53 million in fees from the Argentine government (Blustein 2005).
20. These banks were reputable institutions such as Barclays, Morgan Stanley, Credit Suisse First Boston, JP Morgan, and Salomon (Bonelli 2004). In July 2001, a leading publication in the financial industry, *Euromoney*, reported that Argentina's US$29.5 billion sovereign debt exchange deal was "a great

coup for the banks lead-managing it." By that time, it had already become obvious that a default would have been a less costly alternative than a swap that raised interest rates on payments for a country already suffocated in debt obligations. Yet the profitability of the deal for some investment bankers found in Argentina's economy minister Domingo Cavallo's reluctance to accept the inevitability of a default fertile ground to extract large fees from the government in yet another multi-million dollar operation (*Euromoney*, July 2001).

21. See Datz (2004b, 2007) for a detailed analysis of the pension fund industry before and after the restructuring of 2005.

Works Cited

Alexander, Kern, Rahul Dhumale, and John Eatwell. 2006. *Global governance of financial systems: The international regulation of systemic risk*. Oxford: Oxford University Press.

Andrews, David.1994. Capital mobility and state autonomy: Toward a structural theory of international monetary relations. *International Studies Quarterly* 38:193–218.

Armijo, Leslie Elliott (ed.). 2001. Mixed blessing: Expectations about foreign capital flows and democracy in emerging markets. In Leslie Armijo, ed., *Financial globalization and democracy in emerging markets*, 17–48. New York: Palgrave:.

Beers, David T., and John Chambers. 2002. Sovereign defaults: Moving higher again in 2003? Standard & Poor's, September 24.

Bloomberg, several reports.

Blustein, Paul. 2005. *And the money kept rolling in (and out)*. New York: Public Affairs.

Bonelli, Marcelo. 2004. *Un pais en deuda: La Argentina y su imposible relacion con el FMI*. Buenos Aires: Planeta.

Bulow, Jeremy, and Kenneth Rogoff. 1989. LDC debt: Is to forgive to forget? *American Economic Review* 79:43–50.

Calvo, Guillermo, and Enrique Mendoza. 2000. Rational herding and the globalization of financial markets. *Journal of International Economics* 51:79–114.

Calvo, Guillermo, Alejandro Izquierdo, and Ernesto Talvi. 2003. Sudden stops, the real exchange rate and fiscal sustainability: Argentina's lessons. National Bureau of Economic Research, Working Paper 9828, Cambridge, MA.

Cerny, Philip. 1993. American decline and the emergence of embedded financial orthodoxy. In Philip Cerny, ed., *Finance and world politics: Markets, regimes and states in the post-hegemonic era,* 155-185. Northampton: Edward Elgar.

Cerny, Philip, Georg Mens, and Susanne Soederberg. 2005. Different roads to globalization, neoliberalism, the competition state, and politics in a more open world. In Susanne Soederberg, Georg Menz, and Philip Cerny, eds., *Internalizing globalization: The rise of neoliberalism and the erosion of national models of capitalism,* 1–30. London: Palgrave:.

Chiodo, Abbigail J., and Michael T. Owyang. 2002. A case study of a currency crisis: The Russian default of 1998. Federal Research Bank of Saint Louis, November–December, 7–18.

Cole, Harold, and Patrick Kehoe. 1997. Reviving reputational models of sovereign debt. *Federal Reserve Bank of Minneapolis Quarterly Review,* Winter, 21–30.

Datz, Giselle. 2004a. Reframing development and accountability: The impact of sovereign credit ratings on policy making in developing countries. *Third World Quarterly* 25(2):303–18.

———. 2004b. Pension privatization and the politics of default in Latin America. Paper presented at the annual meeting of the American Political Science Association, Chicago: September 2–5.

———. 2007. What life after default? Sovereign debt restructuring and market access in Argentina. Ph.D. diss., Rutgers University.

Dombrowski, Peter. 1998. Haute finance and high theory: Recent scholarship on global financial relations. *Mershon International Studies Review* 42:1–28.

Dow Jones Newswires, several reports.

Eaton, Jonathan, and Mark Gersovitz. 1981. Debt with potential repudiation: Theoretical and empirical analysis. *Review of Economic Studies* 48(2):289–309.

Eichengreen, Barry. 1991. Historical research on international lending and debt. *Journal of Economic Perspectives* 5(2):149–69.

Eichengreen, Barry, and Ashoka Mody. 1998. What explains changing spreads on emerging-market debt: Fundamentals or market sentiment? National Bureau of Economic Research, Working Paper 6408, Cambridge, MA.

Eichengreen, Barry, and Richard Portes. 1989. After the deluge: Default, negotiation, and readjustment during the interwar years. In Barry Eichengreen and Peter Lindert, eds., *The international debt crisis in historical perspective*, 12-47. Cambridge, MA: MIT Press:.

Euromoney. 2001. Bankers celebrate as Cavallo buys a little time, July 1.

Fernandez-Arias, Eduardo. 1996. The new wave of private capital flows: Push or pull? *Journal of Development Economics* 48:389–418.

Financial Times, several issues.

Gelos, R. Gaston, Ratna Sahay, and Guido Sandleris. 2004. Sovereign borrowing by developing countries: What determines market access? International Monetary Fund, Working Paper 04/221, Washington, DC.

Gelpern, Anna. 2005. After Argentina. Institute for International Economics, Policy Brief in International Economics PB05-2, Washington, DC.

Gill, Stephen, and David Law. 1989. Global hegemony and the structural power of capital. *International Studies Quarterly* 33(4):475–99.

Gourinchas, Pierre-Olivier, Rodrigo Valdés, and Oscar Landerretche. 2001. Lending booms: Latin America and the world. *Economía*, Spring, 47–99.

Graham, John R. 1999. Herding among investment newsletters: Theory and evidence. *Journal of Finance* 64(1):237–68.

International Monetary Fund (IMF). 2002. Sovereign debt restructuring and the domestic economy: Experience in four recent cases. Washington, DC: IMF.

Jorgensen, Erika, and Jeffrey Sachs. 1989. Default and renegotiation of Latin American foreign bonds in the interwar period. In Barry Eichengreen and Peter Lindert, eds., *The international debt crisis in historical perspective*, 48–85. Cambridge, MA: MIT Press:.

Krueger, Anne. 2002. Should countries like Argentina be able to declare themselves bankrupt? *El Pais*, January 18.

La Nación, several issues.

Lachaman, Desmond. 2004. Chasing yield. *International Economy*, Spring, 61–3.

Martinez, Jose Vicente, and Guido Sandleris. 2004. Is it punishment? Sovereign defaults and the declines in trade, manuscript, Columbia University, New York.

Marx, Daniel. 2003. Sovereign debt restructuring: The upcoming case of Argentina, manuscript, AGM Consultants, Buenos Aires.

Mauro, Paolo, Nathan Sussman, and Yishay Yafeh. 2002. Emerging market spreads: Then versus now. *Quarterly Journal of Economics* 117:695–733 (May).

Moody's Investors Service. 2005. 2004 Review and 2005 Outlook, January, New York.

Mosley, Layna. 2003. *Global capital and national governments.* Cambridge, UK: Cambridge University Press.

Pauly, Louis W. 1997. *Who elected the bankers? Surveillance and control in the world economy.* Ithaca, NY: Cornell University Press.

Pettis, Michael. 2001. *The volatility machine.* New York: Oxford University Press.

Phillips, Nicola. 1998. Globalization and the paradox of state power: Perspectives from Latin America. Centre for the Study of Globalisation, Working Paper 16/98, University of Warwick.

Porter, Tony. 2001. Negotiating the structure of capital mobility. In Timothy Sinclair and Kenneth Thomas, eds., *Structure and agency in international capital mobility*, 153-167. London: Palgrave: 153–167.

Reinhart, Carmen, Kenneth Rogoff, and Miguel Savastano. 2003. Debt intolerance. *Brookings Papers on Economic Activity* 1:1–59.

Reuters, several reports.

Rose, Andrew. 2001. One reason countries repay their debts: Renegotiation and international trade. National Bureau of Economic Research, Working Paper 8853, Cambridge, MA.

Roubini, Nouriel, and Brad Setser. 2004. *Bailouts or bail-ins? Responding to financial crises in emerging economies.* Washington, DC: Institute of International Economics.

Santiso, Javier. 2003. *The political economy of emerging markets: Actors, institutions, and financial crises in Latin America*. New York: Palgrave.

Sassen, Saskia. 2003. Globalization or denationalization? *Review of International Political Economy* 10(1):1–22.

Sinyagina-Woodruff, Yulia. 2003. Russia, sovereign default, reputation and access to capital markets. *Europe-Asia Studies* 55(4):521–51.

Tomz, Michael. 2004. Finance and trade: Issue linkage and the enforcement of international debt contracts, manuscript, Stanford University.

———. 2001. How do reputations form? New and seasoned borrowers in international capital markets. Paper presented at the 2001 annual meeting of the American Political Science Association, San Francisco: August 30-September 2

Wall Street Journal, several reports.

World Bank. 2006. *Global development finance.* Washington, DC: World Bank.

Wright, Mark L.J. 2002. Reputations and sovereign debt, manuscript, Stanford University.

Contributors

Anne Bartlett (Ph.D. candidate, sociology, University of Chicago) is a research associate at the Transnationalism Project of the University of Chicago. Since 2004 she has been a director of the Darfur Centre for Human Rights and Development (London). Her current research focuses on the politics of the Darfur crisis. Bartlett has been involved in rights-based issues for more than twenty years, has been active in the "Protect Darfur" campaign, and has traveled with the Darfur delegation to the United Nations Human Rights Commission in Geneva where she spoke on the crisis in both 2004 and 2005. Her publications include (with Clark, T. N., and D. Merritt) "Measuring Political Change: The New Political Culture and Local Government in England" (*The City as an Entertainment Machine* ed. T. N. Clark; JAI Elsevier 2003); "Greening London: Politics, Sustainability and the Third Way" (*UNESCO Volume on Human Settlements and Sustainability*, eds. Saskia Sassen and Peter Marcotullio; Oxford and EOLSS, 2005).

Simone Buechler currently teaches in the Department of Urban Studies at Barnard College and is a visiting scholar in the Department of Social and Cultural Analysis at New York University. She received a three-year faculty fellowship in the Metropolitan Studies Program at New York University. Her research focuses on industrial outsourcing, the informal sector and gender. She received her Ph.D. at Columbia University, where she studied under Saskia Sassen and Peter Marcuse, and was subsequently a doctoral fellow in the Transnationalism Project at the University of Chicago. Her publications include: "São Paulo: Outsourcing and Downgrading of Labor in a Globalizing City" (*Global City Reader*, eds. Neil Brenner and Roger Keil, Routledge, 2006) and "Sweating It in the Brazilian Garment Industry: Bolivian Workers and Global Economic Forces in São Paulo" (*Latin American Perspectives*, May 2004). She was a consultant for the National Academy of Sciences, Panel on Cities, and was invited to write a background paper on the informal sector in São Paulo used in their volume entitled *Cities Transformed: Demographic Change and Its Implications in the Developing World* (2003), http://www.nap.edu/books/0309088623/html/300.html/. She is currently finalizing a book manuscript based on her dissertation on labor market restructuring in São Paulo, Brazil. Before returning to get her Ph.D. she worked at the United Nations Development Fund for Women, focusing on women and microcredit.

Anthony D'Andrea (Ph.D. anthropology, University of Chicago, 2005) is a research associate in the Transnationalism Project of the University of Chicago. His main research interests are in cultural globalization, subjectivity, and lifestyle. Among his publications are "Mobilities, Culture and Religion" (Journal of Humanistic Psychology) and "*Global Nomads: Techno and New Age as Transnational Countercultures in Ibiza and Goa*" (Routledge 2007 (International Library of Sociology).

Giselle Datz is a visiting professor of political science at the University of the District of Columbia and a Ph.D. candidate, global affairs, Rutgers University. She was a visiting fellow of the Transnantionalism Project at the University of Chicago in 2006. She received an M.A. in international relations from the University of Chicago in 2001. Articles on sovereign debt restructurings and credit ratings have been published in the *Review of International Political Economy* (forthcoming) and in *Third World Quarterly* (2005). She is currently completing her thesis entitled "What Life after Default?: Sovereign Debt Restructuring and Credit Access in Argentina."

Gracia Liu Farrer (Ph.D. candidate, sociology, University of Chicago) is a research fellow in the Center for the Study of Social Stratification and Inequality at Tohoku University in Japan. Her dissertation examines the recent student migration from Mainland China to Japan, their migration experiences, and their mobility patterns. She has published "Chinese Catholic Center in Tokyo: Institutional Characteristics in Contexts" (*Religious Pluralism in Diaspora*, ed. P. Pratap Kumar, Brill, 2006), "The Chinese Social Dance Party in Tokyo: Identity and Status in an Immigrant Leisure Subculture" (*Journal of Contemporary Ethnography*, vol. 33, no. 6), and several papers and book chapters in Japanese. Her current research project focuses on the career trajectories and strategies of Chinese employees in corporate Japan's transnational economic practices.

Rachel Harvey (Ph.D. candidate, sociology, University of Chicago) is a research associate of the Transnationalism Project at the University of Chicago. Her dissertation examines the impact of sociocultural processes in the transformation of the London Gold Fix from an international market to a global market. Based on her master's paper, which focused on the impact of the processes of economic and cultural globalization on a small rural town, Elko, Nevada, in a major gold producing region, she published "The Jarbidge Shovel Brigade" (*Uncovering Nevada's Past: A Primary Source of History of the Silver State,* eds. John Reed and Ron James, 2004). She was the recipient of the University of Chicago's department of sociology's *Century Fellowship* and the University of Chicago's *Overseas Dissertation Research Fellowship.* She was also a member of both the *American Journal of Sociology's* book and manuscript review boards.

Matthew J. Hill (Ph.D. anthropology, University of Chicago, 2004) is a research associate in the Growth and Structure of Cities Program at Bryn Mawr College. His research focuses on globalization and urban redevelopment in late socialist Cuba. He is interested in issues of global heritage, spatial scale, and urban revitalization strategies in Latin America and the Caribbean, Eastern Europe, and the United States. He is completing a book entitled *Globalizing Havana: World Heritage and Urban Redevelopment in Late Socialist Cuba.*

Heather Hindman (Ph.D. history and culture, University of Chicago, 2003) is assistant professor of anthropology at Northeastern University. Trained as an interdisciplinary scholar, she uses theories and methods from postcolonial studies, globalization, and science, technology, and society to illuminate issues of power, gender, and history among mid-level global actors. Her dissertation focused on Nepal as a nexus of historical and political novelty; the resulting forthcoming book considers the influence of everyday life interactions of diplomats, development workers, and their local staff on the implementation of policy and projects. Her current research projects take off in two directions: one explores issues of race and gender among diplomats in Nepal and the United States; the other focuses on theoretical issues of alterity and culture under neoliberalism. Her publications include articles in *The Journal of Popular Culture, Himalaya, and Studies in Nepali History and Society* and in the forthcoming book *Beyond the Incorporated Wife.*

Jennifer L. Johnson (Ph.D. sociology, University of Chicago, 2005) is assistant professor in the department of sociology at Kenyon College, where she teaches courses on globalization, vigilantism, and the law. Among her publications are "What's Globalization Got To Do With It? Political Action and Peasant Producers in Guerrero, Mexico" (*Canadian Journal of Latin American and Caribbean Studies,* vol. 26, no. 1, 2001) and the coedited *Moviendo Montañas: Transformando la Geografía del Poder en el Sur de México* (Colegio de Guerrero, 2002), with Beatriz Canabal Cristiani et. al. Her current research focuses on changing understandings of citizenship in Mexico and on the U.S.–Mexico border.

Josh Kaplan (Ph.D. history and culture, University of Chicago, 2006) is a research associate in the Transnationalism Project at the University of Chicago. Broadly trained in the social sciences, particularly in anthropology and politics, he is now completing a Diplôme d'études approfondies (DEA) in international law at the Graduate Institute of International Studies in Geneva, Switzerland. Most of his current research interests lie in the anthropology of international law, human rights and security, and the socio-legal constitution of ethical dilemmas. As part of his ongoing attempt to reconceptualize human rights advocacy, he wrote an article on the political economy of human rights in Israel/Palestine, published in the *Mediterranean Journal of Human Rights,* and he is currently completing manuscripts on the rationalization of human rights violations and a critique of existing theories of state compliance with international law.

Richard Lloyd (Ph.D. sociology, University of Chicago, 2002) is assistant professor of sociology at Vanderbilt University. He is author of *Neo-Bohemia: Art and Commerce in the Postindustrial City* (Routledge, 2005), and has published articles on cultural production, urban tourism, and theories of culture, subjectivity, and instrumental labor from Max Weber's Protestant ethic to the present. Lloyd is coeditor of the culture section of *Contexts* and is on the editorial board of *City and Community.* His current project, *Honky-Tonks and Skyscrapers*, examines downtown development in Nashville, Tennessee.

Rami Nashashibi (Ph.D. candidate, sociology, University of Chicago) is working on a dissertation exploring the encounter of Islam with hip-hop and black street gangs in the post-industrial urban ghetto. His project addresses notions of alternative cosmopolitanisms, transnational communities and the role of urban space in shaping contemporary Muslim identity. He received a Robert Park fellowship, for which he developed and taught a course entitled "Theorizing the Global Ghetto" at the University of Chicago. Among his publications is a forthcoming article on the legacy of the Black P. Stone Nation's encounter with Islam in *Souls: A Critical Journal of Black Politics, Culture, and Society.* He is currently completing an article for publication entitled "Hip in the Holy Land: The Rise of a Global Ghetto." Rami is also a full-time community activist on Chicago's South Side where he organizes around criminal justice reform, immigrant rights, and public safety.

Marina Peterson (Ph.D. anthropology, University of Chicago, 2005) is assistant professor of performance studies in the School of Interdisciplinary Arts at The Ohio University. Her work explores the intersection of performance and the city, addressing issues of citizenship, the contemporary urban public, and civic space. Articles on musical performance and the production of space, world music festivals, global city formation, and urban civilities have been published in *Space and Culture, Journal of Popular Music Studies,* the Korean ethnomusicology journal *Music and Culture,* and the French geography journal *Géocarrefour.* She is currently completing a manuscript on public concerts in downtown Los Angeles entitled "Sounding the City: Public Concerts and Translocal Civilities in Los Angeles."

Kamal Sadiq (Ph.D. political science, University of Chicago, 2003) is assistant professor in the Department of Political Science at the University of California, Irvine. He specializes in comparative politics, immigration, and international relations. Specifically, his research focuses on immigration from and within developing countries, cultural implications of immigrant and refugee flows, globalization, conflict and war in Asia, and international security. His regional expertise is in Southeast Asia (Malaysia, Indonesia) and South Asia (India, Pakistan). He knows Bahasa Indonesia/Malaysia, Hindi (India), Urdu (India, Pakistan), which he has put to use in his interviews and archival research.

Saskia Sassen is the Ralph Lewis professor of sociology at the University of Chicago. Her new book is *Territory, Authority, Rights: From Medieval to Global Assemblages* (Princeton University Press 2006). Other recent books are the third edition of *Cities in a World Economy* (Sage 2006), *A Sociology of Globalization* (Norton 2007), and the co-edited *Digital Formations: New Architectures for Global Order* (Princeton University Press 2005). *The Global City* came out in a new fully updated edition in 2001. Her books are translated into sixteen languages. She serves on several editorial boards and is an advisor to several international bodies. She is a member of the Council on Foreign Relations, a member of the National Academy of Sciences Panel on Cities, and chair of the Information Technology and International Cooperation Committee of the Social Science Research Council (USA). Her comments have appeared in *The Guardian, The New York Times, Le Monde*

Diplomatique, the *International Herald Tribune*, *Newsweek International*, *Vanguardia*, *Clarin*, *The Financial Times*, among others.

Sarah Busse Spencer (Ph.D. sociology, University of Chicago, 2003) studies the interaction of social and economic factors in post-socialist society and the role of reproduction and inertia in explaining trajectories of change in these societies. Other research interests are social capital in the workplace and in the informal economy and global influences on organizational change. Recent publications include "Globalization in Siberia: Novosibirsk and the Role of Place" (*Russian Transformations*, ed. L. McCann, RoutledgeCurzon, 2004) and "Economic Imperialism" (*Encyclopedia of Economic Sociology*, ed., J. Beckert and M. Zafirovski, Routledge, 2005).

Evalyn W. Tennant (Ph.D. political science, University of Chicago, 2006) is currently at the Chicago Center for Contemporary Theory, working on a book based on her dissertation, "The Transnational and the Grassroots in the Making of a 'National' Social Movement: Scale, Structure, and Strategy in U.S.-based Anti-Apartheid Activism." She is the former associate director of the University of Chicago Center for International Studies, and has taught in the human rights and environmental studies programs. Among her publications is "What can the Immigrant Rights Agenda Learn from the Free South Africa Movement?" (ColorLines, Vol. 7, no. 1, Spring 2004). In addition to the geographies and geographic capabilities of transnational activism, her research interests include the international human rights regime and the proliferation of rights-based claim making, and the terms and consequences of corporations' inclusion in the international human rights regime.

Index

D

F

G

J

O

P

T

U

X

Y

Z